SPACE LAW PERSPECTIVES

Commentaries Based on

Volumes 1–15 (1957–1972)

of the

COLLOQUIA ON THE LAW OF OUTER SPACE

Sponsored by

The International Institute of Space Law
of the International Astronautical Federation

Compiled and Edited
by
Mortimer D. Schwartz
Professor of Law, University of California
Davis, California

South Hackensack, New Jersey
Fred B. Rothman & Co.
Distributed for the University of California
Davis, California
1976

© Mortimer D. Schwartz 1976

ISBN 0-8377-1106-1

L. C. card no. 76-26814

Printed in the U.S.A.

EDITOR'S NOTE

The International Institute of Space Law has held conferences each year since 1957, the purpose being to provide members of the space law community with an opportunity to discuss and exchange ideas relative to the problems and hopes created by man's launch into space. Participants in these conferences have become increasingly aware of the value of disseminating the information and philosophies advanced at these colloquia--not only as a vehicle for explaining technical advancement, but as an unusual expression in international cooperation. No other achievement, either social or technical, has nurtured the degree of vision and cooperation accomplished by these considerations of space law, as so accurately predicted by one of the Institute's founders, the late and beloved Andrew G. Haley.

The contents of this volume are based on the contents of the first fifteen volumes containing the proceedings of the Colloquia on the Law of Outer Space, conducted annually since 1957 by the International Institute of Space Law in conjunction with the annual meetings of the International Astronautical Federation. Many of these early volumes are out of print. The chapters in this volume correspond to the sequence of those first fifteen Colloquia volumes, 1957-72, so that Chapter One refers to the First Colloquium, Chapter Five to the Fifth Colloquium, Chapter Ten to the Tenth Colloquium, etc. The scholar responsible for the specific chapter has taken from its corresponding Colloquium volume one or more of the original articles and reproduced them as originally published or excerpted them especially for this project. At the end of each chapter, the scholar has added commentary on other items in the original Colloquium volume and reflections on the material contained here. Hence, this volume is not a mere reprinting of earlier items but rather a review of the published accomplishments of the International Institute of Space Law as perceived through current perspectives.

Narrow nationalism in space law has been countered by a few who initially argued for global identification of these space problems. Their voices were heeded. Now, having achieved such recognition, the International Institute of Space Law offers this volume as a reaffirmation of its objectives.

Mortimer Schwartz

Davis, California
June 1976

TABLE OF CONTENTS

EDITOR'S NOTE

The International Institute of Space Law has held conferences each year since 1957, the purpose being to provide members of the space law community an opportunity to discuss and exchange ideas relative to the problems and hopes created by man's launch into space. Participants in these conferences have become increasingly aware of the value of disseminating the information and philosophies advanced at these colloquia--not only as a vehicle for explaining technical advancement, but as an unusual expression in international cooperation. No other achievement, either social or technical, has nurtured the degree of vision and cooperation accomplished by these considerations of space law, as so accurately predicted by one of the institute's founders, the late and beloved Andrew G. Haley.

This volume is a collection of abstracts taken from the colloquia held from 1957 to 1972. Members of the International Institute of Space Law graciously agreed to act as editors for individual colloquia, excerpting those portions they considered most in keeping with the goals set forth. At the conclusion of each volume, these editors comment on other contributions and the colloquium as a whole.

Narrow nationalism in space law has been countered by a few who initially argued for global identification of these space problems. Their voices were heeded. Now, having achieved such recognition, the International Institute of Space Law offers this volume as a reaffirmation of its objectives.

Mortimer Schwartz

Davis, California
June 1976

PREFACE

by

Fr. W. von Rauchhaupt

The team for the establishment of outer space law has, of necessity, changed its membership since the First Colloquium on Outer Space Law was held in 1958. The two pillars who framed the original twelve-member team, however, have remained from the beginning: Prince Welf Heinrich von Hannover, or, as our old friend Andrew G. Haley always presented him, the first doctor of space law; and Dr. Werner von Braun, the equally famous architect of outer space exploration. It is appropriate that these two have written the introduction and conclusion to this compendium.

Our purpose has been to abridge fifteen volumes into one general reference source recapitulating all major themes on outer space law presented at the colloquia. Our hope is that the publication will strengthen interest in and knowledge of outer space law so that the international community will comprehend its significance and urgency.

The nature of outer space affords no air, no water, no clouds, no nourishment, no latent warmth, no force of gravity; yet stars and light plunge through space with baffling velocity and permeability for untold distances. Mankind will experiment with these phenomena and bend them to his purposes. And just as international law followed the exploration of the earth, outer space law must bring order to the reconnaissance of space.

In essence, the formation of our team was an experiment in international concert. The group germinated through cooperation in national and international congresses of the International Astronautical Federation. As the idea of the space law colloquia grew, we sought the cooperation of many different states; in general we were successful. There were those who assumed a negative attitude, but there were those also whose industry, dedication, and good sense made possible the work culminating in this compendium. Although at times the effort to create new congresses, new institutes, and, indeed, this compendium has seemed superhuman, there is great satisfaction in realizing that outer space law is being recognized as an international reality.

Outer space law is a relative newcomer to the growing confederacy of medical and technical conferences on outer space science. We therefore appreciate the reception given jurists on their many visits to U.S. space stations where new material was presented and practical initiatives discussed. Heartening also was the emerging cooperation between the United States and Russia, and in Europe, the merging of ELDO and ESRO into the European Space Organization (ESO). The time is ripe for further cooperation.

The creation of mankind, its reason and initiative, dates back at most one million years; yet the first creation, light and stars, predates man by billions of years. The younger mankind has formulated his laws and patterned them to his needs: "And God blessed them . . . replenish the earth and subdue it." (Genesis 128) Where once God's eternal creation afforded only a short walk on the moon, now sky laboratories and unmanned satellites extend time and space and afford our own Earth a new view of itself.

February 8, 1974

INTRODUCTION

BY

Dr. W.H. Prince von Hannover

I am honoured and pleased to write the introduction for the compilation of the Proceedings of the Space Law Colloquia. The topic suggested to me was the theme of my dissertation, "Luftrecht und Weltraum" (Airlaw and Space), accepted in 1953 by the Georg-August University in Göttingen. The theses advanced in that study later became the theme of an invitational lecture tour to twenty American universities and other institutions in 1957.

According to Article 1 of the first International Convention of Air Traffic, concluded in Paris after World War I in 1919, all nations have exclusive sovereignty of their airspace--a regulation which was accepted in Article I of the Chicago Convention of 1944.

As nothing had been mentioned about an upper boundary of this national sovereighty, most jurisprudence supported the view that national sovereighty reaches vertically only as far as human influence will allow. This limit was the height being reached by anti-aircraft missiles which, at that time, were still brought down by guns. Rockets penetrating outer space had not yet been invented.

When the United States and the USSR announced the intention to send off satellites to circle the earth, the public accepted this news with enthusiasm and did not protest. I then drew the conclusion that, as a necessary consequence, national sovereignty demanded some vertical boundary. Otherwise the earth-circling satellites would permanently fly over foreign territories, and the countries having sent off these satellites would be guilty of constant violation of international law. Therefore, the legal problems had to be submitted to critical investigation to determine the potential exploitation of outer space. Considering that penetration of outer space by mankind using space vehicles or other projectiles would soon be realized, and further, that the problems posed by Air Law would partly reappear in outer space, it seemed appropriate to call this study "Air Law and Space."

The probable application and comparison of air law theories and concepts to outer space necessitated a clarification and evaluation of air law problems. This analysis further served as a logical starting point in researching the problems of space.

First, the legal nature of outer space as defined both by science and the existing air law must be dealt with. Only the airspace above the high seas and regions outside the sovereignty of any country could be considered free territory. As to airspace above national territories, both the "freedom of the air" and the "zone" theories promulgated with the advent of balloon aviation were discarded. Natural law, legal constructions, and legal policy dictated the acceptance of the extension of sovereignty into airspace. Moreover, this theory had been incorporated into international convention and national laws relating to air traffic. Concerning height limitations, states were entitled to claim sovereignty over the entire air-filled space above their territories. The argument that such sovereignty should be exercised only within the limits dictated by national interest in no way contradicts this doctrine.

The region beyond the atmosphere, however, does not lend itself to the theory of sovereignty over the airspace above national territories. The Kármán-Haley height, limiting the national sovereignty at 80 kilometers distance from earth, is, I believe, an acceptable control; great numbers of satellites now circle the earth, some already at a distance of only 100 kilometers and less. Having free access to the area beyond the atmosphere, space vehicles should be governed by the principles of nationality (the law of the flag) as are the ships on the high seas.

With regard to legal questions arising in the course of space journeys, we concluded that it would be right and proper to apply by analogy the national, multilateral or bilateral air traffic regulations in force in the country over which the space vehicle might be flying unless otherwise dictated by the nature of the circumstances. I am aware that this problem is at present the subject of much debate. So also is the definition of projectiles and their behavior while ascending or descending in airspace, and questions of liability for damages thereby caused to national territories or people. Going into further details would surpass the intention of this study.

Applying the provisions of aviation laws to traffic of space vehicles in regions beyond the atmosphere appeared impossible because of the difference between such regions and airspace. I emphasized, however, that the pilot of a space vehicle could never be "Legibus solutus," even in the absence of special provisions for space traffic. His actions would have to be conducted in a manner unlikely to cause damage to third parties or things. This is the principle universally recognized, both in international and national laws, as the "obligation to ensure traffic safety." Therefore, any passage or stay in the area beyond the atmosphere, "free territory," would be subject to definite legal obligations and rules.

Legal opinion on the probable construction of space stations occasioned the comparison to seadromes. These sea stations were propagated during the 1920's to serve aeroplanes as bases while crossing the oceans. Ample use was made of the questions raised concerning their use on the high seas by the "Comité Juridique International de l'Aviation" at its meeting in Budapest in 1930. My thesis was that many solutions to legal problems posed by seadromes could be applied to space stations. Space stations in regions beyond the atmosphere should not be classified as "res communes"; their legal nature, therefore, should be determined by their mode of construction. There should be no obligation to open any completed space station to the general public. However, once released for use by the general public, no discrimination whatsoever should be allowed.

All of my conclusions on space traffic in this study were based on the premise that the area beyond the atmosphere is considered "free territory." This must, indeed, be the case when one considers the law of nature, of legal constructions and legal policy referred to herein. An even more cogent consideration is this: applied to a journey into space, the usual "geocentric" idea of flight traversing the national territories of various states could hardly be defended because of the altitudes in which such a journey would take place. One would find it highly illogical to be told that a space vehicle traveling from a certain point of the globe to the moon, traverses the national territories of many terrestrial states in the course of its journey in regions beyond the atmosphere.

Subsequent to my dissertation men have walked on the moon, and space vehicles have been sent to Mars and Venus. The space law which governs nations exploring space was created by the United Nations. It is the first codified law of nations of its kind accepted by East and West.

In 1957 here in Western Germany, Chancellor Adenauer was trying to re-establish the confidence of foreign nations in our country. It was an honour, therefore, to accept the invitation to lecture on my dissertation in the United States. My journey lasted six weeks, and I was accompanied by my most esteemed friend, Andrew G. Haley, one of the founders of the American Rocket Society and the International Astronautical Federation.

The people in Eastern Germany acknowledge their appreciation of aid from Russia. We, of Western Germany, accepted gratefully the help offered by the United States, especially the reconstruction of our country under the Marshall Plan. The opportunity in 1957 to express my country's gratitude to a wide public on my lecture tour gave me great pleasure. During my stay in the United States, I gained a great number of new friends who, like me, work for friendship and understanding among all nations. This alone is reason enough to be grateful to my Lord that He gave me the inspiration for these ideas.

This compilation of Proceedings of the Space Law Colloquia will further, too, a worldwide cooperation.

FIRST COLLOQUIUM ON THE LAW OF OUTER SPACE
THE HAGUE 1958

I. Texts Reproduced

DEFINITIONS AND SUBDIVISIONS OF SPACE
BIOASTRONAUTICAL ASPECT

by

H. Strughold

Whenever matters of astronautics are discussed, the word space is used in a great variety of ways, such as outer space, deep space, free space, interplanetary space, cosmic space, and so on. But space is an immensely vast area even within our solar system and its environmental conditions are by no means uniform. We need an exact definition of what is meant by these terms, where above the earth's surface space begins, and what subdivisions of space may be conceivable and practical. In brief, we now need a kind of "geography of space", - what we might call spatiography. This field refers, of course, only to the empty space itself. The description of the environmental conditions on the celestial bodies is called planetography, of which geography (Earth), areography (Mars), and selenography (Moon) are special cases. Both spatiography and planetography are subdivisions of an all embracing cosmography. In the following we shall confine our discussion to the space of the solar system based essentially on space medical considerations or on bioastronautics. A spatiography of this kind may also be useful for other aspects of astronautics such as space technology and space law.

The first and perhaps the most important question that interests us is: Where above the earth's surface does space begin? According to theories in astrophysics, the atmosphere as a material continuum extends to about 1000 kilometers, or 600 miles. In this region collisions between air molecules or atoms become very rare and the atmosphere thins out in the form of a spray zone (exosphere) into the nearly perfect vacuum of space. But this astrophysical aspect is not relevant to astronautics and expecially not to manned space flight. In this respect the cessation of the atmospheric functions and effects determine the border between atmosphere and space. Without going into details -

As low as 15 km (about 10 mi.) and 20 km (12 mi.), the atmospheric pressure functions to provide the lungs with oxygen and to keep the body fluids in the liquid state are no longer effective.

At about 25 km (16 mi.) the air, due to its low density, can no longer be utilized for cabin pressurization; instead we need a sealed cabin the same type as is required in space.

At 40 km (24 mi.) we are beyond the region of absorption for cosmic rays.

The same is true at 45 km (28 mi.) concerning ultraviolet of solar radiation.

The 50 km (30 mi.) level is about the limit for aerodynamic lift and navigation even for the fastest winged craft.

At about 100 km (60 mi.) the rarified air ceases to scatter light and to transmit sound, resulting in the strange darkness and silence of space.

At 120 km (75 mi.) we are beyond the meteor absorbing region of the atmosphere.

This is practically also the aerodynamic heat limit.

And, finally, at about 200 km (120 mi.) air resistance approaches zero. This mechanical border of the atmosphere is its final functional limit. At this altitude the "appreciable" or effective atmosphere terminates.

For the whole atmospheric range within which the various atmospheric functions for manned flight cease, the term "aeropause" has been suggested.

We can also explain the environmental situation in this region by saying that with the vanishing of its functions the atmosphere becomes partially space equivalent at 15 to 30 km and progresses step by step to total space equivalence at 200 km as far as the effectiveness of the atmospheric functions is concerned.

Three of these steps on the ladder to space, or in the intra-atmospheric space equivalent region, where atmosphere and space overlap, deserve our special attention:

1. The physiological zero line of air pressure at about 20 km, at which the environment for the unprotected human body attains the equivalent of a vacuum;

2. The technical zero line for useful aerodynamic support and navigation by control surfaces at 50 km (30 mi.). Above this line we deal exclusively with ballistics, and navigation by control surfaces has to be replaced by reaction control. This altitude is considered by some law experts the limit for national authority over the air space; and

3. The mechanical zero line of air resistance at about 200 km (120 mi.). Here we enter the region of the "KEPLER Regime" where the laws of celestial mechanics, unhindered by air resistance, are fully effective. It is here where space in its connotation "outer space" actually begins.

Such is the picture of the border between atmosphere and space based on a physiological and technological analysis.

For astronautical purposes, what are the possibilities of subdividing the void of our solar system beyond the earth's "effective" atmosphere?

At first glace it may seem strange to draw borderlines or demarcation lines in an environment in which emptiness is the rule and concentrations of matter, in the form of celestial bodies, are the exceptions. There are, however, several ways to subdivide space based on environmental-ecological, on gravitational and on topographical astronomical considerations.

First, of vital interest to the astronaut are the environmental-ecological differences in the environment of space itself, before he considers the celestial bodies.

To begin with, the space environment in the vicinity of celestial bodies is different from that in free interplanetary space. It shows some peculiarities caused by the mere presence of their solid bodies, by optical properties of their surfaces, and by forces originating in these bodies and extending into space.

In the vicinity of the earth, for instance, on one side we are protected from cosmic rays and meteorites by the solid body of our globe itself - just as we are protected on one side of a house against rain, hail, or wind. Other peculiarities of the space environment near the earth are its shadow, its own radiation, and reflected solar radiation, which influence the heat balance of a space vehicle and pose special visual problems.

The forces which cause special regional environmental differences in the space near the earth are those of the geomagnetic field. The magnetic field of the earth strongly influences the influx of corpuscular rays of solar and cosmic origin by channeling them into the polar regions and storing them or deflecting them back into space over the equatorial regions. The polar lights and the high intensity radiation belts, above 600 miles over the magnetic equator, recently discovered by VAN ALLEN by means of the Explorer Satellites, are manifestations of this geomagnetic influence upon the density distribution of ray particles in earth near space.

For all these reasons, space in the vicinity of the earth is distinctly different from open interplanetary space. If we wish to emphasize this fact, we might use for that region in which the earth's influence upon the environmental-ecological qualities of space is distinctly recognizable the designation "circumterrestrial space." The same consideration applies more or less to the other planets and the moons (for instance circumlunar space.) For the circumterrestrial space, or nearby space, we might assume an extension up to 5 earth radii, depending on the outer boundary of the great radiation belt. Beyond this region we enter deep space.

In a certain respect, however, the earth's influence reaches much farther into space than explained above. The factor in question is gravitation, the environmental dynamical substrate for space navigation.

Theoretically, the gravitational field of the Earth, as of every other larger celestial body, extends, of course, to infinity in terms of celestial mechanics; but the astronaut is especially interested in those areas in which the gravitational force of a celestial body prevails over those of other celestial bodies. In the astronautical literature they are known as spheres of gravitational influence. We might call them, briefly, gravispheres.

The gravisphere includes the potential satellite sphere which in case of the earth reaches as far as about one and one-half million kilometers, or nearly one million miles. This is the reach of the earth's satellite holding power. Beyond this distance, at which interplanetary space begins, the gravitational field of the Sun becomes predominant for a space vehicle, and the Earth can exert some influence upon it only in the form of disturbances. The potential satellite sphere of our Moon, according to O. RITTER, extends to about 60,000 km from its center; that of Venus 1 million, and of Mars one-half million km; Jupiter's potential satellite sphere is more than fifty million km in radius.

The first order gravisphere in our solar system is, of course, the gravitational empire of the Sun, which blends far beyond Pluto with the gravitational no-man's-land between the stars. As second order gravispheres then can be considered those of the planets, and as third order gravispheres, those of the moons, the smallest gravitational provinces in our solar system. Thus we arrive at a subdivision of space based on the extension of the gravitational territories of the various celestial bodies.

This dynamographic aspect of space may be useful for a better understanding of the nature and spatial extension of satellite flight and (gravitational) escape operations such as lunar, interplanetary, and planetary space flight.

But we can subdivide space on still a larger scale based on intensity variations of solar electromagnetic radiation as we encounter them when traveling through the whole planetary system from Mercury to Pluto--in other words, as we encounter them as a function of the distance from the Sun. Because this function follows the inverse square law, these variations are very extreme and they involve, of course, all important portions of the solar electromagnetic spectrum (heat rays, light, and ultraviolet rays). In fact, we would not go too far by speaking of a zonation of interplanetary space in this respect, an analogue to the torrid, temperate, and cold zones in the earth's climate.

Such a line of thinking leads to the assumption of a zone which is not too hostile to space operations and in which the conditions on planets are compatible with the possibility of life as we know it. This zone may extend from the region of Venus to Mars and can be called ecosphere of the Sun. A further discussion of this ecological subdivision of the space within our solar system, however, and also that of a topographical astronomical subdivision of space [such as cislunar, translunar space (KRAFFT EHRICKE), interstellar, intragalactic, and intergalactic space] goes beyond the scope of this colloquium.

*   *   *   *   *

A DEFINITIVE STUDY OF THE CONCEPT AND SCIENTIFIC STRATEGY
OF OUTER SPACE. THE CHALLENGE TO ALL NATIONS TO SUPPORT
A JUST SYSTEM OF SPACE LAW

by

. . .

J.G. Fulton

History of Outer Space Legislation in the United States Congress

I have hereinbefore stated that I believe that the United States Congress is proceeding upon the correct course in its legislative program relating to outer space. Much criticism was heaped upon the legislative and executive branches of government when the USSR successfully launched its first Sputnik. It was suggested that possibly we were lax in our efforts to affect legislation relative to fostering a progressive program in outer space. Let us search the legislative record of our Congress in this respect.

On August 2, 1955, during the 1st session of the 84th Congress, Mr. FRANK M. KARSTEN, a member of the House of Representatives, introduced a bill, House Resolution 7843, to establish a Joint Committee on Extraterrestrial Exploration to be composed of nine members of the Senate, and nine members of the House of Representatives. The proposed purpose of this Joint Committee was to make continuing studies of activities and problems relating to the development of extraterrestrial exploration and travel. Action was not taken on this bill.

On August 29, 1957, during the 1st session of the 85th Congress, I introduced House Joint Resolution 460, to establish a Joint Committee on Earth Satellites and the Problem of Outer Space. This Joint Resolution proposed the following purpose: Whereas the developments of high altitude mechanisms and earth satellites capable of supersonic speeds by

7

remote control are proceeding on many fronts; and the problems of outer space and the many investigations of this area have opened a new field whose impact on our civilization shows tremendous capabilities for good or for ill, and

Whereas, for the protection of the general welfare and security fo the United States of America, there is needed a joint and continuing comprehensive study in such fields: Now, therefore, be it resolved... that there is hereby established a Joint Committee on Earth Satellites and the Problems of Outer Space.

On January 9, 1958, in the 2nd session of the 85th Congress, I again introduced a House Joint Resolution which was designated as House Joint Resolution 489, and again proposed the establishment of a Joint Committee on Earth Satellites and the Problems of Outer Space.

Including my Joint Resolution there were 29 bills introduced which related to outer space. The first group of bills listed below is concerned with the establishment of congressional committees, for dealing with legislation:

House Resolution 9668 (KEATING of New York), House Resolution 9901 (BOGGS of Louisiana), House Resolution 9613 (BROOKS of Louisiana), House Joint Resolution 489 (FULTON of Pennsylvania), and Senate Concurrent Resolution 53 (JAVITS): All of these measures would establish a Joint Committee on Outer Space patterned after the Joint Atomic Energy Committee. The first two (House Resolution 9668, and House Resolution 9901) would establish an 18-man committee while the others would call for 14 men.

Senate Resolution 256 (JOHNSON): Sets up a special 13-man Space Committee in the Senate. (Passed February 6, 1958.)

House Resolution 473 (COAD of Iowa): Identical language as Senate Resolution 256, but setting up a 31-man Space Committee in the House.

House Resolution 474 (BROOKS of Louisiana): Same as House Resolution 473 except it calls for a 13-man committee.

House Resolution 496 (McCORMACK of Massachusetts): Similar to House Resolution 474. (Passed March 5, 1958.)

House Resolution 478 (KEATIN of New York): Amends rule X of the House by establishing an 11-man Committee on Outer Space.

The following bills have been introduced to establish or expand existing agencies for operation of projects concerned with outer space:

House Resolution 9874 (LANE of Massachusetts) and House Resolution 9966 (COAD of Iowa): These bills are similar and would establish a separate Outer Space Commission patterned after the Atomic Energy Commission.

House Resolution 10271 (DURHAM of North Carolina), House Resolution 10352 (HOLIFIELD of California), and S. 3117 (ANDERSON) are identical bills. This proposal would amend the Atomic Energy Act to give the responsibility for outer space development to the Atomic Energy Commission. Authorizes an initial $ 50 million for this purpose.

S. 3000 (GORE): Contains a provision authorizing and directing the AEC to accelerate existing programs for the development of nuclear rocket propulsion and a manned vehicle powered by nuclear propulsion and capable of sustained travel outside the earth's atmosphere.

House Resolution 11188 (FRELINGHUYSEN of New Jersey) and House Resolution 11860 (FULTON of Pennsylvania): Gives the National Advisory Committee on Aeronautics (NACA) the authority to conduct experiments involving outer space and to coordinate the Government's activities in this area. A second title of this bill establishes an 18-man Joint Committee on Astronautics. (See House Resolution 9668 above.)

S. 3233 (YARBOROUGH): Authorizes the National Science Foundation to undertake programs in communications and weather modification.

S. 3604 (CASE of South Dakota): Gives the responsibility for development of outer space to the NACA changing its name to the National Astronautics Agency. Governed by a 17-man Board appointed by the President and a Director appointed by the Board.

S. 3609 (JOHNSON and BRIDGES, by request), House Resolution 11881 (McCORMACK of Massachusetts), House Resolution 11882 (A. RENDS of Illinois), House Resolution 11887 (HASKELL of Delaware), and House Resolution 11888 (KEATING of New York): This is the President's bill. Gives the responsibility for development of outer space to the NACA changing its name to the National Aeronautics and Space Agency. Governed by a 17-man Board and a Director appointed by the President. The Director consults with the Board but is not bound by their decisions.

Two related bills have been introduced which would establish a new Department of Science.

S. 3126 (HUMPHREY, McCLELLAN, and YARBOROUGH): Groups together into a new Department of Science and Technology several existing scientific agencies of the Federal Government, such as the Atomic Energy Commission, National Science Foundation, Bureau of Standards, etc. A Government Operations Committee print analysis of the bill, dated March 26, 1958, recommends amendments which would also include the NACA in the new Department and would create standing committees in the House and Senate to handle these matters, including astronautics and space exploration.

S. 3180 (KEFAUVER): Similar to S. 3126. The Secretary of the new Department of Science would be authorized to carry out programs involving development of outer space.

Resolutions were offered which would state a policy of Congress concerning outer space.

House Concurrent Resolution 265 (KEATING of New York), House Concurrent Resolution 268 (HILLINGS of California), House Concurrent Resolution 329 (FULTON of Pennsylvania) and House Concurrent Resolution 330 (NATCHER of Kentucky). These Resolutions would have the Congress express in strongest terms its desire that the regions of outer space be devoted to peaceful purposes through the United Nations or by such other means as may be appropriate.

The above resolutions and a similar House Concurrent Resolution 326 (McCORMACK of Massachusetts) were referred to the Committee on Foreign Affairs. After hearings on the above resolutions they were revised into House Concurrent Resolution 332, which called for the exploration of outer space by peaceful means and that such exploration be dedicated to peaceful purposes. The Foreign Affairs Committee, of which I am a member, favorably reported the above revised Resolution, and it was adopted by the House of Representatives on June 2, 1958.

Therefore, it is very apparent on the record that the Congress of the United States has recognized the far reaching importance of the outer space effort. The interest it displayed, and the immediate definite action it effected, clearly establishes that our Congress did not, and does not, minimize the urgency of immediate measures, both for national defense and for attaining scientific supremacy. It is our endeavor to develop a long-range approach to the space effort--an approach which will encourage an orderly program of development and exploration, facilitate public understanding of our purposes, and promote international cooperation.

I feel that it is the intelligent overall outlook of our Congress and government that will ultimately achieve the intellectual and technological potential of the United States with the utmost force and efficiency.

* * * * *

THE NEED FOR A NEW SYSTEM OF NORMS FOR SPACE LAW AND THE DANGER OF CONFLICT WITH THE CHICAGO CONVENTION

by

M. Smirnoff

In view of everything which has been said and written about space law in the United States, Canada, Europe and in other parts of the world, some points are now quite clear, and, in theory, there is almost unanimous accord on the essential elements of the law of space.

These basic principles are as follows:

(1) It is commonly agreed that the system created by the Chicago Convention is not adequate to solve the problems of law presented by the advent of space flight. For many reasons, the terms of the Chicago Convention, which repeat the principles of the Paris Convention of 1919 concerning the sovereignty of States over the air space above their territory, cannot be applied to conditions in outer space.

First of all, there are many formal arguments and technical reasons why the Chicago system cannot be applied to outer space. In Article 1 of the Chicago Convention, we find the concept of the "complete and exclusive sovereignty" of the State "over the air space above its territory." Article 3 states that the Convention applies to civil aircraft, and the definition of the term "aircraft" is the same as that contained in Annex A of the Paris Convention of 1919: "all machines which can derive support in the atmosphere from reaction of the air." Both the word aircraft and its definition are hardly applicable to conditions in space since in space there is no air or atmosphere.

Apart from these purely formal arguments, there are important technical facts which prevent the application of the principle of State sovereignty to outer space. The sovereignty of the State has two main characteristics: Sovereignty must be real in the sense that it can be defended by the State which claims it; furthermore, if the claim is to be based on a fact, one must know exactly where this fact occurred. Neither of these characteristics can be determined in outer space. In view of present technological developments, no State can defend its right of sovereignty at an altitude of 2,000 miles, for example. Furthermore, it is impossible to so locate an occurrence 2,000 miles in space that one could say it took place in the sovereign region of Belgium or of neighbouring Holland.

The majority of theorists agree that the system of the Chicago Convention is not applicable to the conditions of outer space. Therefore, with flights in space being more and more common, we are presented with the dangerous possibility that outer space is at present a legal vacuum. This fact became obvious when the satellites began their journeys round the earth. Article 8 of the Chicago Convention was completely forgotten, and no one protested against the flights of the satellites. The International Geophysical Year agreement can only partially be regarded as a juridical basis for flights in outer space or as a tacit consensus of all the nations of the world. The real reason why no one protested the orbiting is based on two facts. First, the nations were psychologically unaware of the imminent dangers which space flights presented to mankind. This state of unawareness was also apparent at the beginning of the 20th century when no one seriously protested against the flights of the WRIGHT brothers, BLERIOT and others. Secondly, because of the legal vacuum in outer space, no one who might have wished to make such a protest could find any firm and stable principles in the law upon which it could be based.

This lack of rules or regulations concerning outer space creates a very serious danger for all of the States and nations of the earth. If the launching of the satellites only partially revealed the existence of this danger, the peril will be reinforced by future developments in space flight. One need only point out certain problems inherent in the present state of space technology. For example, States can, without warning, launch rockets and satellites which may pass through the flight lanes of the innumerable airlines which cross their territories. In time, the lack of regulation will cause this danger to increase. We can easily visualize a rocket or satellite going astray because of some technical defect and causing heavy damage to the civilian population of another country. For the moment we shall pass over the military uses of spacecraft and the dangers they present.

What Professor MEYER calls "Verkehrssicherungspflicht," or what may in English be called a mutual obligation not to disturb or endanger national and international air transport, necessitates bringing this vacuum in the field of space law to an end.

(2) While almost everyone agrees in theory that there is a need for filling this legal vacuum, the question of how to do so is another problem. To the large majority of writers, the only way to solve this problem is an international convention. All authors are not united in the choice of the organization to convoke a conference for the elaboration of this agreement. But after the official initiatives taken in the United Nations, we think that the most convenient way to solve, or to begin to solve, this problem is by holding a conference under the auspices of the UN. We do not forget, however, that not all nations are members of that body; yet, it is clear every nation is interested in solving this problem. Therefore, we think that the invitations to this conference on the problems of outer space should be sent by the UN to all of the nations of the world. Thus, the name of this gathering in reality would be the World Conference on Outer Space Problems.

At this point we should, of course, mention the possibility of giving the ICAO the mission of summoning such a conference. In view of its experience, the ICAO would normally be the most appropriate organization to deal with this matter. Nevertheless, there are two reasons why we prefer that the first conference be held by the UN. Although the ICAO has a great number of members, its membership is smaller than that of the UN. Secondly, this is a new problem which, besides its technical novelty, contains many elements of a political nature. Although we think that it is better that the first conference be under the auspices of the UN, this does not in any way exclude the possibility that the ICAO could be of considerable assistance in the work of any organization formed by the conference to deal with these problems.

Everyone agrees that the Chicago Convention cannot serve as a basis for the new regulation of outer space and that an international convention to deal with this matter should be convoked. Discord appears only when a solution to this problem is proposed.

This is quite natural when we consider the novelty of the question and the political importance attached to any discussion of the legal problems of outer space. Although the principle of sovereignty (with recently indicated limitations) is generally agreed to apply to air space, it is not as acceptable when applied to outer space or even to limited areas in space.

We are indeed aware of the difficulties which the proposed international conference will encounter. When last considered, the application of state sovereignty to the air space itself was modified and limited in the interest of air traffic and cultural ties between peoples and nations. Therefore, and this is the focus of our paper, the new convention or agreement on the legal status of outer space will be based on principles differing substantially from those of the Chicago Convention. Herein lies the danger: the creation of systems, different in their essential elements, which will regulate two phases of the same transport entity. Expressed in another way, we fear that the two systems will be in conflict arising from the fact that an airship in the first stage of its ascent will be under the terms of the Chicago Convention; the same airship having left the atmosphere will be under the prescriptions of the new convention.

When we add the almost insolvable difficulties which exist in determining a frontier between air space and outer space, this possibility of conflict becomes much more serious. We have seen that, in theory, all of the proposed delimitations of space in a vertical sense are ingenious fictions, but fictions nevertheless. To base the legal solution of a problem, such as the responsibility for acts along these borders, on this kind of delimitation creates an insolvable legal conflict. This dilemma will be one of the crucial questions before the proposed conference; we do not see any possible solution. However the conference may adopt one of the several proposals which follow:

(1) A system for outer space based on absolute rights of sovereignty;

(2) A system based on the freedom of the whole of outer space. This is the best solution in a world based on collaboration among the peoples, but it is a very dangerous thing in a world divided in two. It is clear that it is this system which may be in eventual conflict with the norms of the Chicago Convention;

(3) A system based on different zones of outer space (the COOPER system) which would
be ingenious if a line could be traced in space as easily as a frontier is drawn on the
ground. This system also presents a possibility of conflict with the Chicago Convention.

Therefore, we do not think a solution can be found for the legal status of outer space
which will not be in conflict with the system of rules embodied in the Chicago Convention.
In short, any solution proposed before an international conference on outer space would
be in danger of so conflicting.

The logical and natural consequence of these thoughts is that any draft of a new convention must bear a close and narrow connection with the Chicago Convention. That is, in
creating a new system of legal rules for outer space, the new conference must amend the
Chicago Convention in such a way that a common system of rules applying to air space and
outer space is created. Although at present it may seem difficult to change the Chicago
Convention, it is the only plausible way to deal with this problem.

To simplify, the basic law of outer space is freedom of passage with the necessary
provisions for sound and reliable transport activities, for the safeguarding of the legitimate interests of the States, and for the free development of the science of astronautics.
On the other hand, it is possible to arrive at a single system of laws which will be a
synthesis of these two different systems: by a further and consistent limitation of the
now slightly obsolete principle of absolute and exclusive sovereignty; and through an
absolute guarantee to the State below the air space that its interests will be safeguarded.
We do not say that this synthesis will be easily achieved. Divergent interests on a
national basis will intervene to delay this agreement. However, any concession of sovereign
rights in an atmosphere of mutual confidence, will be compensated a hundredfold. The un-
interrupted progress of astronautics and the other sciences will be advanced as a result
of the exploration of outer space.

We are also aware of the danger that revision of the Chicago Convention may jeopar-
dize the consensus which that Convention represents. Similar fears were expressed during
the revision of the Warsaw Convention, but we saw that they were unfounded. Therefore,
we hope that conversion of the Chicago Convention into a general system of space regulation will bring into the circle of contracting parties those States still outside it.
This general system, avoiding a conflict between the law of airspace and that of outer
space, will be the best solution. Everything must be done to overcome difficulties
which will surely lie in the path of such a solution. However, these difficulties should
not be allowed to hamper this work, it being in the interests of all mankind for a more
prosperous future on earth and in outer space.

PRINCIPLES FOR A DECLARATION WITH REFERENCE TO THE
LEGAL NATURE OF THE MOON

by

A.A. Cocca

INTRODUCTION

In contrast to past methods of procedure, law today must anticipate technical progress and foresee the legal implications. The consequences which follow from a _faît accompli_ cannot be permitted in the present stage of the development of civilization.

The jurist is faced with this duty, as has been pointed out in the publications by CONSTANTIN A. STAVROPOULOS, head of the United Nations Legal Department, when he referred to the legal problems of space, exploited by artificial satellites.

The duty of the legal profession is to work out general principles which may serve as a basis for future regulation in the use of space and the planets.

The immediate objective of astronautics is to reach the Moon; therefore, it might be useful to anticipate a few concepts in order to draw up a final draft declaration regarding the legal nature of the earth's natural satellite.

To this end, the proposal should be divided into three parts: I. _Prior considerations to be discarded from a legal point of view_ (Our intention is thus to facilitate the work of others who are either co-operating with us or who will follow in our footsteps); II. _Legal possibilities and recommended principles_ (This section is intended to anticipate the results of our initial thoughts on this problem in seeking a workable solution); III. _Draft Declaration_ (This will be a summary of previous work and a material contribution to the preparation of Interplanetary Law).

I. PRIOR CONSIDERATIONS TO BE DISCARDED FROM A LEGAL POINT OF VIEW

The eminent United States jurist, Andrew G. HALEY - the present IAF Chairman - proposed at the VIIIth International Astronautical Congress (Barcelona, 1957) that the Moon be declared a free territory or zone, independent and autonomous. On the basis of this proposal we would like to offer the following observations for consideration:

1. The Moon Does Not Constitute Either a Territory or a Zone in Space

The word _territory_ cannot justly be employed when referring to the Moon, for this term, stemming from the latin _terra_, has been created for application only to our own planet. By extension, this word is applied to the different surfaces of our globe: land territory and sea territory. The expression "air territory" is used by some authors, but always with reference to some part or zone of our planet which constitutes indispensable and inseparable elements in the life of mankind: earth, water, air.

The Moon, on the other hand, is Earth's natural satellite. There is, therefore, a relationship of dependence or of physical subjection, but not of continuity or adjacency, responding to the laws of nature. This fact must be taken into account by jurists in order to study its legal position under the aspect of servitudes, and not under the aspect of annexation of territory in space.

The expressions "lunar continent" or "lunar surface" might be employed, but not "lunar territory" or "lunar zone." These latter concepts are the result of a forced combination of words, and they are also grammatically and legally defective.

The Moon does not constitute a "territory" or a "zone" in space, but a celestial body, a different world within the cosmos.

2. The Moon Cannot Be Declared Independent by the States of the Earth

The Moon presents a limited place which could be occupied; it is a possible site of State power of the Nations of the Earth – but never of the Moon itself, as it has no population of its own. In the event of an effective occupation and supposed "colonization" of the Moon, the power to declare itself independent of the States of the Earth could only be derived from the "colonists," who could vote to sever all ties of political dependence from the States of the Earth.

3. The Moon Cannot Be Declared Autonomous

The term autonomy has two interpretations in law: the etymological and the traditional meaning is that of a State governed by its own laws and not subject to any foreign power. In this conception, autonomy is the equivalent to independence and can therefore only be applied to independent States. The other more modern interpretation represents the unified conception of government with a legislation and internal organization of its own; it is applied to internal Provinces or States as related to a central State or Nation. The Moon has neither a "government," legislation nor an "internal organization" of its own. Any declaration of autonomy, as in the case of a declaration of independence, must come from the Moon's inhabitants, or, as there are none, from inhabitants of the Earth who may later on be transported there and become permanent residents.

4. The Moon Cannot Be Declared a Sovereign State

If we hold that the Moon cannot be declared independent or autonomous of the Earth, then it cannot be declared a sovereign State either. The legal definition of sovereignty (at present under discussion) has two aspects regarding its effectiveness: internal and external. However, it is generally interpreted to mean the quality of a State whose power admits no other superior to itself. The Moon has no organized power which can oppose Earth's superior strength through the sovereignty of its States.

Neither can any terrestrial nation which might be able to carry out the successful occupation of the Moon extend its own sovereignty to cover it. Such nation will have temporary supremacy in the sense that it will reap the benefits derived from the occupation of the Moon, but will not have sovereignty in the strictest sense.

5. There Are No Rights of Ownership on or over the Moon

Ownership is an institution of private law, which does not extend to the Moon. Eventual occupation of the Moon would by no means imply the rights of ownership, but, at most, would entitle Earth - not a particular State - to preferential domination in the event of legal claims being put forward by political organizations from other planets.

II. LEGAL POSSIBILITIES AND RECOMMENDED PRINCIPLES

1. The Moon Must Be Declared Free for Utilization by the Different States of the Earth

The term "free" is not used in the political sense - such as national freedom. It refers to the freedom to make use of a natural phenomenon within the universe. In this connection, we share the opinion of Professor AMBROSINI, President of the Legal Committee of the ICAO, on postulating a simple declaration on the freedom in the utilization of space and the recommendation to establish disciplinary regulations to enforce such a declaration.

It is our belief that, as far as the Moon is concerned, it is necessary:

1. To declare the Moon open for utilization by the Member States of the Community of Nations of the Earth.

2. To draw up regulations for the utilization of the Moon for peaceful purposes.

2. Exploitation of the Moon's Resources

The existence of natural resources on the Moon is an evident fact. It is therefore necessary to lay down regulations for their exploitation. In this connection, it would be advisable to refer to the principles governing the exploitations of those regions on Earth which are acknowledged to be free, such as the high seas, and to be guided by the established regulations for the utilization of the sea's resources.

3. Establishment of a Right of Way on the Moon for the States of the Earth

Servitudes (servitutes) were already clearly defined under Roman law. Relevant easements (rerum praediorum) were for passage, the use of roads and aquaducts. Road easement - right of way - included the right to enter, drive along and pass through (Via est jus eundi et agendi at ambulandi; nam et iter et actum in se continet via: Instutionem Justiniani, Tit. III, De servitutibus praediorum).

Applying this concept to the universe, and bearing in mind the fact that the Moon is a natural satellite of the Earth, the premise that a right of way on the Moon for States of the Earth in space travels should exist can be legally justified.

III. DRAFT DECLARATION

The States of the Earth . . . hereby agree and declare:

Firstly: That the Moon is free for utilization by the States of the Earth, and adequate regulations for this purpose and for peaceful objectives are recommended.

Secondly: That, regarding the exploitation of its natural resources, the procedure shall be the same as that governing the exploitation of the resources of the high seas.

Thirdly: That, with regard to interplanetary travel, and in view of its position as a natural satellite, a right of way is to be established on the Moon for States of the Earth.

* * * * *

Additionally, very detailed papers:

A.G. Haley, Space Age Presents Immediate Legal Problems (p. 5-27) particularly on radio communication and band widths; and

Welf Heinrich Prince of Hanover, Problems in Establishing a Legal Boundary between Air Space and Space (p. 28-30). He earned the first doctorate in Space Law in Göttingen in 1953.

Important also:

J.C. Cooper, The Problem of a Definition of "Air Space" (p. 38-44)

G.J. Feldman, An American View of Jurisdiction in Outer Space (p. 45-50)

E. Galloway, The Community of Law and Science (p. 59-62)

R. Jastrow, Definition of Air Space (p. 82)

E. Pépin, Observations (p. 91-92) for the Permanent Legal Committee

P.B. Yeager, A Code for a New Frontier (p. 116-121)

II. Other Contributions and Comments

The Substance of Outer Space Law.

1. Modern Public International Law began in Spain with Francisco de Vitoria's "De Indis et de jure belli relectiones" in 1539, and Francisco Suarez's "De legibus seu legislatore Deo" in 1612. From Holland came Hugo Grotius, whose "De jure belli ac pacis" was published in 1625. The first thesis on Outer Space appeared in 1932, written by W. Mandl, "Der Weltraum, Ein Problem der Raumfahrt."

In 1950 the International Astronautical Federation was founded in Paris. The first doctoral thesis on Space Law was published in 1953 by Welf Heinrich Prince of Hanover. The following year the Argentinian, A.A. Cocca, wrote his thesis on the law of Outer Space. The Geophysical Year of 1957 began with many new discoveries. On October 4, 1975, the Russians shot the first small satellite into Outer Space. The USA apparently had already done so before, but unofficially, and they have continued since with remarkable success. Leaders in the field of Space appeared - technologists, mathematicians and astronomers like Oberth,[1] von Braun,[2] von Kármán, Haley, Sanger and many more throughout the world. Astronauts were trained and were propelled into Outer Space eventually landing on the moon. They brought back scientific specimens for research on when and how our family of stars around the great sun were created, and low long they may live, and where they travel on their marvelously regular ellipses and circles. Today, the USA and USSR are working together on sky laboratories and shuttles.

2. The forces that create Outer Space Law are science and technology and the philosophy of law.[3] The opportunity to create this vast new law is unique. And all the jurists called upon to cooperate in the forming of it must accept an unusual, but fascinating task: the grasp of scientific facts and their impact on society. Crucial to the new law are fundamental statements and definitions. For instance, taken simply, there are three layers of atmosphere above the surface of our earth. The breathing air extends to about 5,000 meters or more (but less than 10,000 meters). The second, thinner, layer of air, in which airplanes and airships fly is limited by such jurists as Professor von Kármán to to 50 sea miles, or about 83 km. Technologists put this limit at 40 km. because most air travel confines itself to this area. However, there have been experimental exceptions, the most notable being the X-15 which reached almost 120 km. After these results, experiments were stopped. But the USA-Russian agreement of 1971 fixed the level at 110 km. and maximal height for related manoeuvres at 145 km. These are respectably high altitudes, clearly in Outer Space. Where the frontier of Outer Space really begins is still an open question delimited differently by jurists, technicians and politicians. In any event, we know that

---

1. H. Oberth, Die Raketen zu den Planetenräumen, München, 1923.
2. Werner von Braun, Das Marsprojekt, Frankfurt-Main, 1952.
3. Eilene Galloway, p. 59 ff.

Outer Space differs from Air Space in many ways. In Outer Space there is no air, no water, no nourishment for human beings, and no gravitational force. Space is characterized by intense cold, immense distances, and tremendous velocities. Fortunately, all forces follow fixed rules ensuring precise calculation. We are not describing a fourth dimension (cf. K. B. Keating, "Space Law and the Fourth Dimension of Our Age," p. 88). The fourth dimension is supposed to be time. Quite remarkable is the permeability of Space by rays of lights from far away stars or worlds, or by radio waves emanating from certain large stars, like our sun. Our satellites, provided with automatic scientific instruments or manned by living astronauts, also are permeating space. Still, it is not yet known if life exists in Outer Space. For instance, bacteria might bring dangerous illnesses to earth or carried from earth into Space if in fact they could survive Outer Space. With this unknown in mind, satellites to the moon were disinfected carefully, and astronauts had to undergo a quarantine for several weeks. Thus far there has been no substantiated need for this precaution; there was only precautionary fear of contamination. K. W. Gatland in his Contribution for 1958 (p. 63) mentions a number of problems, suggested by the IAF Committee on Space Law, which require urgent attention: (a) upper limit of effectiveness of present air law; (b) upper limit of national sovereignty; (c) radio frequency rules affecting artificial satellites and other space vehicles; (d) rules governing the re-entry of falling satellites; (e) rules affecting the operation of satellites for weather observation, radio and TV relays, and other public services; (f) quasi-military function (e.g., reconnaissance satellites); (g) military conventions; (h) contamination of extra-terrestrial bodies; (i) rules of discovery and occupancy affecting extra-terrestrial bodies; and (j) deleterious effects caused by as yet unknown physical phenomena and techniques. This is a qualified list of interesting and necessary questions. Most of them affect present law or future law, the range of which must be broad and imaginative.

3. The law must finally decide who is competent, and who is to execute it. Is it one person or many; or is it nobody or everybody? Stephen Gorove in his "Toward Cosmic Law" (p. 69) answered the question with:

> He who controls the Cosmic Space,
> Rules not only the Earth
> But the whole Universe.

However, he leaves open the question who will be "He." F. A. Pereira (p. 93-95) speaks of the unification of world astronautical strategy and the "ecumenical" nature of astronautics. He also mentions in his text the terms Human Biosphere and Cosmos. Ultimately the UN is the best ruler and ecumenical legislator. Nevertheless, an ecumenical character of Outer Space organization, taken from church law, has not taken root. The UN has behaved more neutrally than would be expected from an ecumenical premise. Partial conclusions are substantially ecumenical. No state can win sovereignty on the moon or other celestial bodies, nor can a person obtain private property. Of course, there are certain exceptions. For example, exceptions might be allowed in the interest of science, if in a restricted time and place, or where values involved are negligible. Outer Space Law begins in the sphere of Public International Law and includes criminal law and needed protection and assistance.

a) The first legal problems in space matters arose with the building of factories for space vehicles and satellites; the construction of ports for take-off and landing; and the training of the highly skilled staff. Astronauts are trained directly under and by NASA. It is charged with all organization of outer space research. Journeys from star to star may follow later. A. G. Haley called this further part of Outer Space Law the Metalaw. He even hoped that the astronauts on these journeys might meet the angels of God. We did not make technical advances with this religious hope. But the so-called "saucers" stimulated religious and other ideas. To date, three explanations for them seem possible. Possibly they are guided by extraterrestrial intelligences possessing greater knowledge and technical abilities. Or they might be a kind of electricity or air-filled balloons. Electrical forces might account for surprising changes of shapes, colors, and velocities, as with some unusual lightning effects. Finally, they may have something to do with international espionage. There are clubs in the USA and in West Germany that publish papers with authentic photographs and statements. Even now (in 1973)[1] the explanation for "saucers" is not yet solved; yet manifestations of them are increasing.

b) There was no codification of Outer Space Law in view in 1958. The Frenchman, R. Homburg, has described a program for it (p. 79-81). Section 1 deals with terminology. Section 2 defines the purpose of law. Section 3 on Public Law has six parts: Space Statutes; Statute for Natural Satellites and Planets; Artificial Satellites; Traffic and Navigation; Juridical System for Astronefs (Star-Ships); and Radio Communications. Section 4 deals with Private Law (handling wrecks, etc.). The Juridical Committee of the IAF is to prepare appropriate international and - if possible - universal conventions.

c) A few special problems have been dealt with in this first volume. The principle of "Verkehrssicherungspflicht," formulated by Professor Alex Meyer-Koln, is discussed by the Dutch Professor, I.H.Ph. de Rode-Verschoor (p. 103-104). Also Haley's detailed explications have to be mentioned again, more particularly his brave fight at the Warsaw Congress for better band widths for new services in Outer Space (p. 24).

J. Rivoire of Paris touches lightly on military problems (p. 101) and proposes that the jurisdiction of Space Law might be limited to the height of 1,500 km. - and that was in 1958. The same author (p. 98) argues against the claim of sovereignty over a planet by comparing it with the situations of France and Switzerland concerning the deep sea. Nationals from these two countries were the first to penetrate the ocean depths in bathyscaphes. They expected no further rights.

The moon, Cocca states, cannot constitute a territory or a zone in Space; be declared independent by the states of Earth; be declared autonomous; or be declared a sovereign state. However, its resources could be considered for utilization and exploitation. He concludes with a suggested draft declaration covering such usage. His views are about the same today. He views the UN as spokesman for nation-states on the Earth. In later years, Professor Cocca elaborated on the theory of the _res communis humanitatis_ and incorporated the concept of the common heritage of mankind at the UN into the Draft convention in Geneva in 1970.

---

1. C. Sagan at Cornell University and Thornton Page in NASA - UFO's, A Scientific Debate. (26. III. 1973); and K. Luzast - Die Deutschen Waffen, 4 ed. München 1962 (p. 189 - Fliegende Untertassen).

4)   The first volume of the colloquia ends with P. B. Yeager's "A Code for a New Frontier" (p. 116-121). It contains not only a praise of the new Outer Space Law, but also a warning against the overwhelming power of the monopoly of modern technology. He quotes Aldous Huxley (p. 121) on the danger of permitting technology to regulate without establishing the rules of freedom first. The remedy is good, but strict, law for everyone's welfare. Such law depends on commitment to the principles of freedom, equity and civil settlement of disputes in areas beyond the atmosphere. Morals and intellect must work together. To this expectation everybody on Earth - and in Outer Space - can agree and consent.

SECOND COLLOQUIUM ON THE LAW OF OUTER SPACE
LONDON, 1959

I. Texts Reproduced

FOREWORD

by

A.G. Haley and Dr. W.H. Prince von Hannover

The Proceedings of the First Colloquium on The Law of Outer Space held in The Hague on August 29, 1958, and now these Proceedings of the Second Colloquium, held in London on September 4, 1959, set a very definite pattern of important areas of thinking on the problems of cosmic law. We are now at the threshold of a highly serious attempt to define and even codify the problems that have been discussed in a somewhat disorganized fashion in the past. The problem of organization and logical coordination has received much serious attention during recent months. With characteristic wisdom, Dr. E. PÉPIN introduced a resolution at the Plenary Session of the Xth Annual Congress of the International Astronautical Federation, held in London in 1959, which provided:

> That the General Counsel of the I.A.F. is authorized to establish imme-
> diately such working groups as are necessary to consider the legal
> problems of space, which are today considered perhaps capable of resolu-
> tion, for example, space radio allocation frequencies, now being con-
> sidered by the International Telecommunication Union in Geneva,
> Switzerland.

This resolution was unanimously approved by the Council. In the spring of 1960, the following working groups were constituted:

Working Group 1

Chairman: John Cobb Cooper (U.S.A.); Vice Chairman: ... (U.S.S.R.) --- Antonio Ambrosini (Italy), Cezary Berezowski (Poland), Kurt Grönfors (Sweden), Alex Meyer (Germany), Milos Radojkovic (Yugoslavia), R.V. Wilberforce (U.K.), Karl Zemanek (Austria).

1. What theories have been advanced by recognized commentators as to the point at which airspace (atmosphere) ends and outer space begins?

2. Under treaty and international custom, practice and procedure, what generally by definition and judicial precedent is considered to be the upper limit of national sovereignty?

3. What are the jurisdictional and sovereign rights of nations in the airspace (atmosphere) above the terrestrial boundaries of their sovereign territories?

4. What are the rights of passage, if any, of peaceful scientific rocket (centrifugal force) vehicles, through such airspace both on the occasion of launching and on the occasion of reentry?

5. What is the legal status of a rocket vehicle traveling in such airspace?

6. What rights, if any, do nations have with respect to a rocket vehicle penetrating such airspace, such as the right to capture or destroy a rocket vehicle penetrating therein?

7. What is the present legal status of outer space, namely, the area of the universe beyond the airspace (atmosphere) of the earth, giving consideration to the legal effect of the acquiescence of nations to the free use of outer space by space vehicles as the result of the International Geophysical Year and of subsequent informal and formal understandings among nations?

8. Does the legal status of extra-solar space or extra-galactic space differ from the legal status of outer space comprised in our solar system or any portion thereof?

Working Group 2

Chairman: Alfred Verdross (Austria);   Vice Chairman: Ichiro Narahashi (Japan) --- ... (U.S.S.R.), Victor Jose Delascio (Venezuela), Nathan Feinberg (Israel), Leon Lipson (U.S.A.), Jacek Machowski (Poland), N.A.M. MacKenzie (Canada), N.M. Poulantzas (Greece).

1. What are the legal definitions of (a) rocket vehicles, space vehicles, or any other type of man-made instrumentality intended to depart from earth and to operate in outer space; (b) any such instrumentality which is intended to return to earth?

2. What should be the legal status including nationality of (a) rocket vehicles, space vehicles, or any other type of man-made instrumentality intended to depart from earth and to operate in outer space; (b) any such instrumentality which is intended to return to earth?

Working Group 3

Chairman: Michel Smirnoff (Yugoslavia);   Vice Chairman: Aldo Armando Cocca (Argentina) ---...(U.S.S.R.), Luiz de Gonzaga Bevilacqua (Brazil), Welf Heinrich Prince of Hanover (Germany), K. Kirilov (Bulgaria), Borko Nikolajevic (Yugoslavia), Petros G. Vallindas (Greece), Philip B. Yeager (U.S.A.).

1. What theories have been advanced by recognized commentators as to sovereignty over celestial bodies?

2. What should be the legal status of the sun, the moon, the planets, and other natural objects in outer space?

3. Can individual nations obtain sovereignty over celestial bodies?

4. What acts are necessary to establish the sovereignty of a nation over a celestial body? For example, what would be the legal effect of contact between: (a) a manned space vehicle and a celestial body; (b) an unmanned space vehicle and a celestial body?

5. What is the extent of sovereignty over a celestial body?

6. How far does the sovereignty in a celestial body extend beyond the physical substance of the body?

7. What theories have been advanced by recognized commentators as to property rights in celestial bodies?

W o r k i n g   G r o u p   4

Chairman: Mario Matteucci (Italy);   Vice Chairman: William Strauss (U.S.A.) ---
Vincenzo Alessandrone-Gambardella (Italy), Manu Amatayakul (Thailand), K.M. Beaumont (U.K.),
Antonio Francoz Rigalt (Mexico), Eilene Galloway (U.S.A.), Alec Mellor (France), Ingo V.
Münch (Germany).

1. As to each terrestrial sovereign nation, state the treaties to which such nation adheres, and its domestic laws, rules and regulations concerning air space and outer space, and those treaties, laws, rules and regulations which would have to be amended, revoked, changed or superseded because of the adoption of any treaty, law, rule or regulation.

2. What new situations in the area of domestic law are created by space activities to which existing laws are not applicable?

3. Should national codes of domestic law be developed to meet problems arising out of space activities? For example, should those nations which hold themselves to be immune from suit by reason of sovereign immunity permit suit against themselves in the case of actions arising out of space activity?

W o r k i n g   G r o u p   5

Chairman: Christopher Shawcross (U.K.);   Vice Chairman: ... (U.S.S.R.) --- Yasuo Abe
(Japan), Ralph E. Becker (U.S.A.), Henri T.P. Binet (Canada), Sphrang Devahastin (Thailand),
Ernst Fasan (Austria), H.R. Hahlo (U.S. Africa), Marek Zylicz (Poland).

1. What should be the nature and scope of regulations governing the following aspects of space flight:

a) registration requirements for public and private space vehicles;

b) inspection of space vehicles before launching;

c) air traffic rules to be followed by spacecraft while passing through airspace and through outer space [in particular, what regulations should be made to cover the following:

(i) announcement of proposed space vehicle launchings together with information on the vehicle's trajectory;

(ii) the passage of vehicles in outer space so as to avoid collision];

d) safety of life and property in airspace and in outer space;

e) search and rescue;

f) emergency landing of space craft;

g) emigration and immigration;

h) prevention of contamination of airspace and outer space [e.g., by atomic radiation, refuse, abandoned vehicles, and the like];

i) prevention of contamination of earth and celestial bodies;

j) collection and dissemination of information as to the weather, radiation, meteorite activity and similar conditions encountered in space flight.

Working group 6

Chairman: E. Pepin (Canada);   Vice Chairman: Otto Riese (Luxembourg) --- ...(U.S.S.R.), O. Hadjivassiliou-Evgenidou (Greece), A. Beatty Rosevear (Canada), A.C. Russell (Australia), Hassan Safavi (Iran), Branislav Supica (Yugoslavia), Takashi Yoshida (Japan).

1. Are existing international organizations able to administer and enforce appropriate regulations which may be adopted for the regulation of activities in space?

If not, is it feasible: (a) to adapt existing international organizations so that they would be able to administer and enforce appropriate regulations; or (b) to create new international organizations to administer and enforce such regulations?

2. What authority should be delegated to the international organization or organizations which would be responsible for the administration and enforcement of space regulations?

3. What provisions for arbitration should be included in any international agreement concerning the use of airspace and outer space? What situations, if any, should be subject to compulsory arbitration?

5. What is the present and potential role of the International Court of Justice in the settlement of legal problems of space activity?

Working Group 7

Chairman: Andrew G. Haley (U.S.A.);   Vice Chairman: ... (U.S.S.R.) --- J. Busak (Czechoslovakia), Sverre Holsten (Norway), Jean-Pierre Houle (Canada), J. Ivanyi (Hungary), Manfred Lachs (Poland), Digeddine Saleh (U.A.R.), Peter S. Triantafillidis (Greece).

1. What provisions should be made for the determination by national and international organizations of the nature and extent of the requirements for the use of radio in space flight activities? What is the status of current knowledge as to the extent of such requirements at present and in the foreseeable future?

2. What provisions should be made for the determination by national and international organizations of the radio frequencies available for use in space flight activities? What is the extent of current provisions in national and international law for allocations for such uses of radio frequencies?

3. What provisions should be made for international agreement on interference involving radio frequencies used in space flight, including the following subjects:

a) Interference to radio transmissions in space flight activities;

b) Interference from radio transmissions in space flight activities to other uses of radio;

c) Termination of transmissions from radio transmitters in space, expecially those operating unattended;

d) Establishment of priorities for transmission and reception involving space flight activities where interference would result from simultaneous transmissions from several sources;

e) Identification of transmissions to aid in the determination of the sources of transmissions and of interference.

4. Is the International Telecommunication Union [I.T.U.] presently constituted so as to be capable of regulating the use of radio in space flight activities? To this end, what are the present legal capabilities of the I.T.U. with regard to the matters listed below, and in what respects should the International Telecommunication Convention and the Radio Regulations of the I.T.U. be enlarged, or modified, so as to permit the resolution of these issues:

a) In what manner should radio frequencies be allocated for use in space flight activity, i.e., on an exclusive basis, on a shared basis involving other uses, to individual nations, to world organizations, and the like?

b) What is the extent of the I.T.U.'s jurisdiction? Can frequency allocations be enforced by the I.T.U. as to uses outside the earth's atmosphere?

c) Are the existing agencies of the I.T.U. capable of making continuing studies of the uses of radio in space flight activities? In what respects should the agencies of the I.T.U. coordinate such studies with other bodies such as the I.A.F.?

Working Group 8

Chairman: Robert Homburg (France);   Vice Chairman: John Hogan (U.S.A.) --- Alvaro Bauzá Araújo (Uruguay), Arno Barber (Austria), Manfred Bodenschatz (Germany), Maxwell Cohen (Canada), S.W.L. De Villiers (Union of South Africa), Kyozi Funada (Japan), Flávio A. Pereira (Brazil).

1. What situations are created by space activities affecting private rights, to which existing treaties, conventions, agreements and laws of sovereign nations are not applicable? Specifically, what effect will space activities have upon private rights and duties in the following areas: nationality, citizenship, customs, domicile, crimes, immigration, emigration, ownership of property, torts, contracts?

2. What regulations should be adopted for the protection of private interests or for national proprietary interests in outer space?

3. What types of international forums or adjudicatory bodies should be set up by international agreement to decide upon the liability for, and the extent of the compensation applicable, in case of any violation of private rights caused by a space flight activity?

Working Group 9

Chairman: Spencer M. Beresford (U.S.A.);   Vice Chairman: I.H.Ph. de Rode-Verschoor (The Netherlands) --- George J. Feldman (U.S.A.), M. Ferreira de Lima (Portugal), Vicente Gumicio (Chile), Eitaro Komabayashi (Japan), Tsuyoshi Mano (Japan), Friedrich W. von Rauchhaupt (Germany), Jean Rivoire (France).

1. With specific reference to damages caused as a result of space flight activity, what provisions should be included in international regulations or agreement governing (a) the establishement of responsibility and (b) rights of recovery for injury or damage caused by space vehicles:

a) to property and life on the surface of the earth;

b) to airborne property and life;

c) to space vehicles and property and life contained therein? What should be the basis of liability for such damage? In particular, should liability be based upon a theory of gross negligence, reasonable care, strict liability, or some other rule?

2. What requirements and instrumentalities should be created through international agreement to assure the compensation of individuals entitled to relief for any violation of private rights? In connection with this question, will financial guarantees of sovereign states suffice? Would compulsory insurance suffice? Should a specific compensation fund of an international character be created to which public and private agencies would be required to contribute in advance of any form of space flight activity?

Working   Group   10

Chairman: Fritz Gerlach (Germany);   Vice Chairman: Mortimer Schwartz (U.S.A.) --- Gisli G. Isleifsson (Iceland), V. Kopal (Czechoslovakia), C. Lohananda (Thailand), Hector Perucchi (Argentina), Björn Tuneld (Sweden), J.E. Van Der Meulen, (The Netherlands), Hans-Herbert Wimmer (Germany).

1. What international organizations, governmental and nongovernmental, are presently concerned with the regulation of space activities?

2. To what extent may these existing organizations (such as the I.A.F.) serve as agencies for the regulation of various activities in space?

3. Should new international organizations be established for the promotion and co-ordination of activity in outer space?

4. Should a committee be formed to draft an international agreement, modeled on the Antarctic Treaty of December 1, 1959, to limit the use of outer space to peaceful purposes?

Working   Group   11

Chairman: ... (U.S.S.R);   Vice Chairman: C. Wilfred Jenks (U.K.) --- Antonio Ambrosini (Italy), John Cobb Cooper (U.S.A.), Augusto R. Füster (Paraguay), Arthur F. Garmaise (Canada), Elena Genova (Bulgaria), J. Hübener (Germany), M. Potocny (Czechoslovakia).

What arrangements should be made for the creation of international agreements covering:

a) cooperation in space exploration;

b) prohibition of the use of artificial satellites and celestial bodies for certain purposes;

c) cooperation in the development of space law;

d) provisions that space problems not covered by existing law be settled by negotiation or arbitration;

e) establishment of methods for dissemination of basic scientific data regarding space flight;

f) establishment of space data centers and research institutes;

g) operation of international satellites and space platforms;

h) prompt return to the launching country of space vehicles, their equipment and personnel which have landed or crashed on the territory of another sovereign state;

i) use of satellites as charting aids to ship and aircraft navigation;

j) inspection and control of armaments on space flights, particularly nuclear weapons, as well as controls suggested for policing the peaceful uses of atomic energy;

k) the adoption of an "International Space Navigation Code," analogous to the "International Code of Signals on the High Seas"?

We look forward to the papers, which will be presented in these Proceedings during the next several years, for guidance, reference, research and history.

June 1960.

* * * * *

SPACE EXPLORATION - THE PROBLEMS OF TODAY, TOMORROW AND IN THE FUTURE
by
A.G. Haley

. . .

Therefore, in scientific terms there are three distinct regimes of flight, each possible within certain ascertainable, but by no means ascertained, limits: (1) the aeronautical regime; (2) the corridor of atmospheric escape; (3) the astronautic regime. The aeronautical regime is well regulated by law, and the jurisdictional problems it presents have been solved by treaty. The third, the astronautic regime, has been described as a legal "no-man's world" over which the nations of the earth have no jurisdiction. This leaves the question of the escape corridor. Is it to be free for all to use or are there reasons for extending terrestrial jurisdiction to encompass it?

Dr. Eugène Pépin thinks that "it should be taken for granted that over and around the surface of the earth (land or sea areas) there is what the scientists call 'atmosphere' over certain parts of which national sovereignty is extended; and above the atmosphere there is 'space' .... Therefore, from a legal point of view, there are only two zones: one, the air or atmosphere which has a legal status already defined in an international instrument, and the other, the space of a still undefined status."

C. Wilfred Jenks expresses the same view when he states: "Space beyond the atmosphere is a res extra commercium incapable by its nature of appropriation on behalf of any particular sovereignty."

It would appear that both Dr. Pépin and Mr. Jenks would place the escape regime in the same category as either airspace or the astronautical regime and thus refuse to recognize it as requiring a separate treatment in the law.

John Cobb Cooper recognized the need for special consideration of the escape regime when he proposed an international convention which would, inter alia, "extend the sovereignty of the subjacent state upward to 300 miles above the earth's surface, designating this ... area as 'contiguous space,' and provide for a right of transit through this zone for all non-military flight instrumentalities when ascending or descending." Such an extension would, in terms of Dr Sängers diagram, extend jurisdiction from approximately 37.3 miles above the earth's surface to 300 miles. This would be only a small segment of the escape regime which extends 37.3 miles to about 3,728 miles.

It is clear that "contiguous space," as used by Professor Cooper, and the escape region shown in Dr. Sängers diagram, are not the same thing. Basing a jurisdictional area on the concept of "contiguous space" is quite unnecessary, although wisely precautionary, and is not susceptible of implementation. On the other hand, under certain conditions, national jurisdiction will be quite indirectly, but effectively maintained over what might be called "contiguous space." The recovery of the full-scale nose cone of the Jupiter rocket hastens the day when the nations of the earth will be offered point-to-point rocket communications involving many services. Some scientists believe that the first commercial use of rocket vehicles will be for mail transportation between New York and London. This service and other services will gradually be extended to the four corners of the world - Melbourne to London, Moscow to Los Angeles, Buenos Aires to Chicago, Los Angeles to New York. The trajectories of each of these routes will be different, and will involve different altitudes. Some of these rockets will describe a trajectory requiring heights of 300 miles or less, and others will probably require heights in excess of 1,000 miles. National jurisdiction will be effectively maintained by the granting of launching and landing rights, and thus there will be indirect national control with respect to point-to-point earth rockets over contiguous space. With the advent of manned rocket ships, this control undoubtedly will become more severe because of vastly increased considerations of safety and other problems.

More study of the escape corridor and the problems it presents will be necessary before any final decision can be made on whether, as Dr. Pépin states, territorial sovereignty should cease at the aeronautical frontier - the Kármán Line - or whether some measure of direct control over this region should be provided, perhaps along the lines suggested by Professor Cooper. Whatever the final decision may be will depend on the data produced by the scientist and the creativity of the lawyer acting with full understanding of the scientific facts.

The most pressing current astronautical problem is making adequate international provisions for space radio communications. The IAF initiated its program for the development of a plan to control the use of radio in outer space with a formal proposal to the International Telecommunication Union (ITU) dated April 16, 1956. The IAF urged that working arrangements be set up between the IAF and the ITU "looking toward the optimum plan for allocation of frequencies in the radio spectrum for ... communications in outer space."

The IAF proposal contained a five point plan along the following lines:

1. The International Radio Consultative Committee (CCIR) of the ITU should study the requirements of radio in space.

2. The International Frequency Registration Board (IFRB) of the ITU should study the frequencies available to meet the requirements developed by the CCIR.

3. The IAF should send representatives to the sessions of the CCIR and the IFRB.

4. The ITU should send representatives to the IAF's meetings - including the Rome Congress on earth satellites and space flight, September 1956.

5. After completion of the four steps outlined above, the ITU should initiate formal steps to effect radio allocations for use in space.

The ITU responded negatively to the IAF proposal. On June 11, 1956, the Secretary-General of ITU advised the IAF that the Union viewed the matters raised by the IAF as appropriate for the administration of individual member nations.

Thereafter the IAF renewed its proposals - both in presentations to the ITU itself and in proposals to the constituent organizations of the ITU. The first of the latter category to which a formal proposal was made was the CCIR.

The International Astronautical Federation, on September 3, 1956, submitted to the CCIR a proposal that the CCIR establish a new Study Group for extra-terrestrial communications. In this proposal the IAF reviewed the progress up to that time in earth orbital satellite programs, and in the development of Cislunar and Circumlunar space vehicles. In the IAF proposal the importance of radio communications and guidance in such space flight activities was also discussed.

The IAF document thereupon concluded with the statement that the CCIR is the only international body authorized to study the subjects of communications and guidance in extra-terrestrial projects. The IAF urged that such a study be completed and a report rendered in time for presentation to the International Radio Conference of 1959 (Administrative Radio Conference, International Telecommunication Union, Geneva, 1959).

...

In addition to its work with the CCIR, the IAF has effected close cooperation with the ITU, parent body of the CCIR. The current activity of the two bodies, IAF and ITU, is centered around the preparations for the Administrative Radio Conference, commencing August 17, 1959 at Geneva. The duties of the Conference will be to

i) revise the Radio Regulations of the International Telecommunication Convention (Atlantic City, 1947).

ii) deal with all other matters deemed necessary within the terms of the Convention and the General Regulations and any directives given by the Plenipotentiary Conference.

iii) elect the members of the International Frequency Registration Board.

iv) review the activities of the Board.

* * * * *

THE UNITED NATIONS AD HOC COMMITTEE ON THE PEACEFUL USES OF OUTER
SPACE. ACCOMPLISHMENTS AND IMPLICATIONS FOR LEGAL PROBLEMS.

by

E. Galloway

...

Results of the Legal Committee

Under the chairmanship of Mr. Ambrosini (Italy), the legal committee held five meetings, considered the working papers which were submitted by the delegations from Italy, Mexico, and the United States, and maintained a liaison with the technical committee as well as with various representatives of spcialized organizations with space programs. The final report of the legal committee was incorporated into that of the ad hoc committee and unanimously approved on June 25, 1959.

The task of the legal committee was to analyze and submit to the full committee "The nature of legal problems which may arise in the carrying out of programs to explore outer space." This assignment was necessarily related to the terms of reference of the entire resolution passed by the General Assembly (1348, XIII) and therefore was concerned solely with the peaceful uses of outer space. There was considerable discussion, however, as to just what would be involved in reporting adequately on this matter, and three points of view were put forward.

One viewpoint was that the committee should confine itself to identifying and listing legal problems without offering solutions.

A second school of thought favored adding to the list the reasons why the problems were significant and arranging them in order of priority.

A third view was that legal problems could be studied in accordance with general principles of justice from which deductions could be made and applied to specific space laws.

The prevailing opinion was that the committee should proceed with caution and patience, Mr. Ambrosini pointing out that "the legal committee, by the very nature of its functions, would not be working on as firm a basis as would the technical committee, especially as the sphere of work assigned to it was often affected by political considerations." The lack of sufficient experience and scientific information was given as the reason for not being too ambitious. There emerged a consensus that since it was obviously impossible to define all the legal space problems that might arise, the committee would proceed by identifying and classifying problems on a priority basis, distinguishing between those which would respond to early treatment and those whose solution appeared to be in the more distant future. Furthermore, it was decided that the determination of priorities would include some analysis of how the problems could be met, but would not involve recommendations for their solution.

Some general observations were made by the committee which considered that the United Nations Charter and the Statute of the International Court of Justice were not confined to earth and that their provisions could be extended to include activities in outer space. Special attention was called to the fact that the United Nations Charter is based upon the sovereign equality of all its members and that the General Assembly had expressly resolved that international space programs for peaceful uses should be considered in connection with the benefit of States irrespective of the state of their economic or scientific development.

Opinion was unanimous regarding the necessity for studying the principles and procedures which apply to the sea and to airspace in order to determine their relevancy for outer space regulation. Various types of space activities by governments and private groups might engender different kinds of legal problems - administrative, procedural, and regulatory.

There was a firm commitment to the idea that it is neither practicable nor desirable at the present time to devise a comprehensive code of space law. The committee report stated that "... the rule of law is neither dependent upon, nor assured by, comprehensive codification and that premature codification might prejudice subsequent efforts to develop the law based on a more complete understanding of the practical problems involved." At the same time, it is necessary to keep the law in pace with the facts and to insure close cooperation between scientists and lawyers. The committee suggested that its list of legal problems should continually be reviewed by whatever means the General Assembly should deem fitting.

Six problems were listed by the committee as being susceptible of priority treatment.

First, the committee came to the conclusion that the satellite programs of the International Geophysical Year were based upon the premise that nations had permission to launch such vehicles even though they traversed an orbit above national boundary lines. It was concluded, therefore, that within the context of strictly peaceful uses, "with this practice, there may have been initiated the recognition or establishment of a generally accepted rule to the effect that, in principle, outer space is, on conditions of equality, freely available for exploration and use by all in accordance with existing or future international law or agreements."

Second, the problem of liability for injury or damage caused by space vehicles raised a number of legal questions. Answers are needed to such questions as the type of injury and kind of conduct which should establish liability. Should the fact that damage occurred on land, in airspace, or in outer space be a governing factor? Should a launching nation be liable for unlimited damages? Should joint international projects carry with them liability that is joint or several? On the question of who will determine liability and insure payment for damages, the committee considered that study of an agreement providing for compulsory jurisdiction of the International Court of Justice should be given priority. Also, the experience of the International Civil Aviation Organization on such matters should be analyzed to determine to what extent the Convention on Damage Caused by Foreign Aircraft to Third Parties on the Surface could be applied to space vehicles.

Third, the problem of the allocation of radio frequencies to space vehicles follows the scientific and technological evaluation of this important matter. The legal committee called attention to the fact that the International Telecommunication Union is already qualified to function in this area and that documents concerning frequencies for earth satellites will be considered by the Administrative Radio Conference of the ITU, which opened in Geneva on August 17, 1959, for meetings which are expected to last for several months.

Fourth, the avoidance of interference between space vehicles and aircraft is a problem whose legal implications require early study by governments.

Fifth, the identification and registration of space vehicles and the coordination of launchings would necessarily imply the formulation of rules and regulations of vital interest to the legal community.

Sixth, the reentry and landing of space vehicles will create the necessity of making arrangements with nations affected by the descent and landing. Multilateral agreements would be desirable to take care of situations involving accidental landings. The committee also thought that the rules of international law which now apply to aircraft landing in distress might also be made applicable to space vehicles.

In addition to these six top-priority problems, the committee analyzed a number of other areas which can be expected to involve legal measures. Official definitions of airspace and outer space were deemed premature at this time, and the committee believed that the problems to which it had given highest priority did not depend for their solution on a legal distinction between these two areas in the space environment. It was suggested, however, that one approach to the problem would be to establish the limits of airspace and outer space within a practicable range. Another idea which could be explored is use of the type of space activity as a basis for legal control.

The legal questions which might arise in the exploration of celestial bodies were not ranked with high-priority problems at this time, but a number of interesting suggestions for meeting this situation were advanced: That sovereignty should not be claimed by a nation over celestial bodies; that such area should be used solely for mankind's benefit; and that an international administration might handle such matters.

The committee believed there was not much present danger in space vehicles interfering with each other, but thought this was a future possibility. The rules and regulations which now apply to air traffic might be related to space travel.

And, finally, the committee thought that international legal measures might be required to handle technological achievements, particularly in the case of meteorological satellites.

Implications for the Legal Profession

The ad hoc committee report has made a significant contribution toward the orderly development of science and law in the peaceful uses of outer space. From this report, scientists and engineers can be apprised of the legal problems incident to space exploration; and the legal profession has been given the latest scientific and technological evaluations to assist in advancing solutions to present and future problems. Both groups may profit from the description and analysis of the international organizations now operating in this field and determine ways in which coordination can best be achieved.

The report has delineated a rich field for research and analysis which can be of practical value to the International Astronautical Federation in considering the appointment of committees to study the problems of space law. The way is also open for individuals to contribute their thinking to the first historic guidelines for international cooperation in outer space.

The main legal problems which might arise in space exploration and require study directed toward their solution have been identified:

1. To what extent is the recognized international law of the sea and in airspace analogous to the problems of outer space, and in what ways is the space environment unique?

2. What can we learn from the administrative and procedural methods of existing intergovernmental organizations which might have an application to space activities?

3. How can it be determined whether the practices established and observed by the International Geophysical Year may have resulted in international recognition of the freedom of outer space for exploration under present and future international law?

4. What are the advantages and disadvantages of the various proposals made, for the solution of the problem of liability for injury or damage caused by space vehicles?

5. Should the International Court of Justice be given compulsory jurisdiction over disputes between nations concerning liability for damage from space vehicles?

6. Is the experience of the International Civil Aviation Organization concerning surface damage caused by aircraft applicable to space vehicles?

7. What contributions can be made by the legal profession to the International Telecommunication Union in dealing with the problem of allocation of radio frequencies to space vehicles?

8. What proposals can be made for the solution of the problem of interference between aircraft and space vehicles?

9. What legal factors are involved in the identification and registration of space vehicles and the coordination of launchings, both for individual nations and for international arrangements?

10. What rules of existing international law might govern the legal problems which are likely to arise in the reentry and landing of space vehicles? What are the areas in which new substantive agreements between nations may be needed?

11. Is there a requirement in terms of national sovereignty for differentiating between airspace and outer space, and, if so, what are the advantages and disadvantages of the various proposals which can be advanced to meet this problem?

12. What are the international legal implications of the task required for the formulation of safeguards against contamination of celestial bodies and the earth as a result of space exploration?

13. What is the relation of the concepts of national sovereignty to the exploration and exploitation of outer space, and what proposals would have to be considered in arriving at a solution of the problems involved?

14. What legal arrangements of administration, regulation and control would be involved in meeting the problem of coordinating existing international organizations which have space programs or whose activities can logically be extended to include space activities?

* * * * *

LEGAL PROBLEMS OF OUTER SPACE.
USA AND SOVIET VIEWPOINTS.
by
S. Kucherov

...

The Resolutions

The Soviet government presented to the 13th General Assembly of U.N., in March 1958, a proposal "for ensuring that cosmic space is used only for peaceful aims for the good of all mankind." This proposal contains the following points:

1. Prohibition of use of cosmic space for military purposes, and the pledge by the states to launch rockets into cosmic space only in accordance with a preconcerted and agreed international program.

2. Liquidation of military bases on territories of foreign states in Europe, in the Near East, Middle East and North Africa.

3. Establishment of appropriate international control within the framework of the United Nations in order to watch over the fulfillment of obligations mentioned under 1 and 2.

4. Creation of a United Nations organ for international cooperation in the field of cosmic space studies enabling the fulfillment of the following functions:

    a) to develop the preconcerted international program on launching of intercontinental and cosmic rockets for the purpose of studying cosmic space and watching over the fulfillment of such programs;

    b) to continue on a permanent basis those studies of cosmic space which are now being carried out within the framework of the International Geophysical Year;

    c) to serve as a world center for the collection, mutual exchange and dissemination of information concerning cosmic studies;

    d) to coordinate national research plans in the field of cosmic space studies and to extend every possible help and cooperation for their fulfillment."

This resolution was, naturally, fully supported by Galina and Korovin.

The U.S.S.R. proposed at the 13th United Nations General Assembly a recommendation for the creation of an international committee within the framework of the U.N. to promote cooperation in cosmic research for peaceful purposes; a preparatory group of states (the U.S.S.R., the U.S.A., Britain, France, India, Czechoslovakia, Poland, Rumania, and the United Arab Republic) should be formed in order to work out the program and statutes of the committee, as well as define the functions of the future international committee and to present its report to the 14th General Assembly.

The U.S.S.R. proposal was not passed, but a resolution presented by the American delegation was carried, creating a group of other nations "which would give the United States complete control in it," according to Mr. Korovin. In his opinion, by this procedure the United States government again showed its intention to subordinate cosmic research to its expansionist and aggressive plan; this is why the Soviet Union refused to participate in this body.

Thus the U.S.S.R. and the U.S.A., as on many other questions, disagree over the neutralization of outer space and over the composition of the group of nations charged with the working out of the statutes and the program of an international committee at the United Nations to promote cooperation in common research for peaceful purposes.

The Role of the Permanent Legal Committee

It is evident that the differences existing between the U.S. and the U.S.S.R in regard to the questions of the use of outer space and its legal status are basically of a political character and closely related to the general questions of disarmament, and the use of nuclear weapons. As long as an agreement on some "level" will not have been achieved with regard to these basic questions, there will be no effective cooperation between these powers on the solution of the problems of outer space.

What can our Committee do in the presence of such a situation? Certainly nothing to help these countries come to terms. However, the legal status of outer space involves many special questions the clarification and solution of which the Committee can do its best. I have in mind such questions as the delimitation between airspace and outer space and civil and criminal responsibility for damage to body and property caused from outer space. There is a score of such questions which have been debated in literature and sessions of legal societies; it is not necessary to enumerate them here.

While reviewing agencies and international organizations which might do "spacework" for the study of space law, the authors of the Staff Report of the Select Committee on Astronautics and Space Exploration of the U.S. House of Representatives remarked that "the International Astronautical Federation, although experienced in astronautics, is relatively loosely organized and at present does not possess the same degree of official recognition as the other group." The reproach of "loose" organization seems to me to have some ground with regard to the Permanent Legal Committee.

In order to eliminate this defect, I move that the Committee decide:

1. To elect a chairman and a secretary;

2. To organize subcommittees in every country represented on the Committee;

3. To charge every subcommittee with the study of questions pertaining to the legal status of outer space;

4. To charge the Chairman with the coordination of this work;

5. To request that the subcommittees present to the Colloquium of the Committee at the XI Congress of the IAF reports on the problems studied by them.

* * * * *

THE ROLE OF IAF IN THE ELABORATION OF THE
NORMS OF FUTURE SPACE LAW
by
M.S. Smirnoff

...

Therefore, we submit to the attention of the Permanent Legal Committee of IAF and of the Second Colloquium on Space Law the following Project of an International Convention of Space Law:

"... The High Contracting Parties persuaded of the usefulness of the exploration of outer space for the well-being of mankind, desiring to avoid all sorts of conflicts between the peoples and to avoid the creation of a customary law in the field of space flight which could make the international codification of these norms more difficult, conscious of the greatest interest in preventing the military use of outer space, believing more and more in the possibility of transportation in outer space and seeking an international solution in such an important field which will rightly delimitate the obligations and rights of everybody in outer space,

Agree on the following principles of the legal status of outer space:

Article 1

The use of the outer space is free for peaceful purposes only.

Article 2

The outer space begins where the possibility to fly ceases for propelled and jet planes[1], deriving support in the atmosphere from reactions of the air[2].

Article 3

A special Organization acting as a Specialized Agency of the United Nations Organization and in close contact with the International Civil Aviation Organization and other appropriate international organizations will be created to apply Art. 1 and the other articles of this Convention.

Article 4

The High Contracting Parties take the solemn obligation to inform in advance the International Organization, created in accordance with Art. 3, of every space flight with all the necessary details of such a flight consisting of precise data about the spacecraft which will perform the flight, about the place and exact time of the flight and its duration, and about its aim.

Article 5

Upon information mentioned in Art. 4, the International Organization, created in accordance with Art. 3, can, for the reason of coordination of efforts in space exploration and for security reasons, make some remarks which must be taken into account by the High Contracting Parties which plan the flights.

Article 6

Every spacecraft must be individually marked and have a distinctive nationality's mark. The International Organization, created in accordance with Art. 3, can also have its special spacecraft registered as belonging to this Organization. Each High Contracting Party must have a special Register of spacecrafts and all the data of this Register have to be communicated to the above mentioned International Organization.

Article 7

The inscription in a national Register of spacecraft is a basis for the responsibility for all acts and damages which could be done by a spacecraft during its flight in the outer space, in the atmosphere, and on the ground of the earth or on other planets.

Article 8

The right of occupation and discovery does not exist in the space which is considered as res communis and put under the authority of the International Organization created in accordance with Art. 3.

Article 9

This International Organization shall issue all the necessary special Regulations based on the principles of this Convention and aimed toward the regulation of all problems created by space flights. This Organization shall also issue its own Rules of Procedure and its Internal Regulations.

Article 10

All conflicts that may arise from space flights will be solved by appropriate organs of the International Organization created in accordance with Art. 3. If this cannot be achieved, the decision will be taken before the Court of International Justice. The preliminary ad hoc arbitral tribunal procedure is recommended.

Article 11

With the development of space flights and its application in the regular transportation flights from the earth to other planets, with a view to avoiding the conflicts with the principles of Chicago Convention, the space transportation flights will be regarded as being wholly, from the take-off on the earth until the landing on the earth, under the rules of this Convention even for the part of flight performed in the airspace. With the further development of space transportation flights, a common legal regime for the outer space and airspace is to be created.

Article 12

The International Organization, created in accordance with Art. 3, will take the necessary measures to prevent the contamination of outer space with earth microbes and illnesses which may occur during the space flights.

Article 13

The International Organization, created in accordance with Art. 3, will have the authority to punish by appropriate sanctions the contraventions against the rules of this Convention.

The project we propose for the attention of the Second Colloquium on Outer Space Law is far from complete. However, by utilizing all that has been written on the problems of outer space law and, more particularly the works of Mr. John C. Hogan and Mr. Lewis S. Bohn, which encompass practically all problems which can be codified internationally in space law, it will be easy to augment this Project, and to add the details to the principles it proclaims.

But these principles must be agreed upon on the largest possible scale even in the Permanent Legal Committee of IAF, which includes members of different countries and different legal opinions. Only after such an agreement on the basic principles of this Project can discussion go further to broaden the basic text of the Project.

In our mind the basic principles are the following:

1. There is no state sovereignty in the outer space.

2. There is no place for absolute liberty of flights in the outer space.

3. There must be an International Organization to govern the circumstances in outer space and to limit in certain degrees the right of the States to launch spacecrafts to outer space.

4. Only peaceful uses of outer space can be permitted.

5. Measures must be taken to avoid the conflict of norms of the Chicago Convention for airspace and the norms of the new Convention on outer space.

When agreement can be reached in the Permanent Legal Committee of IAF, the first stage of our work will be accomplished.

It is very difficult to tell which method for this work is the best. Perhaps the system of certain rapporteurs for special questions with further discussion of such reports is the most convenient one. But the system of working is not so important. The most important thing is to reach an agreement on the principles which will be the fundamental part of the future Convention. This agreement must be as broadly defined as possible and should include, if possible, all members of Permanent Legal Committee of IAF. When a compromise should be advisable, we propose to support that compromise in the interest of the final success of our work which is so important in the present situation of mankind.

---

[1] The problem of delimitation of airspace and outer space, despite the marvellous work of Professor Cooper and others in this field, is not solved. We chose therefore the system proposed by Mr. Bevilacqua and the Brazilian delegation at the First Colloquium of the Law of Outer Space in The Hague in August 1958. This system gives the solution for one problem at least: the problem of responsibility, which, with this system of delimitation, could be easily solved.

[2] We used the formulation from Annex A of Paris Convention of 1919.

* * * * *

II. Other Contributions and Comments

The Working Groups.

Eleven groups composed of eight to nine members (cf. Eug. Pépin, p. 123) met to consider legal problems of outer space and possible codification (cf. v. Rauchhaupt, p. 125 ff. - International Administrative Community). The groups worked on:

1) End of airspace and beginning of outer space.
2) Space vehicles and instruments.
3) Sovereignty over celestial bodies. (cf. Smirnoff, p. 151-152 - cf. texts)
4) National treaties on outer space. (cf. Galloway, p. 37-40 - cf. texts)
5) Registration for public and private space vehicles.
6) International organizations to enforce regulation of activities in space.
7) National and international organizations for the use of radio in space. (cf. Haley, p. 53 ff., - cf. text)
8) New influence by space activities affecting private rights.
9) Responsibility and liability for damages.
10) Use of international organizations.
11) Arrangements for further international agreements such as an International Space Navigation Code analogous to the International Code of Signals on the High Seas.

It is noteworthy that individuals both within and outside these groups sent contributions of their own on these themes as well as other subjects for this volume--five contributions were sent from the 9th group alone. Extensive contributions were offered by S.S. Lall from India (p. 75-110) and by Haroldo Valladao from Brazil (p. 156-168), who weren't members of any of the eleven working groups. Differing nationalities and divergent national laws all seemed to merge into the framework of international law, which bound them together. The contents of these working-group contributions deal with immediate problems and philosophies for the future:

1. For the present (1959).

   a) The shooting of a rocket into space produces varying effects, as Madame de Rode-Verschoor (p. 134-138) points out, and has revolutionaized many aspects of the life of mankind. She then discusses the educational, military, and political aspects of these changes. In the political consideration, much attention is given to a resolution passed by the General Assembly of the UN in 1958 on establishing an ad hoc committee on the peaceful uses of outer space. This is followed by short comments on the following aspects: astronomical, juridical, economic, sociological, medical, religious. She concludes with a comment about the opening up of a whole new field for imaginative writing.

   b) E. Fonseca (p. 25-26) discusses the establishment of national boundaries of states in space, using as a criterion the dynamic delimitation of the freedom of outer space: "All bodies over which the gravitational field of the Earth does not predominate will be considered free with respect to the Earth and its laws ... All bodies over which the gravitational field of a given planet does not predominate will be considered free with respect to that planet." He concludes by analyzing how the various types of space vehicles would fit into this proposal.

   c) P. H. Furfey (p. 28) states that man and his environment contain all the factors that explain behavior. Human nature, therefore, will react to his change in environment in the space age. He discusses various aspects of this change, but emphasizes the effects of stress.

   d) One of the most difficult problems remaining to be solved is the juridical solution of the sovereignty problem in outer space. Logically, sovereignty cannot exist there. This is the opinion of Professor Alex Meyer (p. 120-122) in contradicting Loftus Becker, legal adviser to the State Department of the USA. Becker stated that his nation's sovereignty extends over the total USA airspace and that with reference to the higher regions of outer space, the USA has never conceded that its sovereignty doesn't exist. Professor Meyer points out that sovereignty can only be exercised in a defined area - an impossibility when applied to outer space. He reasons further that ownership of unmanned space vehicles, launched into outer space, is not lost by the act of launching them. Such vehicles must be returned to the owner state.

   In like manner, S. Kucherov compares American and Soviet viewpoints on some of the legal problems of outer space. He concludes that the USSR and USA "as on

41

many other questions, disagree over the neutralization of outer space and over the composition of the group of nations charged with working out of the statutes and the programs of an international committee at the United Nations to promote cooperation in common research for peaceful purposes."

Valladao (p. 157-168) pleads for an autonomous interplanetary extra-atmosphere space law divorced from Maritime Law, Air Law, and International Law. He sees solar or interplanetary space as immune from appropriation, a "res communis omnium Universi," a common "res" for all intelligent creatures of the universe.

M. Seara-Vazques (p. 139-145), on the other hand, questions whether space is a "res." He agrees with the French lawyer, M. Homburg, who states that astronomical law should be qualified by function rather than by space itself.

2. For the future.

a) Optimists, like V. L. Anfuso (p. 1-4) perceive peace and abundance, if Earthmen can get together on the peaceful exploration of outer space.

b) The cautious politician, S. M. Beresford, considers the counterbalance in national defense between the leading powers, USA and USSR (p. 5-10). He reminds us of the statement of J. Robert Oppenheimer "two scorpions in a bottle, each capable of killing the other, but only at the risk of his own life." He therefore suggests that international agreements should be made which defer the question of national sovereignty. Sovereignty in outer space is not necessary to protect the interests of national states.

H. T. P. Binet from Canada (p. 11-16) argues for one UN agency to supervise the administration of one multilateral treaty based on one doctrine only -- freedom of all-inclusive space, subject to agreed restrictions.

J. Machowski (Poland) presents a contribution on the "Legal Status of Un-manned Space Vehicles" (p. 111-119). Since air law distinguishes the pilotless aircraft from aircraft with a crew, the legal status of unmanned space vehicles should be separated from that of manned vehicles. He feels that the launching of unmanned space vehicles should be allowed and that it is, and remains, the property of the launching state and should be returned to the state of ownership. However, the logical consequence of such ownership is that the owner state must accept the liability for injuries or damages by the unmanned space vehicle.

R. A. Javitch (p. 61-63) from Canada stresses the necessity to create technical regulations regarding landing and starting procedures for high velocity missiles and other space vehicles. He defines three classes of transport systems: Earth-to-Earth vehicles, Space-to-Earth vehicles, and Earth-to-Space vehicles. He feels these definitions would be useful in a future Space Transportation Act, as well as a future Space Law Manual.

P. B. Yeager (USA) in his "Space and Cognopolitics: A Third World Force in World Affairs" (p. 169-176) points to a new path to international cooperation through what he calls the concept of cognopolitics. Heretofore, the course of history has been swayed by "(1) the physical power that could be summoned at any given time, or (2) the resources or wealth at the disposal of the state involved." With the fission of the atom, however, and the Hiroshima bomb, a whole new world opened up --knowledge as a power. "The race to know was on," and thereby the conception of cognopolitics. We may find knowledge, accompanied by understanding, producing the gradual development of cognopolitics as a third force in international relationships.

The two great powers gained entrance into outer space and to the moon separately. But now, in 1973, they join in space ventures. So the hope of peace grows. Nevertheless, we must be cautious lest science and technology create an Orwellian nightmare. Knowledge and understanding can prevent this and can promote prolonged mutual cooperation and a prosperous future for all earth-dwellers.

THIRD COLLOQUIUM ON THE LAW OF OUTER SPACE
STOCKHOLM, 1960

I. Texts Reproduced

THE INTERNATIONAL CONTROL OF OUTER SPACE
by
C. Wilfried Jenxs

...

Man in Space

While adequate international arrangements for the control of instruments in space re-present the most urgent problem and would constitute a major advance, they will be liable to be outdated overnight by the appearance of man in space.

It is now widely and responsibly believed that we are on the threshold of man venturing in space. How many further political and legal problems man's venture into space will bring with it cannot be foreseen with any accuracy until we know much more of the nature and extent of his probable activities in space. Scientific expeditions, military activities, and exploitation of the resources of space in a manner still undefined would create entirely different situations and problems; brief ventures into space, continuous residence in space for substantial periods, and permanent residence in space with reproduction of the species there would likewise involve wholly different problems. We can perhaps envisage three successive phases, which for purposes of convenience, I propose to describe as the Monroe Doctrine for the Moon phase, the Antarctic Analogy phase, and the United Nations control phase.

The first phase will presumably be one of hazardous and intermittent exploration with at most a handful of people in space at any one time. I have suggested in The Common Law of Mankind that for this phase we need a Monroe Doctrine for the Moon concept. The expression is of course a metaphor, and I recognize that the term may be unacceptable in view of its historical associations with one of the space powers, but the concept of hands off, which it conveniently expresses, is a fundamental one, and its validity does not depend on the acceptability of the term. In this first phase we cannot reasonably hope to have evolved either adequate institutional arrangements or sufficiently accepted legal principles to meet longer-term needs, nor will it be practically necessary that we should have done so. However, it will be vital to have established the position that such arrangements and principles will be evolved by common agreement on the basis of growing experience as they become necessary and that meanwhile no unilateral claim to extraterrestrial sovereignty or jurisdiction or to exclusive access to or use of any extraterrestrial place or resource will be recognized. An immediate declaration of policy to that effect, preferably by the General Assembly of the United Nations, is eminently desirable. The Monroe Doctrine for the Moon concept represents a holding operation designed to ensure that longer-range plans are not prejudiced by unilateral action before they have had time to mature.

Such longer-range plans also need immediate consideration, but as it is desirable
that they should be embodied in treaty obligations, they will presumably take longer to
mature. In formulating them we may usefully be guided by the Antarctic analogy. The usefulness of the Antarctic analogy has been fully discussed in Jessup and Taubenfeld, Controls
for Outer Space and the Antarctic Analogy, and I therefore do not propose to recapitulate
their analysis and argument, but since their book was published, the Antarctic Treaty of
1 December 1959 has been signed on behalf of all twelve of the countries which participa-
ted in the Antarctic programme of the International Geophysical Year. The Antarctic Treaty
recites that it is in the interest of all mankind that Antarctica shall continue forever
to be used exclusively for peaceful purposes and shall not become the scene or object of
international discord. The Treaty further proclaims that the establishment of a firm foundation for the continuation and development of international co-operation in scientific
investigation in Antarctica on the basis of freedom of scientific investigation, as applied
during the International Geophysical Year, accords with the interests of science and the
progress of all mankind. The Treaty provides that Antarctica shall be used for peaceful
purposes only and that any measures of a military nature, such as the establishment of
military bases and fortifications, the carrying out of military manoeuvres, and the testing
of any type of weapons shall be prohibited. Freedom of scientific investigation in Antarctica and co-operation toward that end, as applied during the International Geophysical
Year, are to continue. The Contracting Parties agree that, to the greatest extent feasible
and practicable, information regarding plans for scientific programmes in Antarctica shall
be exchanged to permit maximum economy and efficiency of operation, scientific personnel
shall be exchanged in Antarctica between expeditions and stations, and scientific observation and results from Antarctica shall be exchanged and made freely available. In implementing these principles every encouragement is to be given to the establishment of cooperative working relations with those specialized agencies of the United Nations and other
international organizations having a scientific or technical interest in Antarctica. Territorial claims are frozen without prejudice for or against for the duration of the Treaty.
Any nuclear explosions in Antarctica and the disposal there of radioactive waste are prohibited. Each Party may designate observers who are to have complete freedom of access
at any time to any or all areas of Antarctica; all stations, installations, equipment,
ships and aircraft are to be open at all times to inspection by such observers and aerial
observation may be carried out at any time; such observers and their staffs are to be subject only to the jurisdiction of the Party of which they are nationals while they are in
Antarctica for the purpose of exercising their functions. There is to be advance notification of all expeditions to and within Antarctica. There is provision for periodical
meetings of representatives of the Contracting Parties who may recommend to their governments measures in furtherance of the principles and objectives of the treaty. The negotiation at an early date of a similar treaty concerning space, based on the same general
principles, but containing any necessary adaptations, appears to be desirable. It may be
desirable to formulate at an early stage in the proposed treaty or otherwise a legal duty
to give mutual aid against the common dangers of the unknown and proceed to the assistance
of persons in distress. The principle is fundamental in the ethics of mountaineering and
polar exploration and has already received legal expression in the Safety of Life at Sea

Convention and the Search and Rescue Annex to the International Civil Aviation Convention. A Space Treaty analogous to the Antarctic Treaty would represent a bold and constructive advance. If such a Treaty is possible for Antarctica, why is it not possible for space?

As activities in space develop, arrangements analogous to those provided for in the Antarctic Treaty may prove to be inadequate, and more comprehensive arrangements for international control of space may be necessary. We must therefore envisage a third phase, that of the United Nations control. The type of institutional arrangements appropriate for such control must be determined in the light of how the United Nations has developed when that phase is reached, but there are certain general principles which it is not premature to foreshadow now.

We may start from the general point of departure defined by Jessup and Taubenfeld:

> It is clear on a moment's reflection that now, and probably for some time to come, many of the problems connected with outer space are more closely connected with earth and with man on earth. Earth is still the launching site and the base for sending and receiving communications. The needs or desires which inspire the exploration of outer space are earth-born and earth-centered. The use or misuse of outer space of which we speak is man's use or misuse. In speaking of "controls for outer space" we are thinking of man-made and man-applied controls; of controls not of space, but of man-made objects and also of men in space, and ultimately of men on planets in space.

When man ventures into space he takes with him much of his earthly heritage, including the established rules of international law in so far as they are applicable. The Charter of the United Nations is not earthbound. The General Treaty for the Renunciation of War and the Statute of the International Court of Justice, "international custom as evidence of a general practice accepted as law" and "the general principles of law recognized by civilized nations" are all applicable to human relations in space. Within this framework the special political and legal arrangements necessary for the effective international control of space, when the intensity and complexity of space activities has passed beyond the stage at which arrangements analogous to the Antarctic Treaty are adequate, can and must be evolved.

* * * * *

DAMAGE TO THIRD PARTIES ON THE SURFACE CAUSED BY SPACE VEHICLES

by

Eugène Pépin

A more elaborate paper on the problem of damage which may be caused by space vehicles was presented in August 1958 at the First Colloquium on the Law of Outer Space held in the Hague by Madame de Rode-Verschoor, Professor of Utrecht, with the following title: "Responsibility of the States for Damage Caused by Launched Space Bodies." She submitted three possible solutions:

1. Adoption of the principle of absolute liability;

2. Adoption of the principle of liability for fault; and

3. Establishment of an international guarantee fund for paying damage caused by satellites (except in the case where damage is intentionally caused, in which case the state responsible will always have to pay).

Certain of today's speakers proposed, as a new solution, one quite similar to the proposal of Madame de Rode-Verschoor.

Since August 1958 a number of papers dealing specifically with damage caused by space vehicles have appeared in legal periodicals. Among these papers, I wish only to mention an article of Mr. Andrew Haley on "Space Vehicle Starts," published in the <u>University of Detroit Journal</u> in February 1958 and another of Mr. Spencer Beresford in "Liability for Ground Damage Caused by Space Craft,"which appeared in the <u>Federal Bar Journal of United States</u>; this later article discusses specially the applicability of the USA legislation to these problems. The survey of space law, published at the beginning of 1959 by the Select Committee on Astronautics and Space Exploration of the USA House of Representatives, also referred to the problem of liability as an imminent problem.

Furthermore, USSR legal writers are also dealing with the same problem. In an article published in 1958 in the periodical <u>Soviet State and Law</u>, Galina included, among proposals for an international agreement on space, the liability for injury or damage caused by space vehicles. In January 1959 in <u>International Life</u>, Korovin said that governments should bear full responsibility for personal injury or property loss caused by satellites and other space vehicles. During the same year 1959 the UN legal Subcommittee on Peaceful Uses of Outer Space considered in its report that the problem of liability is one of those which should be studied with priority. The Subcommittee suggested at least five questions:

1. Which kind of damage should give rise to compensation?

2. The nature of acts or negligence involving liability.

3. Should the principles be different when damage is caused on the surface, in atmospheric space or in extra-atmospheric space?

4. Should the liability of the launching state be unlimited?

5. If several states are participating in the launching of space vehicles, should their liability be joint or separate?

The Subcommittee suggested also that in order to secure the payment of any compensation, the states should agree that questions of liability for damage caused by space vehicles should be under the competency of the International Court of Justice. Reference was also made by the Subcommittee to the Rome Convention of 1952 on Damage Caused by Aircraft to Third Parties on the Surface, which might be taken into account for the consideration of damage to be caused by space vehicles. Up to now we may say that almost all the writers on the question agreed on the necessity to study the problem of damage, and some of them add that it is necessary to adopt at an early stage an international convention.

From this very short historical statement, which is obviously incomplete, it appears that up to now no real and general discussion of the problem has taken place among lawyers of the several countries; and I wish to say that the Organizing Committee of this Colloquium has been very wise in giving us today such an opportunity. Several papers have been prepared on the subject, and their publication in a volume will certainly be a great contribution for future studies. But it seems to me - and I am sure that I am in agreement with the Chairman - that a comprehensive exchange of views on the most important aspects of the problem, in order to arrive to some common views or agreed principles, would certainly be a great advantage. Here we are not in a controversial or political problem. There is a common agreement on the necessity to pay certain compensation in case of damage; but it has never been discussed how such compensation is to be paid; how it should be calculated and so forth. Today we have here the possibility to have a more complete exchange of views than before. Such a discussion will not present any difficulty, for the distinguished lawyers participating to the Colloquium are quite familiar with the fundamental issues.

I think that we should not complicate the problem. If a damage has been caused by a vehicle of or pertaining to a certain state, in the territory of the same state, this is a national problem; but if we have in a damage elements of different nationalities-that is to say concerning the author of the damage, the victim of the damage, or the territory itself - we have here an international problem on which we should concentrate.

With your permission, I would suggest that we consider successively six important points of that problem and that some speakers may express on each one their personal views.

Those points are the following:

1. Should any damage caused by a space vehicle on any part of the surface of the earth give rise to compensation? Or should some distinction be made according to the category of damage, the type of space vehicle, the place of occurrence or the victims and so forth?

2. In case of damage, who is liable for compensation? For the present, the launching state in question; in the future, state or private organizations or persons, as the case may be?

3. Should the state be considered in any case internationally liable or nationally liable for compensation according to the principle of absolute liability, or should the responsibility be restricted according to the fault principle?

4. Should the liability of the launching state or of the responsible person be unlimited, or limited as regards the amount of compensation?

5. Which jurisdiction, national or international, existing or to be created, may be commonly agreed for consideration of claims arising from such damages?

6. Would it be necessary to conclude a new international convention on this subject? Would it be possible to extend to such claims the application of any existing convention, concerning damages to third parties on the surface?

* * * * *

THOUGHTS ON THE IMPORTANCE AND TASK OF SPACE LAW

by

Franz Gross

> Give me a fixed point outside the earth,
> and I will lift her from her hinges.
>> (Attributed to Archimedes of
>> Syracuse, 282-212 B.C.)

The problems of space law cannot be solved just from the earth, i.e, by applying earthly standards to the universe, but only from the universe, i.e. by the application of new standards both to the universe and to the earth.

Therefore it is not possible to limit either the contents or the area, where space law standards are recognized; for those standards must be the fundamental standards for any other standards in a gradual arrangement of laws.

Thus the sphere of space law standards is not limited either by a limitation of height or by a practical limitation of these standards by astronautics.

The importance of space law standards lies in the fact that they must contain the constitutional standards of the earth, appearing as an entirety against the universe and the celestial bodies.

At present, only international treaties about administration can be made, because we stand only at the beginning of this great human revolution.

I believe that the true significance and thus also the task of space law is still underestimated. This is also the reason why, for certain of its problems, no satisfactory solution has yet been found. Among these problems must be reckoned, in particular, the type and contents, as also the range, of the regulations to be issued.

When Professor Kelsen, discussing Article II of the Chicago Convention, stated that the sphere of authority and the legal system of any one state is not confined to a surface, but exists in three-dimensional space, he did no more than take into account the global shape of our planet. We must remember, however, that our legislation must from now on take cognizance of the position of our earth in space. We must henceforward, in our legal thinking, make a final effort to progress from Ptolemy to Copernicus.

In other words, the legal problems of space can no longer be properly judged and solved from the starting point of the earth but only from that of space itself. Thus we cannot simply apply terrestrial norms to space but must, on the contrary, see to it that the norms of space are valid on the earth.

This corresponds to the laws of natural and human life as I should now like briefly to sketch them.

We understand by the word "law" the sum total of the norms regulating the human behaviour necessary for the preservation of life, but law is always dependent upon man and upon space. If living space is restricted, social relations and legal standards become more condensed; if it is extensive, individual freedom increases and private law gains in importance. Thus, in the spatial confines of the ancient and mediaevel world men formed "society-states," while in the wide, earth-spanning modern age they formed "surface-states."

In those days there was also born the concept of sovereignty, of which Professor Alfred Verdross says in his work on International Law:

> The concept of territorial sovereignty was formed in conjunction with the Roman conception of property. Both are absolute rights, effective against all and sundry. They differ, however, in that territorial sovereignty is a right of disposal under international law, while property is a right of disposal on the basis of the international law of any one state and is therefore subject to numerous restrictions unknown to International Law.

"Unknown to International Law" _as yet_, because the condensation of society took place at first only within the confines of the surface states, while the condensation of the globe, and with it the juxtaposition of the surface states and the increase in the number of these, has happened only as a result of the development of political and communications factors within the past fifty years.

While at the Paris Conference of 1919 the various nations asserted their absolute property rights in three-dimensional national space by means of exclusive and unlimited air-sovereignty, their citizens had already been restricted for some time in their private right as handed down by the commentators. An evolution had occurred which had led from property and the absolute power of the individual via the limitation of this power by the usufruct rights of all and sundry to its final stage in the restriction of this usufruct by state-power.

A social ordering of airspace had thus already arisen within the various states, while the governments themselves did not as yet recognize this ordering as absolute sovereignty.

Only increasing air traffic and with it the growing significance of the basic right in International Law to unrestricted world-communications compelled the Chicago Conference of 1944 to concern itself more closely with the concept of exclusive and unrestricted national sovereignty.

Here the concentration and interweaving of the sovereignty claims of the individual states was already visible. The workings of the following evolutionary principle were already becoming apparent: as men thrust forward into new spaces the individual is unconscious of his partnership with other individuals and with the whole as one limb among many. It is for this reason that the conviction of individual freedom at first prevails. This freedom and individual sovereignty then becomes limited to an ever increasing degree by the freedom and sovereignty of others, while the shape taken by this limiting process forms the basic law of a higher order, namely the order of the whole. This higher order was in the present case national sovereignty in airspace. The state possessed the same unrestricted rights as had been previously enjoyed by the individual.

However, according to the natural principle of entelechy, this process must repeat itself as sovereignty regulations are merged in a higher order while life thrusts forward into space. That is to say that as nations press upward into outer space their respective sovereignties must be restricted in exactly the same way as individual property rights were once restricted by governments, and this takes place, moreover, according to a social order which corresponds to the position of our earth as a planet in space.

As soon as man leaves the earth, he must realize that it is not the centre of, but merely one planet in, the solar system.

Thus space can never assimilate itself to the earth, but only the earth to space--which means that our terrestrial order must adapt itself to this higer order.

Clearly it is this fact which Professor E. Korovin also means when he states in his treatise on "The International Status of Outer Space" that space sovereignty signifies a return from Copernicus to Ptolemy.

The fact, however, that national sovereignty can no longer be exercised in outer space, while on the other hand space works upon national sovereignty, is clearly shown in connection with the problem of neutrality, for in order to preserve its neutrality a national state would have to fly, in the exercise of its defensive sovereignty, over the territories of other neutral states with its defensive weapons and also, as a result of the rotation of the earth, cause belligerent actions above the territories of a number of nations. This would result in the involvement of a neutral state in war with other states by virtue of the very fact that it was defending its neutrality.

From this it follows, however, as Dr. Welf Heinrich Prince of Hanover has several times shown - most recently, I believe, in his contribution to the First Discussion on Space Rights - that the preservation of sovereignty on the earth, if violated from outer space, is virtually impossible.

It is clear, then, that what I might call this "ionisation" of national states must set the same forces in motion as those which our own age has to face as a result of the social revolutions of the past.

As far as the threat of atomic warfare is concerned, it is thus a question of life or death, according to the natural law that life tends continually to expand and must, as it presses forward into new regions of space, either adapt itself to its surroundings or perish.

This fact is also recognized by Professor Oberth in his book "Menschen im Weltraum" (Men in Space). He writes:

> The question of the future of space-travel is at bottom part and parcel
> of the question of human civilisation as a whole. If this collapses there
> will be no space-travel either. Research and progress will, to an ever in-
> creasing extent, be still possible only when human society is able to do justice
> to itself, and when all stand together instead of dissipating their strength
> in quarrels about language, religion, party, system of government, clients
> and export markets and anxiously trying to keep their knowledge and experi-
> ence from others.

From the above observations the following conclusions can be drawn respecting the type, contents, and sphere of validity of the norms of spacial legislation:

1) These must, following the gradations of the legal system, contain basic norms to
which our terrestrial norms must adapt themselves.

2) In their contents they cannot confine themselves to astronautical traffic, but must
contain at the same time the constitutional norms of our globe.

3) Their sphere of validity is of an all-inclusive nature and cannot be limited to any
particular height. It follows:

4) that we should, in the sense of Mr. Haley's and Professor Cooper's proposals, confine
ourselves for the time being to creating international administrative norms because
we are only at the beginning of the greatest revolution in the history of mankind.

* * * * *

WORLD SECURITY AND THE PEACEFUL USES OF OUTER SPACE
by
Eilene Galloway

The objective of the United Nations in establishing the Committee on the Peaceful Uses of Outer Space is to safeguard the right of peoples of all nations to beneficial results from space exploration. Attainment of this objective requires international cooperation which can be furthered by UN assistance for research, exchange and
dissemination of information, encouragement of national research programs, and the study of legal problems arising from space exploration. Solutions proposed for legal problems can be evaluated in terms of whether or not they are likely to contribute to the
betterment of mankind.

Organization for international scientific space activities exists in certain specialized agencies of the United Nations and in recognized non-governmental organizations. Space activities are highly diversified and whether the approach to their development is scientific or legal, the main problem is one of coordination of personnel,
resources, facilities, rules, regulations, statutes, treaties, and agreements.

The state of the art of science and technology in space exploration will determine,
in many cases, what controls are feasible and practicable. Scientists and engineers
need to be informed of the impact of national and international laws upon the conduct
of their projects. Lawyers formulating guidelines for the future need to keep abreast
of fast-developing space sciences. The problem of culling the scientific facts essential to the solution of legal questions may be met by establishing a close working relationship between the IAF's International Institute of Space Law and the International
Academy of Astronautics.

I. International Objective and Role of the United Nations.

The Third Colloquium on the Law of Outer Space meets at a time when the International
Institute of Space Law has been organized into working groups for the study of specific
problem areas. The ideas we generate may lead to action for a system of world security
wherein the people of all nations can be assured that space activities will be conducted

for peaceful purposes. The challenge we face now is to study the legal problems, already so well identified, in conjunction with the developing facts of science and technology, in awareness of the need of policymakers to know the advantages and disadvantages of alternative courses of action, and in recognition of the objective that space exploration should be undertaken for the benefit of mankind.

As we expand from general and theoretical studies of space law and plunge into the detailed research and analysis required for the solution of particular problems, it is essential to understand the existing international situation as it relates to outer space. Our present position has been shaped by an international objective, a pattern of organization and administration which may contribute to the desired result, and the dynamic force exerted by space science and technology upon international ideas and relations.

The international objective of space exploration is contained in the United Nations resolution "International Co-operation in the Peaceful Uses of Outer Space" which was adopted unanimously in a plenary session of the General Assembly on December 2, 1959. In establishing the Committee on the Peaceful Uses of Outer Space, the resolution states that the General Assembly,

> Recognizing the common interest of mankind as a whole in furthering the peaceful use of outer space,
> Believing, that the exploration and use of outer space should be only for the betterment of mankind and to the benefit of States irrespective of the stage of their economic or scientific development,
> Desiring to avoid the extension of present national rivalries into this new field,
> Recognizing the great importance of international co-operation in the exploration and exploitation of outer space for peaceful purposes,
> Noting the continuing programmes of scientific co-operation in the exploration of outer space being undertaken by the international scientific community,
> Believing also that the United Nations should promote international cooperation in the peaceful uses of outer space
> <u>Establishes a Committee on the Peaceful Uses of Outer Space.</u>

In brief, the objective is that space activities should be conducted for the benefit of all people. The methods to be used in attaining this objective are implicit in the resolution: promotion by the United Nations of cooperation between nations and assistance for space programs of the international scientific community.

The directives given by the General Assembly to the Committee also indicate the role of the United Nations and the means of achieving international cooperation: UN assistance for research, exchange and dissemination of information, encouragement of national research programs, and the study of legal problems arising from space exploration. The Committee was also called upon to arrange an international scientific conference of interested members of the United Nations and the specialized agencies.

The objective and general methods of procedure are substantially the same as those adopted by the United Nations General Assembly on December 13, 1958, when the Ad Hoc Committee on the Peaceful Uses of Outer Space was established. One difference in wording is that the 1958 resolution stated that it is the common aim that outer space "should be used for peaceful purposes <u>only</u>," whereas the 1959 resolution creating the permanent committee recognized that the common interest of mankind would be served by "furthering the peaceful use of outer space...[which]...should be only for the betterment of mankind..."

The present position of the United Nations has several points of significance for those concerned with space law.

<u>First</u>, the international declaration of policy seeks to safeguard the rights of the peoples of all nations to beneficial results from space exploration. This worldwide concept of human welfare must necessarily affect the character of controls for strengthening peaceful conditions and avoiding national rivalries which might lead to hostilities. A primary objective has therefore been provided whereby solutions proposed for legal problems can be evaluated in terms of whether or not they are likely to contribute to the betterment of mankind.

<u>Second</u>, problems concerned with outer space and with disarmament are being considered separately by the United Nations. This policy determination was made so that lack of agreement on an effective system of inspection and control of armaments need not delay progress in analyzing the unusual effects of space exploration upon international relations. A unique feature of the space age is that it began and is developing under auspicious patterns of cooperation established for the International Geophysical Year.

<u>Third</u>, the role of the United Nations will be further clarified after the Committee on the Peaceful Uses of Outer Space reports on its review of areas which "could appropriately be undertaken under United Nations auspices," including, inter alia:

Assistance for the continuation on a permanent basis of the research on outer space carried on within the framework of the International Geophysical Year;

Organization of the mutual exchange and dissemination of information on outer space research;

Encouragement of national research programs for the study of outer space, and the rendering of all possible assistance and help toward their realization;

And, furthermore, the Committee was requested;

To study the nature of legal problems which may arise from the exploration of outer space.

Fourth, cooperation between nations and coordination of programs undertaken by organizations of the international scientific community are envisaged as elements of the pattern for space research and operations. This position is based upon the desire to continue, and to build upon, the organizational and administrative practices by which space activities have been, and are being, developed.

II. Organization of International Scientific Space Activities.

The years of planning which preceded the International Geophysical Year laid a firm foundation for international cooperation on scientific projects which were worldwide in their scope. When the International Council of Scientific Unions (ICSU) established its Special Committee for the International Geophysical Year (CSGI) in 1953, the forces set in motion carried through the period of the IGY (from July 1, 1957, to December 31, 1958) with such success that organization on a permanent basis was stimulated.

When the eighth General Assembly of the International Council of Scientific Unions met in Washington, D.C., October 2-6, 1958, the Committee on Special Research (COSPAR) was provisionally established "to provide the world scientific community with the means whereby it may exploit the possibilities of satellites and space probes of all kinds for scientific purposes, and exchange the resulting data on a cooperative basis."

The Charter for COSPAR's permanent organization was adopted at a meeting in Amsterdam on November 13, 1959. The provisions concerning membership and the election of officers are especially significant because of the key role performed by this international non-governmental organization in planning and coordinating space research and development. National members and international scientific unions which adhere to ICSU are eligible for membership if they wish to participate in COSPAR and are actively engaged in space research. The Executive Council is composed of nine representatives of scientific unions, and a seven-member bureau operating under a President, two Vice Presidents who alternate in precedence, and four other members chosen from lists of names furnished by the vice presidents. The United States National Academy of Sciences and the Academy of Sciences of the USSR present separate nominating slates for the two vice presidential positions.

When COSPAR held its first meeting under the new Charter in Nice, France, January 8-16, 1960, the election of officers resulted in the representation of nations identified with both the West and East. The President is a citizen of The Netherlands, the two Vice Presidents are from the United States and the USSR, while the four members elected to the Executive Council represent the United Kingdom, France, Czechoslovakia, and Poland.

COSPAR carries out its functions by means of working groups, now organized on the subjects of Tracking and Telemetering, Scientific Experiments, Data and Publications. In addition, COSPAR depends upon reports of national space activities, and at its January 1960 meeting received information on the status of twelve national programs concerned with space research and operations.

The relation of COSPAR to the United Nations is especially significant. Under an agreement made by ICSU, the United Nations Educational, Scientific and Cultural Organization (UNESCO) stimulates space research by promoting both international and regional arrangements. UNESCO supports COSPAR in its work, undertaking only those requests for space research which COSPAR cannot perform and those requiring intergovernmental agreement. By invitation, the President of COSPAR consulted with the United Nations Ad Hoc Committee on the Peaceful Uses of Outer Space, UNESCO's Department of Natural Sciences, and with the Administrative Radio Conference of the International Telecommunication Union. COSPAR sent an observer to the ITU conference which was held in Geneva from August 17 to December 31, 1959. This conference is noteworthy for having reached agreement on the terms of a treaty which includes provision for the allocation of radio frequencies to space vehicles. Both the United Nations and individual national governments depend upon COSPAR to perform functions of international coordination of scientific space activities.

In addition to UNESCO and the ITU, it can be anticipated that a number of other intergovernmental organizations will be concerned with various aspects of outer space research and development, e.g., the World Meteorological Organization (WMO), the International Civil Aviation Organization (ICAO), the International Atomic Energy Agency (IAEA), the World Health Organization (WHO), and the Inter-Governmental Maritime Consultative Organization

(IMCO).

Harmony between the objectives and organization of national and international programs is vital for successful coordination. The policy objectives and organization of the United States for international space activities are in consonance with those of the United Nations and the world scientific community.

By unanimous vote the Congress of the United States passed a resolution declaring:

That it is the sense of Congress:

That the United States should strive, through the United Nations or such other means as may be most appropriate, for an international agreement banning the use of outer space for military purposes;

That the United States should seek through the United Nations or such other means as may be most appropriate an international agreement providing for joint exploration of outer space and establishing a method by which disputes which arise in the future in relation to outer space will be solved by legal, peaceful methods, rather than by resort to violence;

That the United States should press for an international agreement providing for joint cooperation in the advancement of scientific developments which can be expected to flow from the exploration of outer space such as the improvement of communication, the betterment of weather forecasting, and other benefits; and

That the Congress respectfully requests the President to effectuate in every way possible the objectives set forth in this resolution.

In establishing the National Aeronautics and Space Administration, Congress declared that "it is the policy of the United States that activities in space should be devoted to peaceful purposes for the benefit of all mankind." The law further provides that the aeronautical and space activities of the United States shall be conducted so as to contribute materially to "cooperation by the United States with other nations and groups of nations in work done pursuant to the Act and in the peaceful application of the results thereof." Implementation of this policy is found in the provision that:

The Administration, under the foreign policy guidance of the President, may engage in a program of international cooperation in work done pursuant to this Act, and in the peaceful application of the results thereof, pursuant to agreements made by the President with the advice and consent of the Senate.

Informal arrangements for cooperative programs may also be undertaken by NASA.

In accordance with these policy directives, NASA cooperates with the United Nations and, working through the USA National Academy of Sciences, with the Committee on Space Research (COSPAR). An Office of International Programs has been established by NASA to develop cooperative activities.

International NASA programs that are now under way fall into four main categories: the worldwide network of tracking and telemetry stations so essential for the acquisition of data from satellites and space probes; joint programs with scientists and engineers of nations cooperating in space research; exchange of scientific and technical information, making data available for evaluation to scientists throughout the world; and training programs and exchanges with foreign scientists.

These programs are being conducted in accordance with a policy of freedom and openness which is truly international in matching the scientific and technological requirements of the space age. A case in point is the offer by the United States to the Soviet Union of the use of the special tracking facilities designed for the man-in-space program, Project Mercury. Dr. T. Keith Glennan, Administrator of NASA announced that:

> As an evidence of our interest in international cooperation, we would be most happy to offer the services of our tracking network in support of the scientists of the Soviet Union when and if that nation undertakes a manned space-flight program. Data could be acquired and transmitted in its raw state to the Academy of Sciences in Moscow. A precedent for this sort of thing has been established in the IGY operation when the United States supplied to the Soviet scientists, as of July 1959 some 46 tape recordings of Sputnik I, II, and III. Should special recording or data read-out equipment be required, I am sure that we would be happy to provide them or to utilize equipment furnished by the Soviet scientists. In such a cooperative venture we could help them to keep in continuous or essentially continuous contact with their astronaut.

Another example of the unity which is sought by NASA in generating international cooperation in space research is the offer to launch for other countries individual experiments or complete scientific payloads in artificial earth satellites. NASA authorized the delegate from the National Academy of Sciences to make this proposal at the second meeting of COSPAR held at The Hague in March 1959. Scientists from a number of countries are interested in the opportunity of developing their space projects in cooperation with the United States. Agreements on joint programs of this type have already been reached with the United Kingdom, Canada, and Italy, and are in the process of being worked out with scientists in additional countries.

III. Scientific and Technological Facts of Space Exploration.

The most striking fact about the advent of the space age is the rapidity of the pace of scientific and technological development since the first earth satellite, particularly when comparing present achievements with distant scientific goals as yet unattained. But by practically any other criterion of measurement, the accomplishments made by scientists and engineers, in substantially less than three years, are impressive.

The urgency with which activities are being expanded into the space environment is revealed by the numbers of successfully launched satellites and space probes. Between October 1957 and August 12, 1960, 28 space vehicles were sent into orbit around the earth; 3 were launched into solar orbits; and one lunar impact was made. On August 12, 1960, there were 13 earth satellites still in orbit; 3 space vehicles in solar orbit; and 7 of these devices were still transmitting information from outer space to the earth. The international summary of satellites and space probes was published by the National Aeronautics and Space Administration.

Current Summary (August 12, 1960)　　　　　Complete Summary (Successfully launched
　　　　　　　　　　　　　　　　　　　　　　　　　to date)

Earth Orbit:　　USA .... 12　Earth Orbit:　　USA 23

　　　　　　　　USSR .... 1　　　　　　　　　USSR 5

Solar Orbit:　　USA .... 2　Solar Orbit:　　USA 2

　　　　　　　　USSR .... 1　　　　　　　　　USSR 1

Transmitting:　 USA .... 7　Lunar Impact:　USSR 1

　　　　　　　　USSR 0

Information on the distances from earth reached by orbiting space vehicles affords a factual basis for considering controls that might be applicable to spatial areas and space-craft. Eighteen satellites established a perigee lower than 300 miles, one of the figures theoreticaaly suggested as a demarcation between airspace and outer space. Of these 18 satellites, 10 had a perigee of 156 miles or lower. Going into an elliptical orbit, many satellites come comparatively close to the earth for a few minutes, only to be thousands of miles away a short time later. For example, the US Explorer I satellite, with an estimated lifetime of 3 to 5 years from its launching date (January 3, 1958) has a perigee of 221 miles and an apogee of 1573 miles. Explorer VI, with a life expectancy of 1 year from August 7, 1959, has a perigee of 156 miles and an apogee of 26,357 miles.

This type of scientific information raises questions concerning definitions which have been offered in the hope of clarifying national sovereignty in airspace and outer space. Is the space vehicle, or space itself, to be controlled? Some idea of the complexities of this question can be gleaned from considering an example such as Lunik III, a Soviet translunar earth satellite, which had an elliptical orbit of 625,000 miles for 15 days. Another example is that of the US Pioneer V space probe, launched on March 11, 1960, with an expected lifetime of 100,000 years, a perihelion of 71 967,000 miles and a aphelion of 92 358,000 miles. Jodrell Bank in England received information from Pioneer V from a record distance of 22.5 million miles from the earth.

Time as well as distance must be considered in establishing the necessary correlation between scientific facts and proposals for the solution of legal problems. While the time required to complete an orbit naturally varies with different satellites, many have been circling the earth in approximately $1\frac{1}{2}$ to 2 hours. Speed may be the controlling factor in determining the feasibility of some of the proposed controls.

The nature and amount of information being obtained from scientific exploration constitutes another criterion by which achievements may be measured and evaluated. Several examples will illustrate the yield which can be anticipated from a study of research sources, which are easily available to the international legal profession.

Information from the USA Explorer I satellite, launched on January 31, 1958, led to the discovery of the radiation belt around the earth. From the solar-powered signals of Vanguard I, launched by the United States on March 17, 1958, with a life-expectancy of 200 to 1000 years, the shape of the earth and the locations of Pacific islands are being measured more exactly. Great strides have been made in communications satellites. The Project Score satellite (December 18, 1958) transmitted from outer space a recorded message from President Eisenhower. The USA Pioneer V space probe achieved several scientific "firsts" in transmitting 138.9 hours of data from the space between the orbits of Venus and the earth. Outstanding results from weather experiments have been recorded from the USA satellites Explorer VII (October 13, 1959) and the Tiros television and infra-red observation satellite (April 1, 1960). Circling the earth at a speed of 99.19 minutes, Tiros relayed 22,952 cloud cover photographs, which are considered highly successful.

The Soviet Lunik I (January 2, 1959) went into orbit around the sun on a 15-month cycle. Lunik II (September 12, 1959) impacted the surface of the moon with scientific instruments and the Soviet coat of arms. Lunik III (October 4, 1959) took high precision photographs of 70 percent of the dark side of the moon and transmitted them back to earth.

Obviously, this paper can do little more than indicate the main categories of facts which are available for study, and emphasize the necessity for a thorough evaluation of the impact of scientific knowledge upon problems requiring legal measures for their solution.

IV.   Implication for the Analysis of Legal Problems.

Highlights of the existing international objective, organization, and scientific facts have been provided as a background for the analysis of legal problems arising in space exploration. As the working groups of the International Institute of Space Law begin their studies of the past and present in order to formulate guidelines for the future, it is necessary, also, to consider the assumptions which may underlie their work.

For purposes of discussion, we may consider the validity of the following basic assumptions. Most of the legal problems concerning outer space have been identified, but intensive research and analysis are now required for the solution of specific questions. The international legal profession must find ways of keeping abreast of the rapid development of space science and technology so that legal controls may be logically correlated with space activities. Space law, now in its earliest stage of developments, is a stimulating challenge to non-governmental working groups and individual thinkers who have an opportunity for creative thinking and analyzing proposed objectives, assumptions, and solutions of legal space problems. We have entered a period when policy decisions are in the process of being made by officials of national and international political and scientific organizations. Private groups and individuals are free to think of the alternatives by which specific questions may be mitigated or solved, and to offer the policymakers, at a critical time, some well-reasoned estimates of the probable consequences of each course of action.

Within the context of such terms of reference, what are the implications for space law of the United Nations resolution embodying an international objective for space exploration? The objective, that mankind has a common interest in outer space and its peaceful exploration for his betterment, constitutes a standard by which the probable effects of national and international actions can be measured. Every proposal could be analyzed as to whether or not it might contribute to the betterment of mankind. Proposals affecting national sovereignty or international control could be tested for their likelihood of advancing or retarding benefits for the people of all nations. Particular theories of national sovereignty, concerned with dividing jurisdictions according to zones of altitude or cones of space or free areas, would face the testing question of whether their adoption would help or hinder international cooperation in the peaceful uses of outer space. In terms of achieving the objective, what are the advantages and disadvantages of a system of controls for defined areas of space as contrasted with controls primarily designed to apply to space vehicles? Another question to which little attention has been paid is the legal implication of the growing scientific concept of aerospace in which there is no differentiation between airspace and outer space.

A problem of significance to those concerned with formulating laws for outer space is whether that area is to be used only for peaceful satellites or for both peaceful and military space vehicles. It would be necessary, of course, to define what is meant by "peaceful" and "military." But beyond that, two alternative approaches to law may be envisaged: one would be concerned with permitting peaceful and prohibiting military spacecraft; the other would consist of rules for the regulation of both civilian and military space vehicles. A better understanding of the implications of this situation could result from legal studies undertaken by the International Institute of Space Law.

We may next inquire concerning the implications for space law of the organization for space exploration established by the United Nations and by the international scientific community.

International cooperation rather than international control is now called for in the resolution establishing the United Nations Committee on the Peaceful Uses of Outer Space. There is no official suggestion for a supranational agency to control or conduct the space programs of nation states. Nor is there any official development toward an outer space organization comparable to the International Atomic Energy Agency. The possibility of such developments might be studied by individual lawyers intent upon exploring the pros and cons of different types of organizational arrangement. In the absence of a centralized world authority over space activities, we may expect cooperation between nations to be achieved by the normal method of bilateral and multilateral treaties and agreements.

The specialized agencies of the United Nations and the organizations established by the international scientific community will also be used for the necessary coordination of space activities. From this practice, functional controls may be expected to develop over such areas as weather prediction, the allocation of radio frequencies, and navigation. Many specialized agencies already have rules and regulations which may apply in some degree to space activities.

The problem created for international law is how to coordinate the administrative regulations of various agencies concerned with specific functions of space exploration. To what extent need such rules be made uniform? Will international administrative regulations be coordinated by COSPAR, by the International Council of Scientific Unions, or by the United Nations Committee on the Peaceful Uses of Outer Space? Space activities are highly diversified and whether the approach is scientific or legal, the main problem is one of coordination - coordination of personnel, resources, facilities, rules, regulations, statutes, treaties and agreements.

The state of the art of science and technology in space exploration will determine, in many cases, what controls are feasible and practicable. What can and cannot be done technologically may determine what can and cannot be done legally. But it is also possible that the application of certain historic legal concepts to space activities might preclude courses of action which are technologically possible.

We need to establish a bridge between the legal and scientific professions in order to ensure their coordination. Scientists and engineers need to be informed of the impact of national and international laws upon the conduct of their projects. Lawyers who are formulating guidelines for the future need to keep abreast of the developing facts of space science and technology. There is a tremendous outpouring of scientific data, not all of which is pertinent to problems of law and jurisprudence. The problem of culling out those facts which are essential to the solution of legal questions may be met by establishing a close working relationship between the International Academy of Astronautics and the International Institute of Space Law. By mutual effort and cooperative procedures we shall be able to make a contribution to world security through the peaceful uses of outer space.

* * * * *

Il faut également noter comme textes importants et détaillés - International control of outer space. Some preliminary problems de John Cobb Cooper - FARIA,Y.E. Draft to an international covenant for outer space. The treaty of Antartica as a prototype. - VERPLAETSE, J.G. Conflicts of air and outer space law.

* * * * *

II. Autres Contributions et Commentaires

Contrôle international de l'Espace et des véhicules spatiaux.

Ce volume comprend d'ailleurs deux parties distinctes: La première de loin la plus importante correspondant à la 1ère session intitulée Contrôle international de l'espace, la seconde, plus restreinte, concernant les dommages aux tiers en surface causés par les véhicules spatiaux. En realité, les differents auteurs étudient d'abord un cadre général et leurs approches à la fois théoriques et pragmatiques, servent une realité de tous les jours. Ils bâtissent ensuite quelques essais théoriques sur ce qui n'est encore que pure hypothèse. De toutes façons, leur merite est de préparer une voie d'études, de poser des séries de questions plutôt que de les resoudre. (Wilfried Jenks p.3).

Il est vrai qu'en 1960 3 ans à peine viennent de s'écouler depuis le lancement le 4 Octobre 1957 du premier spoutnik soviétique. Les deux blocs sont tourjours antagonistes et, en fait, les programmes scientifiques servent les programmes militaires de deux super-puissances. Ce livre a le merite de s'inscrire dans une periode de découverte de l'espace et d'un éventuel droit s'y appliquant. Ce fut une base utile pour les traités élaborés dans la dernière decennie. Il est habituel de dire que nous sommes ici placés dans un domaine jeune. Cette idée de jeunesse de l'espace et de son droit se révèle dans l'ouvrage que l'on pourrait résumer - au-delà des 2 parties formelles citées plus haut - en 3 idées sur lesquelles portent les différentes communications
    1) l'idée de découverte et la recherche d'une philosophie de paix,
    2) l'idée d'internationalisation
    3) les premières bases techniques d'un "modus vivendi".

Reprenons ces trois points.

I. <u>L'idée de Découverte et la Recherche d'une Philosophie de Paix.</u>

Les problemes de l'espace ne peuvent être règlés uniquement par des standards "terrestres" mais par l'application de nouveaux standards associant terre et univers. (Franz GROSS p.113).

Cette découverte récente de l'espace - pressentie malgré tout depuis longtemps - (De Jules Verne auteur de fiction au savant Von Braun) pose dès le départ des problemes de définitions. A juste titre le mot espace a prévalu sur des expressions trop techniques (ainsi astronautique ou trop ambitieuses (ainsi cosmos).

"En disant simplement "espace" on ne préjuge pas de l'étendue qui est en cause; on peut englober le domaine traditionnel du droit aérien, mais aussi des zones de plus en plus éloignées de la terre à mesure que les progres de la science et les besoins humains qui en résultent se précisent" (1)

En dehors de tout aspect militaire, les conséquences d'une découverte pacifique de l'espace sont innombrables. On peut néanmoins citer comme exemples

a) les connaissances météorologiques au plan international et les influences sur l'économie en general, le tourisme en particulier,

b) les progrès technologiques communs avec les différents satellites,

c) l'expérimentation des techniques de création humaine,

d) l'information de l'opinion publique (Donald Michael, p. 28).

Dès lors comme pour toute activite humaine, un droit, le droit de l'espace. Un droit se détachant du droit aérien. En effet, le droit aérien puise ses origines dans le droit de la guerre en premier lieu (1914-1918), dans le droit de la paix ensuite (Conventions relatives aux cummunications). Mais une difference fondamentale s'impose d'avec le droit de l'Espace. Les activités aériennes furent très nombreuses et vraiment internationales avant la mise au point définitive d'un droit très élaboré et dont les actuels problèmes sont mineures même s'ils sont parfoit angoissants (Piraterie). Rien de tel pout le droit de l'espace: quelques expériences très localisées (USA, URSS et dan une mesure très faible: Europe) et toujours expériences de découverte. Le droit aérien est un droit de commerce, le droit de l'espace est actuellement un droit de la découverte.

C'est pourquoi toutes les hypothèses imaginatives sont permises. Et avant tout - au dela des idées guerrières sans cesse présentes a l'esprit - une recherche de philosophie de la paix. Ici tous les espoirs sont permis - Eilene Galloway (p. 93 et supra) associe sécurité mondiale et utilisations pacifiques de l'espace. Dès lors, l'O.N.U., théoriquement garant de cette sécurité, pourrait centraliser les informations et même obtenir un pouvoir directionnel. En ce sens la résolution du 14 November 1957 prévoyait déjà l'étude d'un "system de controle destiné à s'assurer que le lancement d'engins dans l'espace extra-atmosphériques ne sera effectué qu'à des fins pacifiques et scientifiques." On a pu dire qu'il y avait danger à associer les questions de sécurite mondiale par le désarmement et problèmes de l'espace. Par la suite, l'Assemblée générale de l'O.N.U. de 1958 fut saisie par l'URSS et les USA du problème de la coopération internationale en matiere spatiale. Mais si l'URSS envisageait à la fois le problème de l'utilisation militaire de l'espace et la coopération

_____

(1) Charles Chaumont. Le droit de l'Espace. Presses Universitaires de France 1960sq.

internationale pacifique, les USA ne prévoyaient qu'un problème de coopération internationales. En fait les 2 requetes d'abord liées par l'Assemblée amenèrent un consensus sur la
base de l'unique coopération internationale pacifique. L'O.N.U. poursuivant sur cette lancée, se donnait des instruments de contrôle groupant au depart 19 états et d'après les
termes du rapport du comité des Nations Unies (1) "chacun peut dans des conditions d'égalité,
librement explorer et utiliser l'espace", consacrait l'internationalisation du droit de l'espace.

II. L'idée d'Internationalisation.

L'idée d'internationalisation doit se réaliser dans un traité, ne serait-ce que pour
combler un vide juridique et confirmer les travaux du comité ad hoc de l'O.N.U. (Michel
Smirnoff p.116). Cette internationalisation revêtira deux formes: bilatérale et multilatérale. La forme bilatérale ou restreinte entre URSS et USA s'est concretisée le 8 Juin 1962
par la conclusion - après de difficiles négociations - d'un premier accord réitéré en Juillet 1963 et en Novembre 1965, pour une coopération dans le domaine de l'utilisation pacifique de l'espace. La forme multilatérale s'est développée lors de l'adoption par l'Assemblée Générale de l'O.N.U. le 13 Décembre 1963 de deux importantes résolutions: la première
(n° 1962) intitulée "Déclaration sur les principes juridiques régissant les activités de
l'Etat en matière d'exploration et d'utilisation pacifique de l'espace extra-atmosphérique",
la seconde (n° 1963) relative a la coopération internationale touchant les utilisations
pacifiques de l'espace". Ces deux résolutions étaient précédées le 5 Août 1963 par le traite de Moscou interdisant les expériences nucléaires dans l'air, l'eau et l'espace.

En realité jusqu'a 1973, l'internationalisation n'est que "pseudo-multilatérale".
Certes, les juristes ont élaboré une voie technique très intéressante (voir Wilfried Jenks
texte reproduit et Y. Escobar Faria p.122) et très élaborée. (cf traité sur l'Antarctique
comme prototype) mais la réalité est différente: les relations ne sont que bilatérales entre
les deux super-grands. Cette bipolarite, "recherche d'une entente à deux s'est surtout
manifestée - malgré la forme multilatérale que revêtait l'instrument (2) dans la conclusion
en 1967 du traité sur les principes régissant l'activité des Etats dans le domaine de l'exploration et de l'utilisation de l'espace extra-atmospherique, y compris la lune et les
autres corps célestes. Il ne faut pas oublier en effet que ce quasi-monopole de l'activité
spatiale s'impose aux autres Etats, crée un dialogue quasi-exclusif (3) entre les USA et
l'URSS maîtres des données techniques et matériellement préparés.

En definitive, le traité du 24 Mai 1972 sur la collaboration dans le domaine de la
science spatiale et de ses applications consacre cette bipolarite. Nous pouvons dire, dès
lors, que si le principe d'internationalisation est posé en droit, il est loin d'etre réalisé en fait. Pourtant, les idées, les théories développées dans l'ouvrage ont beaucoup

---

1) Doc. A. 4I 4I, 3e partie, par. 9.

2) Simone COURTEIX. Historique et contexte du Traité sur l'espace. Politique étrangère
   no. 3, 1971.

3) Cf. Space Agreements with the Soviet Union. Hearing before the committee on Aeronautical
   and Space Sciences US Senate, 92nd Congress, 2nd session, june 23, 1972. Washington,
   U.S.G.P.O. 1972 pp.4-5, 7-8

aidé les juristes chargés d'élaborer les instruments que nous avons cités. La spécialisa-
tion est par ailleurs très importante et certaines techniques juridiques sont retenues.

III. Les Premières Bases Techniques d'un "Modus Vivendi".

Deux questions sont posées:

A) Première question: la délimitation de l'Espace et le régime des vols spatiaux. (Vladimir Kopal, p.108). La charte des Nations Unies permet la pénétration pacifique de l'espace
des véhicules de tous les Etats. Il n'est pas encore possible, malgré les apparences, de
définir exactement les limites supérieures des couches atmosphériques. La notion de frontière revêt ici l'aspect le plus incertain et l'on est obligé de se refuser à tracer une
limite précise et même approximative entre atmosphère, stratosphère, trophosphère, iono-
sphère, c'est-à-dire, en fait, entre atmosphère et espaces interplanétaires. D'autre part
connaît-on deja avec suffisamment d'exactitude la nature physique de ces espaces? Il semble
qu'il y ait encore sur ce point bien des doutes (1).

B) Deuxième question, plus réaliste: les dommages causés aux tiers par les véhicules spatiaux. Cette hypothèse ne s'est pas encore réalisée. Heureusement d'ailleurs. Mais les
problèmes évoqués par E. Pepin sont valables. Nous ne reprendrons ici que l'intervention
du Professeur Von Rauchhapt (2) relative a la juridiction compétente en la matière.

Les notions de tribunal national ou de tribunal international spécialisé ne peuvent en
fait se développer.

Il appartiendrait dès lors, a la cour internationale de justice de La Haye. (Juridiction ou arbitrage) de régler d'éventuels différences.

Quant au fond les difficultés surgissent immédiatement: depuis le maintien de la Lex
Rei sitae jusqu'a l'application d'un accord sur les dommages compensés.

L'éventuelle jurisprudence a de très grandes possibilites juridiques.

– – – – –

(1) Pr. Dt Von Rauchhaupt, p.136

FOURTH COLLOQUIUM ON THE LAW OF OUTER SPACE

WASHINGTON, 1961

I. Texts Reproduced

OUTER SPACE - THE KEY TO WORLD PEACE UNDER LAW

by

David F. Maxwell

...

II. Background of the Problem.

The first warning of the impending danger was sounded by the United States Government on January 14, 1957, when it proposed to the United Nations that:

... the first step toward the objectives of assuring that future developments in outer space would be devoted exclusively to peaceful and scientific purposes would be to bring the testing of such objects under international inspection and participation.

This proposal was implemented by specific recommendations upon which no action was taken. President Eisenhower personally took cognizance of the problem when in January of 1958 he wrote former Premier Bulganin in part as follows:

I propose that we agree that outer space should be used only for peaceful purposes. We face a decisive moment in history in relation to this matter. Both the Soviet Union and the United States are now using outer space for the testing of missiles designed for military purposes. The time to stop is now.

I recall to you that a decade ago, when the United States had a monopoly of atomic weapons and of atomic experience, we offered to renounce the making of atomic weapons and to make the use of atomic energy an international asset for peaceful purposes only. If only that offer had been accepted by the Soviet Union, there would not now be the danger from nuclear weapons which you describe.

The nations of the world face today another choice perhaps even more momentous than that of 1948. That relates to the use of outer space. Let us this time, and in time, make the right choice, the peaceful choice.

In testifying to these facts before the United States Senate Committee on Space and Astronautics on May 14, 1958, the Honorable Loftus Becker, then Legal Adviser to the Department of State of the United States Government, said in part:

Basically, it is the position of our Government that the law of space should be based upon the facts of space and that there is very much more that we have to learn about the conditions existing in space before we shall be in a position to say what shall be the legal principles applicable thereto.

Whatever justification there may have been for that conclusion in 1958, I submit no longer exists in 1961. Since the electrifying launching of Sputnik I on October 4, 1957, the record shows the Soviets have rocketed 15 objects into space including Yuri Gagarin and Gherman Titov. The United States has fired 41 objects into space since Explorer I on January 31, 1958, including Commander Alan B. Shepard, Jr., and Major Virgil I. Grisson. In the course of these explorations, important discoveries have emanated pertaining to wind, velocity, pressure, temperature and density of air, atomic and molecular structure of air, the magnetic field and iconosphere, the aurora and the rings, the stellar and x-ray radiation. In the United States four Rangers are planned. The first is scheduled at an early date to explore the Moon in anticipation of a manned landing later.

The development of the technology makes it clear that soon there will be manned orbiting bombers, military space stations and huge booster rockets with millions of pounds of thrust.

What more do we need to know to realize that unless the rule of law is established soon for the control of outer space, the prospects are bleak indeed for a peaceful solution of the myriad of problems these terrifying inventions will bring in their wake.

Meanwhile, what is the scorecard of the world's political leaders?

By resolution 1348 (XIII) of December 13, 1958, the General Assembly of the United Nations established an Ad Hoc Committee on the Peaceful Uses of Outer Space consisting of representatives of Argentina, Australia, Belgium, Brazil, Canada, Czechoslovakia, France, India, Iran, Italy, Japan, Mexico, Poland, Sweden, the U.S.S.R., the United Arab Republic, Great Britain and the U.S.A.

The Soviet Union, Czechoslovakia, and Poland refused to participate in the deliberations of this committee. Nevertheless, it met and completed a report, which was filed July 14, 1959.

Although recognizing that the conduct of space activities should be effectively "open and orderly." the committee "considered that a comprehensive code was not practical or desirable at the present stage of knowledge and development." It was pointed out "that the rule of law is neither dependent upon nor assured by comprehensive codification and that premature codification might prejudice subsequent efforts to develop the law based on a more complete understanding of the practical problems involved."

This conclusion, it is submitted, begs the question. A "complete codification" is not essential to the adoption of an international treaty which would limit the uses of outer space to peaceful purposes.

Nevertheless, the United Nations General Assembly, recognizing that the exploration and use of outer space should be "for the betterment of mankind" on December 12, 1959, established a Committee on the Peaceful Uses of Outer Space to serve during 1960 and 1961. The mandate of that committee included, inter alia, a directive "to study the nature of legal problems which may arise from the exploration of outer space." Unhappily that committee has never met due to differences between the major powers on the composition of the committee.

There, any attempts by our political experts to evolve a solution to the problem seem to have died while the machinery of industry continues to grind out larger and more powerful rockets.

III. <u>Suggested Solutions</u>.

As pointed out, all scientific and political organizations of international composition
have agreed that cooperation among all nations in the exploration of outer space is necessary for dedication of spaceways to peaceful uses. It is only the means of accomplishing that
objective which has thus far proved elusive.

In the early stages of the quest for a suitable formula, much stress was placed upon
the Chicago and Paris conventions, vesting in each nation sovereignty in the airspace above
it. Qualified scholars sought to delineate an arbitrary boundary between airspace and outer-
space on the theory that a nation's sovereignty should extend no farther than to the upper
boundary of the airspace. These theorists contended that no state has a legitimate right
to claim sovereignty into the distant regions of space.

Priority need not be given to this problem in marking out an agreement to limit the use
of space to peaceful purposes.

I agree with General Thomas D. White, former Chief of Staff of the United States Air
Force, who said:

> In discussing air and space, it should be recognized that there is no
> division, per se, between the two. For all practical purposes air and space
> merge, forming a continuous and indivisible field of operation.

The nature of space flight is such that the instant a satellite or rocket is released,
all the nations of the Earth are involved. It is folly to say that the trajectory of the
particular ship in flight is within the exclusive domination of the launching state in derogation of the rights of all other states.

* * * * *

CERTAIN ASPECTS OF THE RIGHT OF INNOCENT PASSAGE OF SPACE VEHICLES

by

Jacek Machowski

I. <u>The meaning of the term "innocent passage."</u>

There are serious reasons for doubt and objections to the use of the term "innocent
passage" both in air law and in the law of outer space, and even more to its application.

The term originates from the maritime usage. Strenuous efforts have been made to trans-
plant it by analogy from the law of the sea into air law. The only substantial argument
which the supporters of this analogy could provide is that it would be unjust if the airspace over states and airports was placed in a relatively less favourable situation for certain aircraft than territorial waters and harbours under maritime regulations.

No wonder, therefore, that the term "innocent passage," its meaning and its scope have
been subject to a heated dispute since the early days of the foundation of the air law. When

67

in the first decade of this century, Westlake, defending the idea of sovereign rights of States over their airspace, said that it is "subject to a right of innocent passage by aircraft," his chief opponent, Fauchille, replied that the term "innocent passage" used by Westlake was too vague.

It is noteworthy that in air-navigation agreements the term "right (or freedom) of innocent passage" has been used without being defined. It was not defined in either the Paris Convention of 1919, nor the Havana Convention of 1928. Furthermore, when the Chicago Civil Aviation Conference was convened in 1944, the United States Delegation objected even to the inclusion of any reference to the right of innocent passage because of the uncertainty as to how the term would be applied in practice in the future conventions.

Finally, the term was not included in any of the air-navigation conventions at Chicago in 1944. Neither has it ever been made quite clear what was actually intended to be accomplished by the use of the term "innocent passage" in international air-navigation agreements.

The temptation to make analogies is admittedly hard to resist, and the possibilities of such analogies are quite broad. Nevertheless it is not possible mechanically to apply the rules and notions of air law to the law of outer space, just as it was not possible years ago mechanically to transpose the provisions of the law of the sea into air law. For while air law is mainly based upon the recognition of the complete and exclusive sovereignty of a State over the airspace above its territory, there is a strong tendency to base the system of law of outer space upon the acceptance of the view, that outer space is res omnium communis, the common property of mankind, available for peaceful utilization by all, and not subject to acquisition by any state. As yet this entirely new branch of law is considered to be affected only by the basic principles of international law.

II. <u>The right of innocent passage and the sovereignty over airspace.</u>

During the initial stage of its flight after take-off, every space vehicle must pass through airspace. This gives rise to the legal question of rules governing this part of space flight.

The principle of complete and exclusive sovereignty of a State over its airspace is now so firmly established throughout the world, both in international and comestic law, that it is no longer open to question. Even the opponents of the theory of freedom of the airspace have conceded that under this principle, the States whose airspace has been used for flights have the right to adopt and apply such measures as they deem necessary for the security of persons and property on their national territory.

When discussing the right to use airspace of a sovereign State, be it by aircraft or spacecraft, one must bear in mind that the theory of complete freedom of the air has been generally rejected in favour of sovereignty over airspace and that it is for the Government concerned to extend or refuse permission on, and to determine conditions for an entry of foreign craft of any kind into its sovereign airspace.

There is no need to quote here all the official papers which proclaim national sovereignty over airspace. The principle of State sovereignty over airspace finds also support amongst the overwhelming majority of international law experts all over the world.

May I be permitted to confine myself at this point to quoting only two prominent Soviet experts on this subject, Kislov and Krylov, who have written:

Recognition of the sovereignty of a state in its airspace signifies recognition of the full right of each state to regulate <u>all</u> the airways over its territory; that is, the right of the country not to allow flight over its territory by <u>any</u> foreign airships, both those with crews and those guided from a distance, those heavier than air, and those lighter than air including balloons of any size, unless otherwise stated in special conventions and agreements relating to the airships of any definite state or states. The principle of sovereignty in air space presupposes also the right of a country to prohibit transportation of definite categories of cargoes over its territory, and also the use of one or another apparatus, etc., equally, also the right to take any measures to cut short violations of sovereignty by foreign airships.

More detailed views of this subject, with explicit reference to space vehicles passing through airspace, have been expressed by two Czechoslovak scholars. One of them, Dr. Kopal says:

The principle of sovereignty of the subjacent state over the airspace fully applies to rockets while they are passing through this space and before they leave it. The problem now is what is their status the moment they are outside this sphere.

Similarly, as early as in 1932, Dr. Vladimir Mandl, another Czechoslovak jurist and author of the first treatise on the law of outer space, wrote that "as soon as the cosmic craft enters the sphere of air sovereignty, it is subject to the state competence."

According to contemporary practice based upon the principle of national sovereignty over airspace, the right of innocent transit flights through it is not a principle <u>pleno iure gentium</u>, but rather of <u>iure contractus</u>. Such provisions as stipulated in Article 5 of the Chicago Convention of 1944 confirm rather than contradict this principle.

III. <u>The right of innocent passage of space vehicles through outer space.</u>

On leaving the airspace, the cosmic vehicle enters the outer space. The content of the future rules that might govern this part of a cosmic flight will depend primarily on the legal status of outer space, which still remains to be settled.

If we accept the now prevailing idea that outer space is <u>res omnium communis</u> and hence, just as high seas cannot be appropriated by any State, there seems to be no obstacle for assuming the existence of the right of innocent passage of space vehicles through this part of space, providing that this passage is truly innocent, i.e., harmless to peace, security and good order of the territory of the subjacent state. This last requirement will be completely fulfilled on reaching an agreement on disarmament, providing for the exclusively peaceful use of outer space.

It should be noted, however, that the absence of a disarmament agreement and of a formal solution of the problem of the legal status of outer space cannot in any way serve as justification for a complete denial of all the sovereign rights of states, some of which do not cease to be valid even beyond the boundaries of our planet; the right of states to security is one of them. To conclude, we must agree that in outer space as elsewhere, countries are obliged to refrain from threatening and violating the sovereign rights of other states. In other words, each state has full right to make such use of outer space as it sees fit, as long as it does not thereby infringe upon the sovereign rights of other states.

IV. <u>The right of innocent passage of space vehicles and the "theory of zones."</u>

The simplest solutions in respect of the right of innocent passage, which I have just mentioned, based upon the traditional division of space into airspace and outer space, do not seem to satisfy all the jurists dealing with problems of the law of outer space.

Some of them, advancing "the theory of zones" also called "the theory of territorial airspace," would like to see an intermediary space zone created between the airspace and outer space. This zone, according to their suggestions, ought to be governed by special rules, different from those of airspace and outer space. A considerable number of promoters of the theory of zones express the opinion that space vehicles should enjoy special rights of innocent passage through this intermediary zone.

The theory of zones and the right of innocent passage emerged as a compromise solution from the famous controversy which took place about the turn of the twentieth century between the supporters of absolute freedom of the air and the adherents of absolute national sovereignty over airspace. The authors of this compromise theory, profiting from the analogy with the law of the sea, made an attempt to divide airspace into two zones, one subject to national sovereignty and a free zone above it; this was after the pattern of the division, made by the law of the sea, into "territorial sea" and "open sea." Although fervently discussed by scholars, the theory of zones has not gained much backing in the practice of air navigation or legislation.

In connection with the first space flights and the opening of debates about the basic principles of the law of outer space, the theory of zones and the right of innocent passage have been revived by certain jurists, who are now advancing them in new forms, perhaps more in line with the requirements of space age, but built upon the same old principles, so strongly criticized for years. They are requesting now the right of innocent passage not for aircraft, but for space vehicles.

One of the earliest theories in this series was advanced by the prominent American jurist, John Cobb Cooper, who by analogy with the law of the sea proposed to divide the space up to an altitude of 300 miles (480 km) into two zones. The first of them called "territorial space," would remain subject to the traditional, exclusive State of sovereignty. The zone beyond, extended up to 300 miles and called "continuous space," would be granted the right of innocent passage for non-military space vehicles. Beyond the limits of "continuous space" would begin outer space, as free as high seas.

Another version of the theory of zones in respect to the law of outer space was recently advanced by the Inter-American Bar Association, which at its Twelfth Conference held in February 1961 at Bogota (Colombia) adopted a <u>Magna Carta of Space</u>. Its Paragraph "g" reads in part:

> ... since it is impossible to set out a boundary line with physical
> qualities such as characterize boundary lines on land and on the sea, that there
> be established a neutral zone between the upper limits of Air Space and the
> lower limits of Outer Space to be known as "Neutralia" in which the right of
> innocent passage shall be recognized without offense to sovereignty. In this

area of "Neutralia" there shall be the right of innocent passage of all craft, vehicles and objects of transit and movement without any such incident being deemed an invasion of sovereignty. In the event of any such innocent passage no nation shall have the right to attack or destroy such vehicle or object in transit or the nation from which the said vehicle or object was launched or to destroy any occupants thereof without prior, sufficient warning and notice of claim of invasion of sovereignty and without prior opportunity for determination of the merits of such complaints by peaceful methods.

It should be noted that what perhaps detracts the most from the value of the theory of zones are the attempts to establish intermediary zones at the expense of complete and exclusive sovereignty of States over the airspace above their national territory. In his comments on the theory of zones one of the co-sponsors of the Magna Carta, William A. Hyman, does not even try to conceal this when saying that:

... the sovereignty of a state would not be violated by the passage through outer space or the upper regions of airspace above its territory even of a strictly military satellite or space vehicle if the theory of innocent passage is applied. The nature of the vehicle or object creating such trespass would, of course, bear upon the interpretation of the act. In this connection it would seem desirable to establish a middle area between airspace held to be within the sovereign jurisdiction of a subjacent land on the one hand, and, on the other hand, outer space extending above the area of airspace towards heavens and including the planets. This neutral territory could be classified as area of innocent passage and thus avoid subjecting the vehicle to the action which might be taken in other circumstances in the area of airspace.

The theory of zones has been presented in various forms by a number of jurists who often refer explicitly to the analogies provided by the law of the sea. Analogies between the sea on the one side and airspace and outer space on the other, hardly acceptable in the physical sense, seem even more unacceptable in the legal sense. The essence of the problem lies in the difference between the horizontal contiguity of airspace. The former can be separated from the land (as in the case of landlocked countries) while the latter cannot. There does not exist on our globe any land or sea without airspace contiguity. These physical distinctions are of utmost significance from the point of view of security of States, since vertical contiguity creates conditions much more difficult for protecting the safety of the States concerned and more conducive to control and domination over the land than does horizontal contiguity. Security of States has always been the key problem when defining the legal status of areas having various physical characteristics.

During World War II, the "principle of effective control" was advanced in support of the theory of airspace zones. Under a restrictive interpretation of the said principle territorial sovereignty over airspace can be expanded to such an altitude only as can be reached by the effective power of the subjacent state. It was in accordance with this interpretation that during the last war British military aircraft flew over the territory of neutral States, such as Switzerland.

This restrictive interpretation was generated by the "theory of zones"; based upon analogies with the law of the sea, it was the result of a mechanical transfer into the sphere of the law of airspace of the old principle "dominium terrae finitur ubi finitur armorum vis," formulated two centuries ago by Bynkershoek for the purpose of delimintating territorial seas.

Disregarding the well-established principle of full and exclusive sovereignty of States over their airspace, certain Western statesmen and jurists even after the end of World War II, tried to revive the old "theory of zones." Though presented in another form, its basis remained the same; it was the principle of effective control.

Only very recently, and to be more precise, after the launching of the first Soviet Sputnik and other space vehicles, a remarkable evolution occurred in these Western views. Concepts of "free zones," "low altitude flights," and such like were hastily abandoned by most of their former supporters to be replaced soon enough by other ideas tending to extend the sovereign rights of States as far up as into outer space.

Such an extensive interpretation of the principle of complete and exclusive sovereign rights over airspace was first advanced in works, published before World War II, expressing the view that the notion of airspace and, therefore, that of sovereignty of States extends usque ad sidera - up to the stars. It should be noted, however, that such an extensive interpretation of the notion of airspace does not find any corroboration in contemporary rules of internationa law.

Resulting from political and military rather than legal considerations, the lack of consistency in respect to the limits of airspace in the official doctrine of some of the Western powers, of the United States in particular, does not contribute to the search for a solution of the unresolved problems of the law of outer space, which ought to be based upon solid scientific methods and facts.

* * * * *

LEGAL STATUS OF THE ASTRONAUT
by
Aldo Armando Cocca

...

VIII. Military reconnoitering and espionage by the cosmonaut.

According to statements of the cosmonauts, it is easy to find their way about--mentally--during an orbital flight, by reference to the surface of the Earth. The topographical features of the mountains, large rivers, seas, islands and larger lakes, as well as the line of the occidental coasts, can be easily made out. The cosmonaut can take photographs of a place that is judged interesting for a certain purpose, draw graphics of that zone, form a mental scheme of the situation and accomplish similar tasks.

On the 12th of August, 1961, the N.A.S.A. confirmed that approximately half of the seventeen circumnavigations of Vostok II were made over American or Canadian territory and, in most part of the cases, over both of them. Thus a widely crossed net of orbits was made covering a large northern zone of the American continent.

Among regions passed over by Titov and his cosmoship are included the Eastern coast of America, with its big metropolitan zones and military bases, the corridor to the south of the missile testing sector on the Pacific and the general zone of the testing sector of the Atlantic, stretching to the southeast, from Cape Canaveral, Florida. The Vostok II also went over the United States to the latitude of New Mexico, where missiles testing and nuclear investigation are made, and over Montana where the U.S. Air Force has its launching bases for intercontinental missiles. The orbit of the cosmoship passed over Alaska, too, where there are air and military bases, and over a part of Greenland where there is a radar station for detecting the presence of ballistic missiles.

Whatever has been said up to now suggests ample possibilities for reconnoitering and espionage operations, tasks that law cannot neglect.

Let us remember that on May 1, 1960, Francis B. Powers, of the U-2 airplane of the American Air Force, was shot down on Soviet territory, taken prisoner and tried for espionage. Powers "was accomplishing a photographical mission at great height." Two months later, the 1st of July, the American R.B.-47 airplane was also shot down, over the Barents sea, while "accomplishing an electromagnetical mission for the drawing of maps." The airplane's crew - with the exception of its commander, Captain Willard G. Palm, who perished in the operation - followed Powers' fate.

What difference is there between the activity, considered espionage, deployed by the U-2 pilot or by the commander and crew of the R.B.-47, and the one that a cosmonaut can effect with identical purpose? Higher altitude, from the physics point of view, which owing to perfection reached with regard to electromagnetical and photographic apparatus, cannot be technically considered as an obstacle. From the legal point of view it may be said there has been violation of the air border by the pilots of the airplanes. Meanwhile, the cosmonaut would operate through the space border, which has not been legally determined or ruled and, consequently is not susceptible of violation.

We arrive at the conclusion that present military reconnoiterings and espionage actions can be made from space with impunity, and this, Law cannot permit to go on without legal regulation.

If the cosmonaut goes ahead on a mission of military reconnoitering he loses his character as a civil explorer, which we have indicated as the essential legal condition that confers him tutelage and protection, and falls into illegality and clandestiness. He would not be a cosmonaut but a qualified spy, because the expression "cosmonaut" has a precise legal meaning within the Interplanetary Law, which is, above all, a code of conduct and universal law and is placed above national interests in consequence of the four dimensional policy.

That is why it is necessary to forbid, through an international agreement, espionage practiced from space; and if this proved impracticable, countries ought to get used to the notion of the relative value of geographical position of casting bases, weapons factories, barracks and further military installations.

IX. The cosmonaut's salvage.

Since the cosmonaut is a civil explorer of space who answers to a policy, whose character is to be at the service of mankind, it must be established without any further consider-

and afterwards proceed to its corresponding regulation.

The cosmonaut's aid and salvage may happen on land, at sea, and in space. The rules of rescue in space are at present impracticable. Rules of assistance refer to land and to sea when the descent is actually in parachutes or space vehicles. We echo now the Brussels Convention, 1928, for the unification of certain rules regarding assistance and salvage at sea of airships or by airships.

Pilots' or air commanders' obligation to assist a cosmonaut in danger must be established. Assistance will be in proportion to technical means available. The same obligation should be established for ships' captains with regard to cosmonauts who are in danger at sea in the cosmoship or as a consequence of the cosmoship's damage.

* * * * *

II. Autres Contributions et Commentaires

Le quatrième colloque du droit de l'espace étudie particulièrement l'idée de paix dans la société internationale par le développement du droit de l'espace.

What difference is there between the activity, considered espionage, deployed by the U-2 pilot or by the commander and crew of the R.B.-47, and the one that a cosmonaut can effect with identical purpose? From the point of view of physics, higher altitude technically cannot be considered as an obstacle because of the perfection reached with electromagnetical and photographic apparatus. From the legal point of view, it may be said there has been violation of the air border by the pilots of the airplanes. Meanwhile, the cosmonaut would operate through the space border, which has not been legally determined or ruled, and consequently is not susceptible of violation. We arrive at the conclusion that present military reconnoiterings and espionage actions can be made from space with impunity, and this, law cannot permit without legal regulation.

If the cosmonaut goes ahead on a mission of military reconnoitering, he loses his character as a civil explorer, which we have indicated as the essential legal condition that confers him tutelage and protection, and he falls into illegality and clandestineness. He would not be a cosmonaut, but a qualified spy because the expression "cosmonaut" has a precise legal meaning within interplanetary law, which is, above all, a code of conduct and universal law and is placed above national interests in consequence of the four dimensional policy.

That is why it is necessary to forbid, through an international agreement, espionage practiced from space; and if this proves impracticable, countries ought to get used to the notion of the relative value of geographical positioning of bases, weapons factories, barracks and further military installations.

IX. The cosmonaut's salvage.

Since the cosmonaut is a civil explorer of space, who answers to a policy and whose character is to be at the service of mankind, the obligations of assistance and salvage must be established without any further consideration. It is best to fix the principle artion the obligations of assistance and salvage.

The cosmonaut's aid and salvage may happen on land, at sea, and in space. It is convenient to fix the principle and afterwards proceed to its corresponding regulation.

Being salvage in space is at present impracticable, rules over assistance must refer to land and to sea when the descent is parachutes or otherwise. Concerning this last one we could quote now the Brussels Convention, 1928, for the unification of certain rules regarding assistance and salvage at sea of airships or by airships.

Pilots' or air commanders' obligation to assist a cosmonaut in danger will be established. Assistance will be in proportion to technical means available. The same obligation will be established for ships' captains with regard to cosmonauts who were in danger at sea, on the cosmoship or as a consequence of the cosmoship's damage.

* * * * *

II. <u>Le quatrième colloque du droit de l'espace étudie particulièrement l'idée de paix dans la société internationale par le développement du droit de l'espace.</u>

De très nombreuses communications sont consacrées a ces problèmes. La table des matières des Proceedings en fait état.

En réalité, l'on peut distinguer trois aspects fondamentaux dans ces écrits très importants. En premier lieu le thème général de l'interdiction de l'utilisation non pacifique de l'espace, en second lieu, la recherche du principe permettant d'établir un fondement à cette interdiction.

Enfin la recherche de techniques appropriées a cette fin.

1) L'interdiction de l'utilisation non pacifique de l'espace est le problème central du droit que nous étudions. Le problème a été, dès le depart, éludé par l'organisation des Nations-Unies parce qu'il se relie au problème d'ensemble du désarmement. Malgré tout la résolution de l'assemblée générale des Nations-Unies du 14 Novembre 1957 prévoyait: "l'étude d'un système de contrôle destiné à s'assurer que le lancement d'engins dans l'espace ne sera effectué qu'à des fins pacifiques et scientifiques."

En 1961, le Président Kennedy devait non seulement reprendre ces idées mais également proposer un programme. Reprenons ses propres termes:[1]

"The new horizons of outer space must not be riven by the old bitter concepts of imperialism and sovereign claims. The cold reaches of the universe must not become the new arena of an even colder war ...

To this end, we shall urge proposals extending the United Nations Charter to the limits of man's exploration in the universe, reserving outer space for peaceful use, prohibiting weapons of mass destruction in space or on celestial bodies, and opening the mysteries and benefits of space to every nation."

1 Nicholas N. Kittrie, p. 198

Ce qui revient à dire que ce qui appartient à l'humanité tout entière, en tant qu'unité indivisible, sans possibilité de destruction entre groupes humains, ne peut être utilisé que dans des buts pacifiques. En effet, l'utilisation non pacifique ne pourrait se réaliser que par un Etat (ou groupe d'Etats) contre un autre Etat (ou groupe d"Etats). Dès lors, l'utilisation de l'espace doit être exclusivement orienté vers un développement des progrès de la science. En fait, les découvertes devraient être transmises à tous les pays et répandues a leur profit. Dès 1961, on prévoyait les utilisations de l'espace à des fins pacifiques et dans l'intérêt de l'humanité: l'amélioration des prévisions météorologiques, le développement des télécommunications, le perfectionnement des connaissances humaines en ce qui concerne la dimension et la forme de la terre, la répartition des terres émergées et des eaux grâce aux satellites géologiques sont autant d'exemples intéressants. Le 20 December 1961, d'ailleurs, l'Assemblée générale votait à l'unanimité une résolution recommandant au comité des utilisations pacifiques de l'espace extra-atmosphérique de reconnaitre que le droit international et la charte de l'O.N.U. s'appliquaient à l'espace et aux corps célestes et que ceux-ci n'étaient susceptibles d'appropriation par aucun pays. Les Etats étaient invités à donner des renseignements sur le lancement des fusées sur orbite et à échanger leurs informations sur leurs activités dans les espaces interplanétaires. Rappelons que ces premiers principes furent complétés dès Mars 1962 lors de la première session du sous-comité juridique du comité des utilisations pacifiques de l'espace. Mais ce n'est qu'au cours de la XVIIIe session de l'Assemblée générale - le 13 December 1963 - qu'une déclaration concernant les principe juridiques qui doivent régir les activites des Etats en matière d'exploration et d'utilisation de l'espace cosmique, fut adoptée; cette déclaration complétait la résolution votée le 17 October 1963, par laquelle les Etats étaient invités à ne pas placer sur orbite autour de la terre des véhicules spatiaux porteurs d'armes nucléaires ou d'autres armes de destruction massive.[1]

2) Les principes fondamentaux permettant d'établir une base juridique à cette interdiction furent posés dans la déclaration de 1963. Les Etats sont libres - sur une base d'égalité - d'explorer et d'utiliser l'espace et les corps célestes aux conditions suivantes:

a) l'exploration et l'utilisation doivent être effectués pour le bénéfice de l'humanité tout entière. (Cette référence au concept d'humanité est très accentuée dans ce domaine)[2]

b) les activités spatiales doivent être conformés au droit international, y compris la charte des Nations-Unies en vue de maintenir la paix et la securité internationale.

c) les Etats doivent être guidés dans leurs activités par les principes de coopération et d'assistance mutuelle, en tenant compte des intérêts des autres Etats.

d) enfin les textes précisent l'interdiction de non appropriation nationale de l'Espace et des corps célestes (ce qui exclut, dès lors, toute proclamation de souveraineté, occupation et utilisation nationales).

Ces différent principes étaient affirmés lors du quatrième colloque du droit de l'espace dans les différentes communications. En effet, il était nécessaire - dans cette période initiale - de réglementer l'utilisation militaire afin de protéger la liberté, la souveraineté et la securité des Etats non spatiaux. (Ainsi, par exemple, les observations mili-

1 V.J. Simsarian in American Journal of I.L. 1964, p.717

2 David F. Maxwell in Proceedings op.at.

taires par satellites fixes – c'est-à-dire dont la vitesse de rotation est égale à celle de la terre – et les expériences atomiques au voisinage des corps célèstes. Car les Etats non spatiaux ne peuvent accepter les multiplications des activités spatiales que si parallelement à cette multiplication se développe un system de garanties en matière de securité. Ce qui amène à interdire tout système militaire de contrôle afin d'éviter toute idée d'agression. 3) Mais, d'après ces principes, il faut rechercher des techniques d'application. Il est nécessaire de dire que les techniques proposées se présentent en "ordre dispersé" et qu'il n'y a pas à l'heure actuelle de systématisation multilatérale[1]. On ne peut citer que l'article 4 du traité sur l'utilisation pacifique de l'espace du 27 Janvier 1967 qui s'inspire, pour régler la démilitarisation du traité de Washington sur l'Antartique. Mais la guerre peut être évitée lorsque l'on sait s'organiser la paix. Et dans ce nouveau domaine, toutes les procédures peuvent être imaginées. En principe, ces procédures s'organisent autour de trois idées forcées: souveraineté sur l'espace, droit de passage des satellites et responsabilité, statut légal des astronautes.

Il n'est pas nécessaire ici de reprendre d'excellentes études déjà réalisées sur la souveraineté de l'espace[2] sinon pour signaler la dualite du régime juridique de l'atmosphère et de l'espace et les limites verticales d'application du droit aérien.

Quant au régime juridique des satellites, le principe de base est celui qui fixe les limites de la liberté d'exploration par l'obligation de respecter les droits légitimes d'autrui. C'est en principe de bon voisinage qui exige la protection active de la vie dans l'Univers. L'article I bis de la résolution des N.U. du 13 Décember 1963 impose une obligation de but et non de moyen "pour le bienfait et dans l'intérêt de l'humanité tout entière". En fait, dans la mesure ou les satellites de télécommunications sont les plus nombreux, certains auteurs ont critiqué le particularisme des accords à ce sujet.[3] Mais il paraît difficile de se dégager des procédures actuelles. Le point le plus intéressant à noter concerne la responsabilité pour les dommages causés par les satellites: soit avant que l'engin transportant des charges de carburants hautement volatiles, n'ait atteint son orbite, soit que l'engin, quittant son orbite, provoque de graves désastres. Or, ni le droit international traditionnel, ni la loi nationale ne sont adéquates, n'étant pas susceptibles de régler le genre de responsabilité résultant d'activités spatiales et nucléaires. Le paragraphe 5 de la déclaration de 1963 des N.U- traduit la reconnaissance de l'interdépendance des Etats face au risques creés par les développements de la technologie moderne et en conséquence de la nécessité d'un régime de responsabilité absolue. Il est partout admis que cette responsabilité, dont la mesure financière peut atteindre des sommes énormes, doit être nuancée.[4]

Quant au statut de l'astronaute ou du cosmonaute, les problèmes soulevés sont surtout

---

1 Le seul effort de synthèse est bilatéral dans le traité américano-soviétique de 1972.

2 Voir notamment in Proceedings, les écrits du Pr. Dr. Von Rauchhaupt ein Proceedings 1961, Sovereignty in Space, de Welf Heinrich Prince of Hanover.

1 C. Chaumont. Observations sur le régime international des Satellites de télécommunications. Revue générale de l'air et de l'espace 1966, n° 1.

4 Le Comité des Nations Unies sur les utilisations pacifiques de l'espace extra-atmosphérique par Miss J. Gutteridge. Dans Problems in Space Law, a symposium British Institute of International and Comparative law 1966.

relatifs a l'espionnage: si la règle de l'utilisation pacifique de l'espace interdit l'agression, elle ne permet pas encore de préciser très nettement la frontière entre travail spatial scientifique a fins militaires nationales et coopération internationale. Souhaitons le, des Traités pourront pallier cette lacune. Ce quatrième colloque du droit de l'espace concerne l'idée de paix dans la société internationale par le developpement du droit de l'espace.

- - - - -

FIFTH COLLOQUIUM ON THE LAW OF OUTER SPACE

VARNA,1962

I. Texts Reproduced

SOME LEGAL ASPECTS OF THE USES OF RECONNAISSANCE SATELLITES

by

Gyula Gal

In the battle of Fleurus on the 26th June 1794, the fire of French batteries was directed from the reconnaissance balloon "Entreprenant" floating in air above the enemy lines.
Not only balloons, but also aeroplanes were employed in warfare first for reconnaissance
purposes. Technical development enabled them later to fight against each other and against
ground targets. The chain of military uses is unbroken from surveillance flights to indis-
criminate bombing and to the first atomic air attack of history.

Space travel is now in the stage of peacetime uses of artificial satellites for reconnaissance over foreign territories. This military employment of astronautics is a warning
for mankind that this fateful development must be stopped if we do not want to suffer from
the use of this great achievement for global destruction. It is an important task of space
law science to analyze the problems raised by this form of military activity in outer space.

Legal evaluation of reconnaissance satellites is principally connected with the notion
of "peaceful uses." Especially since the U.N. Resolution on the 21st December 1961, /A/Res/
1721/XVI/, this peaceful function is the focus of space law. The problem of delimitation of
airspace and outer space, dealt with by the extended literature on space law, has no chance
to be solved within a reasonable time. Present space activities must be evaluated, therefore,
legally with the presupposition that norms of conduct cannot be derived from the "legal
nature" of the zone from which the activity concerned is carried out. We agree with C.
Chaumont that this functional system is the only one capable of guaranteeing the protection
of all interests involved and promoting, at one and the same time, the progress of science
and the development of international cooperation. We represented from the beginning the
standpoint that legal science and practice must break away from the obsolete schemes of territorial zones. All attempts to establish the law of space must accept the "activity" or
"functional" conception explicitly or implied.

The activity in space presents a great variety both in aims and methods. On the present
technical level of modern warfare the data collected by satellites in their scientific program may also be important from a military aspect. On the lists of artificial satellites,
the categories of "civilian" and "military" satellites have appeared as evidences for purely military activities carried out in space.

Reconnaissance from space as a technical problem has been solved years ago. Since the successful recovery of space capsules (August 1960), it is possible to receive from orbit photos and data otherwise fixed from targets of vital interest from all over the world. The Midas (Missile Defense Alarm System) and Samos (Surveillance and Missile Observation Satellites) systems of the United States are carrying out a 24 hours reconnaissance of great areas of the earth by means of highly accurate TV-equipment, which enables them to spot missile launching bases, airfields, industrial centers, etc. This activity was accelerated after the failure of U-2 flights over the territory of the Soviet Union. Press news characterized Samos as "a veritable 'eye-in-the sky,' which would make such efforts as U-2 information-gathering flights over the Soviet Union wholly obsolete," having the advantage that, "unlike the U-2 which can be shot down, the Samos will be practically invulnerable against an enemy's effort." As J.R. Cownie in Aeroplane pointed out, "The U-2 program gave invaluable information about Russian military power; ... now the U-2 is dead, the Samos reconnaissance program is being accelerated to take its place as far as possible."

From the USAF bases of Port Arguello and Vandenberg since the 22nd November 1961, 20 unidentified satellites carrying "secret equipment" were launched. They were omitted from the list of space launchings in the report by President Kennedy. These secret satellites are undoubtedly carrying out surveillance missions over the territory of the Soviet Union and other socialist countries. These missions consist of detecting and fixing of the position of important "hostile" ground targets for the event of an attack against them.

The activity of the reconnaissance satellites circling the earth is clearly military. Contrary to such functions as meteorological observations or examinations of cosmic radiation, which can be employed for military and purely scientific purposes, this surveillance is only of military character. In the U-2 affair, the United States die not deny the fact that these flights violated the Soviet territorial sovereignty. This violation of the sovereign rights of a state excludes any doubts about illegality of this action, which was denied only by a few theoriticians.

Concerning the legal evaluation of surveillance from outer space, we find that socialist literature of space law unanimously rejects the legality of this activity. On the other side, the opinion of scientists is varied. Space lawyers supporting the legality of space reconnaissance assert three main arguments:

A) Reconnaissance satellites are circling above the spheres of sovereignty of subjacent states. These devices are in a certain sense "above the law" and can operate, therefore, freely from legal prohibitions.

B) If the use of outer space is free for "peaceful purposes" only, reconnaissance from orbit is permitted on the grounds that this activity does not go beyond the limits of peaceful purposes.

C) Espionage does not constitute a delict under international law. It is only a crime according to national law.

Ad A) Some authors attempted even in the "Moby Dick" and U-2 affairs, to describe them as involving the problem of upper limit of territorial sovereignty. Spencer Beresford e.g. pointed out that the U-2 operated at a height of 68,000 feet, higher than man can breath, and "far higher than the balloons of 1956 to which the S.U. objected not only as invasions of

Soviet airspace but as dangers to aerial navigation. Objects at U-2 cruising altitudes would not interfere with any normal use of the air, even by military aircraft."

The Committee on Foreign Relations of the United States Senate in its Report on the Summit Conference has also connected these two separate problems, stating that the incident "has pointed up the need for international agreement on the question of how high sovereignty extends skyward." According to A. Buecking "the activity of reconnaissance satellites cannot be objected to on the grounds of territorial sovereignty." The surveillance from space does not affect immediately the subjacent states. It is carried out without harmful or otherwise illegal effects. Kenneth Gatland points out that "Legally, America has every right to launch reconnaissance and surveillance satellites over the territories of other nations, although the wisdom of doing so at the present critical period of international diplomacy is open to question."

All these opinions are connected with the consequences of an alleged legal vacuum in space. They try to utilize the negative side of theory of sovereignty in a false way. Outer space really does not constitute a part of national sovereignty. It is free and not subject to national occupation. But the declaration of a character of res omnium communis in the above Resolution of the UN General Assembly must be interpreted together with the condition that this use is only possible "in conformity with international law," which - including the U.N. Charter - applies to outer space and celestial bodies, too.

Freedom of space does not mean anarchy in space. This principle is accepted both by interstate practice and theory. No state protested against the peaceful mission of artificial satellites. Such actions, on the other hand, as the Westford Project to place a belt of dipoles in orbit, or the high altitude explosions of atomic weapons met with official protests and scientific criticism.

The extension of international law to outer space is generally accepted in literature on both sides. It is a legal "communis opinio," that the state of res omnium communis may not be interpreted in the sense that it could be abused against obligations under conventional and customary international law. Freedom of space does not mean that space vehicles may shake off the rules of international law regulating the relations of the launching state with other members of international community.

We are aware of the fact, that a series of specific problems of space activities need specific conventional regulations. These future agreements are to be built - as M.S. Smirnoff correctly says that: one, there is no state sovereignty in the outer space; two, there is no place for absolute liberty of flights in the outer space. The latter is not only a principle de lege ferenda. Some authors assert the "legality" of space reconnaissance as a consequence of the lack of treaty prohibitions. Kammerer e.g. says: "A general prohibition of taking photographs from the earth's surface does not exist." We agree, on this point only, with Chester Ward who says that the legal vacuum growing out of the absence of international agreements relative to space and its use creates specific dangers. This is true especially for space reconnaissance! At the Geneva meeting of the Legal Subcommittee of the U.N. Committee on the Peaceful Uses of Outer Space, the Soviet delegation therefore proposed that nations should agree that "the use of artificial satellites for the collection of intelligence information on the territory of foreign states is incompatible with the objectives of mankind in its conquest of outer space."

We must emphasize, that even in absence of such an agreement the activity of reconnaissance satellites constitutes a delict under international law.

1. The 24 hours' surveillance of foreign state territory under conditions of a new strategic idea, which cannot be interpreted according to old patterns, not even to the terms of World War II strategic bombing, is an act which endangers the existence of the states concerned. This new form of global espionage, with continued receiving of data indispensable for an all-out thermonuclear aggression, violates the right of each state to self-preservation.

2. The reconnaissance from orbit as a potential element of a nuclear attack endangers the international peace and security in general. This activity is therefore incompatible with the purpose of the United Nations to maintain international peace and security. (Art. 1. Para. 1.)

3. This activity is, in the sense of modern global strategy, a violation of the obligation of member states to "refrain in their international relations from the threat of use of force against the territorial integrity or political independence of any state." (Art. 2, Para. 4.)

4. For space lawyers who abuse the concept of territorial sovereignty for legalizing of this activity we emphasize that this interference occurs through "zones" which belong without any doubt to the sovereignty of the subjacent state.

Ad B). Some authors try to solve the legal contradictions of orbital reconnaissance by designating the military uses of satellites short of direct aggression as a "peaceful passive" activity. There is in the above mentioned U.N. resolution a statement that "Use of outer space should be only for the betterment of mankind and the benefit of states." This outlining of "peaceful uses" itself gives some instructions in the semantic dispute started by a number of space lawyers who try to justify this activity by saying that "peaceful" use is employed in contradistinction to aggressive and not "military."

Beresford in his work cited above says: "If the use of outer space is restricted by international agreement to 'peaceful purposes', only, ...the satellite surveillance may or may not be permitted, according to what is meant by 'peaceful purposes.'" He quotes George Feldman's interpretation of the U.S. National Aeronautics and Space Act of 1958 that the word "peaceful" as used in the Act means "non-aggressive" rather than "non-military," and the Report of the American Bar Association stating that "Any use of space which did not itself contribute an attack upon, or threat against, the territorial integrity and independance of another state, would be permissible."

The absurdity of this opinion is apparent. It would mean, namely, that all interference in the legally defended rights of the states would be permissible with the only exception of armed attack or threat of aggression. As referred to above, the military reconnaissance itself is a threat against the states concerned. The information collected by global space surveillance is indispensable for a state "which contemplates aggression and intends to strike the first blow and therefore wants to destroy the missile bases so as to avoid retribution after attack." (N.S. Khrushchev)

In our opinion the working of the historical U.N. resolution is clear on this point. It leads a country to the conclusion that all activities in and from outer space which do

not accord with the _only_ legal aim of betterment of mankind and benefit of states are forbidden. We think again that the resolution is also on this point of a declarative character.
It expresses only this consequence of applying the positive rules of modern international
law to outer space. _Peaceful activity is an activity in space only if it does not endanger_
the security of other states and does not constitute a threat of attack against them.

Ad C). Some lawyers quote the Hague Regulations of Land Warfare--espionage is collecting of data secretly and under false pretense - with the conclusion, that: one, reconnaissance
from orbit is not an espionage in the old sense, because it is not carried out secretly; two,
espionage itself violates only national law and does not constitute a crime under international law.

1. Apart from the fact that a great number of unidentified "secret" satellites have been
launched, we refer to an early - technically correct - press commentary on Samos satellites
(N.Y. Times, 26th May 1960): "...the taking of pictures is a silent operation, undetectable
from the ground ... the sending down of its information electronically will not take place
until commanded to do so when it is over U.S. territory, so that its signals could not be
interfered with."

Space reconnaissance is not "openly" carried out. On the other hand, secrecy is not a
necessary element of unlawful intelligence work against which each state has the right to
defend his vital interests. Would the Hague Regulations _relating to war_ mean that an "open"
reconnaissance action in airspace or from outer space would be legal? As _G. Zhukov_ correc-
ly points out, from the viewpoint of the security of a state, it makes no difference from
what altitude espionage over its territory is conducted. The main things are _object and_
results of espionage irrespective of altitude - and secrecy, as we could add to this argument.

Reconnaissance satellites are launched by the states by their armed forces. They are
equipped with such instruments as secure a permanent and systematic radar and photographic
observation of targets all over the world. This is indeed no espionage in the old sense,
but fatally more than all prior forms of espionage.

2. In this respect we refer to our arguments under A) and B). In our opinion the launching
and functioning of reconnaissance constitutes a _delict under international law._

Our conclusion is that the states concerned have the right (whether in airspace or
in outer space is, according to the above arguments, of no importance) to take all necessary measures for the prevention of this unlawful activity against its security, including
the destruction of orbiting reconnaissance satellites. There can be no doubt that technical progress makes possible the interception and annihilation of such satellites. These
measures and possible counter-measures could convert outer space to a battlefield of robot
weapons, which would be able to start a nuclear catastrophe. _Mr. N. Golovin_ suggested last
before the Royal United Service Institution that "a full scale orbital war might well be
the only sane solution of the apparently inextricable East-West ideological and political
opposition." In our opinion, war, even an extraterrestrial war, is no "sane solution" of
international problems. It is no solution at all. Therefore we have the duty to emphasize
the illegality of all such uses of outer space, which in the present stage of nuclear
saturation threaten mankind with the cataclysm of global war.

* * * * *

83

THE ANALOGY OF SPACE LAW WITH AIR LAW -
A LATENT DANGER
by
Michel Smirnoff

Outer Space being above the Air Space it is quite obvious that some analogy between the classical Air Law and the new Space Law must exist. The first authors in Space law were, in fact, the specialists in Air Law and we have to quote Professors Cooper, Alex Meyer, Ambrosini, Dr. Goedhuis, Professor Rinck and many others, who, as outstanding specialists in classical Air Law, wrote the first articles and monographs on Space Law.

This analogy with Air Law was at that time more logical than the analogy with other special laws such as Maritime Law. Therefore, many institutions of Air Law were, in the beginning, transplanted into the new Space Law. One need only quote the problem of sovereignty, of "passage inoffensive," of responsibility and many others. This analogy with the Air Law was quite natural, and it seemed that many institutions of Air Law could be adopted in Space Law. Then began the hesitations in the sense that many authors spoke of the impossibility of applying by analogy the institutions of Air Law to Space Law problems. One of the first authors who denied this possibility of analogy with Air Law was the American lawyer, Loftus Becker, who stressed the necessity to create some special rules for relations in Space.

The arguments of those authors who were in favour of the creation of new rules for Outer Space were based on the assertion that the matter is completely new and that the political moment is highly involved in problems of Space Law. The first set of arguments stressed the necessity to create special rules for Space Law because of the fact that rules of conventional international law could not be applied to relations in Space, and more recently the authors argued the possibility of finding living beings on the planets.

The political arguments differed from the others, stressing the fact that to avoid conflicts in Space, some special rules would be needed. The acceptance of the classical rules of Air Law would bring the conflicts of the Earth into the Space.

The result of those arguments was the setting of special rules for Outer Space based on the conclusion that it is not possible to apply the classical notions of "occupation," "sovereignty," discovery," etc. to Outer Space.

Thus, the majority of authors dealing with Space Law problems came to the conclusion repeatedly in different resolutions of different congresses and conferences that the classical notion of sovereignty is not applicable to the Outer Space which by the nature of things must remain free for the peaceful use of all peoples on the Earth. This conclusion represented the majority view on that problem.

Until that moment we could say that the new Space Law had some analogy with the early development of Air Law, which at its beginning, somewhere about 1910, was based on the idea of the freedom of the air. The further development of classical Air Law proved, however, to be completely different, and the Paris Convention and Chicago Convention were the cornerstones of a theory of air sovereignty which now is the predominant theory in classical Air Law.

Although most recent developments in the theory of air sovereignty show a less rigid interpretation of that theory, the principle is still unchanged and we cling to the Air Law maxim: "complete and exclusive sovereignty of the State in the air above its territory."

Therefore we wanted to present in this paper some remarks and some fears that the analogy of Space Law with the Air Law could turn the development of Space Law on the erroneous paths of the ideas of sovereignty in Outer Space. Our fears are not without basis. We have noticed some authors who are trying to solve the legal problems of Space by applying the principles of classical Air Law.

This idea is simplistic. We only extend sovereignty to the heavens and make a little revision of Art. 1 of the Chicago Convention, and all problems of Outer Space are solved. But the exploration of Space is then practically finished. A little country like Nicaragua or Cambodia could refuse the right to space vehicles of flying over its territory, and the orbit of a scientific satellite is out.

With this extension of state sovereignty another serious danger exists. It is the inevitable consequence that all conflicts of our Earth will be automatically transferred to Outer Space. Mankind, instead of creating a new region without any possibility of terrestrial conflicts, will be confronted with the serious danger of those conflicts in the Outer Space.

Besides the fact that this analogy with the Air Law is absolutely illogical scientifically speaking, it is quite obvious that this analogy could not serve any good purpose. By a caprice of a State, valuable space explorations could be prohibited or endangered. No collective action in Outer Space would be possible. No collaboration in the exploration of Space would be possible, and no financial collaboration in the enormous costs of the space exploration would be realisable. The results of that analogy therefore would be disastrous in every aspect. The only argument which could be supported in favour of that idea is the well-known argument of the security of the State. This argument is universal, and could eventually prevail.

Let us examine the nature of that argument. If we say security, we think of peace-- the insured self-defense of the people, the peaceful future for our children. Could this be realised by a simple declaration extending sovereignty into Outer Space? We do not think so. Only an international convention based on international agreement regulating the relations in Outer Space could guarantee all that what we think of when we say "security"-- a declarative proclamation of the right of sovereignty in space could guarantee it. It is necessary to create an international organisation under the auspices of the United Nations which would be a center of exchange of information about Outer Space and a Bureau where all information about launchings of space vehicles would be registered and the vehicles themselves registered. We hope that with the activity of the Ad Hoc Committee of the UN and with the activity of the new secretary general of the UN, we are now nearer to the actual organisation of the administration by the UN in Outer Space.

Therefore, we lawyers have a great role to play. We have to avoid the analogy between Space Law and Air Law which would be only a detriment to the development of the Space Law. When we say that the analogy between Space Law and Air Law is a danger, we mean the fundamental idea on which Air Law is based. We don't want to deny any possibility of cognation between Space Law with Air Law. After the works of Mr. Beresford, Madame Rode Verschoor and many others, it is clear that the new Convention on the responsibility in Space probably will be patterned on the Rome Convention of 1952 with some amendments perhaps. Many other aspects of Air Law are applicable to Space Law. The principal danger, however, lies in the acceptance of a total analogy between the two laws; all lawyers in Space Law should be forewarned.

* * * * *

SOVEREIGNTY AND NATIONAL RIGHTS IN OUTER SPACE
AND ON CELESTIAL BODIES
by
Robert K. Woetzel

Resolution 1721, which was passed by the Sixteenth General Assembly of the United Nations on December 20, 1961, states that outer space and celestial bodies are "not subject to national appropriation." The United Nations represents the international community and the quasi-totality of civilized states. Consequently, the resolutions of the General Assembly have certain quasi-legal effects. They constitute tangible evidence of what the law is or should be on a particular subject, according to the wishes of a majority of states. They are not generally binding, however, and a violation of them could not necessarily be considered an international delict. A country acting in accordance with the principles laid down in a resolution of the U.N. has the prima facie evidence of right on its side; but to the definitely binding under international law, a resolution would have to be confirmed either by agreement or the continued practice of states or the principles and customs incorporated into the municipal legal systems of different countries. U.N. resolutions may be considered a subsidiary source of international law like the writings of eminent jurists and the decisions of courts, according to Article 38 of the Statute of the International Court of Justice.

In order to determine the effects of U.N. Resolution 1721 on Outer Space, it is necessary, therefore, to examine whether or not the agreements between nations, the practice of states, or the principles of law, as recognized by civilized countries, would confirm the expressed wish of the international community that outer space and celestial bodies should not be subject to national appropriation. In that connection a distinction must be drawn between outer space and celestial bodies, and claims of sovereignty or absolute sovereign control over an area must be separated from the claims of rights to use or explore certain regions. In this discourse, the first part will be concerned with claims of sovereignty in outer space and on celestial bodies; the second part will deal with claims of rights in outer space and on celestial bodies; and in the third section the special problems posed by non-peaceful or military uses of outer space and celestial bodies will be examined.

1. Claims of Sovereignty.

To begin with, it is necessary to determine whether any limits are imposed on the sovereignty of states in the air, according to custom or convention. Conventional international law, as laid down in the Paris Convention of 1919 and the Chicago Convention of 1944, guarantees states "complete and exclusive" sovereignty in the airspace over their territories. Shawcross and Beaumont have interpreted this to mean sovereignty "without limit" - in airspace, that is. In order to determine to what altitude then sovereignty may extend, according to conventional international law, it is necessary to analyze the meaning of the worde "airspace."

The French and Italian texts of the Paris Convention of 1919 use the terms "espace atmosphérique" and "spazio atmosferico," or atmospheric space, while the English text refers to airspace. Similarly, in the French version of the Chicago Convention the terms "l'espace aérien" is used, which in the Spanish version is "el espacio aero." It can be concluded from this that the term airspace was not meant to be an unlimited concept, but referred to the earth's atmosphere.

There are various estimates, however, on how far up the atmosphere extends. They range up to 60,000 miles. This would be a very high limit indeed for sovereignty to extend to; yet taken literally, the conventions on air law provide so. Referring to a possible limit of 10,000 miles, Loftus Becker, former legal adviser of the U.S. Department of State, commented that this left the United States much "elbowroom for discussion," if it wished to claim sovereign rights above the present limits of conventional airflight.

A different limit is indicated, if the probable intention of the framers of the conventions is taken into consideration. This is indicated by the definition of aircraft contained in the Annexes to the Paris and Chicago Conventions which refer to flight instrumentalities that can derive sufficient support from reactions of the air. Aerodynamic lift ceases as a factor in flight support at an altitude between 50 and 60 miles. Andrew Haley, former President of the International Astronautical Federation has, therefore, suggested that national air sovereignty should not extend above that limit.

It must be pointed out, however, that the provisions of the Annexes to the conventions do not represent principles of public law. According to Article 54 (1) of the Chicago Convention the Annexes are "for convenience only" and by the terms of Article 38, states are not obliged to abide by them, if they find it impracticable to do so, except in the case of rules of navigation over the high seas as defined in Article 12. The definition of aircraft in the Annexes is not exclusive, therefore, and it can not serve as a basis for setting a limit on air sovereignty, even though the framers of the conventions probably had this type of flight craft in mind. It appears then that there is no definite limit to national air sovereignty in the conventions.

Next, it is necessary to consider whether states may claim complete and exclusive sovereignty over their territories into space indefinitely or usque ad coelum, as some writers have asserted. National boundaries could be extended into space in two ways: either by projecting upward of the geographic boundaries which would leave wedges of unowned space between contiguous nations from which anything might be dropped on the territories below; or by radial verticals extending from the earth's center through the geographic border to infinity which would leave unowned space only over the high seas and terra nullius. For obvious reasons the second alternative is the more practical of the two, since it would not be of much use to extend national boundaries higher, when it would still be possible for foreign flight craft to hover or pass over the territory below in the unowned wedges of space.

One basis for extending national sovereignty into space for quite some distance would be that air particles can be found in those regions. Thus Loftus Becker made the statement, already referred to, that this fact left the United States much leeway in discussions. It has been pointed out, however, that the airspace referred to in the aerial conventions for all practical purposes did not extend beyond 60 miles. Other grounds than metereological or astronomical definitions of the air must, therefore, be found for extending national boundaries into space.

The two main interests that have guided states in determining what kind of a regime to institute for the air have been national security and economic gain. During the First World War nations became aware of the military potential of the airplane and the threat it posed to the territories flown over, and after the war many of the smaller nations, especially, found it to be in their economic interest to restrict passage of foreign aircraft over their territories. The question that must be asked is whether the same conditions which caused nations to assert sovereignty in airspace pertain to outer space.

The contents of the cones of sovereignty projected would be changing constantly due to the revolution of the earth on its axis, its rotation around the sun, and the movements of the sun and planets through the galaxy. Celestial bodies would be in a certain cone of sovereignty at one moment and in another at the next. Thus a nation placing equipment or personnel on a planet would be violating the sovereign jurisdiction of several countries as it moves in and out of different cones. It seems, therefore, that the security of states would be affected in a quite different way from space than from airspace: not foreign aircraft travelling under human guidance, but the "immutable laws of the universe" would cause the threat to a particular sovereign principality. The stationing of equipment and men on a celestial body would be completely legal at one moment, but it would be a violation of some state's sovereignty and security the next.

Furthermore, while the position of aircraft over a territory affects its ability to threaten or spy against persons and facilities below, this would not necessarily be so with spacecraft flying at very high altitudes. Oblique photography from a position at that height would be just as effective, and the spaceship would not have to be directly over the territory photographed. Rockets and missiles could also be launched from space ships or space stations against a territory on earth, and they would not have to be in the sovereign cone of the territory at the time.

Finally, it should be mentioned that today states are just as vulnerable before modern weapons whether these be in or outside the areas under their sovereign control. Thus a rocket launched from a submarine on the high seas or an intercontinental ballistic missile can be just as destructive as a bomb dropped from a plane. The security of states is equally affected and is not particularly enhanced by zones of sovereignty.

It can be concluded, therefore, that the conditions which caused nations to claim sovereignty in airspace for reasons of security and self-defense are not the same with regard to space. As far as the economic interests of states are concerned, these would retain the right to decide whether spacecraft or missiles used for commercial purposes, like postal rockets for example, could land on their territory; the spaceships or missiles would be passing through national airspace on their way down. Although the day of regularly-operated space lines is relatively far off, it may be said that the constantly changing contents of cones of sovereignty projected into space would make it legal for a commercial spaceliner to be in a certain place at one moment - like on a planet or star - and illegal to be there the next. Again the laws of the universe would be responsible for the violation of sovereignty and not the actions of the spaceship.

Since the conditions which caused nations to claim sovereignty in the air on grounds of security or economic interest are different from those in space, the question must be asked whether nations have a special interest in extending their national boundaries into space. It seems that this is so as long as it is not possible to photograph obliquely or to launch missiles from spaceships that are not directly over the territory they are aimed at. Scientific progress will make these activities possible very soon, however, and then states would have no particular interest in preventing foreign spacecraft from flying over their territory in space. Furthermore, even if cones of sovereignty were projected into space, it should become possible theoretically for spacecraft to navigate around them, unless allowed rights of innocent passage through them; if they stopped on planets or stars, however, they would soon be in the sovereign cone of some nation without any of their own doing, and so be violating the sovereign jurisdiction of some country on earth, - which makes the whole argument of projecting cones of sovereignty into space seem absurd.

According to civil law in various countries, the right of a landowner to interfere with air traffic above his grounds extends only so high as his reasonable interest would justify; above that he is not permitted to interfere with air navigation. The Civil Code of Switzerland contains such a provision, and an American court has also decided that title to airspace unconnected with the use of the land is not possible. Although the problem of sphere-of-interest of the landowner is something quite different from the problem of sphere-of-interest as far as a nation is concerned, some international lawyers have also maintained that a state's sovereignty in the space above its territories can not extend higher than its interests would warrant.

It would seem then, judged by standards of interest, nations would not be entitled to extend their national frontiers into space, since such interests as may exist would not be particularly served thereby, - not more so than if outer space above their territories remained free. On the contrary, freedom of communication in space would be unnecessarily restricted for all states by such an extension of boundaries.

Another argument that has been used for asserting sovereignty in airspace and that has been invoked as basis for extending national boundaries into space, is that of effective control. Thus Kelsen writes, "It stands to reason that a State can enforce the provisions of this convention (Paris Convention of 1919) or of its own national legal order against the aircraft of another State only within that part of the airspace over which it has effective control. The validity of any legal order cannot extend beyond this sphere." And Cooper has maintained with regard to sovereignty in space that "Perhaps the rule should be, in the absence of international agreement, that the territory of each State extend upward as far into space as it is physically and scientifically possible for any State to control the regions of space directly above it."

The argument of effective control could be objected to on grounds that this would allow larger and more powerful states to assert control at much higher altitudes than smaller and not so strong states. Cooper has been careful to explain though that regardless of whether some states could exert effective control at greater heights than others, the limit of sovereignty would be the same for all, in accordance with the principle of equality of states. According to this argument, however, effective control would only indirectly be the basis for claims of sovereignty by smaller states; they could make such claims in areas which they actually could not control.

Furthermore, the doctrine of effective control is not universally accepted as a basic territorial concept. As Cooper himself has later pointed out, the state of Nepal claims territorial sovereignty over many of the highest peaks of the Himalayas; but it can not exercise effective control in many of these areas. Nevertheless its claim has not been challenged by other nations.

This is even more the case with conditions in space. The constantly changing contents of the proposed projected cones of sovereignty would make a normal day to day effective control absolutely impossible. Spaceships and space stations would have to rotate with the earth to remain within the sovereign cone of one nation and not to trespass on that of another. And the planets and stars would be in one cone at a certain moment and in another at the next, as has been described.

Furthermore, the tremendous speeds at which spacecraft would travel, such as 25,000 miles per hour or more, as well as the high altitudes, would make it practically impossible to determine when it crossed the sovereign boundaries in space of one state into another.

It can be concluded then that it is not possible for states to exercise the kind of effective control in space that is customary in airspace. The doctrine of effective control cannot serve, therefore, as a basis for extending national boundaries into space indefinitely, and in any case, it is not universally accepted as a basic territorial concept, as has been pointed out.

Finally, the argument might be advanced that although the conditions which caused states to claim sovereignty in airspace are quite different from those in space, a certain similarity still exists at lower altitudes in space. Furthermore, while it may not be possible for states to exercise effective control at very high altitudes in space, they may still be able to do so at lower heights. It might, therefore, be possible theoretically to extend national boundaries into space for a certain limited distance or to establish a "contiguous" zone of sovereignty in space similar to such a zone in the law of the sea.

In this connection it might be well to refer to the suggestion of Cooper that "contiguous space" should extend to about 300 miles above the earth, because in that area atmospheric drag gradually slows the flight of a satellite until it falls back to earth. Above that limit space should be free. He later changed the limit to 600 miles, in order to give states the right to control missile flight over their territories; that was the height which had been claimed for the Soviet ICBM.

As has been pointed out by Meyer among others, it would be very difficult to establish such a zone or to determine a higher boundary in space, "since between airspace and outer space no determined shore exists." The analogy of the law of the sea could, therefore, not be applied here. It would be almost impossible to tell when a zone ended and another began.

Furthermore, there would be no differences noticeable to flightcraft in passing from one zone into another. Thus the Chief of Staff of the U.S. Air Force has stated that " In discussing air and space, it should be recognized that there is no division, per se, between the two. For all practical purposes air and space merge, forming a continuous and indivisible field of operation."

Similar considerations that mitigate against the acceptance of the theory of zones in airspace would, therefore, apply in outer space. From this it must be concluded that there would be little basis in law and science for nations to extend their national boundaries into outer space.

Next, it must be considered whether space can be treated as an area in which nations might stake out claims of sovereignty. In the fifteenth century different states asserted such claims over large portions of the sea. Thus England claimed the North Sea, the Channels and certain parts of the Baltic, and Venice the Adriatic. Pope Alexander VI in his famous Bill of 1493 divided the world into two halves between Spain and Portugal by a line drawn North to South-West of the Azores; accordingly Spain claimed the Pacific and the Gulf of Mexico, and Portugal claimed the Indian Ocean and the Southern Atlantic. These claims could not be enforced, however, and were then largely abandoned. Thus Queen Elizabeth I answered complaints by the Spanish Ambassador that English freebooters were violating Spanish sovereign rights on the high seas by stating that: "The use of the sea and air is common to all; neither can a title to the ocean belong to any people or private persons, forasmuch as neither nature nor public use and custom permitteth any possession thereof."

Grotius, the "Father of International Law," elaborated the doctrine of the freedom of the high seas in his Mare Liberum. He declared that the sea was incapable of appropriation, since it was not susceptible of dominion; he compared it to the air. He later, however, declared in De Jure Belli ac Pacis that some dominion could in fact be exercised on the high seas by means of fleets or coastal artillery.

This indicates that the exercise of dominion or control was a crucial factor in determining whether nations could claim sovereignty on the high seas. The principle of effective control has also been important in determining whether states had a right to claim sovereignty over land territories. An excellent example of this is the Island of Palmas case: in this instance, the United States asserted sovereignty over the Island of Palmas on the basis of discovery, while Holland had for some time exercised peaceful and effective control over the territory. In the famous Arbitration of 1928 Dr. Max Huber, the arbitrator, decided in favor of Holland, on the grounds that a claim based on discovery must be followed by effective occupation within a reasonable length of time, and the United States, therefore, had forfeited its rights.

In another case, however, the Permanent Court of International Justice at The Hague laid down less stringent requirements for claims of sovereignty. In this instance, Norway had proclaimed sovereignty over Eastern Greenland which Denmark regarded as its own. Denmark showed numerous administrative and legislative acts applying to Greenland as a whole, and in 1931 the international court decided in favor of Denmark's claim, declaring that a title by occupation involves two elements, "the intention or will to act as sovereign, and some actual exercise or display of authority." The natural conditions existing in Eastern Greenland precluded an advanced degree of effective control as it is to be expected in more populated areas; no other state had exercised greater control over the area than Denmark. Nevertheless, effective control could be exercised, if necessary within the set boundaries delimiting the territory claimed.

This indicates that it should at least be possible to exercise effective control over the whole of the area claimed in order to establish sovereignty. It has already been alluded to how the constellations in space are constantly changing, how difficult, if not impossible, it would be to combat spacecraft flying at high speeds and high altitudes. Although states might find means to combat each others flightcraft in space, it is doubtful that they would ever be able to exercise the kind of long-term effective control necessary to stake out claims of sovereignty. Furthermore, it would be extremely difficult to determine boundaries for such claims in space.

Finally, it should be mentioned that while states have claimed sovereignty in the airspace above their territories, they have not regarded the airspace above the high seas as capable of appropriation. In fact, the aerial conventions provide that airspace above the high seas shall be free.

It would also be very difficult to stake out claims of sovereignty in space at lower altitudes where "operation ... are considered more pertinent to earth than to other planets or to interplanetary space travel," as one writer puts it. An example where limited claims were made in terra nullius are the "sectors" of the various powers in the north and south polar regions. These might serve as the basis for claims of sovereignty; a certain degree of effective control can be exercised in them and the claims are usually supported by the principle of contiguity. It might be argued that a similar procedure could be applied in space. But as has been shown, it would be difficult, if not impossible to determine with accuracy the ceiling of such a zone in space as well as the boundaries of various sectors. It is clear, therefore, that measured by these standards, space can not be considered res nullius or an area capable of appropriation by nations. The conditions in space make a long-term and effective exercise of dominion difficult, if not impossible. The vast majority of writers reject the concept of sovereignty in outer space. States may, of course, unilaterally extend their frontiers into space or they might claim sovereignty over sections of space; there is nothing in positive international law to prevent them from doing so. But there would be little basis in fact and law for such claims which would also be contrary to the wishes of the international community as expressed in the resolutions of the United Nations General Assembly.

Claims of sovereignty in outer space must be distinguished, however, from such claims on celestial bodies. Both are opposed in the General Assembly Resolution 1721, but the considerations which affect the situation in outer space are not the same as those pertaining to celestial bodies. Stars and planets are territories in contrast to the vast unlimited entity which outer space represents. It may be possible to occupy celestial bodies, while it is difficult to establish such control in outer space, as has been indicated. It is necessary, therefore, to examine whether or not the traditional rules of conquest and discovery apply to celestial bodies, even if they cannot serve as the basis for claims of sovereignty in outer space.

The discovery of a territory involves more than mere sighting of it. The moon and other planets or stars have long been discovered in that sense. It must be a "purposeful act of exploration or navigation accompanied by a visual apprehension, a landing or some other act marking or recording such visit, but not acts expressive of possession," as Aaronson has explained. The question then arises whether states may follow up claims of discovery with claims of sovereignty over the territories discovered.

Discovery as such has never been sufficient basis for claims of sovereignty; it has to be followed by some degree of effective control. This was already so in the 16th century, and it is still a valid rule today. In the Island of Palmas case, mentioned previously, the arbitrator decided that discovery might give a state an "inchoate title" to a territory, but it has to be followed by some effective control within a reasonable length of time. Furthermore, the Permanent Court of International Justice determined in the Eastern Greenland case that a claim of sovereignty would be sufficiently established, if a state has clearly shown intent to act as sovereign and has also displayed or exercised its authority. This decision indicates that the court was aware of the fact that it was not possible for a state to maintain a constant occupation for effective control in some areas, and it accepted certain administrative acts as sufficient display of authority in ruling in favor of Denmark.

It must be considered, therefore, whether these criteria for asserting claims of sovereignty may be applied to celestial bodies. One author has mentioned the possibility that states might leave scientific instruments behind on planets or stars as signs of discovery, just as in previous times they raised crosses or coats of arms on territories newly discovered. Thus certain plaques bearing Soviet insignia were reportedly left on the moon by the Russian rocket "Lunik." It seems clear, however, that such acts would not suffice to establish claims of sovereignty. According to the rules pertaining to discovery and sovereignty on earth, a state would have to exercise or display more authority than indicated thereby, in order to be recognized as sovereign of territories in space. The Soviet government also did not claim sovereignty or sovereign control over the moon or parts of it following the landing of its first moon rocket.

The question, of course, presents itself whether it is at all possible to exercise or display the necessary degree of sovereignty over planets or stars. It has been shown that it would be difficult for states to exercise effective control over outer space in general. The planets and stars are, however, capable of some occupation like territories on earth; they differ substantially in their nature from space. They resemble more areas of land where it is possible to exercise a certain degree of effective control.

There is no rule of international law which would prevent states from asserting claims of sovereignty over celestial bodies or areas on these, if they are able to show a certain intent and will to act as sovereign and have exercised or displayed some authority to establish a substantial degree of effective control. This will probably be less than on earth during the initial stages of space exploration at least. The question whether these criteria have been satisfied in any particular case can be decided by the International Court of Justice or any other competent international agency to which nations might submit their disputes, just as the Greenland case was decided by the Permanent Court of International Justice. Celestial bodies could, therefore, be considered areas capable of being claimed as the sovereign territories of states on earth.

In contrast to the opinions expressed above, some authors like Aaronson maintain that the rules on discoverey and sovereignty pertaining on earth heretofore cannot be applied in space. Aaronson expressed the opinion that they are no longer really valid in an international society that has been "so closely organized" and in which so many international institutions have been established. He feels that the rules on discovery of celestial bodies should be determined by universal agreement.

Horsford believes that celestial bodies should be placed under an international trusteeship system set up by the United Nations similar to the present Trusteeship Council. This could be done according to Article 59 of the United Nations Charter which provides for the establishment of specialized agencies. The space organization would administer the planets or stars through states as under the present trusteeship on earth.

Even though a greater degree of effective control is theoretically possible on celestial bodies than in outer space in general, the international community is opposed to claims of sovereignty, as expressed in the United Nations Resolution referred to above. Both the United States and the Soviet Union have subscribed to this resolution. The implication is that it would not be permissible for a state to impose its absolute sovereign control over an area in outer space. Future practice and additional agreements between nations may confirm this and make it a binding rule. The members of the United Nations would also be free to establish any other regimen in outer space and on celestial bodies, like a trusteeship arrangement, as recommended by certain writers.

2. National Rights.

While the United Nations Resolution 1721 opposed claims of sovereignty, it does not expressly forbid claims of rights to explore and utilize resources in outer space and on celestial bodies. Furthermore, the right of self-defense is not restricted by the United Nations Resolution. Nations might, therefore, claim certain rights in space, even if they do not attempt to establish sovereign control. In international law there is a difference between sovereign control over a territory or space, and the assertion of a right in a specified case to use such a territory or space. Thus the President of the United States issued a proclamation on September 28th, 1945, claiming for the United States the right to exercise jurisdiction over the natural resources of the subsoil and sea bed of the continental shelf without actually claiming sovereignty over that area. The exercise of such jurisdiction by a "contiguous nation is just and reasonable," but the "character as high seas of the waters above the continental shelf and the right to their free and unimpeded navigation are in no way thus affected." A similar proclamation was issued by the President with respect to protection of coastal fisheries, and various treaties have also been concluded regulating the access to oyster beds outside the territorial waters of Great Britain, France and Ireland. In each case the character of the high seas as _res communis_ was not affected.

Another example of nations reserving rights as to jurisdiction and control without actually claiming exclusive sovereignty is Antarctica. In May, 1958, President Eisenhower declared that "my Government reserves all of the rights of the United States with respect to the Antarctica region including the right to assert a territorial claim or claims." And, other nations have reserved similar rights. The Antarctic, in contrast to the high seas, could be regarded as _res nullius_ capable of being occupied and claimed as national territory. In the meantime all territorial claims in the Antarctic have been "frozen" according to the Antarctic Treaty which was signed on December 1, 1959, by twelve nations, including the United States and the Soviet Union.

Nations have also asserted certain rights in the air over the high seas, which are considered free, according to the aerial conventions. Thus they have established a number of contiguous zones that extend for hundreds of miles. These have been tolerated as reasonable in the interests of national security and self-defense.

States may assert rights of self-defense with regard to space activities without actually claiming sovereignty in space. Such rights could be exercised under Article 51 of the Charter of the United Nations. In this connection Loftus Becker has stated that "the United States is prepared at all times to react to protect itself against an armed attack, whether that attack originates in outer space or passes through outer space in order to reach the United States." In October of 1960 the Executive-Secretary of the Space Law Commission of the U.S.S.R. Academy of Sciences, declared that "In case of need the Soviet Union will be able to protect its security against any encroachments from outer space just as successfully as it is done with respect to air space... Such action will be fully justified under the existing rules of international law and the United Nations Charter." It is possible that countries may claim the right to shoot down in self-defense passing spacecraft which they consider to be dangerous to their security.

In this connection it is necessary to consider the legal problem posed by earth satellites flying in space and over the territories of other states. The United States and the Soviet Union announced that they intended to launch earth satellites in connection with the program of the International Geophysical Year some time before this was actually accomplished. The White House issued such an announcement on July 29, 1955, and the Soviet Academy of Sciences made known its intention on April 15, 1955. No state objected to these announcements; though this cannot be taken as tacit consent to the launching of the satellites, since the declarations were not addressed to states in particular, the fact remains that by making them the United States and the USSR gave other states the opportunity to object and did not merely present them with a "fait accompli."

Since then various satellites have been launched and no state has objected to them, as long as they were regarded as designed for peaceful scientific purposes; these satellites have passed over the territory of most nations. Haley, among others, has suggested that there exists now a tacit consent of nations to the flight of satellites over their territories.

This can be assumed only for satellites which serve peaceful scientific purposes. States could at any time object to other kinds of satellites passing over their territories, such as those for military reconnaisance purposes, and the Soviet Union has in fact protested against the flight of the American satellites Midas, Tiros, and Samos on grounds that they could be used for espionage.

The contention of the Soviet international lawyer Zadorozhnyi that the Russian earth satellites did not fly over other states, but that these passed under them because of the earth's rotation is spurious, since the satellites moving at a speed of some 18,000 miles per hour would have passed over many state, even if the earth did not rotate.

It can be concluded, therefore, that nations have expressed a certain tacit consent to the passage over their territories of such satellites as the Sputnik and Explorer which serve peaceful scientific purposes only. The United Nations in a resolution of December 12, 1958, also indicated its approval of peaceful activities in space of the United States and the Soviet Union by stating that "recent developments in respect to outer space have added a new dimension to man's existence and opened new possibilities for the increase of his knowledge and the improvement of his life." And the UN Resolution 1721, referred to previously, states that "Outer space and celestial bodies are free for exploration and use by all States in conformity with international law."

In the future, states may exercise their rights in space by launching missiles for the delivery of mail or cargo between distant points on earth, or they may send manned rockets on to the moon or other planets, or establish space platforms, TV-relay stations, and realize programs for the acquisition of economic resources in space, the modification of the earth's weather, and further interplanetary exploration. Nations may intend to exploit certain resources in space and on celestial bodies to the exclusion of others. Jenks, among others, indicates that cosmic rays could be considered res nullius which nations might intercept and utilize, if possible, as well as interstellar gas which might be regarded as analogous to sea water in its legal character.

There would seem to be little objection in international law against states claiming exclusive rights to exploit minerals and other resources found in space or on celestial bodies. Such assertions of rights need not be accompanied or based on claims of general sovereignty; in such cases the legal situation would resemble that in the Antarctic region where nations have also asserted certain national rights without actually claiming sovereignty.

It has been maintained that allowing states to claim sovereignty or even national rights on celestial bodies would amount to opening these up to wanton exploitation and national rivalries. Jenks, therefore, concludes that "It is most desirable that sovereignty over unoccupied territory in the moon or in other planets or satellites should be regarded as vested exclusively in the United Nations..." and that "It is most desirable that title to any natural resources of the moon or of other planets or satellites which may be capable of utilization should be regarded as vested in the United Nations and that any exploitation of such resources which may be possible should be on the basis of concessions, leases or licenses from the United Nations." He also explains that if celestial bodies were placed under international control, international rules would be necessary to administer them. They could be derived in part by analogy from such regulations as the land claims provisions annexed to the treaty concerning the Archipelago of Spitzbergen of 1920, and the mining regulations which Norway issued in accordance with the treaty.

Although it is most desirable that wanton exploitation of the resources in space should be avoided, this could be done through a limited form of international regulation as exists under international conventions on conservation of natural resources on the high seas. Such regulation could be restricted to certain purposes, and need not preclude states from pursuing their objectives independently as long as these do not conflict with the common interest of nations. States could, therefore, issue licenses and leases for the exploitation of resources and use territory in space in other ways; but they would be bound in their activities by certain international standards and regulations.

The use of outer space or celestial bodies for broadcasting political propaganda or excessive advertising might be prevented by international agreement. It is possible for the United States at this time to use the Telstar communications satellite for advertising commercial products; there is no provision in the U.S. Communications Satellite Act of August 1962 that would prevent this. The Soviet Union and other countries might resent being subjected to commercial propaganda, however, just as the United States would probably dislike communist political propaganda relayed onto American television screens. In order to prevent serious conflicts from arising, the nations might agree to abstain from using space for such purposes.

In general, leaving to states the major responsibility for developing the potentials of space would have the added advantage of providing them with the incentives of prestige and economic gain. It might conceivably be argued that nations which, for one reason or another, cannot engage in space activities would benefit more, if the resources in space were developed by an international organization of which they were members. Nothing would prevent the active space powers from granting a kind of partnership to other states and their citizens in the development of space travel and resources, when they found this to be in the general interest. Today there already exists a large degree of international partnership in the exchange of scientific information on space research, because this is in the common interest. The United States has launched a number of space research projects in cooperation with other countries. In certain instances, however, nations may find it in their interest to develop space resources more or less independently, and they may claim and exercise national rights in outer space and on celestial bodies, according to the rules of international law.

An associated problem concerns the status of artificial space bodies launched from earth. In that connection the responsibility of states for their space activities would have to be examined. These issues are, however, not directly related to the topics under discussion, namely sovereignty and national rights in outer space and on celestial bodies. They do not fall within the scope of this discourse.

With regard to the law which would be applied in outer space, UN Resolution 1721 "commends to states for their guidance" the principle that international law, including the United Nations Charter, applied to outer space and to celestial bodies. In areas where resources are being exploited or where a state has set up a scientific research station, the law could be the same as that of the sovereign state and the family of nations, or it could be extended by analogy, or new laws would have to be enacted to provide for the special exigencies that may arise in the course of space exploration.

It has been maintained by certain Soviet writers that the "law of peaceful co-existence" should be applied to outer space, especially since the Soviet Union has been a pioneer in the exploration of space. There is no provision in international law which prevents the Soviet Union from applying its legal standards at the installations under its control, as long as they are in accordance with the generally accepted principles of the law of nations. The United States and other powers would be free to do the same on their spaceships and at their space stations. No nation has a monopoly on the law of outer space. In cases of conflict of laws, the United Nations or the International Court of Justice might be consulted. Under the Antarctic Treaty of 1959, differences between states are submitted to the ICJ upon the consent of the parties concerned. A similar arrangement might be established with regard to outer space.

A special problem which deserves mention in this connection concerns the rules which would apply to relations between earthmen and possible sapient beings in space. This subject can only be treated cursorily, since it remains in the realm of conjecture for the time being, and it is not certain whether such beings exist. Even so, there are forty billion stars in our galaxy, and at least forty billion other galaxies, and many scientists maintain that it is very likely that intelligence other than ours exists in space. It is necessary then to at least antitipate the problem of relations with space beings.

The first question that arises is whether such beings should be treated like persons on earth; that is, subject to the same legal and social considerations which govern relations between men, or whether they must be dealt with according to a completely different code. It is very difficult to find an answer without knowing the nature of such beings; they may be some kind of intelligent plantlife or their needs and cares or mores may be completely different from ours. What may please us might displease them and vice versa, psychologically and physically.

Haley has taken great pains in elaborating the subject of metalaw or law that is concerned with "all frames of existence - with sapient beings different in kind." He advocates that the principles of natural law be applied in dealings with space beings and that "no earth-spaceship may land without having satisfactorily ascertained that (1) the landing and contact will injure neither the explorer nor the explored; and (2) until the earth ship has been invited to land by the explored." He further proposes an international authority that would have "the power and resources in space in cooperation with lunar and other planetary authorities to contain violence and to administer and enforce regulations relating to safety, sanitation, health... etc."

Haley's suggestions are very commendable as far as they go. It is clear that according to the principles of international law existing today, it would not be permissible for one nation to wage wars of aggression or conquest against another. Similar principles could be applied by analogy in space, so that conquest and enslavement or domination of other intelligent beings would be contrary to generally accepted precepts of law. It will be necessary, however, to await the results of further scientific explorations which may yield some information about such beings before it is possible to attempt a definitive regulation of sapient relations in space.

3. Military Uses of Space

Finally, the problem must be examined whether or not states have the right to use outer space and celestial bodies for military purposes. It has been indicated that actions in self-defense would be legal, according to Article 51 of the Charter of the United Nations. But can a state establish military platforms, or reconnaisance systems or otherwise use space for military reasons, according to international law?

President Eisenhower, however, in his note to Premier Bulganin of January, 1958, proposed "that we agree that outer space should be used only for peaceful purposes. We face a decisive moment in history in relation to this matter. Both the Soviet Union and the United States are now using outer space for the testing of missiles designed for military purposes. The time to stop is now."

The Soviet government at the time rejected the American proposals, on the grounds that they were aimed at preventing the Soviet Union from using its intercontinental ballistic missiles, or in the words of Premier Khrushchev: "The thought behind this U.S. Proposal is to ban weapons which can threaten U.S. territory but to retain control of all other types of weapons..." The Soviet government proposed that the problem of the peaceful use of outer space be linked with other problems, e.g., the cessation of atomic tests, the ban of nuclear weapons, and the disbandonment of U.S. overseas military bases.

In the resolution on outer space of December 12, 1958, the United Nations General Assembly recognized "the common interest of mankind in outer space and that it is the common aim that it should be used for peaceful purposes only." The resolution coincided in its main points with the draft resolutions supported by the United States and Great Britain among others. The Soviet proposal which linked the problem of peaceful use of outer space with the questions of cessation of tests and disbandonment of U.S. overseas bases was not adopted. The United Nations resolution also expressed the wish of the community of states "to avoid the extension of present national rivalries into this new field."

In the resolution of December 20, 1961, the United Nations recognized "the common interest of mankind in furthering the peaceful use of outer space" and for "the betterment of man" and for the benefit of all countries without regard to their stage of development. These resolutions clearly indicate that it is the wish of the international community to avoid the extension of national rivalries into space. Since United Nations resolutions have certain quasi-legal effects, as has been pointed out, it can be concluded that nations would only have a clear legal right to engage in certain activities in space and that it would contrary to the wishes of the international community for them to exercise controls in space that would extend national rivalries into this new field. The resolutions are not explicit enough to make the extension of such rivalries violations of international law; but this could be confirmed, if they were strengthened by further such declarations, agreements and the practice of states.

In particular, it must be considered then what kind of rivalries would be contrary to the wishes of the international community. The policy declarations of most governments in the course of the United Nations debates indicate that those involving non-peaceful uses of space would be primarily affected. Furthermore, many authors have come out against the use of space for other than peaceful purposes. Thus it can be concluded, that in the first line the extension of national rivalries involving arms and military uses of space can be considered contrary to the wishes of the world community.

This does not, of course, prevent states from acting in self-defense, according to Art. 51 of the United Nations Charter. They may take such measures in space as would be warranted under the doctrine of self-defense, or in execution of an international mandate - for example, as part of a United Nations police force in space.

It must be pointed out, however, that the United States and the Soviet Union are already using space for military purposes. Both countries have tested missiles in outer space for several years. After the space flights of Major Andrian Nikolayev and Lieutenant Colonel Pavel Popovich in August 1962, Soviet Defense Minister, Marshal Rodion Malinovsky, declared: "Let our enemies know what techniques and what soldiers our Soviet power disposes of." The United States has launched several Samos and Midas reconnaisance satellites which are capable of photographing and detecting military operations in the Soviet Union. The Samos is essentially an improvement on the U-2 spy plan and uses high powered cameras to obtain its information. The Midas employs infra-red sensors to detect the heat generated at missile sites at the time of a launching; they can record rocket motor discharges at ranges of 5,000 miles.

One of the major Pentagon research projects concerns the development of a manned or unmanned satellite which would be capable of "inspecting" another satellite in space, and if it proved hostile, either to destroy it or transmit signals which would call for its destruction. This satellite interceptor which was once called Saint, is now officially referred to as a satellite inspector or space counter-weapon system.

Other uses of space for war-like or military purposes would include the establishment of space platforms from which missiles can be launched onto earth; and the construction of military spacecraft that can hover over points on the earth. The high-altitude atomic tests by the Soviet Union and the United States are also designed to serve the advancement of nuclear weapons technology. Such uses of outer space are clearly contrary to the expressed wishes of the international community. The Sixteenth General Assembly of the United Nations passed Resolution 1648 on November 6, 1961, by a vote of 71 to 20 with 4 abstentions, which calls on all powers to refrain from further nuclear testing; neither the United States nor the Soviet Union approved of the resolution, and the tests were continued, in spite of the opposition by a majority of smaller nations.

As has been stated, the United Nations resolutions are not necessarily binding, unless they have been confirmed by continued practice or further agreement between states. The major powers which have launched space instrumentalities have indicated that they are not willing to compromise their security without adequate safeguards. At the same time they have denounced each others actions as violations of international law and comity. The United States considers the Soviet Union's resumption of nuclear testing in 1961 in abrogation of a three-year moratorium a grave offense and a breach of agreements. The Soviet Union explains its action as necessary for the preservation of its defenses. On the other hand, the USSR condemns the launching of the U.S. reconnaisance satellites as aggressive and in violation of Articles 1 and 2/4 of the United Nations Charter. The United States maintains, however, that its satellites are justified by reason of self-defense.

Two main obstacles make it difficult to ensure that space is used for peaceful or non-military purposes only: the difficulty of determining whether a particular satellite or space station is not being utilized for military purposes; the information obtained at a weather station could, for example, be useful to military authorities. In many other instances it is also not possible to distinguish with certainty between a peaceful and a military use of space. Secondly, it is impossible to separate the problems prevailing on earth from the uses of space. Mankind's endeavour in space is an extension of its activities on earth. Soviet officials, on the basis of their own rocket and satellite achievements, have been saying for years that in the event of hostilities, missile and space combat is inevitable. Many United States officials and scientists, particularly in the Air Force and in industries related to the Air Force, have made similar statements. Consequently, it is unrealistic to expect states to neglect their security in space.

The question of regulating the use of ICBMs which fly through outer space has been discussed by the Disarmament Subcommittee of the Disarmament Commission of the United Nations. The other military uses of space also fall within the scope of the disarmament and arms control negotiations. In order to ensure that national spacecraft are not used in violation of international law, it has been suggested that they be subject to some form of inspection. Such inspection could be carried out by nations reciprocally or by an international organization set up under the terms of an international convention or established by the United Nations. The legal aspects of the question would be a matter for consideration by the United Nations that holds a certain responsibility for ensuring that space be used for peaceful purposes only. Any protest against a state for violating international principles of law and comity in space could be lodged with that body.

Another model for international inspection might be the system established under Art. VII of the Antarctic Treaty of 1959, according to which nations participating in the Consultative Conference on the Antarctic can dispatch representatives to any part of the region, in order to inspect stations, equipment, ships and planes at point of loading and unloading. The Soviet Union appears to be unwilling to concede such powers to any authority at this time, however.

In conclusion, it should be stated that until a formula is devised for ensuring the security of states under conditions of controlled disarmament, the development of weapons technologies in outer space and on celestial bodies is likely to continue. It is to be hoped that agreements on different areas of arms control will be forthcoming soon, lest the arms race be further extended into space. Already scientists including Dr. Von Allan are warning about the danger to manned space flight of a radiation belt due to high altitude tests. The United States and the Soviet Union bear the primary responsibility for resolving their differences in this area, so that peace may be assured on earth and in space.

In view of the need to guard against possible breaches of arms control agreements, the nations must decide upon a satisfactory detection or inspection system. But suspicions of each other's motives should not be exaggerated to the point that any agreement becomes impossible. A certain line of thinking is opposed to any accommodation between the nations, even when this is for the common good. Some persons are suspicious of cultural contacts, scientific and educational exchanges, and international peaceful co-operation. It would appear as if they believed that what is favored by the other state cannot possibly be in their country's interest; thus if the other side is against nuclear war, because of the danger of total annihilation of mankind, they feel that it might be in their interest to risk a clash arms. Their thinking is rigid and dangerous; their influence is pernicious. Both the United States and the Soviet Union have repudiated them; but it is necessary to be constantly on guard against them, lest they thwart the efforts to promote international peace.

The differences between the ideologies and economic systems of the countries cannot be ignored; but they should not constitute insurmountable barriers to agreements on arms control which will also extend to space and celestial bodies. The great powers have a limited time within which to reach an understanding before nuclear weapons become part of the arsenal of many countries and the danger of atomic war is increased. It is the earnest wish of all peoples as expressed in the resolutions of the United Nations that such an agreement will be reached soon.

The vision of mankind exploring space is a grand one. Nations should cooperate as much as possible, in order to avoid unnecessary duplication of efforts, waste and inefficiency. The letter of President Kennedy to Premier Khrushchev of March 7, 1962, proposes such cooperation in exchanging information on weather and tracking services among other areas. Furthermore, UN Resolution 1721 advocates such cooperation under the aegis of international organizations, like the World Meteorological Organization and the International Telecommunication Union.

As has been shown, nations may also pursue their interests in space independently in accordance with the principles of international law. Since they may claim certain rights in outer space and on celestial bodies, the incentive for each nation to explore the secrets of the universe as fast as possible will lend added impetus to the space effort. While the military race between the countries should be ended, peaceful competition between the different systems is a healthy thing. Let the different ideologies and systems be tested by their ability to produce the goods and services which will be conducive to the greater happiness of mankind. And in the mean time let us keep up these scientific contacts which mean so much to us personally and professionally, so that we get to know each other better; for it is the human in all this which is most important and connects us in our work per aspera ad astra!

* * * * *

II. Other Contributions and Comments

Contributions were written by 38 authors; 40 reports were presented.

Most articles deal with the question of which principles of international public law should be directly applicable to outer space and the problem of state sovereignty, both in connection with an extensive analysis of UN Resolution 1721 (XVI). Much attention is also paid to the legal aspects of the use of reconnaissance satellites and communication satellites in general in outer space. It cannot be denied, when reading the Proceedings of the 1962 Colloquium, that the solution of space problems or, in general, the setting up of rules for the use of outer space is greatly influenced by the then existing political situation in the world ("cold war" policy). Although the main impression in the respective articles is one of good will and of the importance of international cooperation in this field, the respective authors, as they are members/representatives of different economic systems, do "blame" each other - more or less indirectly - for violations of the principles of Resolution 1721 (XVI), which was passed unanimously by the General Assembly of the United Nations in 1961.

This short commentary is summed up by a quotation from the report of Mrs. E. Galloway, United Nations Committee on the Peaceful Uses of Outer Space, p. 16:

"The difficulties of the Legal Subcommittee in reaching agreement on a report comparable to that of the Scientific and Technical Subcommittee cannot be attributable to lack of knowledge on the nature of legal space problems. It would seem, rather, that the interjection of political considerations creates an unfavorable atmosphere for conducting the work of the Subcommittee by means of reaching a consensus of opinion, rather than by voting .... Meanwhile, scientific and technical progress in exploring and using outer space for peaceful purposes will go on. Observed rules and regulations of the ITU and the WMO will contribute by common law paths to the evolution of space law. Other orderly international procedures will develop from bilateral and multilateral agreements. The situation is a challenge to the members of the International Institute of Space Law to make foresighted proposals leading toward the solution of legal problems."

- - - - -

SIXTH COLLOQUIUM ON THE LAW OF OUTER SPACE

PARIS, 1963

I. Texts Reproduced

INTERNATIONAL SECURITY CONTROLS: FROM THE ATOM TO COSMIC SPACE

by

Stephen Gorove

I am very grateful to the International Institute of Space Law for the opportunity to address this meeting here today. I am sure that those of you who were present with me five years ago at the First Colloquium on the Law of Outer Space at The Hague must have noted the progress which has been made in the development and clarification of ideas regarding cosmic law. I feel certain you will agree with me that this is in no small measure due to the un- tiring efforts of the directors and organizers of these meetings.

My topic today has some bearing on a project in which I have been engaged both in the United States and here in Europe, for the support of which I am greatly indebted to the A- merican Society of International Law, the Ford Foundation and the University of Denver. I would like to address myself to the subject of international security controls over the peaceful uses of atomic energy in the hope that this may be helpful not only in identifying some of the problems encountered, but also in enabling us to draw some parallels which may be useful in the establishment and operation of similar security control systems for cosmic space, an area equally sensitive to national defense.

A glance at the panorama of institutional arrangements in international security control over the peaceful uses of atomic energy is instructive since it reveals broad variations in regard to composition, purpose, methods and achievements.

Structurally, the control systems are incorporated in a network of bilateral agreements as well as in regional and other international multilateral undertakings, such as Euratom, the European Nuclear Energy Agency (ENEA) of the Organization for Economic Cooperation and Development (OECD) and the International Atomic Energy Agency (IAEA). These are complemented by further agreements between individual states and international agencies, and between in- ternational organizations themselves. While the membership of IAEA is diverse and not limit- ed to countries joined together for political or economic reasons, membership in Euratom is confined to the Common Market countries and that in the ENEA of the OECD to those states which have ratified the Security Control Convention of 1957. The bilaterals, on the other hand, are concluded between the atomically more and less advanced countries which have friendly relations.

The general purpose of international security control over the peaceful uses of atomic energy is the prevention of the proliferation of nuclear arms, or more precisely, the prevention of the diversion of certain specifically designated materials, equipment, services and facilities from peaceful to military purposes. In view of the frequently noted difficulty of finding differentiating criteria for what constitutes peaceful in contradistinction to military uses, a question which is equally important both in regard to the atom and outer space, it may be of interest to note that in the ENEA of the OECD an attempt is made to delineate the two fields by the stipulation that military purpose includes the use of special fissionable materials in weapons of war and excludes their use in reactors for the production of electricity and heat or even for propulsion.

It might also be worth bearing in mind, when considering any future agency for controlling outer space, that the field of application of international security control in the peaceful uses of atomic energy is severely limited at present. In case of the ENEA, for example, international security control applies basically only to the operation of joint undertakings and to materials, equipment and services which are made available by the Agency or under its supervision. The IAEA control system is even more restricted, applying primarily only to cases where assistance is provided by the Agency, or at its request, or under its supervision. Apart from these provisions, it is, of course, possible both in the ENEA of the OECD and in the IAEA to apply security control, at the request of the parties, to any bilateral or multilateral agreement, or to any activities of a requesting state in the field of atomic energy. Euratom, in a sense, constitutes an exceptional system in the field of international security controls in that it pledges to ensure the non-diversion of materials from peaceful to military uses basically only if the Community entered into an agreement to this effect with a third country or an international organization. Apart from this, the purpose of Euratom's safety control is to satisfy itself that ores, source materials and special fissionable materials are not diverted from their intended uses (whatever these uses may be) as stated by the users. Furthermore, the system applied by the Community specifically excludes control of any materials which are intended for the purposes of defense insofar as they are in the course of being specially prepared for such purposes or which, after being so prepared, are, in accordance with an operational plan, installed or stocked in a military establishment. Within these general limitations, however, the safety network of Euratom is broader in coverage than its ENEA and IAEA counterparts since the control applies to all other atomic undertakings of the Member States.

The approaches and methods followed by international atomic institutions to ensure peaceful uses cover a wide range and include, for example, the examination of the design of installations, the maintenance of accounting records, the transmission of periodic reports and on-the-spot inspections. In the case of bilateral agreements, where there is sufficient confidence among the parties, a simple written pledge may be all that is required.

The nature of control in regard to the frequency, type and date of inspections and reports may greatly depend on the amount of materials involved, the chances of diversion, the techniques available for its detection, the cooperation of the receiving authorities (government or business) and many other factors such as, for instance, the type of installations involved and even consideration of moderation and balancing of interests. One lesson which may be drawn from the existing network of international atomic control undertakings, which may also be kept in mind as regards international safeguards for cosmic space, is that a hundred percent fool-proof system whereby every possible diversion would necessarily be detected is, for all practical purposes, an impossibility and efforts to reduce the margin of error or undetectibility below a certain minimal level are likely to be prohibitive in terms of cost and become too burdensome, hampering industrial progress. At present, it seems that all international security controls over the peaceful uses of atomic energy have come to realize this fact.

On-the-spot inspection, carried out by persons specially appointed for the purpose, is at the center of all control systems. Inspection itself is a very complex task which includes technical problems, organizational procedures, as well as human relations. While undoubtedly there is a deep-rooted psychological problem involved in the presence of international inspectors on a sovereign state's territory, it has been found that consultations with the domestic authorities prior to the arrival of the inspection teams, their possible accompaniment by national officials, and informal discussions of found discrepencies may help to alleviate any ill feelings. On the other hand, the suggestion that the health and safety inspections be combined with security control inspections, as originally envisaged by the IAEA, though appealing in theory, has proved to be impracticable in actual application, largely for political reasons, and thus no institution has combined them. This is, however, something which would have to be again carefully weighed in connection with control systems for outer space.

The record of security controls in the field of atomic energy has been on the positive side of the scale. No diversions, to my knowledge, have been discovered or reported and the operations of the systems have not encountered serious difficulties. On the other hand, it should be admitted that, even in such a closely-bound undertaking as Euratom, disputes have arisen touching upon national interests such as, for instance, the determination of the particular point at which materials become "specially prepared" for defense purposes and therefore pass beyond the safety system of Euratom. However, such controversies among allies are usually far more easily and quietly settled than those among nations holding diverse political, economic and ideological beliefs as is the case in the IAEA where the sensitive questions of national sovereignty, ideological conflict and the contrasting of the "have" as against the "have-not" nations often magnify them out of proportion.

Even these cursory examples which time and space have permitted seem to indicate that, in order to overcome national barriers in a field so sensitive to defense as international security control over the atom, and most likely also in the equally sensitive area of cosmic space, one has to start out with extremely limited objectives and with delicate operational differentiations based upon a very careful allocation of authority in terms of people, resources and institutions. While it is true that international security control over the peaceful uses of nuclear energy has been on a very fragmentary and limited level, I would like to draw your attention to what may be regarded as the most significant achievement in this field. This is the provision which permits international inspectors to appear on the territory of a sovereign state and which gives them access at all times to all persons, places and data as necessary in connection with the adequate performance of their duties.

This, coupled in many instances with judicial safeguards, is, I believe, a formidable step forward in the development of world institutions.

In conclusion, may I say that I am not sure at all whether I have been able to convince you, let alone myself, that there are some useful analogies between the atom and cosmic space. However, I believe that there is at least one. It seems that the more we are splitting the atom the more problems will arise and the more we are expanding in the universe the more question marks there will be to keep our working groups busy.

* * * * *

THE CODIFICATION OF SPACE LAW

by

F. W. von Rauchhaupt

I.   The beginning of Space Law.
   A.   Some theoretical jurists are still against the existence of Space Law.
   B.   On the other hand, the General Assembly of the United Nations with its resolution 1721 of December 20, 1961, declared that Public International Law is applicable to Space Law. The transposition of Public International Law from Earth and the air into Space above creates some difficulties:
      1.   Some aspects of Public International Law could not be applied in space--for instance, those laws regarding U boats, those pertaining to damages, or those regarding the continental shelf (claimed by several American States), or the law of the adjoining air.
      2.   On the other hand, there remain many gaps in Space Law that Public International Law could not fill totally in the steadily expanding Space Law.

II.   The most conspisuous gaps, though partly closed, follow:
   A.   The problem of sovereignty in Space Law. Sovereignty in Space does not exist because Space is res omnium communis.
   B.   The fact that the limit of damages that can be given in the USA for a single case of damage is the enormous amount of $250,000,000.
   C.   The avoidance of wars by the stopping of certain atom tests, of outright spying, and of the direct confrontation of governmental heads of the USA and the USSR in order to avoid accidental wars.
   D.   At the same time international peace is to be preserved by means of mutual collaboration, for instance, by exchanging the reports of weather satellites (of the Tiros and Nimbus type) and of the Telstar communications satellites, by the favorable distribution of radio spectrum channels, by research of magnetic fields, and in sum, by good intentions and observance of the moral code of civilized peoples.
   E.   Making use of space exploration just for scientific purposes, for example, enlarging our small knowledge of space, of the stars therein, and of their powerful emanations. A certain gain also arises from the indirect influence on national industries.

III. The foundation of space law.

A. The goal of these legal experiments is a complete Law of Space.

So far two bases are prevalent: the continental codification of every part of the law by legislation, and the Anglo-Saxon piecemeal collection of law through the decisions of law courts. The American opinion seems to vacillate back and forth. But with this absolutely new Space Law, it seems advisable to begin by complete codifications, that is, in our case, the logical presentation of the whole of Space Law in one book. The model, followed by most modern States, is the five codes of Napoleon: the civil, the commercial, the penal codes, and the civil and criminal jurisdictions. They exist under the aegis of the constitution. Do not forget, though, that these codes are national codes, whereas the Space Law code or codes would belong to Public International Law, which so far has not yet achieved a complete codification of its own. Nevertheless, the constitution could be transposed into Space Law.

B. The constitution directs the law of--

1. the territory: Space is enormous and does not know frontiers. It begins where it touches the upper limits of air space.

2. the inhabitants: whether they be nationals or foreigners. So far only 14 living people (eight North Americans and six Russians) went up and returned. They are not yet space inhabitants, only visitors. We do not know yet of other inhabitants in Space.

3. the State power: in space it is international and a res omnium communis, but just like any national State, it controls:

   a. Legislation. There is not yet a House of Representatives. Perhaps the International Astronautical Federation or its International Institute of Space Law could fill this gap. The United Nations would have to serve as the last resource and legislator, if its many other duties would allow it.

   b. Administration of Space on Earth is already very comprehensive. This administration is competent for the making and testing of space vehicles of all kinds, both small and large, meant to carry only instruments or astronauts as well; furthermore, it allocates radio spectrum channels, the journey and the return, the preparation of starting and landing places, the employment of the control staff, and the timetables. These tasks are mostly of a technical nature, which allows a comparatively easy understanding among all partners and guarantees fruitful collaboration.

   c. Jurisdiction for Space Law. A competent law court exists in the International Court of Justice at The Hague. It might be advisable to introduce lower national law courts for less important affairs. International law may be applied in these new national law courts just as the national prize courts use Public International Law.

IV. Conclusion.

These considerations in favor of the codification of Space Law might be studied in the groups of our International Institute of Space Law. The Space Law constitution will have to be formulated first. The formulation of other facets of Private International Law and the five codes will then follow more easily.

* * * * *

MORALS AND GOOD INTENTION IN SPACE LAW
by
F. W. von Rauchhaupt

Preface:

(1) Morals and good intention in theory.

(a) Morals were mentioned in the preface to the first volume of our Space Law Colloquium with regard to the Spanish creation of new law for the newly discovered continents of America. The creators of this new law were professors of theology in Salamanca. Their doctrines can be identified with the three principal commandments of the New Testament: love of God, of brother or neighbour, and of the enemy. In our colloquium of 1962, H. Caplan referred to the Old Testament for the same purpose. But we find in the IAF, representatives of many other religions in Asia. A Japanese professor sang, at the 1962 meeting of the Grotius Foundation in Bordeaux, a religious hymn in honour of the collaboration of mankind for Public International Law. There are also people who deny the existence of God. They remind us of children who pretend that they are not afraid in the dark or who want to prove their courage in this way. Nevertheless, belief in God and Christ, as our Savior, grows in our times in many ways. We see it in the form of the New Moral Rearmament (VCAR), in International Christian Leadership, and in other international associations with moral programs.

(b) The essence of morals includes good and honest behaviour--ethics. The philosopher I. Kant and his many followers translate morals into legality; double morals mean dishonest behaviour. Important is the decision of the Paris Tribunal of Arbitration in 1893, in which the counsel for the USA, J.C. Carter, said that "the mutual relations of States ... are based on principles of the law of nature or morality ...." A large portion of international law is rather a branch of ethics, the sources of which are (1) Divine Law, (2) enlightened reason, (3) the consent of nations. Morals are also the canons of professions, the American Bar Association among others.

(2) Morals in practice.

In practising morals, good intention is needed. Egoism and an exaggerated nationalism are not helpful, nor any claim to total world power.

I. Public International Law and Space Law.

The introduction of Public International Law into Space Law was decided by Resolution No. 1721 of the UN General Assembly, dated December 20, 1961, and the Statutes of the International Institute of Space Law were accepted in Paris on March 24, 1963. Public International Law is to serve only peaceful uses; it must not be used for aggressive aims. That means that arms are allowed only for self-protection against an unprovoked attack or for police duties. In Space Law, peaceful satellites are permitted.

A. In Theory.

It would be senseless to make all Public International Law applicable to International Space Law. Only the applicable parts should be used.

1. Sources.

The main sources of Public International Law are contained in Article 38 of Statutes of the International Court of Justice at The Hague. This Article includes the morals we espouse for International Space Law. The philosopher I. Kant calls morals also a law of nature. The contents of natural law (as a human law) depend on the state and meaning of the general culture; whereas morals belong to divine law, which cannot be altered by mankind.

2. Aims.

The intention of uniting International Law with Space Law is to save the rights of mankind in Space—freedom, equality, peace—advancing at the same time the sciences of Space, and to create the proper organisations. The UN and the IAF helped to achieve these first results. We cannot hope to advance International Space Law unless we endeavor to reach a state of mutually good intentions and a useful collaboration that will enable all parties to trust in disarmament and peace.

B. In practice.

1. Results.

We see good results already: the exchange program between the USA and the USSR of March 20, 1963, on weather satellites, including the research accomplishments of the USA through the Tiros satellites; an exchange of the experiences by cosmonauts of both sides; new Cosmos XIV satellites dispatched by the USSR since April 13, 1963; the agreement that dangerous waste material, particularly after nuclear experiments, is not to be dispensed in Space because of the damage it might cause to mankind. Telstar, on the contrary, is a privately owned USA enterprise to distribute news and coloured pictures via Space.

2. Further goodwill.

Further collaborations are shown in a steady exchange in arts and music, in tours, even in discussions on politics. Most important is the Geneva treaty of June 20, 1963, concerning the direct communications between the USA and the USSR in order to avoid the accidental outbreak of a disastrous world war.

3. Collaboration.

Friendly intentions, peaceful collaboration, and mutual confidence and trust are necessary adjuncts to Space Law. Unfriendly actions, even indirectly, are harmful.

II. The application of morals to Space Law is in the experimental stage.

    A. Public International Law.

        1. A Bill of Rights for individuals in Space is still lacking.

        2. Spying is to be avoided, but spying is permitted, even by the UN, in the case of self-defense. The American West Ford Project of April 21, 1961, threw 350,000,000 metal needles into Space which disappeared without any visible effect so far. The experiment was repeated recently. Soviet nuclear explosions might be mentioned here, though their aim was to find out the force and expanse of these blasts.

    B. Penal Law.

        The moral certainty of the jury in criminal law suits is based on the conviction of the conscience, but not on penal law. This legal device might be useful in Space Law, too.

    C. Civil Law.

        Civil law acknowledges moral obligations and just moral considerations. This concept might be used in Space Law regarding damages.

III. Practical consequences.

    Space Law must be based on good intentions and mutual confidence.

    A. Provisional measures.

        New rules have to be established for the registration of Space vehicles, their timetables, and their insurance. Peaceful Space vehicles and their occupants must be returned if they come down in a country other than their own, whether by mistake or accident.

    B. Final results: treaties and mutual control.

        1. We need an international treaty and executive legislation for the most important branches of Space Law: administrative law, criminal law, damages law.

        2. Mutual control and inspections have already been agreed upon in the Antarctic Treaty. These measures should also be introduced into Space Law. It will be the special task of the UN to be the center and the pivot for these provisional and final measures. The smooth functioning of this concert will make easier the needed agreements for disarmament and world peace.

* * * * *

CONCEPTS AND METHODS IN THE LAW OF OUTER SPACE

by

Julian G. Verplaetse

I Terminology

The term "space law" is inadequate. Space is actually any extension characterized by the old concept of the three dimensions completed by the new Einsteinian one of the fourth dimension. The application to the universe is but one meaning of space.

The term "law of outer space" is more cautious, more realistic, confined to actual need: conflicts between air and outer space, corridor connecting both, orbiting.

Many prospects now envisaged under the term of space law go beyond actual need or attempt overtrumped generalizations. Definitely, manifold activities will be covered by different regulations. Such a body as "universal cosmic law" is not within the reach of our present experience.

A most urgent task is to bring more clarity and uniformity in the legal terminology relating to activities directed towards outer space. Conceivably, no full-size list can be drawn up ne varietur. But a good start could be made by a tentative draft of terms and definitions pertaining to the phases located on earth, in the air, and in the escape corridor.

II Concepts

It would be delusive to start from the top. This would be tantamount to beginning with the unknown. No talk on natural law would be able to give real and legal cloth to our imagination. Therefore we cannot maintain that our task is, at present, to create a wholly new branch of the law, even less to state that it would derive from our concept of natural law. But it would also be wrong to resume the elements of vertical law which have developed in the law of the air, and prolong them into outer space.

R.N. Gardner writes:
"...the things that take place in space are inextricably bound up with the things that take place on the surface of the earth. Those people are living in a dream world who think that space can be wrapped up in a nice new sanitary package and insulated from terrestrial reality."

One cannot share the extremes of that opinion. The independent age of the space beyond the outer layers of our earth looms at the horizon of mankind. When that epoch dawns, it is likely that independent bodies of law will govern those spaces. Hence, it is unwarranted to decree that outer spaces are inextricably tied to the earth and cannot be insulated from terrestrial reality. But it is true that, for the time being, all outer space activity starts and is largely guided from the earth. (Proof of independent action by the cosmonaut is now established, but his range of freedom is still limited.)

Therefore the right concept would seem to be that, for concrete purposes, and as far as human endeavor has already penetrated or will soon penetrate a new field of activity, we must, with the tools at our disposal, i.e., with our human knowledge and legal arsenal, try to find out the rules that can apply to human beings within the scope of actual activities directed towards outer space. This would limit our task to concrete topics.

The problems first to be considered could be deduced from the approach of Professors Myres McDougal and L. Lipson and from the Russian suggestions in "Kosmos i Mezdunarodnoe Pravo" (cf. my review of that book in 29 Journal of Air Law and Commerce, 1963, nr 1; Zeitschrift für Luftrecht 1963, 194; Diritto Internazionale 1962, 284).

At present the choice of topics could be taken from the main activities now carried out:

1) Earth orbiting man in outer space.

2) The lunar phase.

3) Interplanetary phase (Venus, Mars flybys or probes).

4) The Cosmos earth satellites as adjunct to phase 1 and/or 2, beginning March 1962.

As an example we may consider the law of war and neutrality.

It would be preposterous to consider neutrality in the light of a war fought on Mars or Venus or in World Space. Please let us keep our fancy clear of the nightmarian infinitudes in order to foster healthy dreams.

Even if we stick to the realistic approach, i.e., to the terms defined above, there would be different situations to take care of:

a) War fought out in outer space itself, without earthly impact (unless accidental).

b) Auxiliary war in outer space, i.e., as a part of land-, sea- and/or air operations.

c) The very particular case of a terrestrial power going up in outer space in order to strafe another terrestrial power.

Moreover the case for neutrality would be different whether outer space is free or subject to sovereignty of some kind, whether neutral Powers are engaged in outer space activity or not.

This does not mean that we must and can cover all those individual cases. We must, of necessity, follow general lines, but always keeping within the bounds of reasonable foresight. Even then, we become clearly alive to the fact that the concepts will not be moulded after the wise or terrestrial rules, but that, on account of essential difference in technique, those rules will be impracticable or subject to profound alterations.

III Methods

At present there is no hope that the Governments involved in outer space activity or the member-States of the UN will reach a general agreement on a general code of legal conduct in outer space.

The latest meetings of the UN Subcommittees have been as disappointing as their predecessors.

The recent meeting of the UN legal Subcommittee, May 1963, did not reach any positive result. After thirteen meetings, the session was described as a "very useful and constructive exchange of views." This euphemism could not smother a divergence in the matter of method, the Soviet Union being in favor of a treaty-type document, whereas the non-communist Bloc would be satisfied with a Resolution of the UN General Assembly. This conflict of method prevented a positive result, even in those questions which were qualified as non-controversial.

Three main groups of questions could be distinguished after the debates:

1) Non-controversial. E.g. freedom for exploration and use of outer space by all States equally under international law, immunity of celestial bodies from national appropriation, applicability of international law, including the UN charter, to relations among States in outer space, retention by the launching authority of jurisdiction over and ownership of space vehicles and their personnel, and on liability for injury or damage that might be caused by space vehicle accidents.

2) Issues capable of agreement and adjustment: willingness of some delegations to enter into multilateral agreements on the subject of assistance, rescue and return of astronauts and space vehicles, including settlement of the damages caused.

3) Issues on which fundamental disagreement persists: space reconnaissance and prohibition of war propaganda in outer space.

Shortly after the meeting of the Legal Subcommittee, the UN scientific Subcommittee adjourned on a very similar negative outcome, although some modest results could be achieved in particular fields.

In view of this failure the Legal Subcommittee requested that the two major powers, the USA and the USSR, should try to settle privately the major difficulties which bore out the persistent opposition.

The USA has submitted a paper to the Soviet delegation stating some proposals. At the moment of writing no answer has been received. It may be supposed that it will be slow-going to attain a broader understanding than that achieved on June 8, 1962, on technical matters of meteorological satellites, mapping of the earth's magnetic field and experiments in space communications.

There are four main differences of approach. The Russian side of that approach may be summarized as follows:

1) Prohibition of the use of outer space for propagating war and racial hatred or enmity between nations.

2) Outer space activity must be a monopoly for States, excluding private undertakings such as the communication satellite Tellstar.

3) Ban against collection of intelligence from outer space, which is called "imcompatible with the objectives of mankind in its conquest of outer space."

4) States must approve in advance experiments by others in outer space. This smacks of a veto system.

As far as is known from the USA proposals, these would attempt a compromise, namely by pointing out that private space operations must be authorized and supervised by the Governments concerned, which should also bear international responsibility for the activity of their nationals. On the other hand, before initiating new projects, they would be willing to enter into "appropriate international consultations." With reference to observation and photography from outer space, the USA considers that they are consistent with international law and the UN charter in the same way as landmasses may be observed and photographed from the High Seas. The USA further claim that it is impossible to distinguish between military and non-military use of outer space (though they would maintain the distinction peaceful-aggressive). American analysts of Soviet attitudes affirm that the Soviet Union is also drawing closer to that line of thought. They cite military people and scientists of the USSR and, among the jurists, the Executive Secretary of the Space Law Commission of the Soviet Academy of Sciences, who stated in July 1962: "... it, by no means, follows that it is forbidden to use this space for striking through it or with its aid a retaliatory blow at the aggressor in the course of legitimate self-defense."

Two facts emergy from the recent discussion:

1) There is a persistent deadlock in the legal field. No global arrangement is in the offing.

2) Limited objectives are now being pursued by a limited number of States.

Thus our task is clear. What the law of the outer spaces will ultimately be is beyond our grasp and imagination. A wholesale transfer of the terrestrial bodies of law would be of no avail. Our duty is to find a concrete norm for the most urgent human necessities in outer space.

Somebody must prepare the exploration of the applicability of some old rules to some parts of the new substance. The International Institute of Space law is the only body working on an international basis in that field. Therefore this Institute should, at this Session, single out one topic or two topics, considered as the most urgent, on which it is likely that a minimum agreement can be reached and that seem to be fairly within the grasp of technical stability, so that no upheaval must be reasonably foreseen in the near future. Next year that minimum consensus should be submitted to the General Assembly of the IAF and should be communicated to all States as well as to the UN.

After listening to the different speakers, I would like to suggest as the choice topic the ideas developed by Mr. Jozsef Ivanyi on a Draft Convention on Safety of Life for cosmonauts and the eloquent plea of Mr. Kenneth A. Finch on the same subject, urging for early consideration of that matter in view of the meetings of the Telecommunication Union next year.

This topic has all the qualities needed for our purpose: it has the human touch, which should leave no jurist indifferent; it is a legal necessity if we want to avoid such accidents as those which nearly befell the American astronaut Carpenter; it anticipates the deadline to which Mr. Finch alluded; finally, it has been recognized as urgent by the Major Powers involved, in their proposals submitted to the Committee on the peaceful uses of outer space at its Second Session, September 1962, as set forth in Annex III of Doc. A/5181. It is also within technical and scientific foresight, since we keep outside cosmic compass, on which experimental facts are too scarce as yet.

* * * * *

FREEDOM OF SPACE AND ITS LIMITS
by
G. P. Zhukov

Six years ago Man for the first time in history overcame the force of gravity, and since then life on earth has acquired a new dimension. The greater cause of Space conquest is

115

gaining in scope from year to year. Mankind is penetrating deeper and deeper into Space, to other planets. Simultaneously our knowledge of the Space in immediate proximity of the Earth is becoming broader and broader.

The extension of states' activities in Space and active development of manned flights into Space raise some vital law problems. Not many years ago the question of legal regulation of state activity in Space was considered to be something verging on fantasy; now this is a question of paramount importance.

Indeed, it is far from the same thing for millions of people on Earth whether Space will become a sphere of international co-operation of states in the interests of all mankind, or it will become the arena of armaments race and struggle for supremacy.

That is why it is important for all mankind and especially for astronauts, the courageous explorers of the expanses of the Universe, not to permit a "jungle law" in Space, but to provide for a solid legal order, precluding any arbitrary or lawless actions, and forbidding any sort of experiments dangerous for man's life or health.

The first step in this direction was made by the United Nations Organization General Assembly in December 1961. The adopted Resolution declared that the study and use of Space should serve the welfare of all mankind. The same Resolution emphasized that international law, including the UNO Charter, covers Space and celestial bodies; that they are free for investigation and use by all states in accordance with international law; and that they cannot be appropriated by individual states.

N.S. Khrushchev, President of the Council of Ministers of the USSR, in his message to President J.F. Kennedy of March 20, 1962, expressed his approval of the fact that the Soviet Union and the United States, who are ahead of all the other countries in Space conquest, had managed to co-ordinate those important principles of space law, which later were supported by other countries. The message also conveyed the idea that we should go further and try to find a common approach to the solutions of vital law problems which are raised by life itself in this space age.

What are the problems that deserve the speediest legal settlement?

There can be no doubt of the urgency of working out the basic law principles of states' activities in Space. Such problems as rendering assistance to spacemen and spaceships and those concerning their return are urgent as well. The question of the responsibility for damage caused by states' activity in Outer Space should be studied too.

The necessity of investigating these problems are stressed in the UNO General Assembly Resolution 1802 (XVII) of December 14, 1962. A Committee on the Use of Outer Space for Peaceful Purposes, consisting of representatives of 28 states, was established within the United Nations Organization framework. Along with solving problems of scientific and technical cooperation, the Committee is supposed to work out Outer Space legal regulations. Precisely for that purpose the Committee established a Legal Subcommittee, the first meeting of which was held in Geneva in June 1962.

The USSR has submitted for consideration of the Legal Subcommittee documents of such paramount importance as the Draft Declaration on the basic principles of states' activities in the field of investigation and use of Outer Space and the Draft International Agreement on rescuing crash landed spacemen and spaceships. The USA delegation in the Legal Subcommittee made attempts to press a discussion on the responsibility for damage caused by a spaceship. Due to wide differences between the members of the meeting, the Legal Subcommittee did not reach agreement on any one of the suggestions.

Nor did the session of the UNO Outer Space Committee held in September 1962 show any substantial progress in his respect.

The General Assembly of the United Nations Organization at the XVII session, held in December 1962, expressed its regret at this fact and called to all states to co-operate in working out legal regulations for Outer Space. Unfortunately no progress has been made in this field so far. The second session of the Legal Subcommittee, held in New York in spring 1963, did not justify the hopes either.

The Soviet delegation made considerable efforts to get things moving. At the very beginning of the session, the Soviet Union submitted for consideration of the Legal Subcommittee a revised Draft Declaration on the basic principles of states' activities in Outer Space. The Draft Declaration took into account the suggestions of other countries, including the USA, the UK and the UAR.

What is the essence of the Declaration suggested by the USSR? Does it protect true interests in Outer Space of all states no matter whether large or small, whether they are conducting investigations in Outer Space or just embarking on this path? Does it provide for a sufficient guarantee of international co-operation in peaceful use of Outer Space?

The public opinion of all countries is unanimous in that free access to Outer Space for all countries is now a universally recognized fact. However, the USSR, as well as the majority of the countries of the West and the East, believe that this freedom in Outer Space cannot be infinite and should have reasonable limits.

That is why the Soviet Draft Declaration, reflecting the opinion of wide circles of international public concerning the necessity of restricting freedom in Outer Space, contains firm guarantees against abuse of this freedom. And what is more, it defines precisely what types of space apparatus and what forms of activities are impermissible in Outer Space. Thus, for example, the Soviet Draft Declaration emphasizes the inadmissibility of the use of Outer Space for the collection of intelligence and for war propaganda, the necessity of preliminary discussion and co-ordination among the states of experiments which may impede peaceful investigations of Outer Space, and declares that any activities in Space should be carried out by states only.

The suggestion to establish guarantees agains abuses of freedom of action in Outer Space was seconded in the Legal Subcommittee by the delegations of the UAR, Brazil, India, Morocco and Chad.

Indeed, what law standards could excuse the launching by the USA of containers with copper needles into the Outer Space last spring? As many international scientific authorities stated, this launching seriously impedes the work of astronomers in many countries, who study celestial bodies with the help of radio telescopes. Therefore it was not accidental that the second session of the Scientific and Technical Subcommittee of the UNO Outer Space Committee, held in Geneva on May 14-29, 1963, paid much attention to the problem of cessation of harmful experiments in Outer Space.

On the initiative of India, the Subcommittee adopted recommendations which emphasize the anxiety of all mankind in connection with the dangerous consequences that may result from unilateral and arbitrary actions in Outer Space. The Subcommittee drew the attention of the

UNO Committee on Outer Space to the urgency and importance of solving of the problem of eliminating all obstacles in the way to the use of Outer Space caused by potentially harmful experiments.

The adoption of this Recommendation was the manifestation of the anxiety of wide scientific and public circles of many countries.

In connection with this, it should be recalled that the Draft Resolution, prepared by the Subcommittee on Outer Space Law Problems of the Inter-Parliamentary Union for the 52nd Inter-Parliamentary Conference, declares explicitly that "it is necessary to refrain from experiments in Outer Space or any other activities that may prevent other countries from peaceful use of Outer Space."

The D. Davis Institute on Studying of International Problems (Britain) favoured a preliminaty international agreement on coordination of experiments which may result in unfavorable effects in the proximity of the Earth. The position of the USSR concerning the necessity of co-ordination of hazardous experiments in Outer Space meets with understanding and wide support.

The Soviet Union believes also that freedom in Outer Space is incompatible with the use of artificial satellites for the collection of military information. Indeed, do such actions answer the purposes of mankind in mastering Outer Space? Do they conform to universally recognized standards of international law? Of course not. It is quite evident that there is no "right for espionage" from Outer Space or anywhere else. Naturally, such a right cannot exist. Moreover, in international practice of relations between different countries, the conviction that espionage is illegal, that the states are responsible for such actions, and that they have the right to take the necessary measures to guard the national security from espionage, has been universally recognized since ancient times.

Sometimes in the West the argument is voiced that "observation" from Outer Space is not forbidden by the international law and consequently is legal. But it is clear to anyone that there are different kinds of observation from Outer Space. The observer may confine himself to survey of clouds and collection of other data necessary for meteorological forecasts. That is one thing. And quite another thing is when the satellite makes photographs of military objects of another state, e.g., rocket bases. That is not the kind of information which is of importance for a state that takes care of its own defense; this sort of information is useful only for a state which is going to be the first to attack, to destroy the rocket bases of the enemy and to avoid retaliation.

Such "observation" of another state's territory is illegal, no matter where it is conducted from - from the surface of the Earth, from the air or from Outer Space.

Such "observation" is prohibited by the standards of air law. As an example we may refer to the Chicago convention of 1944, Clause 36, which says: "Each contracting State may prohibit or regulate the use of photographic apparatus in aircraft over its territory."

The illegality of espionage from the point of view of the international law is confirmed by provisions of other agreements. Thus, for example, the Hague Convention on Laws and Customs of War held in 1907 provides for punishability and illegality of scouts. In time of peace the role of such scouts is performed by satellites when they are used for collection of military information. Defending national interests of all the peoples of the world, the Soviet Union suggests that the Declaration should confirm the prohibitons which

118

were introduced long ago into international law and which are condemned by world public opinion.

The possibility of using artificial satellites for communication and radio and TV broadcasting purposes is acquiring tremendous importance in our age. The question is whether communication with the help of those satellites would serve the development of friendly relations between the peoples and for dissemination of true information or it would become a new path for propaganda of war, racial discrimination and hostility among peoples. This question is raised by life today and it is impossible to evade it. That is the reason why the Soviet Draft Declaration includes a clause prohibiting the use of Outer Space for propaganda of war, national and racial hatred or hostility among peoples. This clause of the Draft Declaration is based on the Resolution of the UNO General Assembly (1948) which denounced war propaganda openly and unambiguously - Incidentally, there is one more circumstance that urges the necessity of this step, namely the plans of some Western states to extend the right to private enterprise to Outer Space.

In 1962 the USA Congress adopted the law on the establishment of a private corporation which has taken into its hands intercontinental television and telephone communication by means of the "Telestar" and other so-called "communication satellites." The establishment of this corporation aroused serious apprehensions even in the USA Congress, where this fact was justly quoted as usurpation of sovereign rights of States by a private company.

It is quite evident that in order to provide proper legal order in Outer Space, all kinds of activities for investigation and exploitation of Outer Space should be performed by States only. Freedom of action given to private companies may lead to chaos and arbitrariness. No argumentations that the State controls and is responsible for the activities of such private companies will change anything.

That is why the Soviet Union suggests including into the Declaration a clause stating that the activities in Outer Space may be performed only by States, acting with due understanding of their responsibility. But in order to reach a clear definition of legal order in Outer Space, firm international obligations should be undertaken by the States.

At the Legal Subcommittee it was suggested that the Declaration should be adopted only as a Resolution of the General Assembly of the United Nations Organization. However, the discussion at the Legal Subcommittee meeting showed again that the legal validity of the Resolution of the UNO General Assembly both in practice and in doctrine continued to cause debates. This circumstance alone may serve as a serious argument against a Declaration in the form of a Resolution of the UNO General Assembly. Consequently the Declaration on the basic principles of states' activities in Outer Space should have the force of an international treaty. The force of international obligations is a question of great importance. The Soviet Union proceeds from the fact that if the governments really want to observe certain principles of behaviour in Outer Space, they must be interested in the Declaration asserting these principles with the force of an international treaty.

The Soviet Union strives for the establishment of a firm legal order in Outer Space and is ready to take upon itself the corresponding legal responsibilities.

The Soviet Union suggests that the existing international practice should be followed according to which questions associated with policies on land, on sea, and in the air are regulated by special agreements. The working of Space law should keep in step with the progress in the field of science and technique so as to promote the expansion of international co-operation in the sphere of peaceful use of Outer Space, the consolidation of peace and friendship among the nations.

* * * * *

II. Other Contributions and Comments

Contributions were written by 35 authors; 38 reports were presented.

Following Professor E. Pépin's advice at the Varna Colloquium, 1962, that mutual agreement on the interpretation of the general principles governing the exploration and utilization of outer space should be reached in the first place before dealing with all the other problems emerging out of space activities, most reports dealt with the general principles of space law and their interpretation as they are set forth in UN Resolution 1721 (XVI), and the use of artificial satellites in context with the term "peaceful." The rest of the reports dealt with liability problems arising out of space activities, European cooperation (Bourely) and Metalaw (Haley).

1. General principles governing the exploration and utilization of outer space.

All authors on this subject stress the importance of international cooperation in this field, that outer space should be open to all states for peaceful purposes, and that the celestial bodies or parts of them shall not be subject to national or private appropriation. Since UN Resolution 1721 (XVI) - containing the basic principles for the exploration and utilization of outer space - was passed, different opinions exist about the legal status of this Resolution: whether it is binding or only of a declaratory nature. Therefore, the UN General Assembly requested the Committee on the Peaceful Uses of Outer Space to continue the elaboration of the basic legal principles as well as to prepare draft proposals for specific technical agreements. Especially, the Soviet delegate insisted on the preparation of "a formally binding instrument" (F.B. Schick, The Political Bedlam of Space Law). Also, many members of the International Institute of Space Law pled for a quick codification of space law, except Mr. C. Boasson, who is of the opinion that too little is yet known about future developments of space technology.

2. Interpretation of the term "peaceful."

Much attention is paid to the expression and interpretation of the term "peaceful use of outer space," on which subject no consensus exists. One of the causes of disagreement or controversies on this subject is the existing "cold war" policy between the United States of America and the Soviet Union. Consequently, the accomplishment of a more definitive formulation of the basic legal principles governing outer space activities is made dependent on the progress of the disarmament negotiations. Although a Partial Test Ban Treaty was signed on August 5, 1963, there still exists another point of difference: the use of artificial satellites in outer space (see the reports of Korovin and Lukin). According to the Soviet Union, the use of artificial satellites is always contrary to the rules of international law, but as Schick writes (p. 26): "It ought to be noted, however, that not every disputed aerospace activity may necessarily constitute a threat to the peace, a breach of the peace, or an act of aggression." He also is of the opinion that there should be a strict division between politics and the setting up of rules for outer space control. He suggests that this control should be given to the Security Council of the United Nations.

3. Articles dealing with terminology in space law.

Among others, mention should be made of Professor Cocca's report "Determination of the meaning of the expression 'res communes humanitatis' in space law." Starting with the Roman concept res communis omnium, he thoroughly analyzes the evaluation of this term in international law throughout the Middle Ages up to the present moment. His summary may be quoted: "The expression res communes without the addition of the word humanitatis does not express the exact meaning one has in mind when referring to the juridical condition of outer space and the celestial bodies, since the traditional expression - according to the etymology and the legal line of thought, prior to the exploration of outer space - may give place to misunderstandings, which could be avoided by the substitution of the word omnium by the word humanitatis."

Also, K.A. Finch, "Territorial Claims to Celestial Bodies," gives an extensive historical review of the term "occupation" and by means of some famous cases before the Permanent Court of Arbitration, the Permanent Court of International Justice, and the present International Court of Justice he shows that the above-mentioned term cannot analogously be applied to celestial bodies. He pleads for internationalization by the United Nations (p. 58).

4. Articles concerning liability problems arising from space activities.

The existing systems of liability in other areas are mainly based on fault, although there is already a slight tendency towards strict and absolute liability, however, with some possibility of exculpation and exoneration. S.M. Beresford notes in his article "Requirements for an International Convention on Spacecraft Liability" that a system "of liability without fault will be much easier both to negotiate and to administer. For the protection of claimants, also, liability should be imposed without fault, primarily because a claimant could not have prevented injury himself or damage to his property, and cannot be reasonably expected to prove fault on the part of the operator or other defendant." (p. 4) Mitigation of liability, however, should be admitted: "The doctrine of absolute liability would impose too harsh a standard on defendants." (p. 5)

G.D. Schrader describes in his article "Space Activities and Resulting Tort Liability" the various methods of recovery presently available to claimants damaged by the U.S. space activities, the role of the International Court of Justice concerning such problems, and the part to be played by international conferences or conventions. He is of the opinion that, as in the early days of aviation, space law shall adopt the doctrine of liability without fault (p. 16/17). An international convention on this subject as a solution seems doubtful to Mr. Schrader at the present "... as there are and will be only two nations engaged in space activities. Hence, any international convention on the subject of liability would be enforceable only if the Soviet Union and the United States were in agreement and accepted the terms and responsibility imposed thereby. To this end, both Nations could promulgate domestic legislation without compromising their national sovereignty thereby allowing adequate recovery .... As the Soviets recognize liability for any damages their space ships might cause ...," the United States should increase the limits of administrative recovery under the National Aeronautics and Space Act, Military Claims Act, Foreign Claims Act and the Federal Torts Claims Act per incident, and, by so doing, "a reasonable recovery may be afforded to claimants ... and perhaps unnecessary litigation can be avoided."

- - - - -

SEVENTH COLLOQUIUM ON THE LAW OF OUTER SPACE

WARSAW, 1964

I. Texts Reproduced

LEGAL ASPECTS OF CELESTIAL BODIES AND SPACE STATIONS

by

Harold Berger

As the Space Age relentlessly advances toward that great and historic moment when an earthling first lands on a celestial body after a long journey from his home planet, it is indeed fitting to discuss current aspects of sovereignty in respect to outer space containing celestial bodies and space stations now being designed for orbital placement.

Existing international flight agreements and customary rules of international law affirm that every state has the absolute right to control all movement in an area called air space above its land and waters and that air space over the high seas is as free for international use as are the high seas themselves. See Article I of the Paris Convention of 1919 on the "Regulation of Aerial Navigation," which sets forth that "the High Contracting Parties recognize that every power has complete and exclusive sovereignty over the air space above its territory."

The Chicago Convention of 1944 adopted a similar restatement of existing international law by providing in Article I "that the Contracting State has complete and exclusive sovereignty over the air space above its territory." Prior to the Chicago Convention, the United States, in both the Air Commerce Act of 1926 and the Civil Aeronautics Act of 1938, asserted sovereignty over the air space above its land and waters. Although the term "air space" is nowhere defined, most commentators agree that the draftsmen of this legislation and of the pertinent sections of the Paris and Chicago Conventions had no thought at the time of space vehicles, space travel, appropriation of celestial bodies and orbital placement of space stations.

It can thus be concluded that existing agreements did not, by their terms as previously understood, apply to cosmic space and, therefore, such agreements left the regime of outer space an open question ... .

* * * * *

AN ANALYSIS OF CERTAIN POLICY APPROACHES IN THE
UNITED STATES TO THE EMERGING LAW OF OUTER SPACE
by
Carl Q. Christol

American policy respecting the formal development of a law for outer space has been much influenced by two opposing schools of thought. The disagreement is not as to goals so much as it is a question of how American interests might be best advanced and protected.

When a subject is regarded as novel there is an almost relentless tendency to advocate caution in treating it. When the subject is better understood there is a noticeable tendency to move more rapidly to resolve remaining uncertainties. Several years ago the counsels of caution were preponderate, and the "wait and see" point of view seemed to prevail. However, with greater experience a new approach seems to have gained acceptance ....

The supreme danger confronting legal policy-makers is that an effort dedicated to providing answers may sometimes result in overly simple answers to complex and difficult problems. A further danger, in the eyes of some, is the effort to provide answers at all, on the score that there are not ultimate solutions and that the attempt to provide answers which are not real is both retrogressive and misleading to the naive and unsuspecting ....

Other more activistically inclined commentators have argued that outer space law is more a political than a scientific problem, and that its principles and rules "like much else in an indeterminate universe, depend on the order of experience in space as well as on the changing political context." Many commentators have remarked about the extensive gap between scientific and technological achievement and the condition of the law. They favor closing the gap through the promulgation of what they regard as present, practical, common sense rules ....

*   *   *   *   *

LEGAL STATUS OF CELESTIAL BODIES AND ECONOMIC
STATUS OF THE CELESTIAL PRODUCTS
by
Aldo Armando Cocca

I. JURIDICAL CONDITION OF THE CELESTIAL BODIES

1. <u>What is understood by "a celestial body"</u>?

It will be necessary to define a celestial body. Some authors consider that celestial bodies are the planets and the Moon; others include the asteroids and meteorites of a considerable size; some others even consider it fit to include in the denomination of meteorites the accidental gaseous formations.

Amongst the authors who have given the problem considerable thought, we must mention the Austrian jurist, Ernst Fasa, who, in a paper presented at the IV Colloquium on the Law of Outer Space made a distinction between objects with no firm surface, like the Sun, and those with a firm surface, like the Moon. The next year, the same author posed again the issue at Varna, when he discoursed on what is a <u>natural celestial body</u>. Fasan considers that the micro-meteorites and other bodies of very small size, which could be used <u>in toto</u>, should be classified as <u>res quae usu consumitur</u>, and therefore be object of exclusive appropriation. On this issue the Bularian jurist, Marco G. Markoff, in a manuscript finished the 1st May, 1963, and not yet published, gives an important warning: the appropriation of a natural celestial body made by a State, with the purpose of "consuming" it totally (e.g.: by destroying a large meteorite or by trying to displace a small asteroid from its natural orbit) may have a disfavorable effect on life and security on Earth.

In the proposed text of the draft resolution sustained by Fasan at the VI Colloquium, we can read: Part C.4): "Pieces of matter, which can be transported as a whole through outer space, such as meteorites, shall not be deemed celestial bodies in the same sense of this Resolution." Furthermore, in the fundamentum of the draft the author says: "To find a limitation, it is submitted, that any piece of matter, which can be controlled and can be transported through outer space <u>in toto</u>, is no celestial body in a legal sense."

* * * * *

PREMATURENESS AND ANTHROPOCENTRICITY IN LEGAL
REGULATION OF SPACE?

by

Pompeo Magno

Knowledge, diffusion, and teaching of space law are undoubtedly facilitated by the fascination of this new legal discipline. Space, in its immensity and with its mysteries, has a deep attraction, especially for young persons, who are attracted by the novelty of the problems arising from it. They have the imagination necessary to every researcher, in all fields, including the field of space.

But in opposition to this generally favorable attitude toward space studies, specifically space law, there is a certain skepticism based on prejudices that must be overcome.

This question is often asked by one who approaches the subject for the first time: Isn't it premature to talk about space law now, in an era in which the conquest of space is still a dream and navigation in the cosmos is still in an experimental phase? Under these conditions, wouldn't it be more opportune to wait until wider and more durable space ventures are carried out, and actual cases of interference or conflict arise among interested parties, in order that legal questions may be created within this framework? Wouldn't a set of laws emerge that would be more suitable and have a relationship to reality?

Such doubts, which reflect a superficial type of good sense and a natural reluctance for schematic and useless theories, create a feeling of disinterest for space law, as we mentioned above, which is the subject of this paper ....

On the other hand, it is a good thing for all concerned to understand ahead of time the limits and the conditions of their future actions. Thus, those countries and individuals preparing for space exploration would know what rules governed their activities and what laws and obligation they would have to meet. Otherwise, they would have to resort exclusively to the law of force and would have to take and hold only those things that they felt capable of defending. Since the law of force has its own rigid logic, and the dynamics of human events determine that the strong of today are never the strong of tomorrow, a chain of mutations in handing down badly constituted interests begins. It continues with the well-known historical consequences of conquests.

This cannot be prevented after the fact: once advantages have been created, it is against the teaching of history to believe that one would renounce success that he had undoubtedly obtained at great personal risk and sacrifice.

Also, in the field of space exploration, we cannot derive a great deal of comfort from the fact that up to the present the two space powers, USSR and USA, have made reassuring statements concerning their lack of material interest and their altruism and have made their findings available to the entire human race. Since, aside from the fact that very little conquest has been made up to now, these statements and generous attitudes are due to the greatness and power of the two above-mentioned nations, as well as to their reciprocal limitations. But when, in the evolution of historical situations, the pre-eminence of the equilibrium of these two countries changes, could the human race depend on the durability of the present lack of egoism?

In addition, the development and the increasing perfection of space vehicles will make them available to many more possible explorers in the future. Will these latter be guided by a similar spirit of autodiscipline and by a sense of responsibility now seen in the two major space powers?

All these considerations, as well as others, make it necessary to launch the legal regulation of space today, and not tomorrow when it could be too late.

* * * * *

THE PRINCIPLE "RES COMMUNIS OMNIUM" AN THE
PEACEFUL USE OF SPACE AND OF CELESTIAL BODIES
by
Enrico Scifoni

The enthusiasm and hope that the beginning of the space age kindled in human hearts were very quickly followed by the fear that these amazing products of human will and genius might be turned into instruments which could destroy, or seriously endanger, the peace of the entire human race.

On October 4, 1957, the United States brought up the question of the use of cosmic space for military purpose before the United Nations General Assembly. In a memorandum of January

126

1957, this country proposed that experiments then underway be integrated in an efficient system of armament control.

Meanwhile, the first Soviet launchings were followed on February 1, 1958, by the beginning of a series of American launchings. Both the major space powers, the Soviet Union (in a note of March 15, 1958) and the United States (in a note of September 2nd the same year), suggested to the United Nations that the complex problem of the utilization of cosmic space be considered as an autonomous question....

But what is the exact significance of "res communis omnium"? According to a detailed analysis by Magno, two considerations are essential:
1) To declare that space is "res communis omnium" is not the same as proclaiming absolute liberalism authorizing anyone to make use of the universe "ad libitum." Otherwise, it would mean sanctioning that state of legal anarchy existing in the universe at present.
2) Such a declaration would create for every individual, and not just for every nation, the right to have an active part in and to be a co-proprietor in the enjoyment of the thing under consideration.

Therefore, in contrast to what is generally held from the definition, we are not dealing with an exclusive right of the states or organized communities, but with a true right of co-proprietorship and recognized common use for individuals. In this case, we cannot speak of co-ownership of property, because the concept of property, in addition to being within the realm of private right, is subject to becoming void through non-use or alienation, and can be limited in various ways by means of the constitution of real rights in favor of third parties....

It can clearly be seen that, among all the possible space uses, those for military or espionage activity should not be permitted. In addition, we must keep in mind the danger of atmospheric contamination resulting from experimentation. The latter may be caused by nuclear experiments, for example, which cause radioactive fallout.

The specific use of celestial bodies infers knowledge of the effective possibilities of exploiting them. In fact, a complete investigation of the probable resources in space should be extended beyond our solar system. However, in spite of the number of facts we have accumulated concerning cosmic space, our knowledge is still limited to our solar system and very little can be said with certainty about the other systems, even those in our own galaxy....

* * * * *

INTERNATIONAL REGULATION OF OUTER SPACE ACTIVITIES

by

Eilene Galloway

An examination of the implications for space law of the present organizational structure and general principles now governing international space activities should help in identifying the ways and means by which certain types of desired regulation may be accomplished. If the purpose and degree of existing methods of regulation can be determined, the result should contribute toward a more specific awareness of the details involved in the subject so often referred to in general terms as "the law of outer space."

The purpose of law is to provide fair rules which are observed so that order rather than chaos prevails--to the extent that principles are observed by nations in the conduct of space activities, to the extent that members of various international organizations make rules for their own guidance. To that extent we have, and are developing, norms which guide all those operations undertaken for the use and exploration of the space environment.

This approach leads to a different result from that which contends that there is no space law or that which holds that no law can be determined until a distinction is made between airspace and outer space. Instead, there is an examination of the premise that some rules have been agreed upon and are being observed, and that with the passage of time a body of controls is developing for the conduct of international space activities....

Most space research programs are carried on by individual nations and in cases of joint projects, coordination and necessary regulation are achieved by adhering to international agreements, treaties, or informal arrangements for cooperation among nations. One of the most outstanding examples of regulation of this type is that provided for in the international convention on the "Partial Revision of the Radio Regulations (Geneva, 1959), and Additional Protocol" adopted at the Extraordinary Administrative Radio Conference on Space Communication in Geneva between October 7 and November 8, 1963, and now ratified by nine nations. The objective of this revision is the allocation of frequency bands for space radiocommunication and radioastronomy. Allocations were made for communication, meteorological, and radionavigation satellites, space research, radioastronomy, and the application of space techniques in the aviation and amateur services. Support functions were also made to space telemetering, tracking, and telecommand....

* * * * *

LEGAL PROBLEMS OF A MANNED LUNAR INTERNATIONAL LABORATORY

by

Andrew G. Haley*

Introduction.

The Lunar International Laboratory Committee was formed at the First Special Meeting of the International Academy of Astronautics held August 16, 1960, in Stockholm. Under the inspiration and guidance of Dr. Frank J. Malina, the Committee was organized to consider various aspects of a lunar laboratory, a project considered desirable and beneficial in the international cooperative effort to better understand our universe....

I. New Lunar Lands and Claims of Sovereignty

Terrestrial Precedents

A) The concept of res nullius.

Res nullius is the property of no one. There is an absence of ownership or "title" in a thing because either: (1) it is abandoned by a former owner, or (2) it was never claimed as the property of anyone, or (3) it is not susceptible of private ownership. In the latter sense, res nullius was a specific term of Roman law.

Commentators treating the question of sovereignty with regard to outer space and celestial bodies, have frequently discussed the concept of res nullius, but very few have seriously considered it applicable in the environment of outer space ....

B) The concept of res communis.

The antithesis of the concept of ownership, exclusive rights, exclusive control and sovereignty is the concept of res communis, which applies to all things enjoyed by mankind in common such as air, light and freedom of movement on the high seas....

---

*) Andrew G. Haley was counsel for the Federal Radio Commission and the Federal Communications Commission, 1933-1939. Primarily a communications lawyer, he did research for Senator C.C. Dill in drafting the Radio Act of 1927, and also the Act of 1934. He has handled scores of cases and proceedings before the United States Courts and the FCC, involving common carrier and television and radio broadcasting matters. He is General Counsel and Past President, International Astronautical Federation; Counsel, American Institute of Aeronautics and and Astronautics (AIAA); Past President and former General Counsel, American Rocket Society (ARS); Academician of the International Institute of Space Law; Vice Chairman of the Committee on the Law of Outer Space of the American Bar Association; Washington, D.C., law firm - Haley, Bader & Potts; co-founder and World War II president of Aerojet; vice-president and director, Axe Science Fund; author of Rocketry and Space Exploration [Van Nostrand, Princeton, 1958]; author of Space Law and Government [Appleton-Century-Crofts, New York, 1963]; author of numerous articles dealing with the legal, sociological and economic aspects of the Space Age; member of the United States delegations to several international radio conferences; past chairman of the Technical Committee on Space Law and Sociology of the American Institute of Aeronautics and Astronautics.

Mr. Haley has received the American Rocket Society Special Award "for distinguished service and untiring efforts" (1954); the Grotius Medal of the International Grotius Foundation for the Propagation of the Law of Nations "for his efforts in lecturing at more than a score of U.S. universities and numerous universities in Europe on the subject of space law and international cooperation" (1958); the Medal of the British Interplanetary Society "for outstanding contributions to astronautics" (1962); the AIAA G. Edward Pendray Award "for a pioneering contribution to the analysis of governmental and international legal questions arising from the rapid development of space travel and space exploration, as exemplified by his book Space Law and Government published in 1963" (1964); and other awards and honors.

*   *   *   *   *

THE CHAMBERS OF THE INTERNATIONAL COURT OF JUSTICE AND
THEIR ROLE IN THE SETTLEMENT OF DISPUTES ARISING OUT
OF SPACE ACTIVITIES

by

Dionyssios M. Poulantzas

The prospects of referring disputes arising out of space activities - or only certain among them - to a judicial organ is a problem which does not depend so much on the competence in abstracto, of that organ to render justice as on other, mostly practical, reasons. Nevertheless, the chances of a judicial settlement of these disputes would be better in a specialized international court, all the more so if the "compromise," i.e., a special agreement of the parties in each case, which in my view is the most probable method of submitting these disputes to a judicial settlement, were chosen by the parties.

In point of fact, for the solution of disputes originating in outer space there is required not only knowledge of the law of outer space - which is only now being formed - but also of technics, of astronautics, etc. Accordingly, the establishment of a specialized international court to this effect would be most useful, and quite consistent with today's trend towards a specialization of International Justice with a view to meeting the requirements of modern life and of the quickly changing the science of international law.

The setting up, however, of a specialized international court, completely independent of the International Court of Justice (I.C.J.),[1] might be somewhat dangerous. Indeed, multiplication of international courts could lead to opposite decisions on similar legal issues, with a resultant confusion in international case law.

Accordingly, the best way for the settlement of the disputes arising out of space activities by a specialized judicial organ would be their solution by a chamber of the I.C.J.[2] ....

---

1) See in general with regard to the I.C.J. and disputes arising from space exploration Andrew G. Haley, Space Law and Government, New York, 1963, pp 149, 259.

2) It is not intended, however, to deny the fact that the I.C.J. has so far met successfully cases where special and technical knowledge was indispensable, as e.g., in the Fisheries case (1951) or in the Minquiers en Ecrehos case (1953). At any rate, the forming of a Chamber for dealing with "space cases" would prove most valuable to this effect (See Dionyssios M. Poulantzas, The Legal Status of Artificial Satellites, Revue hellénique de droit international, January-December 1961, p. 227.

BASIC STAGES AND IMMEDIATE PROSPECTS OF THE

DEVELOPMENT OF OUTER SPACE LAW

by

G. P. Zhukov

It is important for all mankind and first of all for cosmonauts, brave explorers of
outer space, that a stable law should dominate in outer space which would exclude arbitrary
rule and lawlessness and which would ban the conducting there of experiments harmful to
life and health of people.

To achieve such law in outer space, it is necessary to conclude international agreements which would bind states by firm legal commitments and would establish such rules of
states' behavior in outer space that would contribute to the development of friendly relations among states and would ban such activities in space which could cause damage to other
states rights and interests.

In the first stage of the outer space exploration, it was enough to acknowledge that international law, including the United Nations Charter, promoted the penetration of a man into outer space. This was confirmed by the United Nations General Assembly in its resolutions 1721 (XVI) and 1804 (XVII). Practically, it meant that a certain rule of law had been
established in outer space along the lines of which states should conduct their activities.
And first of all, it meant that states' actions in space should be in compliance with the
principles of peaceful coexistence which constitute the foundation both for the United Nations Charter and (all existing actually at present) international law.

Yet, life urgently demanded that these general provisions should be defined concretely
and developed, taking into account the specific features of activities in space. In connection with this a necessity arose to develop just and humane principles of outer space law
calling for the regulation of the activities of states in space. The Soviet Government un-
dertook the initiative in putting this question up for discussion. Guided by the interests
of further progress in space exploration and in the development of international cooperation
in this field, the Soviet Union presented to the United Nations a clear and extended program
which was laid down in the Soviet draft of the Declaration of Basic Principles of States'
Activities in the Exploration and Use of Outer Space, first submitted in May 1962 and then
later in April 1963 in a revised form....

Now it is universally acknowledged that outer space is a "property" of all mankind.
"Achievements in the exploration of space, said N.S. Khrushchev--as well as space itself--
are property of all mankind. That is why the results of exploration of space should be for
universal benefit, benefit for all peoples living on our wonderful planet, the Earth."
It is for these reasons that the Declaration approved the principle that Outer
space and celestial bodies cannot be a national property. In combination with the prohibition to place and to test nuclear weapons in outer space, this provision of the Declaration
forms a legal guarantee of using outer space in the interests and for the benefit of all mankind.

Distinct from celestial bodies, which cannot be a national property, artificial
space objects belong to the state where they are registered no matter where they are. Ac-

cording to the Declaration such objects or their parts, if found beyond the territory of the state where they are registered, should be returned to that state. This particular feature distinguishes them from meteorites falling to the Earth and which are usually called "res nullius."

With the development of astronautics a problem may arise as to what kind of law people on board a space ship or orbital station should obey? In respect to objects in outer space the Declaration solves this problem by analogy with ships in the high seas.

The Declaration says that a state which registered the object launched in outer space, maintains also its jurisdiction and control over such object and its crew during their stay in outer space....

* * * * *

RELATIONSHIP BETWEEN AIR LAW AND THE LAW OF OUTER SPACE
by
T. Verplaetze

Two Opinions.

From the very outset, research on the law of outer space has been primarily conducted by air lawyers.

Nonetheless, it has been generally held that the regime of outer space is entirely different from that of the airspace. Fundamental disparity between them was seen as freedom from sovereignty in outer space against subjection to sovereignty for airspace. In that prospect it might be thought that maritime lawyers, riding the waves of the Free Main, were the proper experts to build the new rules. Since maritime lawyers were not called in, some quirk may appear in the antithetical position....

I. Basic Premise.

One may start from a general rule of law, which has been stated in the context of the law of the High Seas, by Myres McDougal, as follows:

"The regime of the High Seas ... composed of two complementary sets of prescriptions ... one ... under the label of "freedom of the Seas" ... the other ... to honor ... claims ... which may interfere ... . To the initiated, these prescriptions and technical terms are not absolute, inelastic dogmas but rather flexible policy preferences, permitting decision makers a very broad discretion ... for promoting major policies."

A similar pattern can be upheld for a human vision of the law of outer space. Whatever the time of thought and shape of legal construction, any human approach will be based on the bipolarity of freedom and restraint....

II. Peculiar Position of Air Law with Respect to the Law of Space.

There are two vistas leading to the connection between air law and the law of outer space.

The first is the argument of analogy ....

The second avenue from air to outer space is the argument that outer space activity postulates air law....

* * * * *

II.   <u>Other Contributions and Comments</u>

Among other papers included in this Colloquium, some dealt with the legal problems associated with international space communications. A number of significant questions were
raised by I. Cheprov of the USSR, who emphasized that the matter of space exploration is of
concern to states and that a system of international communications by means of satellites
must be established on a truly international basis and on the basis of the principle of
equality of states.

Several writers, including Nicholas M. Poulantzas and Istvan Herczeg, concentrated on
the legal character of the resolutions of the United Nations General Assembly concerning
outer space. Poulantzas took the position that, despite the fact that   United Nations
resolutions have no legal binding force, they may be regarded "as a psychological element
concerning the necessity of a certain practice, the opinio necessitatis." Herczeg, on the
other hand, came to the conclusion that General Assembly Resolutions are "not yet a rule of
international law" and are "not binding upon states which are not members of the organization." However, they are binding "upon member states in the sense at least that they should
refrain from any kind of attitude that could prevent that resolution from developing into a
generally accepted rule of international law."

In addition to giving a comprehensive survey of the legal problems of a manned lunar international laboratory, Andrew G. Haley also discussed various aspects and developments in
the field of medical jurisprudence in relation to outer space. He reviewed scientific developments, including research projects and their developments in the United States and the
Soviet Union.

The various principles incorporated in the resolutions of the United Nations General
Assembly were reviewed by Morton S. Jaffe in a fairly detailed manner. They were also discussed by William A. Hyman in his paper on "Wanted - Law and Policemen in Space..."

Manfred Lachs discussed his 1964 lectures at The Hague Academy of International Law on
"The International Law of Outer Space" in which he dealt <u>inter alia</u> with the extension of
international law into outer space, the special status of outer space as subject of international law, the legal status of celestial bodies, the peaceful use of outer space, disarmament, and the creation of sound foundations for peaceful cooperation.

Other papers reviewed questions of liability for damage caused by spacecraft (I.H.P. de
Rode-Verschoor), the sources and fundamental constitution of space law (Von Rauchhaupt), the
general principles of law (Janos Kiss), the activities of the Space Law Committee of the
Hungarian Lawyers' Association (Szadeczky-Kardoss) and various reports of the working groups
of the International Institute of Space Law (Cooper and Haley).

The paper dealing with liability drew upon pertinent resolutions of the United Nations
General Assembly dealing with outer space, in particular the Declaration of Legal Principles

133

governing the activities of states in the exploration and use of outer space. In addition, the paper also touched upon the question of liability of an international organization, such as, for example, the European Launcher Development Organization (ELDO). The paper also noted the direct bearing that the registration of objects launched into outer space has on the subject of liability for damages.

The article by Zhukov dwelt, in particular, on the various principles incorporated in the Declaration of Legal Principles. Among those were mentioned the principle of freedom of exploration and use of outer space, the principle of international responsibility of states for national activities in space, the principle of free access, the duty of states to refrain from potentially harmful experiments in outer space, the ownership of artificial space objects, the general principle to render all possible help to distressed astronauts and the principle of international responsibility for damage caused by an artificial space object.

The presentation by von Rauchhaupt traced the sources of space law and pointed out that outer space is free "from any sovereignty that could be claimed by any state." In addition to reviewing the beginnings of academic and scientific concern with the legal problems arising out of man's activities in outer space, the report also considered the question of whether judicial decisions or legislative action is the most suitable for the development of space law. Finally, the paper touched upon the questions pertaining to what the writer called "fundamental constitution" of space law.

Most of the discussion by Janos Kiss dealt with various resolutions of the U.N. General Assembly and the International Institute of Space Law and concluded by calling for international regulation concerning the legal status of the moon.

- - - - -

EIGHTH COLLOQUIUM ON THE LAW OF OUTER SPACE

ATHENS, 1965

I. Texts Reproduced

INTERNATIONAL   ORGANIZATIONS FOR COOPERATION IN SPACE AND THE PROBLEM OF LIABILITY

FOR SPACE ACTIVITIES

by

Michel Georges Bourely

Among the host of legal problems involved in the question of liability for space
activities, those created by the existence of international organizations for cooperation in space are particularly likely to repay an attentive consideration.

As you will be aware, there are two organizations of an institutional character now
in being, both formed by European countries imbued by the wish to see Western Europe play-
ing a part in the peaceful contest now being waged in space. They are the European Space
Research Organization (ESRO/CERS) and the European Organization for the Development and
Construction of Space Vehicle Launchers (ELDO/CECLES). But you will also be aware that
another form of cooperation - this time world wide - has just come into being with the entry
into force of the Washington agreements establishing interim rules for a commercial system
of global telecommunication by satellite.

Thus international organizations engaging in space activities have become a present-
day reality whose incidence on the question of liability demands to be examined.

What are, from the standpoint of legal theory, the specific problems arising from the
application to international organizations of the acknowledged principles governing liability in respect to space activities?

What attitude is adopted in practice by the existing organizations for international
cooperation?

These are the two questions which this paper will attempt to answer...

There is only one positive legal text on the subject that can be invoked in the case
in point, namely, Resolution No. 1962 (XVIII) of the United Nations General Assembly entitled the "Declaration of Legal Principles Governing Activities of States in the Exploration and Use of Outer Space," point 5 of which says: "When activities are carried on in
outer space by an International Organization, responsibility for compliance with the principles set forth in this Declaration shall be borne by the International Organization and
by the States participating in it."

Thus an international organization is indeed required to observe the principle of indemnification of the loss or damage referred to in point 8 of the same Declaration, both
under its own responsibility (in the moral and political sense of the word) and under that

of the States who are members of it. The formula used in the Declaration implies recognition that the international organizations have a specific, but non-exclusive responsibility for making good loss or damage caused by their activities in space.

The interlocutory question being thus answered in the affirmative, the fundamental consequence of recognizing the international space organizations to be subject to the Convention on liability is that they are on the same footing as States in respect of their rights and obligations.

Of course, the international organizations are affected by all the provisions that will figure in the agreement, and in particular by the nature, whether absolute or otherwise, of their liability, and by that of the limitation of the total amount of compensation. But what is to be noted here are the consequences that flow from the fact that the rights and obligations stemming from the Convention devolve on an organization and not the member States that compose it.

Thus the style of "owner" or "launcher" of the space vehicle will accrue to the international organizations. Hence the requirements (still to be defined) as regards control identification, registration and notification of launchings will also apply to them. This will greatly simplify the situation and facilitate the claims procedure.

Similarly the international organization will be entitled, if the case arises, to invoke their rights as victims and obtain direct compensation for loss or damage sustained by them ....

*   *   *   *   *

SUMMARY OF GENERAL REMARKS
by
Andrew G. Haley

THE TRADITIONAL BASES OF INTERNATIONAL LAW

The fundamental nature of human law is determined by its anthropocentric character. With this in mind, two traditional schools of international law, the positivist orientation and the natural law theory, can be analyzed, and their fundamental conflict examined. If the writings of leading positivists are discussed, and the general theory of the positivist position explained, and the philosophy of natural law is discussed, it can be shown that the latter is a more desirable basis for the emergence of a new international law of space. Natural law is based upon unchanging fundamental moral principles arising out of the nature of man, and its role as a guide to change of specific rules of law in accord with changing circumstances must be examined. The problem of the need for change in the law must be discussed in light of the counter-balancing need for stability which is an essential character of the law. A brief historical review indicates that the philosophy of natural law was first suggested as a basis for international law at a time when a revolutionary new problem similar to that of our own time had just arisen -- the discovery of the new world. The unfortunate consequences of the failure to adopt such a basis at that time are well known. Consent of the nations, i.e., the process of tacit expression of consent through custom and usage, has been introduced as a basic step in the international law-making process...

136

Through application of accepted practices, the nations of the earth have developed a new principle of international law -- i.e., by common consent to an evolutionary step they have acknowledged that outer space may be used for peaceful and scientific purposes without regard to the national sovereignty of subjacent territory. An extension of this principle is found in recent developments directed toward the creation of satellite systems in the communications, meteorological, and radiation fields ....

* * * * *

THE ORIGIN AND PRESENT STATE OF SPACE LAW
by
Fr. W. von Rauchhaupt

Historical events and technique

1) The usual methods of propulsion about the beginning of the present century were the horse-drawn carriage and the railway, the bicycle, and the often asthmatical motorcar. The airplane followed. Motorcars and airplanes were gaining importance. The names of the rocket-researchers Goddard in the USA, Ziolowsky in Russia, Ganswindt in Germany, Oberth in Rumania, and Werner von Braun were known only much later ....

VI. The legal outlook

A reliable outlook on the future development of Space Law could scarcely be predicted, but a few limits could be marked.

1)a. Space Law is dependent on Space Politics. A sensible cooperation in these two new spheres seems advisable. Some neutral aspects of these spheres promise good results: in the research of the weather, in the distribution of news, and most likely also in medicine and biology. Certain difficulties are still apparent in respect to research and technology. The atom test on Earth and the prohibition of armaments in the Outer Space were accepted because of the fear of otherwise threatening greater dangers.

b. In research the Iron Curtain of politics hinders quick results. Mutual efforts in this regard, though, are tried. These efforts are mostly restricted to collaboration at international congresses, scientific institutes, and through libraries. Slowly the interest in a closer exchange of experiences in Space Research is growing. The centers for such exchange remain, however, with the USA Congress in Washington, D.C., the United Nations in New York and though only meeting occasionally for short periods, the most important meetings in Geneva, Paris and elsewhere in Europe.

c. Keeping pace with technology naturally requires careful attention to advancements in the field. The opposition may hinder fruitful work, but it may, as well, incite better results. The USA publishes much new material. Recent findings are not treated as secret. The information is accessible to everybody in the USA and Western Europe. There is no Iron Curtain to close off the West, but little sign of reciprocity is shown from the East ....

* * * * *

SOURCES OF THE LAW OF OUTER SPACE
by
Julian G. Verplaetse

I. SUBJECT

It has been generally assumed that, starting from our sublunar premises way into the deep horizons of extra-terrestrial spaces, the sources of the law applicable to human activities in this field should be patterned after those of international law in terrestrial society.

This view offers the most reasonable, or the least unreasonable, analogy in a domain where all analogies are shaky and hazardous.

Starting from this assumption, it is only natural, on point of method, to accept likewise the help of Article 38 of the Statute of the World Court, which, although stating a ruling procedural in nature, is a good guideline for any substance of international calibre.

II. CONVENTIONS

There are now at least four main international agreements which apply in small or larger measure to outer space:

1. The Test-Stop Treaty signed at Moscow August 5, 1963, banning nuclear weapons tests in the atmosphere, in outer space and under water, which became effective on October 10, 1963.

2. The limited agreement between NASA and the Soviet Akademia Nauk, beginning June 8, 1962, on technical matters of meteorological satellites, mapping of the earth's magnetic field, and experiments in space communications.

3. The unique experience of COMSAT, the American Corporation of Telecommunication in outer space, which was accepted (reluctantly, as far as Europeans go, who, for the first time in history, acted as an international entity: The European Conference on Space Communications) by most nations of the "Western world" as well as Japan and Australia. This American act was the sole basis of the Interim Agreement for Global Telecommunications signed at Washington, August 20, 1964, both entering into force that very day.

4. The International Telecommunications Convention at Geneva, December 21, 1959, complemented by the Partial Revision of Radio Regulations at Geneva, November 8, 1963, allocated, for the first time in history, frequency bands for space communication purposes, giving approximately 15% of the spectrum (6000 négahers) to those communications.

Those direct applications of conventional international law apart, room for analogy of any earth-bound international convention is tiny ...

V. ACTIVITIES OF THE UNITED NATIONS, CHIEFLY THE RESOLUTIONS AND
RECOMMENDATIONS OF THE GENERAL ASSEMBLY.

Whatever their value as material source, it is generally agreed that, outside the narrow sector of administrative matters and the special case of Chapter VII of the Charter, UN activities are not formal sources by themselves. Even parties thereto have not subscribed to formal commitment and have not intended to do so.

Therefore the Resolutions and Recommendations of the General Assembly have to be granted their own value, and nothing else. Nor can they be likened to customary law, nor even to the teachings of jurists and publicists (Art. 38 (a) Statute).

CONCLUSION

The obvious path to be trodden is the international convention, although a general charter of outer space is definitely premature.

*   *   *   *   *

TO WHOM DOES SPACE BELONG?

by

Pompeo Magno

The imagery and eventually the more concrete conquest of cosmos by man have been heralded to the whole world by the latest well-publicized spacial enterprises. A few days ago, the first man who had been in direct contact with spacial emptiness returned to earth.

Man's first direct entrance into space is not an isolated event; it is the beginning of the realization of a program already predetermined - the moon operation - a program envisaged by the Soviets secretly a few years ago and now openly pursued by the Americans.

Plans for landing on the moon were put into operation in 1957 when both nations passed the borders into space. The purpose of the landing was not one of territorial occupation, nor the innocent examination of a celestial body. The ulterior motive was the establishment on the moon of a spaceship carrier from where the ships could leave with greater ease for voyages and exploration of greater distances.

There are many difficulties in launching space satellites and instruments from the earth. To surmount these, it has been necessary to employ talented men to break through tremendous technological barriers -- i.e., the braking action of atmosphere and the terrestrial attraction force -- at a pace only the two most powerful nations could afford.

The Two Principal Questions.

With the sportsmanlike enthusiasm and with the euphorical climate which followed the spacial activities of these two great Nations still today in competition, we must focus on two principal questions:

What is the purpose of the conquest of the cosmos, and what benefits can be derived from it for man?

Will the spatial enterprises increase or prejudice the possibility of human peace?...

These considerations have formulated the first and most important problem which relates to space: the problem of the space juridical regime. In other terms, to whom does space belong? Whose is it or to whom will it belong?

The first theory which was presented, but is now actually abandoned by the scholars and is not adopted by any state, confirms that the State which lies below the space spreads its sovereignty to the same space. This theory is the application into the outer space of the principles which regulate atmospherical space. It is known that, according to the aeronautical law, each State is sovereign over the air column, or more precisely, over the space above the ground of its own territory. This principle is accepted universally in the aeronautical field enforced by the international conventions and concluded by more diverse national laws existing in each State.

The fundamental convention for the settlement of the Aerial Navigation was stipulated in Paris on 10-13-1919 and confirmed by treaty in Chicago in 1944. Article 1 precisely establishes: "The negotiating members recognize that each power has the full sovereignty and exclusive right to the atmospherical space above its territory and above the territorial waters."

Article 1 of the Italian national law of 8-20-1923 says, "The State exercises its full and exclusive sovereignty on the atmospherical space above its own territory and also that of the territorial waters."

Article 1 of the Soviet aviation code of 4-7-1935, ratifies that "The full and exclusive sovereignty of the space above the USSR belongs to the Union of the Socialist Soviet Republics."

The United States aviation law of 1926, incorporated in the aeronautical civil law of 1938, established that "The United States possesses and exercises complete and exclusive national sovereignty to the space above all internal waters and space above the adjoining far sea."

But the regime of sovereignities adopted and applied to atmospherical space has demonstrated since the beginning that it has been inapplicable in outer space....

The Possibility of Conflict.

We affirm, therefore, that the aeronautical law of sovereignty to the space above the territory of each State is not applicable to the external space stratum.

From the first moment, this doctrine of sovereignty has caused reverberations among those who must apply existing aeronautical laws to outer space. Today States refrain from asking other States for authorization or permission to fly over their territory. Conformance is requested by the international conventions and aeronautical systems. Not only has the request for authorization been neglected, but the States which should grant such authorization have not felt damaged by the absence of their permission. Any future protests could be met with the claim that the State had already renunciated its own sovereignty.

* * * * *

THE FUTURE INTERNATIONAL AGENCY FOR THE

ADMINISTRATION OF COSMOS

The ICAO's Candidature

by

Michel Smirnoff

It sounds pretty otpimistic, not to mention fantastic, if some 3 milliards of little beings called "men" think they can administrate Cosmos. However, all the authors of articles and even books on this problem of the administration of Cosmos think in terms of the administration of human activities in Cosmos, a concept much narrower and much more precise. But the authors who have written on this problem, and they are many, do often speak of the necessity to install order in the Cosmos. It is true that in the last eight years since the first Russian satellite went into the skies, many things have been achieved in Astronautics and many efforts have been made to expand the opportunities for man to reach the Cosmos. However, we are still in the period of beginnings, and we still do not know what occurs on the planets and what kind of surprises are in store for us. Therefore, we shall in this article limit the expression "administration of Cosmos" to the administration of human activities in Cosmos. The development of new projects in Astronautics increases every day, and the USSR and USA are not now the sole States interested in Space activity. The problem of organizing an international and central administration for this activity is important in view of the possible conflicts which could be generated by such activity.

The idea of that organisation was anticipatory, and many authors agreed on the necessity of its being under the auspices of the United Nations Organisation. Among those authors many claimed that this organisation must be truly a world organisation embracing all the States of the Earth, even those which are not members of UNO....

The Candidature of ICAO for the Title of

Specialised Agency for Outer Space

It was quite natural that the International Civil Aviation Organisation (ICAO), an authority in the field of civil air transportation and in general in all problems of aeronautics, should be interested from the beginning in the problems created by the appearance of man in Outer Space. The analogy between aeronautics and Air Law on the one hand and astronautics and the peaceful uses of Outer Space and Cosmic Law on the other hand was natural and logical even to people outside of ICAO. Therefore, this interest in ICAO as an organisation which could help create new norms of law for Cosmos came not only from within ICAO itself, but also from without.

ICAO iteslf declared its interest in the problems of Outer Space as early as 1956 during its Tenth Annual Meeting in Caracas. It was there that ICAO, although with some reserve, underlined its interest in these new problems and especially in the effects cosmic navigation could have on the development of air transportation. Only three years later in a report which the Secretary of ICAO presented to the Ad Hoc Committee on the Peaceful Uses of Outer Space of UNO, on May 15, 1959, ICAO once more spoke of its interest in these problems: "The cooperation must be effected on the international level with the aim to insure the security of air transportation in the moments of launching of Space Vehicles or of their return in the atmosphere." The problems which ICAO is especially interested in are the allocation of frequencies in radio communications in Outer Space, the identification of Space Vehicles and the accidents of those vehicles which could generate the damages on Earth or in the air. To underline this study character of the ICAO's interest to the Outer Space problems it is necessary to say that ICAO edited one of the first Bibliographies of Outer Space....

There are some authors who say that all that is needed is an addition to Art. 1 of the Chicago Convention of 1944, a new paragraph which would continue the control of ICAO outside the Earth's atmosphere. In addition to this simplified approach there are many well known authors (M. Aaronson, Professor Moyer and Professor Pepin, to mention only a few) who also say that ICAO is fit completely to assume this duty of the administration of human activities in Outer Space. Professor Nicolas Mattesco thinks it was a great error that the experience of ICAO was not sufficiently called upon in the past whenever problems of Outer Space were raised. Professor Metteesvos' opinion is that ICAO should have been invited, at least as a member, when the Ad Hoc Committee on the Peaceful Uses of Outer Space was created.

Another group of scientists, besides this group, wants to give full control to ICAO in Outer Space. This is the so-called medium group which advocates that the experience of ICAO must be fully utilised in the study and exploration of Outer Space. They think that full collaboration with ICAO must be achieved, but they think that at the moment ICAO in its present formation could not carry out the role of the specialised UN agency for Outer Space. Among those authors we cite Eilene Galloway, Cyril Horsford and also our own ideas which correlate with the ideas of that group of scientists. Mrs. Eilene Galloway believes that any organ regulating Outer Space should utilise the rich experience of ICAO. Mr. Horsford thinks that any such agency must be patterned after ICAO with the sole difference that such agency will be not based on the Chicago Convention terms, but on the terms of new rules not based on the idea of the sovereignty of different States in Outer Space. In an article written for the First Colloquium on the Law of Outer Space in Amsterdam-The Hague, 1958, we explicitly pointed out that an international conference on Outer Space must be initiated by the United Nations. An entire paragraph of that article was devoted to giving such an initiative to the ICAO: "... On that very place we want to mention the possibility to give to ICAO the initiative for the calling of such Conference. Owing to its experience, ICAO should be the most convenient organisation to treat this problem...."

* * * * *

SPACE ACTIVITY AND INTELLECTUAL PROPERTY

by

Imre Mora

Preamble

In the following short outline an attempt will be made to throw a light upon the relationship between space activity, space law, and the principal forms of intellectual property, copyright and patent law.

For the readers of the present paper there is no need to emphasize the revolution which space activity has brought about in the field of law. Old legal concepts are suddenly in need of being revised and new ones are born; in short, a new science - space law - emerges.

It goes without saying that space activity has its effects in the domain of intellectual property too. The questions arising in this field bear two different characters: a) practical problems, i.e., ones arising already or in the immediate future; b) problems arising in connections with the exploits of the distant future (in other words, hypotheses). We shall deal with the pertinent questions in this order laying emphasis, of course, on the ones belonging to the first category.

Problems of immediate concern are, for example:

1) The legal protection (by copyright or otherwise) of scientific information

   a) obtained in the course of space activity,

   b) transmitted by space objects (satellites),

2) the legal protection of transmissions from earth to earth, but via a telecommunication satellite,

3) the patentable nature of inventions connected with space activity....

I. Space activity and copyright law.

Before we proceed to answer the specific questions raised in the Preamble, a few general remarks seem necessary concerning the nature, content, and extent of a copyright. Most of the readers of the present paper will be acquainted with the basic concepts of copyright law; therefore, we shall forbear proving our theses and to go into details.

In spite of differences in the legislation of various states, copyright, in most legal systems, is the <u>author's subjective right to dispose of the result of his creation - the work - and to exploit it commercially</u>. Very appropriately in many languages copyright is called "author's right."

Now an interesting feature of <u>subjective</u> copyright, which we should like to emphasize, is its coherence, its united character. By this we do not mean that concerning the same work, identical law would apply in every country (this question belongs to the domain of positive substantive law), but that the author's right concerning a given work is unified.

The author may grant part-licences on his work. For instance, he may agree to its being performed, published, translated, etc.; such part-licences may be subjected to different legal systems, but this does not change the fact that the basic right remains unified and, generally, under the rule of a well-defined legal system....

Summing up the problem, we may say that the copyright legal relations of scientific information obtained with the help of space objects are not governed by any special laws (space-copyright law), but by the national law of the interested states and the "terrestrial" international law applicable to them.

The legal protection of transmissions from earth to earth via the telecommunication satellites.

The former problem logically leads up to the present one. The Telstar, Syncom, Molniya - type artificial moons not only are apt to transmit programs, but were expressly built for this purpose. What, then, is the position here?

Once more, there is no need to invoke space law for the solution. The program-transmitting celestial bodies are, essentially, objects placed there by, and belonging to, a state. They are no more than a link in a microwave chain, although a link placed outside the sovereignty of any state. Thus, anybody who can may freely receive their programs, just as one receives a radio station, but not for public performances or relays which fall within the limitations of copyright laws....

II. Space activity and patent laws.

The character of patent law is entirely different from that of copyright. While subjective copyright - as mentioned before - is unified, is coherent, patent law is not and does not attach to the creation of the invention (i.e. the "work"), but to the registration thereof. While in most countries the mere creation of a work ensures copyright for it (even in countries where registration is necessary, some measure of legal protection attaches to the work), the mere creation of an invention never secures protection for it under the patent law.

Independently from the question whether the respective patent law (i.e. the substantive rules) of the various countries are uniform or not, subjective patent right will exist only in that country where the competent Patent Office has recognized it by having registered the patent. Even the Patent Convention (the London Text enacted in Hungary under Decree-Law No. 17 of 1962) only grants priority for patent registration in another union-state (Art. 4) but does not give a patent right beyond the state where the patent was actually registered....

III.(2) Copyright protection in space.

This is not as far-fetched as it seems. Already there is a big hue and cry because a few air transport companies are showing films during air travel, and others plan to engage live comedians. They are accused of unfair competition. And we have heard about space-faring aircraft, in the design stage, which will have no windows. Is it possible that the passengers will be shown films in space in order to divert their attention? If so, to whom are the performing fees due, and which states organizations will collect them? Well, we may venture the statement that this question too will be governed by <u>the law of the flag</u>, and not by the law of the country above which the airspace-craft is flying (or-biting).

III(3) <u>Exploitation in space of inventions patented on Earth</u>.

Without going into details we merely wish to point out that under patent law, "exploi-tation" usually means industrial exploitation used on a larger scale. Simple use of pat-ented inventions does not constitute an infringement of patent. In consequence, this prob-lem will not arise for a long time. We merely mentioned this because there was news about a process enabling extraction of water from minerals also found on the Moon. This might involve exploitation of a patent....

* * * * *

LEGAL PROBLEMS AND GENERAL PRINCIPLES OF SPACE LAW

by

Constantine G. Vaicoussis

The spectacular recent evolution and frequent launching of various types of rockets, spacecraft, and spaceships daily endangers world peace and universal security.

To face this serious danger, multilateral agreements should be signed among nations, especially on the following two most important subjects, namely, legal status of Outer Space and legal status of the celestial bodies.

In launching manned spacecrafts there may most probably occur either bodily injuries or even deaths of persons on board the spacecraft and/or persons and property on the surface of the earth. Responsibility in such cases for indemnities to the persons in question should be closely related to the nationality of the spacecraft. The aforementioned legal questions will call for future regulations to be agreed upon by international agreements or conventions.

For this reason, I should like to submit the following draft agreements or conventions as a basis for further discussions.

LEGAL STATUS OF OUTER SPACE

For a scientific and peaceful research of Outer Space a multilateral international agreement should be adopted under the auspices of the United Nations ....

* * * * *

145

II. Other Contributions and Comments

As in the Proceedings of the Seventh Colloquium on the Law of Outer Space, in this Colloquium we also find discussions of the legal character of the United Nations General Assembly resolutions. In addition, more space is devoted to the legal problems of communications by satellites. Among the writers discussing the latter topic may be mentioned Professor Aldo Armando Cocca, Andrew G. Haley, William A. Hyman, Jozsef Ivany and Marco G. Markoff.

Professor Cocca's contribution consisted of an "introductory report" in which he addressed himself to the question of whether a single global communication system or a plurality of systems should be established. He raised the question of what provisions should be adopted to assure maximum cooperation in case of the creation of several systems. He touched upon the procedure for fixing, approving and controlling international communications programs as well as the question of which authority should make decisions in case of interference with communications. He also posed the question of relations between national regulatory bodies, the International Telecommunications Union, and the consortium or international organizations. Finally, he drew attention to the necessity of evaluating problems of patent, copyright and national cultures.

In addition to addressing himself to some of the aforementioned problems of space communications, Andrew G. Haley drew attention to the technical, economic and political aspects of the consideration of the convenience of a single vs. a plurality of communications systems.

William A. Hyman's paper dealt with the background and development of the communication satellite corporation and the controversy surrounding its establishment.

The paper presented by Jozsef Ivany dealt with aspects of the protection of radio astronomy in the legal framework of telecommunications, the results of the International Telecommunications, the results of the International Telecommunication Conference of 1959, and the actions taken to satisfy frequency claims. He raised the question of whether or not outer space is a free area for radio activity and discussed the role of telecommunications by communication satellites on a global scale. He also reviewed the telecommunication policy connected with the new technology and touched upon problems of monopolies, charges, the role of the ITU and the International Institute of Space Law in developing the law of communications.

Professor Markoff's discussion acquainted the reader with the American and Soviet positions concerning communications by satellite and pointed to the element of novelty of such communications and their effect on international relations which he felt should serve the noble cause of international understanding and rapprochement.

In addition to the papers dealing with legal problems of space communications, the papers presented by Eugène Pépin, F.B. Schick and Jerzy Sztucki may be mentioned. The article by Eugène Pépin concentrated on the important topic of the teaching and study of space law of the world. The paper listed the names of countries and institutions at which space law had been taught either as part of a course on Public International Law or as a complimentary subject to Air Law, or as an idependently taught course. In addition, the paper also included a list of organizations, both permanent and non-permanent, listed by countries, concerned with the study of the legal problems of outer space.

In his article on the subjective approach, Professor Schick discussed both the fundamental principles applicable to aerospace activities as well as the development of specific norms for aerospace. In addition, he examined the interrelationship between space law and the problem of national security. The concluding part of the presentation dealt with the common law of outer space.

Some of the initial problems pertaining to the legal status of space objects were discussed by Jerzy Sztucki. The writer analyzed the relevant discussions of the United Nations Legal Sub-Committee as well as various provisions of the International Radio Regulations and raised some significant questions with respect to the name, definition, and classification of space objects.

Both the Seventh and Eights Colloquia have significantly contributed to the clarification and development of the law of outer space, and a brief review can hardly do justice to the wealth of thoughts and contributions included in them.

- - - - -

NINTH COLLOQUIUM ON THE LAW OF OUTER SPACE

MADRID, 1966

I. Texts Reproduced

COMMUNICATIONS IN ORBIT: A PROGNOSIS FOR WORLD PEACE

by

Jerome Morenoff

I. Introduction: The majority of space law literature to date dealing with communications satellites has been concerned primarily with such tangible concepts as frequency control, the Communcations Satellite Act of 1962, the International Consortium, and so forth. Although many of the fundamental legal issues concerning space communications have already been partially resolved, inadequate attention has been focused upon the status of Communications satellites in the context of an emerging customary law for outer space. It is my intention to remedy this inadequacy and place in proper perspective the effect of customary international law on the future of communications satellites. Once this has been accomplished, I will indicate a positive trend which may eventually form the basis for world peace through space law and order.

Already, the skeleton of international space law has been constructed in a series of United Nations resolutions. Basic to this law is the concept that outer space is regarded as free for "peaceful" purposes, and that no one nation or group of nations has the right to "appropriate" outer space for its own use. In light of these stipulations, the implications of a military communications satellite system such as that advanced by the United States Defense Department, or of some future system which may combine both military and commercial functions, must be considered. The legal question involved becomes one of definition and reflection of political ideologies: Is a system serving military purposes antithetical to the concept of "peaceful" purposes? A comprehensive investigation of the subject based on evolving customary law indicates that this could become a point of contention among world powers. However, experience in the analogous situation of reconnaissance satellites has shown that expediency may persuade governments to enter into a state of "mutual concession" which would gradually evolve into customary law, thus converting the semantic distinction into a moot issue.

Directly related to this question of "peaceful" versus "military" uses of outer space and the concept of "mutual concession" is the subject of existing and potential patterns of management control of communications satellites. Possible systems of management may be classified into the following categories:

(1) Unilateral -- such as state-owned or privately-owned systems;

(2) Multilateral -- such as cooperative ventures among various states, i.e., International Consortium;

(3) The desirable International Global-Cooperative Space Communications System.

Within the context of this problem, we are again confronted with the dilemma of legal definition. Could a unilaterally or multilaterally managed system be vulnerable to the accusation of "appropriating" outer space? The Soviet objection to the Consortium as being controlled by American interests indicates that it might.

A possible prognosis for these legal implications may be found, again, in a comparison with reconnaissance satellite systems, which seem to be progressing through a state of mutual acceptance toward a hoped-for, eventual system of international control. In like manner, we may expect communications satellites to become an accepted and conceded reality both under unilateral and multilateral management. Only when these hurdles of minor though significant objections are overcome can we expect that the East and West will be able to fully realize the disadvantages inherent in individual "global" systems. Once this point is reached it must logically be followed by constructive negotiations to form a single global communications satellite system under the auspices of an international organization, such as the United Nations. This paper will demonstrate the trend toward this desirable goal. To effectively accomplish this task, the concept of customary international law and its effect on the development of a code for outer space must be comprehensively analyzed and thoroughly understood in order to demonstrate its applicability to communications satellite developments.

II: An Emerging Law for Outer Space: I will not belabor this audience with a detailed discussion of the elements of customary international law. I will, however, briefly indicate the criteria which must be satisfied before a custom can be considered law in the international sense. Basically, there are two elements necessary to the formulation of customary law: usage and opinio juris. Usage is generally referred to as the "material" element which encompasses the actual practice of a stipulation. This may be either a positive act, or the omission of such, functioning according to the variables of duration, frequency, and uniformity, and being initiated by the so-called "resource" states, or those who have the opportunity and capability of participating. Opinio juris is the "subjective" or psychological element in customary law. It is the feeling or "mental" attitude on the part of the resources state that the action which it is undertaking is necessary and legally just or is required for future legal order.

Although these requirements are definitive, they are still subject to various interpretations. Usage, for example, may vary in the required frequency and duration. The subjective element may relate to various norms, extending to all aspects of prior authority, morality, natural law, reason, and religion. It is interesting to note that the sources to which authorities determining such viable law may turn for concurrence are not limited to international agreements, but include every written document, every record, act, or spoken work, which presents an authentic picture of the practice of states in their international dealings.

At one time, an extensive period was required to incorporate a principle into the body of customary international law. Present world affairs have a more inclusive effect on the entire community. Of primary significance in this modern era is the existence of international bodies such as the United Nations, which play a vital role by giving nations an open opportunity to express their particular community expectations. As such, these organizations become an important new source of international law.

In the realm of outer space, it is generally agreed that a large order of definitive law would only handicap the natural development of this vast area of infinite potential. The trend, therefore, has been toward the gradual evolvement of a customary legal structure from which to control activities in outer space. Such a body of customary prescriptions insuring freedom of access to outer space has been developing during the past decade. It is important to emphasize, however, that this freedom of exploration and use of outer space is expressly limited to "peaceful purposes." It is clear that all the requirements necessary for establishing the customary law, which maintains this freedom, have been acceded to. Concerning the material requirement of "usage," the resource states have uniformly and continuously utilized this claimed right in launching numerous satellites, and those states who were not able to actively participate have made use of the doctrine either by their open support of this activity or by their failure to protest and claim sovereign rights. As for the subjective requirement: opinio juris, that the employing states had rightful intentions is confirmed by the extensive support given this doctrine by states in international meetings and conferences, by high-ranking officials in their position as representatives of opinion, and by legal organizations and by scholars from many nations.

III: <u>Military versus peaceful uses of outer space</u>: This concept, unfortunately, is imprecise with respect to the meaning of "peaceful" purposes. In some instances, the characterization of an activity as peaceful or non-peaceful is easily discernable. Thus, the placing in orbit of nuclear weapons is considered a non-peaceful use of space. On the other end of the compendium are the obviously peaceful uses of space which have met with no complaints, such as manned space flights or communications satellites expressly designed for commercial applications. Between these two extremes lies an ill-defined, gray area into which falls the issue of military and quasi-military communications satellites. To determine the legal status of these space vehicles, it is first necessary to define the concept more expressly. There are, essentially, two divergent definitions of peaceful purposes. According to the American view, the term is synonymous with "non-aggressive" purposes. The Soviet view, on the other hand, contends that peaceful purposes are the same as "non-military" purposes. It appears that before a viable definition of peaceful purposes can be reached, it is first necessary to define military purposes, and in so doing, to distinguish between those activities which are of a purely military nature, and those which may, under certain circumstances, serve military purposes. If this distinction is not drawn, then any resulting ban on military activities might seriously prohibit most scientific endeavors in outer space. Taking this into consideration, it seems likely that the only viable definition of peaceful purposes would be one that included military activity of a non-aggressive nature. If this definition is finally accepted, then communications from outer space, consistent with non-aggressive missions, would be considered as a peaceful use and hence, justifiable under this tenet of customary law.

There is evidence to support the contention that this definition has implicitly been adapted. However, its acceptance has not come about as a result of resolving this semantic distinction. Rather, it is based upon the gradual evolution of a state of "mutual concession" between the two "resource" states: a development which will gradually result in customary law with respect to communications satellites. The ultimate stage in this evolution is a truly international global satellite system, serving the needs of all inhabitants of the earth. It therefore behooves us to trace this gradual evolution, and compare it with a parallel development of reconnaissance satellites in an effort to provide a basis for an effective prognosis.

IV: _Communications satellites and space-law_: This evolutionary development to which I have made reference may be conveniently divided into four phases: Phase 1: Unilateral implementation--is characterized by unilateral implementation on the part of the first "resource" state, the United States. Its Communications Satellites activity actually began in 1958 with Project SCORE, and continued with the Telstar, Relay, Syncom, and Early Bird Satellites. The Union of Soviet Socialist Republics, apparently lacking the technological capability to become a resource state in the area of communications satellites, until recently, has busied itself by turning out a series of adverse propaganda remarks concerning the American activity. The same situation, according to unconfirmed reports, existed with respect to reconnaissance satellites. Thus, Phase I may be categorized as one of unilateral implementation on the part of the United States and unilateral propaganda attacks on the part of the Soviets.

The Second Phase or "Mutual Concession" is characterized primarily by a basic change in attitude on the part of the Soviet Union, brought about not by a shift in idealistic orientation, but rather by an expediency necessitated by their own active participation in this field. Thus, on April 23, 1965, when the Soviets launched their first Communications Satellite--MOLNIYA I, a state of mutual concession was entered into, in which both the United States and the Union of Soviet Socialist Republics existed as resource states. Soft-pedaling of accusations that American communications systems were to be used for military purposes was certainly to be expected when one considers that a similar Soviet state-owned system would inevitably inherit this function, and thus, such objections would be contrary to the Soviet's own interests. This pattern of adjusting ideological dogma to the practical necessities of technology was similarly evidenced in the field of reconnaissance satellites, in which both resource states tacitly agreed to the conducting of satellite surveillance. According to published reports, the Soviets developed their own reconnaissance satellite capability early in 1964. Shortly after this, Soviet propaganda attacks on United States reconnaissance satellites ceased and the public concessions reflected in the most recent United Nations documents indicate that the Soviets no longer object to this activity.

Certainly, Soviet ideology has had a direct bearing on the formulation of their policy in outer space. Basic to the Communist approach is the adjustment of policies and outlooks to best serve their ends. Similarly, the Soviets have adjusted their interpretation of international law to suit their own needs. For the Union of Soviet Socialist Republics, the legality of aerospace activities has depended primarily on the nature and function of the activity as opposed to the general application of the legal concept. In conducting their campaign of peaceful-coexistence, the Soviets have sought to avoid military conflict which would only inhibit their intentions, and to use international law to serve their own ends. It is obvious, then, that this apparent recent adjustment of the Soviet attitude towards both communications and reconnaissance satellites has been felt to be in their best interest. If this is so, and the Soviets feel they have much to gain by sanctioning these activities from outer space, then the indicated trend from "mutual concession" appears to be toward the official authorization of such unilaterally conducted activities.

151

<u>Phase III: Officially authorized unilateral implementation</u>: This now brings us into a discussion of the third phase of this program. By official authorization, we mean that the tendency is toward the actual establishment of custom which would officially declare satellite communications and reconnaissance to be in accordance with international law. If such a custom is established, then there would be no need to justify these activities under any other legal doctrine. Furthermore, with the establishment of this customary law, the question of what constitutes "peaceful" uses of outer space becomes unimportant with respect to these non-aggressive activities as they would become officially sanctioned regardless of their categorization. In regard to the requirements of customary law, there is definite evidence that the subject requirement or rightful intent is being satisfied. Usage must be gleaned from public reports concerning both communications and reconnaissance satellites. Thus, barring any serious objections by the international community, it is evident that a customary law officially sanctioning what is, at present, merely tacitly accepted, is in the process of being developed. That such a law would be derived from the activities of only two resource states may mean that the required period of time for its establishment would be more extensive than ordinarily expected. However, the immediacy of the problem may belie the aforementioned obstruction to its acceptance.

<u>Phase IV: Cooperative open space international implementation</u>: The final phase in this evolutionary process for communications satellites will follow logically from the preceding phases if this activity is ever to develop to its optimum potential. Preliminary steps toward a system of international cooperation have already been taken. The International Consortium now consists of almost 50 nations. Although the experience to be gained by this attempt at international cooperation is invaluable and praiseworthy, it is not, unfortunately, without serious shortcomings; that is to say, the Consortium is not a truly global-international organization, the most obvious flaw being the absence of Soviet bloc representation. According to Soviet spokesmen, their objection to the organization lies in the dominant role played by the United States therein. It may therefore be expected that the Soviet bloc will establish their own global system in the near future. To further complicate the situation, other Western European nations have also spoken of instituting their own independent satellite communications system, to say nothing of similar plans on the part of the United States Department of Defense. This hodge-podge of systems can only lead to confusion, conflict, and inhibition of the potential of any satellite communications system. Similar problems exist in the area of reconnaissance satellites. The majority of nations have neither the technological competence nor the economic resources to undertake such activities. Consequently, the need for a universal warning system and the goal of reducing world tensions through reliable information on the imminence of the threat is not fulfilled. All states are equally subject to the threat of a nuclear attack. To force underdeveloped nations to be dependent upon the resource states in order to maintain their security would only produce resentment in the world community.

The only answer for both the communications and reconnaissance dilemmas lies in the formulation of a truly cooperative open-space international control organization, most likely to be formed under the auspices of the United Nations. For example, the creation of a United Nations Communications Satellite Agency (U.N.C.S.A.) or a United Nations Reconnaissance Satellite Agency (U.N.R.S.A.) or, on a more comprehensive level, a United Nations Satellite

Control Agency (U.N.S.C.A.) would be deemed as a necessary step in the quest for a lasting world peace.

I shall not attempt to discuss the details of a program of this nature at this time, since these would depend completely on the prevailing circumstances at the time of its inception. In any case, the primary function at hand is to indicate that such a trend does exist. It was, initially, a desire for a broader, more efficient means of communications throughout the world that stimulated interest and experimentation in the field of communications satellites and it will be that same desire for global understanding that will eventually lead us to true international cooperation in space.

*   *   *   *   *

COMMENTS ON SALVAGE AND REMOVAL OF MAN-MADE OBJECTS FROM OUTER SPACE

by

R. Cargill Hall

Introduction: Space traffic congestion is developing in the near-earth regions of outer space from the increase in space-vehicle traffic and the accumulation of orbiting man-made debris. Removal of man-made debris from outer space and the salvaging of valuable spacecraft hardware involve legal problems that are primarily international in scope.

Before long it will become mandatory for states to remove from orbit unmanned space vehicles and debris that pose a hazard to spacecraft navigation. The need to prevent cluttering of outer space, before the requirement for deorbit-removal of this material became necessary, was first recognized in 1958. Andrew Haley then recommended that "no object should be placed in orbit in outer space which cannot be guided back to earth or destroyed by some other means, such as being guided into the sun..." Although the problem was recognized by Haley and by several other observers, it was not acknowledged by those responsible for the space programs in major states. Since 1958 the proliferation of spacecraft and debris remaining in orbit for extended periods has reached a point where near-term interference with orbital spaceflight can be foreseen, and the problem of congestion has become a popular topic. In a recent article Life Magazine noted that there are now "some 1,200 satellites, burnt-out rockets, and just plain junk orbiting the earth," including a trash bag thrown overboard while on orbit by Gemini astronauts Young and Collins in a manner reminiscent of earth-bound motor car travelers.

Coincident with the need for deorbit-removal of debris from orbit, advanced technology will soon demonstrate that salvage/retrieval of spacecraft hardware from near-earth orbital altitudes is feasible and economical. While the cost of retrieval is high, salvage of specific items for reuse or analysis (such as a J-2 rocket engine from the second stage of a Saturn 1B, for example) can pay the cost and more. At higher altitudes, in circular orbits of 1,500 statute miles and beyond, prolonged exposure to radiation in outer space will have damaged or degraded the performance of much equipment, and salvage may not prove economical as the major goal. Nevertheless, as the increasing size of spacecraft increases allowing for stowage of additional gear, salvage may also be effected at these higher altitudes incidental to deorbit-removal or inspection operations.

Several important legal questions require international attention if potential disturbance between states is to be avoided in the conduct of space salvage and removal operations. Specifically, with respect to space salvage, when, if ever, is an unmanned orbiting space vehicle considered abandoned--with no intent on the part of the launching state to return and reactivate it--and therefore a derelict object? In the event that ownership and national jurisdiction continue permanently, what of inactive craft or debris that constitute a hazard to spacecraft navigation and are not removed from orbit by the state of registry--would good cause exist for another state to board these objects to deorbit them or otherwise remove them from all traffic patterns? Since a vast majority of space vehicles are public craft, they represent for states "a national asset of the greatest importance, directly related to their most exclusive bases of power." These legal questions become, therefore, intimately connected with politics of national prestige and security.

Space salvage and removal operations will create international friction if they are undertaken in the absence of international consensus on these questions. The repercussions of unregulated space salvage and removal activity are apparent; unless the political and legal issues inherent in these operations are amicably resolved and international standards of practice agreed to, we can expect that any unauthorized attempt on the part of one state covertly or overtly to salvage or remove inactive "abandoned" spacecraft of another state from orbit will trigger international incidents or, possibly, military conflict between the major space powers.

This paper will review the legal status presently accorded unmanned spacecraft, discuss the principles of maritime law that may be applied in instances of salvage and removal of these craft or their component parts from earth orbit, and attempt to determine national rights to and legality of space salvage and removal activity. Finally, several alternate approaches that can be taken to resolve the political and legal issues involved in the preceding operations are investigated, and a recommendation is made for the approach which the author believes most appropriate.

LEGAL STATUS OF UNMANNED SPACECRAFT ON ORBIT

Most Soviet and American jurists agree that objects launched into outer space belong to the state of registry, that they carry the flag state nationality, and that jurisdiction over them resides with the state or origin. This opinion is reinforced by informal agreement reached by the United Nations General Assembly in Resolution No. 1962 regarding the legal status of spacecraft on orbit, and by the customary practice of states with respect to public and private vessels and aircraft. It appears already established beyond doubt in space law that states have immediate title to and jurisdiction and control over all registered manned and unmanned spacecraft in earth orbits and beyond, and may exercise their prerogatives to protect and prescribe policy for these vehicles.

There has not been, however, in the expressed opinion of jurists, in General Assembly Resolution No. 1962, and in recent international deliberation aimed at establishing a convention governing the conduct of activities in outer space, any distinction made between national jurisdiction and control over active and inactive space vehicles or their parts. At present, with respect to space salvage operations, it is not possible to determine with certainty whether jurisdiction (1) obtains permanently regardless of an absence of continued effective physical control or the state of being of the object, or (2) lapses with the conclusion of effective physical control--in abandonment of the object--as in maritime law. With unqualified national or international fiat on this question lacking, it is appropriate to review the characteristics of "active life-span" exhibited by unmanned spacecraft, and analogous legal precedent that may be applied from maritime law, which may indicate whether national jurisdiction ceases or is nullified when a space vehicle's useful life is ended. (There is no question raised over national jurisdiction in the case of manned spacecraft.)

Contemporary unmanned space vehicles have an "active life span" on earth orbit varying from several weeks to several years, dependent upon the programmed period of performance and the reliability of their mechanical and electronic subassemblies. After this active life span is terminated (by ground command, by technical malfunction, or by the breakup of the craft), a space vehicle is in a permanently inactive state, that is, its transmitters are shut down, and all equipment ceases to function. At this time there is no possibility of reactivating the craft's equipment, effective physical control ceases, and the vehicle is dead and becomes, for all intents and purposes, a large piece of debris--unresponsive to further commands from the launching state. It is left free to orbit the earth silently, a potential hazard to spacecraft navigation for many years or until the friction of the upper atmosphere slows it sufficiently so that it reenters and incinerates or impacts the ground.

In classical maritime law any piece of property on navigable waters exhibiting the characteristics just enumerated for our permanently inactive unmanned satellite is considered derelict, i.e., "abandoned and deserted by those who are in charge of it, without hope on their part of recovering it (sine spe recuperandi), and without intention of returning to it (sine animo revertendi)." To be considered derelict, Judge Story asserted in Rowe v. The Brig, "it is sufficient that the thing is found deserted or abandoned upon the seas, whether it arose from accident or necessity or voluntary dereliction." Fragmented debris also may be equated with derelict flotsam from a wreck, or, in certain instances, jetsam that is thrown overboard while on orbit. It is significant that derelict property does not have to be lost (its location unknown), only abandoned without intent to return, for inactive, unmanned spacecraft in earth orbit are not necessarily lost--most can be tracked and their positions computed and projected into the future for many days. (Smaller pieces of debris or objects in certain trajectories can be lost to ground-based skintrack radar.)

From the preceding analogy, can permanently inactive unmanned spacecraft and debris be juristically considered abandoned? Is it correct to assume that once their active life-span is ended, and they are at least technically abandoned, that they become derelicts? Two French lawyers adopted this position--without specifying whether the unmanned spacecraft were physically controlled or inactive--in 1955, and suggested that they were res derelicta, like a shipwreck, or a kind of "bottle in the sea." This approach has been strongly criticised--but not refuted--by the other jurists, and it has not received any international support. In fact, the question of continuity of national jurisdiction and abandonment remains open, and until it is satisfactorily answered it is a potential source of international friction.

SALVAGE ON MAN-MADE OBJECTS FROM OUTER SPACE

With the legal question of dereliction of inactive unmanned spacecraft unanswered, can we determine what international rights to salvage of these craft or their component parts do exist? Let us assume, for the purpose of discussion, that these craft are abandoned. Maritime law accords distressed and derelict private vessels or property on navigable waters as subject to salving by anyone who, in good faith, takes possession of the property as a salvor. The salvor is not considered an interloper or trespasser, and he may claim a salvage reward if the craft is conveyed to shore. While title to the abandoned or distressed property is not relieved from the legal owner, the salvor may, by the act of successfully salving the property, claim a lien against it.

For public vessels, however, whether derelict or in distress, there is no equivalent international recognition of contract or voluntary salvage. Article 14 of the Brussels Salvage Convention of 1910, now ratified by the United States and the Soviet Union, specifically excludes "ships or war or . . . other government ships appropriated exclusively to a public service" from provisions of the Convention. Although this restriction has drawn criticism and proposals for revision to include these vessels, no international suit to recover a reward, either in rem or in personam, presently is granted for salvage services rendered public craft. (This does not hold true in all municipal law; some states permit suit for recovery of a salvage award where public property is rescued and returned.)

Most American and all Soviet unmanned spacecraft are public vehicles, and may be considered akin to government-owned scientific research vessels. It would seem indicated by analogy with maritime law that an international suit for remuneration for salvage services rendered foreign space vehicles or their parts would not be permitted even if they are determined in distress or are abandoned and derelict. Foreign spacecraft equipment recovered on earth or returned from outer space would, under customary law, have to be turned over to the state of registry without compensation. Conversely, should it be held that permanently inactive space vehicles are not abandoned and derelict, then any attempt at unauthorized or voluntary salvage by a foreign state becomes trespass, international theft and piracy, or an unwarranted act of aggression, depending upon the circumstances.

REMOVAL OF MAN-MADE OBJECTS FROM OUTER SPACE

Municipal laws of maritime states normally require that when a vessel is wrecked or sunk in a navigable channel or territorial water, posing a hazard to navigation, it is the duty of the owner to immediately mark it with a buoy or beacon during the day, and a lighted lantern at night. In United States Admiralty law, if the owner does not diligently remove the craft "it will be considered abandoned and becomes subject to removal by the United States Government." Hazards to navigation on the high seas of a similar nature, however, involve application of norms derived from international custom and compacts.

Derelict objects on the high seas without a legal title or national flag, such as icebergs and unidentifiable flotsam and jetsam, can be mined and sunk by any nation. Derelict vessels in the same region still carry the indicia of their national origin, are possessed of a titled owner, and retain some residual value. Neither the multilateral Convention on the High Seas (1958) nor the Convention for the Safety of Life at Sea (1960) accord a legal right to any nation to sink or otherwise destroy these vessels, other than the nation of the derelict vessel's nationality, irrespective of the hazard they represent for maritime navigation. Chapter V, Part D, Regulation 2 (a) of the latter Convention directs the master of a ship which encounters "dangerous ice, a dangerous derelict, or any other direct danger to navigation . . ." to communicate information regarding the hazard to authorities ashore. In maritime law the legal right to destroy abandoned vessels of another nation on the high seas in peacetime is only received from that flag state, and is normally accorded, if it is a private vessel, after permission is secured from the titled owner and insurance company.

Equivalent hazards to spacecraft navigation in near-earth space can be at least temporarily minimized by obtaining precise information on the changing positions of space objects. Vast economic resources and advanced technology permit the major states to establish and maintain large networks of ground-based radar to track and account for most orbiting spacecraft and inactive debris. In the United States ground-based radar tracking and correlation of spacecraft and debris is handled by the North American Air Defense Command, which maintains a Space Detection and Tracking System (SPADATS) for defense purposes to detect, track, identify, and catalog all satellites and orbiting metallic debris in earth orbit. Although developed for defense purposes, SPADATS tracking information can be employed by American space agencies for launch planning in order to prevent a collision in outer space. Technical limitations to SPADATS, however, restrict the number and kinds of objects that can be successfully observed by skintrack radar, additional difficulties are introduced by the increase in space traffic and by vehicles capable of changing orbits.

The accumulating debris, the introduction of vehicles that can change orbits, and the technical limitations of ground-based radar systems will eventually force states engaged in space exploration to provide for deorbit-removal of inactive hardware that remains in orbit for an extended length of time. In the near-earth regions this task may be accomplished by (1) space systems consisting of manned, recoverable spacecraft capable of orbital rendezvous-docking and equipped with spare solid-propellant rockets that can be "strapped on" inactive, unmanned vehicles or their fragments by astronauts during extra-vehicular movement for the purpose of "braking" the objects into a reentry trajectory, and (2) for flights yet to be launched, programming spacecraft with the capability for controlled deorbit at the conclusion of their mission. As spacecraft are constructed of more durable metals, however, large pieces survive to impact the earth. The time selected for initiating reentry destruction will have to take into account acceptable reentry zones for given orbital trajectories. Reentry would have to be triggered to occur over uninhabited areas unless the angle of attack can be effectively controlled to ensure that no fragments survive air-friction heating. When deorbit-removal of man-made objects from earth orbit becomes a practical necessity and space systems to accomplish this task are created, states will also have to determine what inactive debris may be legitimately removed from orbit if they wish to avert international incidents.

Outer space, like the high seas, is generally acknowledged to be free for the use of all; it is not subject to the exclusive competence of any one state as is national airspace. It is reasonable to infer from maritime law that title to indentifiable, inactive, man-made objects in space is retained by the flag state and is not affected by abandonment. (The legal question of dereliction--central to space salvage operations--does not obtain in the case of deorbit-destruction missions.) The growing number of man-made objects in near-earth space that will remain in orbit for periods ranging up to thousands of years represent a threat to the safety of spacecraft navigation in the future. Under customary law, authority to deorbit and destroy--or to permit others to deorbit and destroy--identifiable space debris would be confined to the state of registry in times of peace and in the absence of any convention governing the conduct of this activity.

Still, should future traffic congestion in near-earth polar and low-inclination orbits occur so that intolerable navigation difficulties result, and in that circumstance a state refuses to remove its debris, would another state be within its rights to board and deorbit the foreign debris?

McDougal, Lasswell and Vlasic suggest that "states can be expected to claim competence to make applications to the spacecraft of other states for violations of inclusive prescription, such as with respect to minimum order or the authorized exclusive protection of the underlying state." While a course of direct interference with identifiable property of another state in outer space may eventually be determined necessary by national policy-makers as a result of collisions there, it will not be undertaken without careful consideration of the tradeoff between the benefits that may be achieved for spacecraft navigation and the potential international disturbance that will result from this action, compared to the continuing navigation hazards created by the orbiting debris. International protest and threats to take action to deorbit hazardous foreign debris would logically precede such activity, and should afford an interval in which the offending state could take action on its own initiative.

CONCLUSION

The contemporary international community is composed of separate, independent states, with the states most active in the exploration of space possessing a proponderance of power. In the absence of an effective centralized authority, resolution of the political and legal issues involved in space salvage and removal activity can be secured by one of two principal modes: through agreement among the states concerned, or by reliance upon custom and precedent derived from actual practice. For these projected operations, however, custom and precedent can only proceed at the risk of conflict. Even if a nation initiating unrestricted salvage and removal activity were willing to accept similar claims in kind against its own inactive craft, reciprocal response is not guaranteed. Direct interference with or destruction of inactive public property of another nation in outer space, instead of establishing a permissive norm, may well cause the state offended to react by implementing sanctions it considers sufficient to force cessation of this activity, such as escalating interference to include removal of active unmanned spacecraft. The more rational--and more likely--approach to resolution is by formal international agreement in which mutually acceptable standards to regulate space salvage and removal operations are formally established in convention. Growing space traffic congestion in near-earth space and a technology that now permits rendezvous and docking on orbit will increase the urgency for recognized acceptable procedures and should work to force international settlement of established standards.

Should precedent and custom prevail, however, in the case of removal-destruction of inactive man-made objects where a state retains title to its hazardous debris in earth orbit but refuses to remove these objects, and where other states refrain from interfering with the debris to the peril of spacecraft navigation, it would seem that a corresponding corollary should obtain: absolute liability is imposed upon the state of registry for any damage caused by its debris in outer space, or at least some form of the _res ipsa loquitur_ doctrine should follow in which automatic negligence is attributed to the launching state. When related to space salvage operations, reliance upon custom and precedent may influence states to program a capability for controlled deorbit into their vehicles to prevent any opportunity for salvage; this eventuality also would provide direct benefit to future space navigation. However, for spacecraft placed in orbit at higher altitudes, where the weight penalty imposed in carrying additional propellant for deorbit purposes is unacceptable, we may expect that states will begin "booby-trapping" their vehicles in order to discourage foreign tampering or salvage attempts.

In the event that national decisions are made in favor of seeking international agreement to resolve the political and legal problems of space salvage and removal activity, any international conference convened for this purpose will have to arrive at suitable definitions for "spacecraft," "satellite," and fragments thereof, for example, and establish the legal status of these items, including the duration that national title and jurisdiction is effective, the vehicle type (public or private), and the recognized state of being (active or inactive). Salvage and removal of inactive man-made objects in outer space may be legally prohibited by finding that national title to and jurisdiction over recognizable material is not affected by the passage of time. This kind of determination, however, should be accompanied by assurances that the launching state will remove its own inactive debris from earth orbit within a reasonable period or stand liable for any damages they may cause others. Conversely, if some form of space salvage and removal activity is found commonly acceptable, various articles will have to determine when such activity is permissible and for what kinds of vehicles or fragments, and establish procedures for obtaining permission to proceed, for presenting salvage claims, and for returning material to the state of registry, among the more important considerations.

Space salvage and removal systems are presently under study by several aerospace firms in the United States. A definitive answer to the legal question of abandonment of inactive unmanned spacecraft as it affects space salvage operations, and international procedures for removal of hazardous inactive debris from earth-orbit traffic patterns cannot afford to wait on attainment of these technical capabilities and inauguration of these programs if international discord is to be avoided. In a decentralized international political arena, the minimum acceptable resolution is a statement from national policy-makers regarding their nation's position on the question of abandonment, together with pledges to remove their own inactive debris from near-earth space. Such statements would provide a basis for community expectations. The final resolution that states must work for it normative regulation of these activities reached in convention.

*   *   *   *   *

II. Other Contributions and Comments

The papers in this volume are grouped under the several subjects dealt with at the Colloquium, and they are reproduced approximately in the order that they were presented by the participants.

a. <u>Introduction</u>: Thus, the volume starts with an introductory part, in which one will find consecutively the opening remarks of Pépin, the inaugural speech of Tapia Salinas, Chairman of the Colloquium, followed by a homage to Haley by Pépin, and concluded with a "Report of the President of the International Institute of Space Law," also by Pépin; the last mentioned report gives a brief account of the activities of the Institute, and the state of affairs of its membership.

b. <u>Celestial Bodies</u>: In 1966, one of the major goals of space activity is a landing on the moon. It is therefore not surprising that governments and private space lawyers alike pay much attention to the legal consequences of such landings; as for the latter, <u>ten</u> contributions on the subject "celestial bodies" testify to this interest within the IISL. While at the same time the UN Outer Space Committee and its legal sub-committee go through the final stages of drafting a treaty which covers celestial bodies, members of the IISL Working Group III on the <u>Legal Status of Celestial Bodies</u> formulate a resolution on this subject. In his introductory report, Smirnoff, chairman of the working group, can note with satisfastion that the legal principles contained in the 9-article UN draft treaty and in the IISL-draft resolution prove to be very similar. In both documents the 1963 Declaration of Legal Principles shows its influence. Discussing the brand new Space Treaty, <u>Brooks</u> comes to the conclusion that an international regime as the working space model has not been accepted and may not be regarded with favor; for this he blames <u>inter alia</u> "the desire for national prestige in the context of the cold war, an inertial clinging to old habits, and the mesmerizing influence of the Antarctic experience." (p.19). In case the international climate on earth does clear, Brooks explores extensively various forms of international organization, and scrutinizes treaty techniques to facilitate "cosmic management." He finally concludes that an International Planetary Organization with wide but well defined jurisdiction over activities on celestial bodies and lunar and planetary launches is desirable. It should be noted in this respect that the author prudently limits his legislative appetite to the planets of our solar system. <u>Csabafi</u> and <u>Rani</u> argue that the agreements reached on certain basic legal principles concerning the general legal status of outer space and celestial bodies will result in a shift of attention towards the <u>specific</u> issues of the law of celestial bodies, which are not (yet) regulated sufficiently. A list of such problems is added, and, as for the methodology of future research, the authors suggest continuing with the work group method.

In a short contribution Horsford gives some attention to registration and identification of space vehicles, and outlines the provisions of a space treaty with special reference to the moon, drafted by some members of the David Davies Study Group.

The imminent landing on, and exploration of the moon leads <u>Navarro</u> to formulate some specific rules on such matters as sterilization of space vehicles to avoid contamination of both moon and earth, the status of scientific establishments on the moon, and the legal aspects of the exploitation of its natural resources.

<u>Fasan</u> identifies several problems to be dealt with by the IISL without further delay, such as: the definition of a celestial body, the question of their appropriation (in whole or in part), the right of self defense, and such questions as mining rights and safety regulations. This urgent need for regulation is also felt by <u>Gal</u>, who rightly warns, however, to stick to reality and to avoid science fiction problems.

160

Rusconi arrives, after some research, at the following definition of heavenly (celestial) bodies: "A heavenly body, juridically considered, is every corporeal and organic structure, separated and individualized, that is found in the ultra-terrestrial space, and can be subject to the possession and property of man, and that has an economic value" (p.58). In her second paper, Rusconi obviously shares the concern of her colleagues with respect to the not yet regulated aspects of the exploration and use of celestial bodies, i.e., in particular the rights and duties with respect to natural resources.

c. Telecommunications: The list of contributions on the legal aspects of telecommunications by satellites opens with the introductory report of Cocca. In the face of the possible establishment of several (global) communication systems the author explores ways to assure maximum cooperation between these systems. Other problems mentioned are such as that of program control in the case of direct broadcasts, interference with communications and subversive broadcasts, and the question of possible sanctions. No specific recommendations are given by the rapporteur. (It should be realized in this connection that many of these problems are hardly new, but simply old ones in a new setting.)

The Intelsat Agreements of 1964 were only of a temporary character; they obliged the Interim Committee to submit recommendations for definitive arrangements for an international global system. Doyle proposes in this connection to give the IISL an advisory role in the matter; his suggestion to adopt a special study program to that end would - if adopted - have led to an interesting precedent with respect to the IISL's task and activities in general.

A contribution of Rodoreda deals with the subject of communications under the following subject-headings (inter alia): la competencia territorial en el espacio y en el espacio libre en relacion a los satellites de communicaciones, normas de aplicacion a los satelites de communicaciones, viabilidad de tratados de tipo comercial relativos a las comunicaciones via satelite, etc.

The trio Ivanyi, Szadeczky-Kardoss & Mora gives a clear picture of space telecommunications as an extension of the traditional means of transmission of transportation. The question whether the existing regulations (of the ITU) also cover the earth-outer space-earth connections is raised and - rightly it is believed - answered in the affirmative. The authors take the same position in the case of transmission of signals wholly outside and beyond the atmosphere, in outer space (e.g. between satellites, or between moonstation and satelite). The main argument used, which is also the official ITU position, is that the ITU is the specialized agency of the UN charged with the task to regulate communications without any restrictions as to its area (cf. also UN Resolution 1721(XVI) which provides that international law is applicable to outer space).

Morenoff's interesting treatise on the customary law which is being developed regarding communications and reconnaissance satellites has been reprinted in full.

Zhukov gives an idea of how a world-wide telecommunications system by satellites should look, by focusing on the rights and obligations of states with respect to such a system. However, the obvious candidate for this role, Intelsat, does not meet with approval. The author does not give his reasons, but the views of most socialist jurists on this point are well known. The possibility of using direct broadcasting satellites for propaganda constitutes another source of concern for Zhukov. Finally, he makes some suggestions for legal measures aimed at the protection of satellites, not only against harmful interference - which the author considers not sufficiently dealt with by Art. 47 of the International Telecommunication Convention - , but also against the putting out of commission of equipment of the satellite or the latter's destruction.

d. Liability: Part IV of the Proceedings opens with Berezowski's introduction of a draft convention on damage caused by foreign flightcraft, i.e. aircraft and space craft, to third parties on the surface, a concept which, as the rapporteur admits, is an extremely controversial one. In 1966, the Legal Subcommittee of UNCOUPOS is already preparing a convention on space liability, while the Rome Convention of 1952 regulates cases of damage caused by aircraft on the surface. A third instrument would create many problems, although the idea of one treaty covering flightcraft has, as such, the advantage of simplicity (e.g., definition problems with respect to aircraft and spacecraft as separate instrumentalities would not exist). De Rode-Verschoor suggests in this respect considering Berezowski's draft part of a larger convention, in which another practical problem, that of salvage of astronauts, could also be regulated.

Papacostas on the other hand describes some new principles that have already developed in this field, and the legal consequences resulting therefrom. The author discusses inter alia the concept of state liability independent of any violation of an international obligation, or, to use a different term, liability without fault, justified according to the author by the seriousness of potential damages. There is already in 1966 hardly any disagreement with respect to this principle. In the Legal Subcommittee many delegates appear to be in favour of it, and also IISL author, Scifoni, approves of what is also known under the term "absolute" or "objective" liability. The last paper on liability shows the same preference, although its author, Machado, also argues that such liability should be limited in value.

e. Space vehicles: Of the contributions collected under this heading, the detailed and interesting working paper of Sztucki deserves attention. His view that the necessary legal link between a state and its space object should not be established by the application of the traditional concept of nationality (as used in aviation), is apparently not shared by Ferrer, who believes that space ships ("naves espaciales") - as distinguished from space objects ("objetos espaciales") which are not constructed by man - should have a nationality. This is not merely a matter of terminology. Thus, another author, Lopez-Cutierrez, speaks of the "flag" of space craft to describe its legal link with a state. But, where Sztucki notes a tendency for basing this link on a factual criterion, that of launching, Lopez-Gutierrez seems to prefer registration, a formal criterion known in shipping and aviation (id. Herczeg, p.131), and quotes with approval Art. 18 of the Tokyo Convention, which in the case of international organizations operating aircraft provides that the member states "shall...designate the State among them which, for the purposes of this Convention shall be considered as the State of registration."

Quite a different problem is that of salvage and removal of space objects from outer space, which may become urgent in the future because of the increase in space vehicle traffic and the dangerous accumulation of orbiting man-made debris. Hall reviews in a well-written paper on the subject the legal status presently accorded unmanned spacecraft, discusses the principles of maritime law that may be applied, and attempts to determine national rights to and legality of space salvage and removal activity. (His paper has been reproduced except for its introductory part).

f. <u>Terminology</u>: <u>Kopal</u> introduces briefly the problems of legal terminology used in space papers as a new item on the agenda of the colloquia, whereas <u>Araujo</u> attempts to find the correct term to designate this new branch on the legal tree sometimes called "cosmic law," astronautical law or interplanetary law. <u>Machado</u> finally discusses such words as space ship, space vehicle, space object and spacecraft.

g. <u>Various</u>: This last part contains a series of papers which, though not falling under one of the previous subject headings, nevertheless deal with questions which deserve the space lawyers' attention. After the contribution of <u>De Montella</u>, entitled "Imperio de la ley y libertad del espacio en el derecho astronautico," <u>Larsen</u> eloquently advocates ICAO involvement in the regulation of space activities, the legal basis for which he sees in the fact that anything which affects civil aviation is its proper concern, and almost all space activities now affect aviation (coordination of aircraft and spacecraft navigation, communication satellites, meteorological satellites, etc.). A paper of <u>Magno</u> on "Il diritto spaziale di fronte ai problemi della collaborazione internazionale" follows. <u>Marcoff</u> analyzes Paragraph 3 of the Preamble and Art. 1 of the 1963 Declaration of Legal Principles, and concludes that the notion of "peaceful" use of outer space should be interpreted as meaning that <u>all</u> activities of a <u>military</u> character are forbidden in outer space, and not only those that are of an <u>aggressive</u> nature.

<u>Naiman</u> suggests the creation of an international meteorological data collection and distribution system headed by an organization. Annexed to the paper is a suggested agreement outlining the set-up of the organization. Also questions as dissemination of space data, radio spectrum management and liability are extensively dealt with.

The scientific and technical accomplishments of the space powers and their cooperation in the space field are impressive, according to <u>Shiffer</u> and <u>Snyders</u>, but little progress has been made by the nations of the world in the legal management and control of space. Examples to illustrate this view are given and the authors warn that war in and over space is inevitable unless equitable rules are formulated immediately. Regrettable is the author's suggestion that "mankind as a whole, the Planet Earth as a unit, formally claim Space and assert that all space activity must serve all men"; mankind may not be the only inhabitant of outer space!

<u>Von Rauchhaupt</u> gives some thought to the way in which ELDO and ESRO, through combined space activities and theoretical research of the member countries, create new law, which must fit into general and international - as distinct from European - space law.

Finally, <u>Vereshchetin</u> presents a paper in which various forms of cooperation of the USSR in the exploration of outer space are shown. Bilateral agreements with France, USA and UAR and some multilateral agreements, together with the international organizations in which the USSR plays a role, are given as examples of such cooperation.

h. <u>Report and Summary</u>: The last part of this volume contains the tentative results of Pépin's questionnaire on the teaching and the study of space law in the world. A growing interest in space law becomes apparent in view of the number of universities and institutions, as well as the books and other publications dealing with the subject. One important obstacle hindering this development should be singled out, namely the scarcity of available official documentation, which should be of special concern to the members of the IISL.

TENTH COLLOQUIUM ON THE LAW OF OUTER SPACE
BELGRADE, 1967

I. Texts Reproduced

THE RECORD UP TO THE PRESENT TIME
by
Stephen E. Doyle

The International Telecommunications Satellite Consortium (INTELSAT) came into being in
August 1964. The organization and operation of this unique enterprise have been determined
by two agreements: (1) An Agreement Establishing Interim Arrangements for a Global Commercial Communications Satellite System; and (2) A Special Agreement now incorporating a Supplementary Agreement on Arbitration. During the initial three years of operation INTELSAT has
made remarkable progress. It has established international communication satellite facilities by the joint effort of more than fifty nations. These same nations generate more than
90 per cent of the world's international telecommunications.

During the initial period, INTELSAT has had a variety of legal, technical and other
problems, most of which have been overcome, so that up to the present time the fledgling
organization has established a praiseworth record of achievement, strong growth, and rapid
development. This paper presents s synoptic review of some of the alleged problems and
legal problems which INTELSAT has faced during its infancy.

During the organizational period and early months of INTELSAT (1963-1964), commentators,
particularly in the U.S.S.R., presented views strongly criticizing the establishment of
interests in space activities by private enterprise. G. Zolotov commented in one article
that, "Free enterprise in space can lead to chaos and arbitrary acts." G. Stashev has commented that "The organization for managing and operating the international communications
satellite system is not conceived as a genuinely international body." Referring to the
INTELSAT agreements of 1964, I. I. Cheprov has written that "True, it is hard to tell from
the text of these agreements what is in question: a new international organization, a
joint stock company with the participation of foreign capital or an unusual hybrid of the
two. Perhaps these formal shades of difference would have not been worth discussing had
they not concealed a vital and alarming fact: encroachment by U.S. monopoly capital on the
interests of mankind in the exploration and use of outer space, specifically by setting up
a global communications satellite system." These statements require careful analysis.

In an earlier paper, I have noted that the next major milestone for implementing decisions with regard to the permanent organization for international satellite communications
will be reached in 1969. During the interim, diplomats and lawyers will accomplish much
more understanding and agreement if they clarify in their discussions the nature of the
topic being discussed. Legal, political, economic, and technical problems should not be

164

confused.

The 1964 Agreements, as duly drawn and executed international agreements, are a part of the body of international law of direct bearing on signatory states. Discussions of their efficacy, political desirability, economic soundness, or social significance are all in order. What must be avoided, in order to prevent confusion and pointless bickering, is the treatment of political aspects of the problems as "legal," or the voicing of economic criticism of organizational structures as challenges to legal validity.

In a recent article by Professor Jean Voge, of the University of Brussels, a man with two years of experience in the conduct of affairs of INTELSAT speaks out with his opinion of some major problems involving INTELSAT. Professor Voge makes reference to provisions contained in Article X of the 1964 Agreement which reads as follows:

ARTICLE X

In considering contracts and in exercising their other responsibilities, the Committee and the Corporation as manager shall be
guided by the need to design, develop and procure the best equipment
and services at the best price for the most efficient conduct and
operation of the space segment. When proposals or tenders are determined to be comparable in terms of quality, c.i.f. price and timely
performance, the Committee and the Corporation as manager shall also
seek to ensure that contracts are so distributed that equipment is
designed, developed and procured in the States whose Governments are
Parties to this Agreement in approximate proportion to the respective
quotas of their corresponding signatories to the Special Agreement;
provided that such design, development and procurement are not contrary
to the joint interests of the Parties to this Agreement and the signatories to the Special Agreement. The Committee and the Corporation as
manager shall also seek to ensure that the foregoing principles are
applied with respect to major sub-contracts to the extent that this
can be accomplished without impariing the responsibility of the prime
contractor for the performance of work under the contract.

It is Professor Voge's view that these provisions are hollow words in light of the fact that United States industry today holds a commanding lead over the rest of the world in the advanced technology of communication satellites. He argues that this situation renders the terms of the agreement, which encourage international distribution or spreading of contracts, unreal and unable to be applied. He recommends that to meet the challenge of United States industry in this regard, interests in other countries, particularly in Europe, should com-bine financial resources, manpower, and technological skills to create truly competitive enterprises capable of producing on a par with United States industry. Professor Voge does not challenge or recommend changes in the wording or nature of the 1964 Agreement.

In another area, however, Professor Voge does see need for changes in the Agreement because, he asserts, under the terms of the Agreement, Comsat, the United States designated entity participating in INTELSAT, is responsible for management of the space segment of the global system, while simultaneously a domestic communications entity in the United States, and therefore subject to certain domestic laws. Professor Voge argues that this dual role places Comsat in "unavoidable" conflicts of interest. As he puts it, "Even though it strives to act in all impartiality, the managing agent of INTELSAT will find it difficult to act against the interests of its own country or against its own interests, and we cannot hold this against it."

One solution which could assure avoidance of conflicts of interests would be to arrange for more multinational participation in the work of the manager of the system. Subsequent to the publication of Professor Voge's views, it may be noted, the President of the United States transmitted a message to the Congress of the United States outlining certain principles for which the United States would be seeking agreement in 1969. Because of the leadership position of the United States in satellite technology, because of its major contributions to international telecommunications traffic, and because it provides the launch services to INTELSAT for the emplacement of satellites in orbit, the United States has played a major role in organizing and establishing the global commercial communications satellite system. President Johnson has clearly stated, however, that:

> We seek no domination of satellite communications to the exclusion
> of any other nation -- or any group of nations. Rather, we welcome
> increased participation in international communications by all INTELSAT
> members. We shall approach the 1969 negotiations determined to seek
> the best possible permanent organizational framework.
>> --We will consider ceilings on the voting power of any
>>   single nation including the United States--so that
>>   the organization will maintain its international
>>   character.
>> --We will support the creation of a formal assembly
>>   of all INTELSAT members--so that all may share in
>>   the consideration of policy.
>> --We favor efforts to make the services of personnel
>>   of other nations available to ComSat as it carries
>>   out its management responsibilities.
>> --We will continue the exchange of technical informa-
>>   tion, share technological advances, and promote a
>>   wider distribution of procurement contracts among
>>   members of the consortium.
> It is our earnest hope that every member nation will join with us in
> finding an equitable formula for a permanent INTELSAT organization.

Thus does the President of the United States present the views of that nation on how INTELSAT can be developed and improved to facilitate even more remarkable achievement than has been seen in the first three years.

The question of appropriate ceilings on national voting power in INTELSAT will receive long, hard study by all member nations, and perhaps others, before the Conference on definitive arrangements convenes in 1969. Whatever criteria are accepted for determining national voting power, those criteria must, as President Johnson has said, constitute an equitable formula for the organization. Up to the present time, the measure of voting power of each participant in the consortium has been determined on the basis of the principle of ownership related to use.

When INTELSAT was being created the organizers diligently sought a reasonable, equitable and realistic set of criteria for determining relative shares of ownership interest for participating nations. It was agreed that at least for the period of the interim arrangements such allocation would have to be determined by some reference base other than exclusively past experience, because it was acknowledged that satellites by their nature offered significant potential changes in rates and system capacity for international communication systems. The criteria finally agreed upon was the relative percentage of each member nation's contribution to long distance telephone traffic as projected by organs of the ITU for the year 1968. Some adjustments in these projected figures was provided for because it was clear that not all international telephone traffic would be handled by satellite in 1968. These ITU figures provided a useful base from which to work and, as nearly as was possible in 1964, a reasonable projection of national expectations as to satellite system usage. Usage of satellite facilities during the early years of service will provide a valuable record of experience as a component of the data to be available during the 1969 Conference on definitive arrangements.

A recurrent apparent problem about which interested observers have frequently commented is the relationship between Comsat and INTELSAT vis-a-vis the relationship between Comsat and the Federal Communications Commission, the domestic communications regulatory agency of the United States.

The 1964 Agreement provides in Article II that:

> Each Party either shall sign or shall designate a communications
> entity, public or private, to sign the Special Agreement which
> is to be concluded further to this Agreement and which is to be
> opened for signature at the same time as this Agreement. Relations
> between any such designated entity and the Party which has desig-
> nated it shall be governed by the applicable domestic law.

Comsat is the designated entity representing the United States in the Interim Committee. As a committee member Comsat has a vote on all matters requiring decisions by the Committee. The rendering of such vote by the accredited representative is accomplished in accordance with established domestic procedures under which necessary governmental advice on issues before the Committee is given. It should be clearly understood, however, that the Government of the United States does not attempt at any time to regulate, control, or at all interfere with functions performed by or in the name of INTELSAT. This distinction is not always clearly drawn by commentators, nor is it well understood by critics of the Federal Communications Commission who have alleged that the Commission attempts to frustrate INTELSAT by the exercise of jurisdiction over that organization. This allegation is not supportable in light of actual experience. It was this very issue which prompted the FCC's Commissioner Cox to append a separate concurring statement to a Commission decision issued in 1966. The Commission order authorized Comsat, as the U.S. representative on the INTELSAT Committee, to participate with its partners in INTELSAT in the procurement of the INTELSAT III satellites. Commissioner Cox wrote:

> I do not wish to regulate the affairs of INTELSAT any more than my colleagues do. However, I think we are charged by Congress to regulate certain of the activities of ComSat, and this may have an impact from time to time on the international consortium. ComSat, first of all, is a domestic common carrier for profit and not an agency or establishment of the United States government. Secondly, it is this country's representative to the international consortium, and in that capacity it must act in such a way as to give full effect to our domestic regulatory scheme -- a fact recognized by Article II(a) of the international interim agreement which provides that applicable domestic law shall control relations between each signatory country and its designated representative. Finally, ComSat is the manager of the consotrium. Obviously its triple role poses problems for ComSat, but that does not excuse it from observing the domestic law which binds all our international communications carriers.
>
> There are established procedures which, if ComSat had followed them, would have permitted the Commission and other agencies of our government to discharge our respective statutory responsibilities as to this application without becoming involved with the international aspects of the matter. Instead, ComSat made a proposal to INTELSAT which it had not cleared with its own government, and now seeks to speed acceptance of this _fait_ _accompli_ without the checks and procedures we would normally require. While these processes take time, I am satisfied that the record will show that the Commission has been much more expeditious in disposing of ComSat's applications than the latter has been in filing them.

Clarification of the areas of responsibility of the FCC and ComSat with regard to INTELSAT has facilitated major improvement and greater effectiveness being achieved in the operations of both entities. Since the Commission's order relating to INTELSAT III satellites was adopted in June 1966, there have been no recurring problems of this kind in FCC-ComSat relations.

The last of the problem areas to be reviewed in this paper involves certain problems which arose under certain procedural rules of the FCC relating to procurement of goods and services by ComSat in the satellite service. The initial wording of Part 25 Subpart B of the FCC's Rules and Regulations, adopted January 8, 1964, presented a problem of apparent applicability to foreign corporations over which the U.S. Government could exercise no regulatory power. In a petition dated December 22, 1965, ComSat called this situation to the attention of the FCC and recommended certain changes in the procurement rules to clarify their applicability and to expressly state that they do not apply to foreign entities. ComSat's proposed revisions were reviewed in a public administrative process and found to be entirely appropriate. By a Commission order released June 29, 1966, Part 25 Subpart B of the FCC's Rules and Regulations were revised in accordance with ComSat's proposal.

In every case where the novelty, complexity and dynamic nature of the emerging global commercial communication satellite system have given rise to problems, resort to appropriate administrative procedure to alleviate such problems has proven successful. The orderly growth of the global system and the cooperative development of a strong, economically viable, efficient and effective organization for control of the system have resulted in remarkable achievements. The record up to the present time of the resolution of real and alleged legal problems associated with creation of international satellite communication facilities has been exemplary. In a true spirit of cooperation the members of INTELSAT has worked together to overcome emerging problems and made substantial progress. This cooperative effort is destined to continue. In 1969 the agreements creating INTELSAT will be reviewed and possibly revised. The end result of the cooperation among nations of the world will be to improve communications among all nations -- a prerequisite to a world at peace under law.

*   *   *   *   *

PROBLEMS OF INTERPRETATION OF THE SPACE TREATY OF 27 JANUARY 1967

INTRODUCTORY REPORT

by

Istvan Herczeg

The "Treaty of Principles Governing the Activities of States in the Exploration and Use of Outer Space, including the Moon and other Celestial Bodies" established on the 27th of January, 1967, and signed by the majority of the existing states (81 until the 10th of July) signifies a milestone not only in the field of the legal regulation of space activity, but also in securing peace for mankind in the boundless Cosmos whose conquest by science and technics for human activity began only a decade ago.

It is this outstanding significance of the Treaty which makes it a signal duty of international lawyers to deal with certain questions of interpretation arising in connection with the agreement, on a scientific level. Thus, it is a momentous task for the International Institute of Space Law to make every effort to clear the relevant scientific views and to arrive - as far as possible - at common standpoints in the questions under dispute.

At its April 1967 session, the Board of Directors of the Institute appointed a three-man working group to study the problems of interpretation. Members of this working group were Mrs. Eilene Galloway, Mr. Michel Bourély and the undersigned as rapporteur. Owing to the shortness of available time and the lack of personal meetings the members of the working group have been unable to agree on every point, and consequently the undersigned rapporteur is submitting this report as his own report to the participants of the Belgrade Colloquium indicating the points upon which the other two members of the working group held different views. Under these circumstances the report will only serve as a basis for discussions by raising the following questions:

1. Does the obligation of use for exclusively peaceful purposes extend beyond the Moon and other celestial bodies, to the entire outer space?

This question will arise because Article IV only mentions the Moon and other celestial bodies when providing that these shall be used by the States Parties to the Treaty exclusively for peaceful purposes.

As an exemplification of this general norm the same Article further provides that the establishment of military bases, installations and fortifications, the testing of any types of weapons and the conduct of military maneuvers shall be forbidden on the Moon and on celestial bodies. This provision, therefore, contains an identical obligation for the complete demilitarization of the Moon and other celestial bodies, as does the 1959 Convention concerning the Antarctic. As regards the entire outer space, Article IV further states only that the States Parties to the Treaty "undertake not to place in orbit around the Earth any objects carrying nuclear weapons or any other kinds of weapons of mass destruction...or station such weapons in outer space in any other manner." The said wording of Article IV leads to the conclusion that - apart from the Moon and other celestial bodies -

the rest of space falls under the obligation of a partial demilitarization only; i.e. restricted to the nuclear weapons and weapons of mass destruction.

QUERY: whether such an interpretation of the text of Article IV can be reconciled with the entire Treaty?

In my opinion, examining the Treaty as a whole, the obligation of exclusively peaceful use will follow therefrom also in relation to the entire space. Such an interpretation is first of all supported by the Preamble which admits "the common interest of all mankind in the progress of the exploration and use of outer space for peaceful purposes," and expresses the wish "to contribute to broad international cooperation in the scientific as well as the legal aspects of the exploration and use of outer space for peaceful purposes," recalling finally United Nations General Assembly Resolution 110(II), which condemned "propaganda designed or likely to provoke or encourage any threat to the peace, breach of peace or act of agression" and considers that the said resolution 110(II) is applicable to outer space. Apart from the Preamble, the exclusively peaceful use concerning the whole of space can be derived - among others - from the general norm expressed in Article I of the Treaty according to which "the exploration and use of outer space, including the Moon and other celestial bodies, shall be carried out for the benefit and in the interests of all countries," but even more from the provision contained in Article III under which the States Parties to the Treaty shall carry on activities in space "in accordance with international law, including the Charter of the United Nations, in the interest of maintaining international peace and security and promoting international co-operation and understanding." Article IX adds to this that "in the exploration and use of outer space, including the Moon and other celestial bodies, States Parties to the Treaty shall be guided by the principle of co-operation and mutual assistance and shall conduct all their activities in outer space, including the Moon and other celestial bodies, with due regard to the corresponding interests of all other States Parties to the Treaty."

Obviously, it would be impossible to implement the benefit and interest of all countries (mentioned in Art. 1), further the interest of maintaining international peace and security (mentioned in Art. III) and finally the principle of co-operation and mutual assistance (mentioned in Article IX), unless the obligation of exclusively peaceful use is valid for the entire space. Under these circumstances there is no other answer to the first question - in my opinion - but that the Treaty as a whole stipulates the obligation of use for exclusively peaceful purposes concerning the entire outer space, regardless of the concrete obligations laid down in Article IV concerning the Moon and other celestial bodies.

Against the above reasoning, Mrs. Eilene Galloway opposed the following views:

> That Treaty is very explicit on the question of exclusively peaceful uses so that it does not present a problem of interpretation. The phrase "exclusively for peaceful purposes" is used in only one operative part of the Treaty - Article IV, Paragraph 2 - which is limited to the Moon and other celestial bodies. Where provisions are intended to have wider application, the Treaty uses the phrase "outer space, including the Moon and other celestial bodies." Preambular languages and Articles III and IX cannot be construed against the clearly expressed language of Article IV, basic canons of treaty in-

terpretation, and the views expressed by the Treaty negotiators. The
Soviet Union, in particular, on a number of occasions in the Legal
Subcommittee and in the General Assembly, rejected the concept of
peaceful uses for all of outer space. By thus limiting the application, the drafters of the 1967 Treaty did not set aside outer space
generally as a sphere for lawlessness and aggression, for Article III
makes international law, including the Charter of the United Nations,
the code governing conduct of States Parties in outer space. Article
III forbids in outer space the uses of force forbidden to States on
Earth by the Charter of the United Nations. Article IV goes further
and forbids on the Moon and other celestial bodies military activities
legal on Earth and in outer space generally under the Charter.

In the opinion of the undersigned, these objections do not lead to a different result
in the question of interpretation. Mrs. Galloway referred to Art. III, which provides
for the application of international law and the U.N. Charter in the exploration and use
of outer space including the Moon and other celestial bodies; this Article makes it obvious that the threat and use of force is prohibited also in the entire cosmic space.
This, again, is identical with the duty of exclusively peaceful use. However, the standpoint taken by the delegate of any state in connection with the use of the _term_ during
the discussions preceding the conclusion of the Treaty is irrelevant. As is known, in
the interpretation of an international treaty, the material of the preparatory work can
only be consulted if the context of the treaty itself fails to provide an answer to the
question which has arisen. In the present case, however, the answer furnished by the
quoted provisions of the Treaty may be regarded as unequivocal.

2. Which State is meant by the term "the appropriate State" used in Article VI?

    Does it refer to the state of the "non-governmental entities," or the state of the

    place of launching, or some other state?

    Article VI declares: "The activities of non-governmental entities in outer space, in-
cluding the Moon and other Celestial bodies, shall require authorization and continuing supervision by the appropriate State Party to the Treaty." However, neither this Article nor
the remaining provisions of the Treaty contain any guidance as to which state shall be considered as the "appropriate State."

    According to the rules of private international law the "nationality" of the legal
entities generally attaches to the country in which they have their seat. This general norm,
however, can hardly be applied in connection with space activities. It may, namely, occur
that the seat of the "entity" carrying on space activity is in one state, whereas the production of the space instrument takes place in another state, and its launching in yet another. In order that the rules relating to authorization and continuing supervision may be
implemented in practice, it would be obviously insufficient if the said obligations were
incumbent on the state of the seat of the entity only; in the case cited in the foregoing,
the necessity of authorization and continuing supervision would obviously concern all three
states. This doctrine appears to be supported by the analogy to be found in Article VII of
the Treaty which declares the international liability of several states in connection with
one launching if such states have had an essential role in one way or other in the launching.

Mrs. Galloway made, in this connection, the following observation:

> The point would seem to be correct that there may be several
> 'appropriate states' with responsibilities under Article VI. Is it
> not doubtful, however, that the State Party whose only connection with
> the particular space activity was that some components or space in-
> struments were produced on its territory would often be one of the
> 'appropriate states'?

3. The term "registry" mentioned in Article VIII - does it denote a national or international registry?

The very text of Article VIII implies that this can only be a national registry. Thus, alone on the strength of the wording of this Article the question of an international regis- tration will not even arise. It should be known, however, that UNO General Assembly Resolu- tion 1721 (XVI) Part B, had recommended the announcing of all launchings of space objects to the General Secretary of UNO; also, Article XI of the present Treaty contains a similar obligation when asserting that "States Parties to the Treaty conducting activities in outer space, including the Moon and other celestial bodies, agree to inform the Secretary-General of the United Nations as well as the public and international scientific community, to the greater extent feasible and practicable of the nature, conduct, locations and results of such activities."

In addition to the foregoing, it is a fact that since the acceptance of General Assembly Resolution 1721 (XVI) both the USA and the USSR have informed - and in three cases France and Italy also - the General Secretary, a fact which poses the further question whether this many years practice can be regarded already as a customary-law rule under international law?

In my opinion, the answer to the latter question must be, for the time being, a negative one. The said practice, namely, has been followed in a repeated and regular manner by two states only. Consequently, such practice - no matter how important the states in question be - cannot be qualified as a customary-law rule which would be universally valid for all states. The less so because neither the extent of information (the date to be communicated) nor the extent of international registration have been defined so far.

Thus, from Article VIII it merely follows, in my opinion, that the states carrying on space activities are obligated to establish and to keep national registries by municipal legal rules; such registries must be kept not only for enabling identification of ownership, but also for determining the facts necessary for salvage and liability for damages. The obligations relating to international registration should be regulated by a separate treaty and until such time as an agreement of this type will come about, only the duty of general information, as laid down in Article XI, will be incumbent on the states.

Mrs. Galloway's objection:

> It does seem that the treaty language clearly refers to national
> registries. But no obligation to keep a national registry follows
> from Article VIII. From Article VIII, it follows that a State Party
> which does not carry a space object on its registry will not benefit
> from the provisions of that article. Failure to maintain a registry
> would be no violation of the Treaty.

The author of this report accepts the above objection, remarking however that at least _de lege ferenda_ steps should be made towards the introduction of the national registries, the lack of which could easily lead to anarchy with space activities growing more frequent.

4. What are the consequences of the failure to comply with the "appropriate international consultations" mentioned in Article IX?

Under Article IX: "If a State Party to the Treaty has reason to believe that an activity or experiment planned by it or its nationals in outer space, including the Moon and other celestial bodies, would cause potentially harmful interference with activities of other State Parties in the peaceful exploration and use of outer space...it should undertake appropriate international consultations before proceeding with any such activity or experiment." QUERY: When the aforementioned "harmful interference" ensues without the State Party previously having initiated appropriate international consultation, what is the kind of responsibility that such state will have to bear?

Under the general rules of international law, when a state commits a breach of international law, it will become liable to sanctions determined by international law to be applied against such state by the other states, particularly by the state having suffered injury. It is doubtless that a contracting state which, defying Article IX of the Treaty, fails to initiate international consultations before engaging in a potentially harmful space activity or experiment, and particularly if such neglect actually causes "harmful interference," such state will have violated its international contractual obligation committing thereby a breach under international law. However, the sanctions applicable against such state will be limited by Paragraph 4, Art. 2, of the United Nations Charter, which prohibits the use of force in international relations. Consequently, only retortions could be applied as sanctions against the law-breaking state, but it is disputed whether non-armed reprisals are allowed, considering the above-quoted provision of the Charter.

Mrs. Galloway's observation:

"The only question relating to Article IX might be whether or not it is an essential article whose breach would be material, giving rise to consequence which might differ from breach of a non-essential article."

5. What is the legal nature of the provision of Article X under which "the States Parties to the Treaty shall consider on a basis of equality any requests by other State Parties to the Treaty to be afforded an opportunity to observe the flight of space objects launched by those States?"

The answer to this question can essentially be found in Paragraph 2 of the same Article which provides that the respective conditions shall be determined by agreement between the States concerned. Under such circumstances the rule relating to the opportunity for observation as defined in Article X can be, at most, regarded as a recommendation. With the addition, however, that if a State Party grants opportunities for observation to another State Party under an agreement concluded with the latter, then - on a basis of equality - it cannot deny the same to other State Parties raising identical claims. In all cases, therefore, bilateral or multilateral agreements are necessary in order that the actual right of observation be constituted at all.

Mrs. Galloway's objections are the following:

I do not agree with the conclusion that, under Article X, if a State Party grants opportunities for space flight observation to another State Party, it cannot deny the same to other State Parties raising identical claims. This conclusion is not in accordance with the understandings of the treaty negotiators. States Parties have undertaken an obligation only to consider requests on a basis of equality. They are not compelled to grant requests of all once they have granted the request of one. A State may find the scientific and technical benefits of participation in operations of one space flight observation facility to be an inducement to enter into the first agreement, whereas the added benefits of a second agreement might not be as attractive. This would be sufficient grounds for a State having considered the second request on a 'basis of equality,' to reject that request. The negotiating history makes clear that the phrase 'shall consider on a basis of equality' was intended to preserve this flexibility for a State Party to weigh each request on its merits in terms of the State's own needs and not compel it to enter any agreement or identical agreements with every applicant. In considering this question, Article X, paragraph 2 must be taken into account, which provides that any such arrangements must be determined by agreement between the parties.

Against this objection the undersigned maintains his standpoint that inasmuch as a State Party has granted observation rights to another, in this case - in principle - a third State Party could claim such rights, although it is doubtless that such claims can only be realized according to Art. X, Paragraph 2, through the agreement of the interested states.

6. <u>What are the rights and duties created by the Treaty in respect to international inter-governmental organizations</u>?

Mr. M. Bourély makes as his starting point Art. XIII, Paragraph 1 which reads:

"The provisions of this Treaty shall apply to the activities of States Parties to the Treaty in the exploration and use of outer space, including the Moon and other celestial bodies, whether such activities are carried on by a single State Party to the Treaty or jointly with other states, including cases where they are carried on within the framework of international inter-governmental organizations."

This prompts the comment that the provisions of the Treaty are rendered applicable to the international inter-governmental organizations through the intermediary of the States Parties to the Treaty who are members of them. However, whereas such a concept is logical in the case of an "inter-governmental organization" in the broad sense of the term, i.e., the case of a Treaty of Association or a governmental conference, it is no longer so in the event of the organization being given a formal status and a legal personality. Such is the case in particular of the two European space organizations, ESRO and ELDO. It would also be the case of any other world or regional organization engaging in sporadic space activities.

Without dwelling on the regrettable fact that these organizations, although endowed with legal personality, were not invited to give their opinion when the draft Treaty was being discussed, it may be noted that the provision contained in the first paragraph of Article XIII constitutes an application of the theory of stipulation and promise pro tertio, under Roman law. Unfortunately, at least two points remain moot:

A. What is the status of the Member States of an organization not parties to the Treaty?

The answer is obviously that they are not bound by the first paragraph of Article XIII, nor therefore will they feel bound by the provision of the Treaty, whether as members of the organization or as sovereign States.

B. To mitigate this drawback, therefore, can the organizations, or at any rate those having legal personality, sign or accede to the Treaty?

The reply is incontrovertibly negative by reason of the terms of Article XIV, which very clearly restricts to States the right to sign or accede to the Treaty.

This manifestly deliberate state of affairs is all the more deplorable because - and this is the second comment - all the Treaty provisions are directly applicable to the international inter-governmental organizations albeit the Treaty has not been signed by them. This is indicated by the wording of the first Paragraph of Article XIII.

Upon a rather closer scrutiny of the situation, a third comment springs to mind, namely, that there is at least one area, responsibility, in which the legal relations stemming from the Treaty begin to be exceedingly complicated.

As already mentioned, Article VI with reference to general, or rather political, responsibility for compliance with the Treaty states: "When activities are carried on in outer space, including the Moon and other celestial bodies, by an international organization, responsibility for compliance with this Treaty shall be borne both by the international organization and by the States Parties to the Treaty participating in such organization." The phrase "and by" indicates plurality of responsibilities between the Member States and the Organization as such. This constitutes therefore a quite remarkable deviation from the basic principle underlying the first paragraph of Article XIII, according to which an organization's rights and obligations under the Treaty are received through the Member States. But is such derogation well founded?

In view of the overall concept of the Treaty it would appear dubious.

To begin with, a mention of the organizations with regard to political responsibility may be warranted in the case of those having legal personality, but not in the opposite case; now, the Treaty does not define what is meant by an international inter-governmental organization.

This article also raises the question already alluded to of an organization's Member States who are not parties to the Treaty.

But the situation is complicated still further by the question of financial liability, i.e. the obligation to compensate for damage according to Article VII, since this lays the obligation equally on each State carrying out a launching, each State procuring a launching and each State from whose territory or facilities an object is launched.

Obviously, however, in many cases such States, even if parties to the Treaty, will not necessarily all be members of the organization whose activities are in question and for them the Treaty will remain a dead letter.

Of course, these difficulties could not have escaped the notice of the States who negotiated the Space Treaty and who agreed to sign it; the conditions in which it came into being made it a political gesture whose importance can never be sufficiently emphasized, but whose price was the creation of a legal situation that is both complex and ambiguous regarding the status of the international organizations in respect to the Treaty.

But a fourth comment that can be made is that the authors of the Treaty believe they were answering this objection when they added a second paragraph to Article XIII. This states:

> Any practical questions arising in connection with activities carried on by international inter-governmental organizations in the exploration and use of outer space, including the Moon and other celestial bodies, shall be resolved by the States Parties to the Treaty either with the appropriate international organization or with one or more States members of that international organization, which are parties to this Treaty.

But this praiseworthy recommendation is strictly speaking superfluous since such a settlement would have been reached necessarily and spontaneously. Moreover, the decisions taken can only result in internally effective measures whereas the true problem is, and remains, these organizations' status in the international community.

Since the Space Treaty only constitutes in sum a general framework, and particular treaties on liability and assistance are already under study in the legal sub-committee of the UN Space Committee, we may be permitted to hope that these other treaties will be able to give realistic consideration to the existence of international inter-governmental organizations engaged in space activities and, after consulting with them, accord them their due rights and obligations independently of and without prejudice to the rights and obligations of the States composing them.

Such a realistic approach to the problem is all the more imperative in that some day – we at any rate may hope – space activities will be conducted by world-wide organizations, notably within the framework of the UN itself. There is no reason to wait until then before granting the organizations, already in existence and already practicing that international collaboration in space aspired to by the Treaty itself, the place in the international community that is their due.

These are the conclusions of Mr. Bourély.

The undersigned rapporteur fully agrees with the above argumentation insofar as the provisions of the Space Treaty do not define in a clear manner the rights and duties of international organizations deriving from the Treaty. The undersigned, however, thinks that the Space Treaty does not stand alone in this respect, as the legal status of inter-governmental organizations is not regulated elsewhere in a general manner either. It is known that the UN International Law Committee first as a sequence to the General Assembly Resolution 1289 (XIII) and next in 1962 has dealt extensively with the question. No decision, however, was reached as to the question whether in addition to the States themselves also international inter-governmental organizations should be recognized as subjects of international law, and if so, under what conditions and to what degree.

It appears that the signatories of the Space Treaty did not want to create a precedent in this question by recognizing the inter-governmental organizations as having equal status with the States. This is the source of the ambiguities which will continue to exist as long as the general regulation of the legal status of international organizations is pending.

$$-\quad-\quad-\quad-\quad-$$

As seen from the foregoing report, even in the midst of the 3-strong working group, differing opinions have been voiced in respect to almost every question. It will be the task of the participants of the Colloquium to contribute to the formation of common standpoints by answering the questions listed under 1 to 6.

$$*\quad*\quad*\quad*\quad*$$

REMARKS ON THE INTERNATIONAL STATUS OF INTERNATIONAL SPACE ORGANIZATIONS
by
Jerzy Sztucki

The problem referred to in the title of this paper has at least two different aspects.

The first one is that of the scope of competence of international organizations with regard to space activities. This aspect of the problem has been given wide consideration in the legal literature, including various private proposals for the institutionalization of all the space activities within the framework of a world organization which would also have exclusive jurisdiction over outer space and celestial bodies. But on the official level this aspect of the problem was practically dismissed as early as in 1958, and with the exception of incidental, loose and marginal remarks during discussions in various U.N. organs has not been touched upon since. The question of competence of international organizations with regard to space and space activities might be, in itself, a subject of a special study. This paper, however, is focused exclusively on the second aspect of the problem - that of the status of international organizations in legal instruments intended to regulate space activities.

The international lawmaking for space activities has been heretofore concentrated on three main issues:

a) general principles, embodied first in the Declaration of 1963 and then developed in the Treaty of 1967;

b) regulations concerning assistance to and return of astronauts and space objects, to be embodied in a special convention;

c) regulations concerning liability for damages caused by space objects, also to be embodied in a separate convention.

During the negotiations on all three issues, considerable attention has been given to problems resulting from the participation of international intergovernmental organizations in space activities.

It is to be recalled that in the Declaration of Principles of 1963 this fact is taken into account in one sentence of Paragraph 5 which provides that:

> ...when activities are carried on in outer space by an international organization, responsibility for compliance with the principles set forth in this Delcaration shall be borne by the international organization and by the States participating in it.

This provision, redrafted in order to comply with formal requirements of a treaty, is repeated in the last sentence of Art. VI of the Treaty of 1967 which, in order to avoid any misunderstandings as to the scope of application of all of its provisions, explicitly states in Art. XIII that,

> ...the provisions of this Treaty shall apply to the activities of States Parties to the Treaty in the exploration and use of outer space, including the moon and other celestial bodies, whether such activities are carried on by a single State Party to the Treaty or jointly with other States, including cases where they are carried on within the framework of international inter- governmental organizatons. Any practical question arising in connection

with activities carried on by international inter-governmental organizations in the exploration and use of outer space, including the moon and other celestial bodies, shall be resolved by the States Parties to the Treaty either with the appropriate international organization or with one or more States members of that international organization, which are Parties to this Treaty.

Before passing to further considerations two points should be made clear at the very outset in connection with this article.

First, it applies only to international intergovernmental organizations and not to international non-governmental organizations. Consequently, in this paper "international organizations" are to be understood as intergovernmental organizations only.

Secondly, it applies only to those intergovernmental organizations which serve as the framework for the joint activities of states in the exploration and use of outer space and not to all international organizations.

It is to be noted that, while in connection with the Declaration of Principles the question of status of international organizations did not give rise to much discussion, it did provoke some arguments touching upon general problems of international law, during the negotiations on the Treaty.

In particular, a proposal was made to the effect that:

...if an international organization which conducts activities in outer space including the moon and celestial bodies transmits ... a declaration that it accepts and undertakes to comply with the provisions of this Treaty, all the provisions except articles (...concerning signature, ratification and accession...) shall apply to the organization as they apply to a State which is a Party to this Treaty.

This proposal envisaged also that:

...the States Parties to this Treaty undertake to use their best endeavors to ensure that any international organization which conducts such activities and of which they are constituent members is authorized to make and will make the declaration referred to in paragraph 1 of this article.

Another similar proposal envisaged that:

The States Parties which conduct space activities through international organizations undertake that those activities will fully comply with the provisions of the Treaty. A declaration to this effect may be transmitted by such an organization to /the depositary authority/.

Proposals of an analogous character are included also in some draft agreements on assistance and return and on liability for damages and in amendments thereto. One of these drafts in its earlier version envisaged even the possibility of an international space organization becoming a Party to the Convention.

Proposals of this type gained support of some members of the U.N. Legal Sub-Committee while a number of other members strongly opposed them. As it is seen from the record of the last session of the U.N. Legal Sub-Committee in June-July 1967, proposals of this character are still pending in connection with the discussion on drafts of the two special conventions though the concept of a separate acceptance of an international agreement by international organizations apparently has already been rejected in the preparation of the Treaty on Principles of January 27, 1967.

Besides the divergency on the question of a separate acceptance of an international agreement by international organizations, there is a certain variety of approaches in formulating the position of international organizations vis à vis specific rights and obligations contained in various material provisions of the documents under review. Roughly speaking, one can distinguish three main patterns here:

1. International organizations are not being mentioned at all; this pattern is followed in all versions of the Soviet draft agreement on assistance and return and also in the early versions of the Belgian working paper on liability.

2. International organizations are not being mentioned in particular provisions or are being mentioned only in some of them (e.g. Art. VI of the Treaty of 1967), but a special article is intended to settle generally the question of the relationship between the provisions of a given document and the activities carried on within international organizations. This, in turn, is being done in two ways:

- either by providing for the applicability of material provisions of a given document to the activities of international organizations;
- or, by providing for a separate acceptance of the material part of an agreement by an international organization.

The first way has been adopted first of all in the Treaty of 1967 and also in the Soviet self-amendment to the second revision of the draft convention on assistance and return. The Hungarian draft convention on liability is also very close to this pattern.

3. International organizations are mentioned side by side with states in all pertinent articles; this pattern has been followed in all versions of the American draft agreement on assistance and return.

The above mentioned proposals touch upon the problem of legal personality of international law. And in the context of those proposals this problem involves two practical questions of treaty-making, i.e.:

1. whether or not international organization should be expressly referred to in a legal instrument (generally in a special article or in all pertinent material provisions) as possible parties to the international legal relationships to be established in that instrument - in order to ensure that the activities carried on within their framework be in compliance with that instrument;

2. whether or not a separate acceptance of an international legal instrument by an international organization is necessary in order to produce this effect.

Although the second question has already been answered in the negative in the Treaty of 1967, the report of the subsequent (sixth) session of the U.N. Legal Sub-Committee (June-July 1967) shows that some members of the Sub-Committee consider this question still open. It has also been recorded in this report that in connection with the draft agreement on assistance and return it was also impossible to reach an agreement with regard to the first question.

As is well known, the problem of legal personality of international organizations as possible subjects of public international law has been widely discussed for a very long time in the legal literature as well as by the U.N. International Law Commission pursuant to the General Assembly resolution 1289 (XIII) and has remained unsolved. The opinions range from considering international organizations side by side with sovereign states as subjects of international law - though the opinions that this quality is in case of international organizations a "sui generis" one, or is limited, secondary, etc. - to the denial of this quality to international organizations.

It is certainly neither the purpose nor the ambition of this paper to solve on several pages the problem which has not been exhausted and still less - solved - in hundreds of volumes of scholarly writings. But it would be hardly possible to avoid any comments on that subject in general, since it has become inherent in practical negotiations.

It is to be noted first of all that regardless of the long lasting controversy over this problem in the theory of international law, never before has it provoked any serious controversy in practical treaty-making. In a number of instances entering into international agreements by international organizations has been taken for granted; in an equal number of instances a possibility of an international organization to become a party to an agreement has never come up at all although the substance of an agreement may have had bearing upon activities of this or that international organization. And the law-making for space activities is probably the first instance in the history of treaty-making when the question of status of international organizations has proved troublesome in practice.

This inevitably brings about some reflections as to the reason of this unusual situation.

A general outlook on the statutory provisions of the existing international organizations with regard to their aims, purposes and general functions leads to the conclusion that, roughly speaking, those functions amount to:

- co-ordination, unification and promotion of progress of national activities
  in a given field;
- some competence to handle international disputes and other political matters
  of international concern, which is the case with international organizations
  of general political purposes.

Both types of functions could be described in a very general sense as regulatory ones. As such, they are of purely international character and by its very nature cannot physically and may not legally fall within the competence or authority of any single state.

On the other hand, operational functions are, perhaps with only several exceptions, either completely lacking from the statutory provisions of international organizations in existance heretofore, or are limited to a kind of sponsorship.

If some international organizations do carry in practice some operational activities, these activities are of a marginal character with regard to their statutory functions - e.g. operating postal service by the United Nations, which has never raised the problem of a possible accession of the U.N. to the Universal Postal Convention. Similarly, nobody has ever raised the problem of an international organization acceding to the International Telecommunication Convention just because it might operate a radio station to specific international labor conventions because they might have a bearing upon the labor relations of the personnel employed by an organization.

Within the field of space activities we are facing a situation which is altogether different.

First of all, the statutory functions of the international space organizations are primarily operational ones. And it is not incidental that the strongest insistence on granting the international organizations a special, separate status with respect to international legal instruments to govern space activities came from the members of those organizations.

Moreover, the operational activities in question are by no means international in their nature. Quite to the contrary, space activities may be - and in fact, are - carried mostly on a national basis, and the international organizations created with a view to carrying on operational activities in space, perform functions falling essentially within the competence of individual states thus creating a certain functional analogy to the position of individual subjects of international law. They represent first of all a pool of resources, their regulatory function almost completely lacking, while their predominant function, operational, is to be in itself subject to international regulations.

This seems to explain why the question of the status of international organizations in the legal instruments to govern space activities has emerged and why it caused some difficulties in practical negotiations.

The concern of lawmakers about the widest possible application of a legal instrument they are to agree upon is perfectly natural and plausible. Since international organizations are an integral part of contemporary international life it is perfectly reasonable to have them included into the scope of application of appropriate international agreements.

However, the way it is to be done is not unimportant and for the practical reasons it would seem advisable to solve this problem on the basis of considerations of expediency rather than in a form implying specific position on the controversial problem of whether or not international organizations are subjects of international law - with all the consequences of this status.

The first approach is being represented by Article XIII of the Treaty of 1967, which, on one hand, provides generally for the applicability of its provisions to the activities carried on within the framework of international organizations; and on the other hand, leaves all practical questions which may arise in connection with activities carried on by those organizations involved. This is the way the matters have been always handled, even without specific treaty provisions to this effect.

The second approach has been represented by various proposals mentioned earlier - especially those providing for a separate acceptance of agreements under negotiations by international organizations. This approach is being based on the assumption that international organizations possess the quality of subjects under public international law and, consequently, by the very virtue of this quality may become parties to international commitments.

The following considerations are usually presented in support of this assumption:

1. Statutes of international organizations usually provide for their legal personality;

2. International organizations are authorized under their constitutive acts to include international agreements;

3. International organizations are, in fact, parties to a great number of international agreements.

It must be noted, however, that all these arguments are challengeable.

Argument sub 1 seems to be based on a misconception. The statutory provisions in question, starting with Art. 104 of the U.N. Charter - through the corresponding provisions in many other statutes - down to Art. XIV of the ESRO Convention and Art. 20 of the ELDO Convention, just to mention expressly space organizations, deal with the question of their legal personality under domestic legal order of the member states and not with the question of the quality of the subject of public international law. In some cases this is indicated expressis verbis, e.g. in Art. 104 of the U.N. Charter, which runs as follows:

> The Organizations shall enjoy in the territory of each of its Members such legal capacity as may be necessary for the exercise of its functions...

It follows no less clearly from the Art. 20 of the ELDO Convention that provides that:

> the Organization shall have legal personality. It shall in particular have the capacity to contract, to acquire and dispose of moveable and immoveable property, and to institute legal proceedings...

In some other cases, including Art. XIV of the ESRO Convention, this particular restrictive meaning of the corresponding articles is worded less clearly and may be only interpreted in the broader context, but it would not be reasonable to draw a conclusion from these differences in wording that some international organizations (e.g. ESRO) are subjects under public international law, while others with differently worded statutes are only legal persons under domestic order of member states and not subjects of public international law. Such a construction - probably contrary to intentions - would mean that precisely the most representative and authoritative organizations, including the United Nations and its specialized agencies, would be - because of the wording of a particular clause in their statutes - deprived of the quality of subjects of international law. This proposition would probably be hardly acceptable. Apparently, however, in all statutes the question dealt with in corresponding articles is exactly the same and should not be confused with the problem of international organizations as possible subjects of international law.

As far as arguments sub 2 and 3 are concerned, it is necessary to draw attention to the following circumstances:

a) the capacity of international organizations to enter into agreements does not stem ipso iure from the fact of their existence, as is the case with sovereign states, ius tractatuum being one of their basic subjective rights, but from the consensus of states - members of a given organization - expressed in an international treaty (the constitution of an organization). This capacity is always limited to the specific types of agreements, which may vary from one organization to another, according to the provisions of the constitution of the organization, or to the special ad hoc decisions by its representative organ.

b) there is not a single case of an international organization being in any form a separate party to a multilateral treaty setting forth general principles, standards and regulations of international conduct, even if its contents has had any bearing upon the activities of the said organization. Conventions on the privileges and immunities of the United Nations and on the privileges and immunities of various specialized agencies - to which respective organizations are not separate parties in any form - are remarkable and very instructive examples in this respect. And this situation has never been construed or interpreted in the sense that international organizations are free to act in defiance of legal rules in force.

c) Under constitutional instruments of the U.N., specialized agencies, which might be reasonably considered as representative examples both on account of the number of their members and of their extensive contracts and administrative apparatus, their capacity to enter into agreements does include agreements also with international non-governmental organizations and even with national institutions, i.e., agreements which do not involve the question of whether a party to such an agreement is a subject of international law, for non-governmental organizations or national institutions certainly are not, and the agreements in question are not international ones under public international law. This, however, only shows that the capacity of these organizations to enter into agreements is of quite different order than the question of possessing the quality of a subject of international law.

d) Practice of international relations tends to prove that the capacity to enter into agreements which are international in character may belong to parties which by no standards might be considered as subjects of international law and never claimed such a quality. By way of illustration one may quote here agreements entered into with individual states by such organs as the Governing Commission for Upper Silesia (a tripartite semi-military organ established under the Treaty of Versailles to carry on the plebiscite), the Governing Commission for the Saar Basin, or by the Council of Ambassadors as one party agreements registered with the League of Nations.

It must be remembered, above all, that international organization is a form of multilateral contracts between states. Quite a variety of forms of such contacts is in use in present day international relations, ranging from ad hoc diplomatic conferences - through periodical conferences of specific groups of states, some times directly envisaged in a treaty, as is the case with the Antarctic Treaty of 1959, Art. IX - further, through standing international diplomatic organs without permanent international secretariat, as the Council of Foreign Ministers established under the Potsdam Agreements - up to the organizations with permanent international secretariats more or less developed.

The question immediately arises: Is it possible at all that a form of contacts (cooperation) between subjects or public international law become in itself another separate subject under the same legal order? The negative answer to this question seems obvious. But should a positive answer be attempted, a further question would immediately arise - namely, at what point does a form of international contacts (cooperation) turn into being a subject of public international law?

An answer that the existence of a permanent international secretariat is a decisive factor would have to be challenged on the grounds that the existence of a specific organ as a condition to acquire a quality of the subject of public international law is a concept totally alien to this legal order.

An answer that the decisive factor would be a statutory provision vesting an organization with the quality of subject of public international law would have to be challenged on the following grounds:

a) An overwhelming majority - if not all - of the existing constitutions of international organizations provide clearly only for their legal personality under domestic legal systems of member states;

b) International organizations whose constitutions provide only for their legal personality under domestic law, nevertheless, do enter into agreements of an international character so that this capacity obviously does not depend upon such a statutory provision;

c) Such a concept would be of no practical value with respect to organizations of more limited number of members since even if their constitution contained an appropriate provision, it would not be binding for non-member states.

Having said all this, we must come back to the fact that international agreements are, nevertheless, being entered into by international organizations and we seemingly find ourselves in a vicious circle. The only consistent way out is in taking a different look upon the phenomenon of entering into agreements by international organizations.

Apparently, this phenomenon should not be regarded as a subjective right of an organization - as is the case with sovereign states - but as a _modus procedendi_ or _modus operandi_ of an international organization agreed by constituent members between themselves. In some cases it is even difficult to call it "a right" since entering into specific agreements may be obligatory. This is the case with agreements between the United Nations and the specialized agencies (Art. 57, para. 1 and Art. 63, para. 1 of the U.N. Charter). Conclusions of agreements as a form of commitment has been also obligatory under Art. 43 and under Chapter XII of the Charter. Members of the organization may agree to adopt this _modus operandi_ also in the cases not envisaged directly in the constitutive document of an organization. And this has been the case with agreements between respective organizations on one part and the respective governments on the other concerning the organizations' headquarters. But it is to be added here immediately that at least five from among the U.N. specialized agencies operate without concluding agreements regarding their headquarters, although probably all specialized agencies would have to conclude such agreements should those be regarded as resulting from the very nature of an international organization as a separate subject of international law. The concept of international organizations entering into agreements, as the _modus operandi_ which may or may not be adopted in particular cases or categories of matters is based primarily upon considerations of convenience, expediency or effectiveness and not upon the recognition of international organizations as subjects of international law _in principle and in general_.

Another question is that an international organization having once entered into an agreement, technically becomes a party to a commitment which may be international and public in character. And, in this purely technical meaning, it may be assimilated to a state in the sense that it may become and becomes subject of specific international rights and obligations.

However, the legal nature of the two technically analogous situations is very different. States are subjects of international law in general by their very existence and by virtue of this quality they may enter into a whole range of international legal commitments. But with regard to international organizations the situation is quite opposite. They enter into specific international legal commitments when the interested states deem it proper, and to the extent they deem proper, - and only when so agreed between the subjects of international law - do international organizations acquire indirectly and in a technical sense only the quality of a subject of specific international rights and obligations.

What are the practical consequences of this approach on lawmaking for space activities?

The first and the most important one is that a legal construction under which an international organization by virtue of its very existence or by virtue of the statutory provision on its legal status is entitled to accede or not to accede to any international agreement as a separate subject of international law is not warranted. The legal title for entering into international agreements by an international organization is created only by the specific consensus of states should they deem such a modus procedendi appropriate in a given case or category of cases. However, in the case of separate acceptance of multilateral treaties by an international organization much is to be said against the appropriateness of such a modus procedenti when confronted with possible practical solutions. Roughly speaking, there might exist three possibilities:

a) All members of the organization are parties to the international agreement in question;

b) None of the members of the organization is a party to such an agreement;

c) Some members of the organization are parties to the agreement;

Let us consider each of these three possibilities:

- In the first situation an accession of an organization to an agreement would be superfluous since member states are integral entities, and the rights and obligations they assume apply to all their activities regulated by the agreement in question; if, however, an organization did not accede to the agreement, this - first of all - would be contrary to the concept of the integrity of member states as a subject of international law; secondly, it would mean that when acting through an international organization, states are not bound by the valid agreements in force. Thus, the practical result would be quite contrary to inventions: limitation of the scope of application of an agreement instead of the assurance of the widest possible scope of its application.

- In the second situation providing an international organization with a choice, to accede or not to accede to an international agreement, is simply pointless; one certainly cannot expect an international organization, no member of which has become a party to an agreement, to accede to such an agreement itself. And this really makes no difference in comparison with the situation when such a choice for international organizations would not exist at all.

- Also, in the third situation it would be difficult to see any useful purpose in envisaging a possibility of acceptance or non-acceptance of a multilateral treaty by international organizations. If the organization does not accede, the results would be . just as undesirable as in the first situation with respect to members being parties to the agreement, while members not being parties to the agreement would be in the same position as if the choice for the organization did not exist at all. On the other hand, if an organization made use of the possibility to accede, it would be still highly doubtful whether this would make the provisions of an agreement binding upon members which otherwise did not sign it, especially if within the organization they also voted against the acceptance of that agreement. Should they have to vote within the organization for the acceptance of an agreement, it would be difficult to find reasons why they would not have to sign this agreement also as individual states.

Proposals advocating a separate acceptance of agreements by international organizations envisage also that parties to agreement which are members of international organizations would do their utmost to ensure that the organization in question make a declaration of acceptance. But in practice, either these members are influential enough and in that case they would be in a position to ensure a de facto compliance with an agreement by their organization, which would be sufficient, or they are not influential enough - and then the reference to their endeavors is pointless.

Anyway, this third situation is by no means different from that in which several states would participate in a common space venture, not institutionalized in international organization, only some of them being parties to an agreement relevant to this venture. And the practical problems involved are exactly the same in both cases.

These are probably considerations behind the already mentioned fact that up to now international organizations have not appeared in any form as separate parties to multilateral agreements establishing legal order for different fields of international activities. And this long established and well founded practice has been also confirmed by the Space Treaty of 1967, in spite of some formal proposals to the contrary submitted during negotiations.

Attempts at a revival of these proposals still later in the U.N. Legal Sub-Committee seem therefore unwarranted not only in the light of general and well-founded international practice but also in the light of the recently signed treaty which should be regarded as setting some binding patterns for further more detailed agreements.

The last session of the U.N. Legal Sub-Committee provided additional material in support of the view represented here - namely, that the question of the status of international organizations in international agreements is the question of convenient and practicable modus operandi rather than the principal question of their quality of subjects of international law in general.

One may refer to draft agreements relating to two items on the Sub-Committee's agenda and presented by one and the same member. Although both drafts might be applicable also to the activities carried on within the framework of international organizations, only one of them envisages a possibility of their separate acceptance by international organizations. Regardless of the author's objections against such a possibility, the very fact of making a distinction in this respect in two drafts seems to confirm the view that the position of the sponsor is based on practical considerations in each case and not on some preconceived principles which as such should have been equally applied in both cases.

The report of the Sub-Committee's last session shows also that while it has been possible to reach an agreement on formal references to international organizations as subjects of specific rights or obligations in connection with two questions relating to the agreement on liability, at the same it has not been possible to reach similar agreement in connection with two articles of the convention on assistance and return. And here again we are witnessing a lack of uniformity in the position of negotiating parties which might be expected as stemming from practical considerations only.

In connection with the question of status of international organizations as shaped in Article VI and XIII of the Treaty of 1967, the Report of the Working Group on "Problems of Interpretation of the Space Treaty of 27 January 1967" contains an opinion of one of its members "that there is at least one area, responsibility, in which the legal relations stemming from the Treaty begin to be exceedingly complicated."

The provisions of the said articles are, undoubtedly, very general in nature and do not dwell on the procedure to be followed in specific situations which may or may not arise in the future practice. And this seems to be the only reasonable way to deal with the problem of status of international organizations in the international space agreements - also in future agreements on particular aspects of space activities. In this connection, it is to be noted that various draft agreements on the assistance and return and on the liability while using the term "international organization" do not contain a clause, similar to that of Article XIII of the Treaty of 1967, restricting the meaning of that term to organizations carrying space activities. Thus, these drafts extend the applicability of the respective provisions of all international organizations. One may wonder whether this obvious departure from the scheme of the Space Treaty of 1967 is intentional or is simply due to the lack of precision at the state of drafting.

It is to be admitted that if this departure is intentional, there might be some good practical reasons for it, since non-space organizations may be also involved in situations falling within the scope of the forthcoming agreements. E.g. a non space organization may suffer damage or may be in a position to render some assistance in rescue operations. However, it is clear that the position of non-space organizations vis-à-vis provisions of those agreements is different from that of space organizations and that, consequently, one can hardly place them on an equal footing with respect to each particular provision. It seems, therefore, that detailing excessively the provisions pertaining to the rights and obligations of international organizations under the forthcoming agreements while - on the other hand - speaking generally of all international organizations is not a very practical method. And this seems to be an additional argument in support of dealing in a rather general manner with the question of applicability of the said agreements to the situations involving international organizations.

One can hardly see any danger for the international legal order in this way of action. Existing multilateral agreements usually contain no specific references to their applicability of international organizations although they may be involved in matters settled by these agreements. And one could hardly quote examples of offences to the international legal order being caused by the lack of a detailed elaboration of the status of international organizations in multilateral agreements.

Quite to the contrary, it may be feared that more troubles may be caused by attempts at the detailed elaboration on this problem which might only further complicate the very process of lawmaking for space activities.

*   *   *   *   *

II. Other Contributions and Comments

The papers are grouped under the several topics adopted for the program of the Colloquium and are reproduced in the approximate order that they were presented by the participants. A very useful feature has been added, namely, summaries of the discussions of the participants. The year 1967 is an important one, not only because ten years have passed since the first artificial satellite was launched into outer space, but also because it is the year of the entry into force of the Space Treaty. The many contributions on this Treaty (14) are a clear indication of the interest of space lawyers in this instrument. As a first collection of commentaries on its provisions, this part of the Proceedings is of great importance for the students of space law. But other subjects also deserve the readers' attention, such as the legal status of stations on the moon and telecommunication by satellites. A veritable plethora of papers have been submitted, but, within the available space, it is impossible to give equal attention to each of these. The following brief comments have to suffice.

After the introductory part I, in which, apart from the annual report of the President and also an homage to Cooper has been included, part II is concerned with a futuristic subject, "Stations on the moon." The subject entails such questions as: can an area be claimed around a station, and if so, what is the extent of the jurisdiction which could be exercised as to acts or disputes involving personnel of two neighboring stations. These and other questions are raised in the introductory report presented by Horsford "to stimulate discussion." The comments (by Machado) and the ensuing discussions show a careful approach to these problems by most commentators ("there are certain rights and jurisdiction in the state of the flag") and a tendency to rely on the provisions of the Space Treaty.

A contribution of Rodoreda (Spain) goes into the question of concessions for exploration of a celestial body, distributed by the UN, and deals extensively with the way in which this should take place and the legal consequences therefrom. Ferrer (Argentina) surveys the issues and ends with twenty conclusions, the last of which states: "La Lay del Estado de Registro de la aventura espacial será aplicable a èsta. Y por tanto, a los vehiculos y en general, estaciones que la componen, asi como al área de ocupación."

A paper by Iványi and Móra on the applicability of patent and copyright laws in interplanetary relations concludes with the thesis that if a "work" is protected in the "mothercountry," it will also be protected at the moonstation, and vice versa (in the case of a work created at a moonstation).

Jurisdiction of a state with regard to a settlement and its inhabitants on the moon, and a state's mining rights with respect to the natural resources of the moon are the subjects on which Zhukov gives his views. Telecommunications by satellites: Some papers of high quality have been submitted on this important subject, and understandably Intelsat plays an important role in the discussions. Thus, where Cocca concludes, in his introductory report, that none of the international organizations known at the present could serve as a model for an organization charged with the administration or operation of an "international public service" supplied by communications satellites, he also excludes Intelsat (and the ITU). Why this unique organization does not meet with general approval is a matter on which Colino, in an excellent and thorough paper on Intelsat's many faces, gives the reader some insight: the main criticism concerns the US domination through the system of voting and the position of ComSat as manager of the system. Some further inside information is provided by Doyle, whose contribution has been reprinted in full. Armstrong, finally, gives an interesting account of the technical possibilities and economic advantages of satellite communication, whereas Dessaucy looks at the consequences of considering direct broadcasting satellites as constituting an international public service.

Interpretation of the 1967 Space Treaty: Most attention at the Belgrade Colloquium goes to the various provisions of the Space Treaty. The importance of its interpretation led the ITSL Board of Directors to appoint a working group to study the matter. The interesting introductory report which is the result of the work of Galloway, Bourely and Herczeg, the members of this working group, has been reproduced in full, together with the summary of the discussions to which the report led. One of the main questions, which divides members of the working group and other participants alike, concerns Art. IV of the Treaty: Does the obligation of use for exclusively peaceful purposes extend beyond the moon and other celestial bodies to the entire outer space? One view, based on an interpretation of the Treaty as a whole, is that the question should be answered in the affirmative (Herczeg, Fasan); others look at the text of Art. IV which appears to lead to a negative answer (Roy, Verplaetse, Galloway). The term "peaceful" in itself is another problem; both Gál and Galloway discuss its meaning, and the former arrives after a solid argument at the conclusion that the term means "non-military," whereas Mrs. Galloway appears to prefer a meaning which is mostly referred to as "non-aggressive." Gál's view, it must be added, is shared by most if not all Soviet authors. The provisions of the Treaty which deal with international organizations (directly or indirectly) are subjected to strong criticism by Bourely; the underlying reason for the fact that those organizations are the poor cousins in the Treaty is obviously a consequence of the different views held by socialist and western countries with regard to an organization's legal status vis-à-vis the international community.

Berger briefly describes the history of the Treaty, and enumerates its provisions; the latter approach is also taken by Diederiks-Verschoor, who adds some useful observations to the articles described. Short contributions of Pompeo Magno, Schrader and Smirnoff and a paper written by Vereshechetin conclude this part of the Proceedings. The latter author examines the question whether scientific and technical agreements on space - e.g. the Dryden-Blagonravov agreement between NASA and the Soviet Academy of Sciences - constitute a source of space law, a question which he answers in the affirmative.

A list of the signatures of the Outer Space Treaty forms a useful extra, although the date of closure of the list should have been added.

Various subjects: The "benefit of all countries" formula of Art. I of the Space Treaty is merely a "general concept," a "goal" and a general purpose, according to Brooks, who presents thereby the official American point of view. More specifically, he asserts, a US satellite is not available for the use of countries other than the USA except by consent; and through an assessment of the other provisions of the Space Treaty, he shows that the Treaty as a whole did little to advance international organization. As a practical example of international organization with respect to a specific activity, Brooks mentions Intelsat, and he concludes that both a universal space agency with an over-all task and ad hoc enterprises with specific tasks can exist together in the future.

The only paper on the important question of liability for damage resulting from space activities has been submitted by Meloni, who discusses, consecutively, the liability of states and international organizations, the various kinds of damage, the principle of liability and the question of its limitation, and, finally, the important question of law and procedure in case of disputes with respect to a claim. A draft resolution follows in which Meloni puts, inter alia, a limitation of liability.

Pelegri (Spain) looks at the consequences of exploration of celestial bodies by one or more states, and comes to doubt that exploration for the benefit of mankind will soon be a reality. Poulantzas discusses Art. IV and XII of the Space Treaty which deal with demilitarization of celestial bodies and supervision and control in the form of a right of inspection of stations and installations on these celestial bodies. (One of the imperfections to which attention is drawn in this paper is the fact that stations or vehicles in outer space can not be inspected.)

Von Rauchhaupt gives an account of ten years of development of space activities and space law culminating in the conclusion of the 1967 Treaty. Frequency allocation and interference with telecommunications, meteorological satellites used for military purposes, and the rescue of astronauts are subjects on which Simic gives his views in his article "Legal problems relating to man-made objects in space." He is followed by a lawyer-scientist team, Shiffer and Snyders, who propose to make international space treaties and inspection and control of space activities enforceable by means of established legal and technical international organizations, namely the UN, ICSU and the ICJ. The authors do not go into the question of whether and to what extent their scheme is feasible to a contribution to the states concerned.

In addition to a contribution on legal aspects of international cooperation in outer space, written by Tapia Salinas, the fifth part of the Proceedings finally contains the paper of Sztucki, which gives an excellent picture of the socialist views with respect to the international status of international (space) organizations. Part V is closed with an interesting paper on "Semantics and space," submitted by Thomas, and a short summary of discussions. Thomas admonishes us that after having concentrated on expanding capabilities of communications facilities, e.g. by satellite, we should now first examine languages and try to determine how they can be used more effectively, and she quotes a CBS vice-president's worry: once we have the world's attention, what are we going to say to them? Semantics, the study of the meaning of words, may be of some help in this connection. In an addendum to the Proceedings a special legal problem which was the subject of a meeting of the scientific-legal liaison committee of the IISL is presented, namely, that of the definition of outer space.

Galloway, in her report to this meeting, recalled that in September 1967 the Scientific and Technical Subcommittee of the UNCOUPOS concluded that at the present time there are no scientific criteria on which to base a precise and lasting definition of outer space. The following questions are raised to stimulate the discussion: (1) why do we want a definition of outer space? (2) why does it seem impossible at the present time to define outer space for the long-run future? (3) is it necessary to have a definition of outer space? (4) what should be our attitude toward this problem in the future? The tentative answers given by Galloway, and further comments on the questions in general from Zhukov and Kopal, give a very useful insight into the many aspects of the problem, thus forming a good conclusion of the Proceedings of this year Colloquium.

ELEVENTH COLLOQUIUM ON THE LAW OF OUTER SPACE

NEW YORK, 1968

I. Texts Reproduced

ANNUAL REPORT OF THE PRESIDENT

OF THE INTERNATIONAL INSTITUTE OF SPACE LAW

During the last year, an increasing interest of lawyers of the world in the activities of the Institute and their cordial cooperation in many respects should be noted.

1. Membership - The total membership of the Institute, which reached 314 on October 1, 1968,
    is largely representative of the worldwide legal community. The members are from the fol-
    lowing 49 countries: Argentina, Australia, Austria, Belgium, Brazil, Bulgaria, Canada,
    Chile, Colombia, Costa Rica, Czechoslovakia, German Democratic Republic, German Federal
    Republic, Denmark, Dominican Republic, Egypt, France, Greece, Hungary, Iceland, India,
    Iran, Israel, Italy, Japan, Luxemburg, Malta, Mexico, Netherlands, Norway, Papua, Para-
    guay, Peru, Philippines, Poland, Portugal, Rumania, Spain, Sweden, Switzerland, Taiwan,
    Thailand, Turkey, Uruguay, United Kingdom, U.S.A., U.S.S.R., Venezuela, and Yugoslavia.

2. Activities of the Institute
    a) Colloquia of Space Law - The Xth Colloquium of Space Law, held in Belgrade in Septem-
       ber 1967 under the chairmanship of Professor Milan Bartos, was a success with the
       participation of fifty lawyers from twenty-six countries.
           The discussions at the XIth Colloquium, to be held during the XIXth I.A.F. Con-
       gress, will be conducted by Mr. Paul Dembling, the distinguished General Counsel of
       NASA.
    b) Participation of IISL Members in International Meetings
       (i) United Nations Conference on the Exploration and Peaceful Uses of Outer Space
            (Vienna, August 1968) - Several members of the Institute took part as Represen-
            tatives of their Governments to the Conference; among them, three IISL Direc-
            tors were present. Another member, Professor Ambrosini, presided over the sec-
            tion on "Economic, Legal and Social Problems." The IISL President also attended
            the first sessions of the Conference.
       (ii) Conference of the International Law Association (Buenos Aires, August 1968) -
            The Conference had on its agenda several questions on space law (lower limits
            of space, telecommunications by satellites, legal status of spacecraft).
            Numerous members of the Institute, also members of the ILA, took part in the

discussion.

c) <u>Promotion of the Knowledge of Space Law</u> - In addition to the efforts made by several IISL members in developing interest for space law in their own countries, the IISL President has been able, after the Conference of the International Law Association, and with the priceless assistance of one of the Directors, Dr. Cocca, to visit some countries of South America (Brazil, Argentina, Chile, Peru and Bolivia). Both delivered lectures on various subjects of space law of immediate and current interest to universities, "Colegios de Abogados," Institutes of Space Law, and "Cortes supremas." They noted the great interest of professors, students, and lawyers in general for this new branch of law. Such visits are a valuable contribution toward the expansion of knowledge of space law in the world.

3. <u>Publications</u>
   a) <u>Bibliography of Space Law</u> - The 1967 issue was printed in early July and distributed to the subscribers.
   b) <u>Legal Terms in Astronautics</u> - The list of these terms to be annexed to the Multilingual Dictionary sponsored by the Academy is now ready in proof form.
   c) <u>Survey of Space Law Teaching</u> - The important material recently collected will permit preparation of a very comprehensive panorama of space law teaching, to be published early next year.

4. <u>Financial Situation</u> - The grant received a year ago from the United Nations for a study on the system of telecommunications by satellites, the contributions received from several donors, and the sale of Bibliographies have permitted and will permit, at least for one year, the Institute to continue its activities, in particular the publication of the Bibliography and the Survey of Space Law Teaching.

5. <u>Andrew Haley Gold Medal Award</u> - The Board of Directors has decided to award the 1968 Andrew Haley Gold Medal to Mrs. Eilene Galloway, senior specialist in international relations, and Special Consultant to the U.S. Senate Committee on Aeronautical and Space Sciences.*

6. <u>Secretariat</u> - Members of the Academy Secretariat, under the direction of Miss Helene van Gelder, have continued their efficient assistance to the Institute.

October 2, 1968   The President of the Institute

                                                          E. Pépin

---

* The Medal was presented to Mrs. Galloway by the President of the Institute at the Banquet of the Congress on October 17, 1968, with the following citation:

   In recognition of her outstanding contribution since the beginning of the
   Space Age as author, lecturer, editor, and commentator in connection with
   the creation and development of space law in order to establish and maintain the rule of law in relation to mankind's activities in outer space.

INTERPRETATION OF THE SPACE TREATY - PART II
SUMMARY OF DISCUSSIONS

The discussion on this item centered on the meaning of the expression "peaceful uses."

Mr. Vereshchetin (USSR) explained that, according to the views of Dr. Zhukov, "peaceful uses" implies "non-military uses," but the Treaty does not prohibit any kind of military activities; it prohibits certain activities enumerated in Article IV. Therefore, what is not prohibited is permitted according to Article IV.

Mr. Dembling (USA) considered that "peaceful uses" implies only "non-aggressive" uses.

Dr. Fasan (Austria) said: "To minimize the obvious difficulties on the meaning of the term 'peaceful uses,' I want to point out the following: viously the authors do not realize that they agree on the question of which kinds of activities are permitted in Outer Space and on the Celestial Bodies, and that the dispute is only a semantic, not a legal one. To prove this, one should look at the following:

	Military Activities	Non-military Activities	Aggressive Activities	Non-aggressive Activities
Military Personnel	not peaceful	peaceful	not peaceful	peaceful if military
Non-military Personnel	not peaceful	peaceful	not peaceful	peaceful if non-military

Major Jaffe (USA) said that he did not clearly see what is not prohibited and therefore what is permitted.

Dr. Markov (Bulgaria) stated that Article I of the Treaty is only declaratory and is not a rule of international law.

Dr. Mankiewicz (Canada) observed that the Treaty contains many contradictions.

Mr. Pelegri (Spain) was of the same opinion and referred especially to the ownership of cosmic objects which is linked to the responsibility of their utilization and linked also to the problem of the registration of such objects. After giving a number of possible situations, he considered particularly Articles VI, VII and VIII of the Treaty and said:

> Who is responsible for the launching? According to Article VI the responsible States are those involved in the corresponding activities in Space; that conclusion seems reasonable and indisputable. But this answer brings us to formulate another question: When is it considered that there exist such activities in Space? The apparent answer seems to be, when it has an object in Space. Is it correct? All preparations effected on the ground are they not oriented to attain the cosmic Space? If an accident derives from them on the ground, as experienced with the vehicle Apollo, is it not derived from the intention of attaining the cosmic Space?
>
> How do we know that a State has placed an object in Space? The correct answer is probably: when it is announced that it is going to

be done. Now this requisite of announcement is never done previously. At the ONU there is a register utilized only when the States deem it convenient. Even in such case the registration is done 'a posteriori,' never 'a priori.'

In its cosmic activities, who is the responsible State? The jurist has to refer to the rules of private law, and the conclusion to which he arrives is that the property over a thing goes together with its responsibility over it. We can apply such principle to our cosmic law. The owner of the object is the responsible one. If this conclusion is the logical one, and nothing is to be found against it in Article VI, Article VII, instead, bars us completely by stating that the responsible one is the State effecting the launching from its own territory, or which facilitates the launching, or launches or procures the launching. The text of Article VII produces confusion due to the fact that there may be many individuals responsible. Even assuming that there were only the one who owns the territory from which the launching is effected, may I ask how to approach the case when it is launched from a seadrome, this being the case of unknown property.

To complete more confusion there, we have Article VIII, which states that the State registering the object or spaceship has the jurisdiction over the object and the person in it. If we connect Article VII and Article VI, it appears that the responsibility falls on the State from which territory has been effected the launching; but, from Article VIII it is seen that the State where the registration has been made has the jurisdiction and the ownership and the right to claim the return of the objects and the cosmonauts. This statement is evidently a contradiction with the previous ones because, assuming it would be acceptable, some rights are recognized to States which have no obligations due to its activities; but we have seen that they are responsible in accordance with their activities.

According to Article VI the States are responsible for their activities in cosmic Space; which ones? Those who can claim the return of their spaceships because they registered them in their own favor? It looks reasonable in face of the responsibility of the owner towards the owned thing. But, is it so according to Article VII? Evidently not, they are those who have launched it. Then, is it admissible that an individual has had all the rights over the thing and gets profit of it, and another one has had all the responsibilities derived of its activity, even if it is not its own? Evidently this is the absurd that bears the examination of the above mentioned articles, and that brings about the mention of such clear contradictions.

There is only one method, registration, as I have explained, and as have many other jurists. In this case there will be no doubt whatsoever on ownership, which creates rights and duties as well. That makes possible, as in maritime law, that all transfers of dominion be publicly known. Then, there is no difficulty in respect to identification of the object in case of accident--all of it without fixing subsidiary responsibilities, and in some instances direct ones, in case of negligence or imprudence on the part of the State that mans at the moment the object, or has chartered it from the owner. Although, as stated by Mr. Arets in his paper on the Responsibilities of the international organizations, the damaged one can sue the State which did the launching and also the State which ordered it; in my opinion that means quite properly the owner.

Finally, Prof. Ikeda (Japan) asked: How could the test of so-called F.O.B.S. (Fractional Orbital Bombardment System) be compatible with the requirement of Article IV, par. 1, i.e., ban of nuclear weapons or weapons of mass destruction in orbit in Outer Space? When the orbit of F.O.B.S. is not completed only by one meter, is that F.O.B.S. legally admissible? Don't you think that F.O.B.S. is at least against the spirit of the Space Treaty?

The answer from the Chair was that F.O.B.S. should be considered to be legal, because the orbit of F.O.B.S. remains fractional, not completely circling the Earth.

Mr. Hall (USA) stated that the goal of ultimate demilitarization of outer space proposed in the Russian presentation was desirable and should be pursued; however, he asked the Soviet delegate, assuming recent press reports can be believed, how he would accommodate American and Russian reconnaissance activity within his postulated categorization of activities in outer space between peaceful uses (non-military) and non-peaceful uses (any military activity).

Mr. Vereshchetin (USSR) responded that ultimate demilitarization, which prohibited all military activity, was the goal toward which all states should work. There was no direct response to the question.

* * * * *

One of the most important discussion of the 11th Colloquium was the discussion on the AGREEMENT ON THE RESCUE OF ASTRONAUTS, THE RETURN OF ASTRONAUTS, AND THE RETURN OF OBJECTS LAUNCHED INTO OUTER SPACE.

(PART III)

The "Special Working Group" (Prof. Pompeo Magno, Chairman; Dr. Jerzy Sztucky, and Dr. Vladimir Kopal) made before the Colloquium the following proposals and queries, which the group presented to the auditorium:

1st: To express a favorable opinion of the Agreement in question and designate the same as the first example of the application and development of the fundamental principles contained in the Space Treaty of 27-1-1967.

Augur the prompt conclusions of the other Agreement regarding compensation for damage caused by the launching of objects into space.

2nd: To give notice that the Agreement confirms the independence of Space Law and to express the hope that the States and Universities – which have not already done so – shall promote studies and set up chairs of Space Law.

3rd: To reaffirm the need for an appropriate terminology, in all languages, and adopt the special multilingual dictionary published by the International Institute of Space Law.

4th: To discuss and assess the following interpretations of the individual Articles of the Agreement:

a) Does Art. 2 stipulate or not that, for the intervention of the Launching Authority in rescue and search operations, a prior decision is necessary, and, if so, from whom?

b) Does Art. 2 bind, or not, third party States (with respect to the Launching Authority and the territorial State) to provide the territorial assistance stipulated in the same Article?

c) Does Art. 3 bind, or not, the contracting parties to perform non-territorial assistance?

d) Do Arts. 1 and 3 refer to the crew only? And does Art. 5 refer to all space vehicles whether manned or not?

e) Do Arts. 4 and 5 stipulate, or not, the return of the astronauts, independently of their mission, and under that aspect do they derogate from jurisdiction on foreign subjects?

f) Does Art. 6 attribute all the commitments provided for in Arts. 1, 3 and 5, Paragraphs 1 and 2, to the inter-governmental organizations and to the relative member States (provided they are contracting Parties to the Agreement)?

g) Does Art. 6 attribute, or not, an independent juridical position, independent of the States forming part of it, to the inter-governmental organizations?

h) Does Art. 7 bind, or not, the contracting parties to the immediate respect of the Agreement independently of the situations and procedures as per the Space Treaty?

Dr. Stephen Gorove, Chairman of the Graduate Program of the School of Law and Professor of Law, University of Mississippi (USA) mentioned:

The Agreement on the Rescue and Return of Astronauts and the Return of Objects Launched into Outer Space, which was unanimously approved by the U.N. General Assembly in December 1967 has been hailed as a momentous accomplishment and a prompt follow-up to the Outer Space Treaty of 1966. The Agreement is broader than the provisions of the Treaty dealing with assistance of distressed astronauts (Art. V of the Outer Space Treaty). The stipulations in the Agreement spell out in detail the right and the obligations of the Contracting Parties as they relate to the rescue, assistance and return of distressed astronauts and the return of space objects. The purpose of this brief review is merely to reflect and raise a few queries in relation to some of its provisions, questions which will some day most likely be answered in more detail, perhaps authoritatively or possibly otherwise. E.g. Dembling and Arons: "The Treaty on Rescue and Return of Astronauts and Space Objects", 9 Will & Mary L.R. 630 (1966). The Treaty was a beginning and Dr. Gorove hoped, that as man's travel in outer Space will become commonplace, the initial agreements will be expanded or revised in the light of experience and need.

*   *   *   *   *

INTRODUCTORY REPORT

by

The Special Working Group

(Dr. Cyril Horsford, Chairman; Dr. Michel Smirnoff, Dr. Ernst Fasan)

Following discussion of the working group's report last year on this subject in Belgrade, the group has desired to consider these problems further at the Colloquium in New York in 1968.

It is not necessary to restste the main principles outlined in last year's report. They are well known, and form part of the U.S. Treaty on Outer Space of 1967.

It will no doubt be agreed that no state will make a successful claim in law to the sovereignty or territory of an area of a celestial body (Treaty, Article 2). Also, it can not be denied that a state is entitled to retain ownership over its property in space and on celestial bodies, and jurisdiction over its own personnel (Treaty, Article 8).

Arising from these considerations and the discussion at last year's Colloquium, there are still some questions for clarification:

1. What particular rights may a state which has established a permanent manned station on the Moon or a celestial body expect to enjoy?

Comment.

It is suggested that jurisdiction over all personnel coming to the station is one possible right, the use of minerals and facilities necessary to maintain the station is another, and also the freedom from interference by other states in the quiet use and enjoyment of the base, including freedom from interference with communications to and from Earth, and support in case of accident or distress.

2. Should a United Nations Agency be created to administer the celestial body concerned either by personnel or observers to see that Treaty obligations are carried out, and to grant concessions to exploring states, or distribute mineral resources, etc. (as suggested by Dr. Kopal at last year's discussion), or should states themselves be responsible?

Comment.

The real question here is the extent to which the United Nations should be directly involved in administering celestial bodies.

3. What action should be taken by personnel of neighboring space stations on a celestial body in the event of war on Earth between their respective countries?

Comment.

In view of the ban on military activities on celestial bodies and the requirement in the Treaty for mutual assistance, are these obligations paramount considerations in international law, or is loyalty to the Earth state more binding?

4. What steps should be taken to ensure conservation of resources and minimum contamination of celestial bodies by exploring states?

Comment.

This is an important problem throughout the whole of space exploration for the future, affecting Earth as well as the celestial bodies, and may involve scientific consultation on the lines suggested in Article 9 of the Treaty and action by international bodies such as COSPAR.

5. Is a station in permanent orbit around the Moon to be regarded as in space or on the Moon for legal purposes?

Comment.

This is primarily a question of jurisdiction and is included so that the matter can be clarified.

* * * * *

John R. Tamm, mentioned that the logical point of departure for a discussion on the Legal Status of National Stations on Celestial Bodies is the Outer Space Treaty and particularly Article VII thereof. This section declares that the State Party that launches an object into outer space shall retain jurisdiction and control over such object and personnel while on a celestial body and that ownership of objects landed or constructed on said body, including component parts, is not affected by their presence on a celestial body. On first reading, this article appears to be clear and complete. As we shall discover, the application of the language to specific situations may be subject to question. Since the Treaty has been approved by the two leading space powers, as well as a considerable number of other states, it would appear that the Treaty may, for most purposes, be considered as controlling.

Although the Outer Space Treaty does not attempt to define the terms "celestial body" or "objects," it is apparent from the language that such terms are meant to include all natural bodies in outer space, excluding the moon, which is referred to especially (see Manuel Augusto Ferre, Argentina: "La Proplematica Juridica de una Estacion Lunar," Proceedings p. 145) and all tangible properties once physically present on earth and subsequently transported to the celestial body. John R. Tamm means now, that in summary a national station located upon a celestial body possesses no more or less legal status than may be endowed upon it by its national owner or sponsor.

* * * * *

SURVEY AND PROSPECTS OF THE LAW OF OUTER SPACE
by
W. von Rauchhaupt

...

The traffic with the Outer Space is the most difficult and dangerous problem. Natural fragments, consisting of rocks and metals, for example, iron or nickel, also dust particles are attracted from Outer Space by the Earth, they burn up or fall down on the Earth's surface. The Max Planck Institut in Heidelberg, Germany, has undertaken the great task to collect, count and analyse these dust bits. In the opposite direction the artificially constructed rockets and satellites are launched from the Earth up into the Outer Space. Many of them are now manned by astronauts.

back from there.

Also discussed is a plan to place in Outer Space a space vehicle as a kind of workshop to assist with repairs, exchange materials and offer help to the astronauts. This may include a walk in Outer Space itself. The astronauts are to be assisted in case of accidents, distress, or emergency landing by astronauts of other states, and they are to be brought back to their own countries.

All space vehicles, manned or not-manned, are to be kept under the control of their own states. The vehicles retain the nationality and protection of their own states, and their flights are always to be registered. The state may also be responsible for damages if the insurance is not sufficient.

Of great importance is the anticipated launching of three astronauts to the Moon and their safe return. Journeys to Venus or Mars or to small asteroids beyond Mars, like Eros, may follow. The creation of colonies is theoretically considered in order to lighten the burden of possible over-population. The practical realisation of such expeditions depends on protection against dangerous radiation in the Van Allen Belt or from the sun. Furthermore, the right gravity, breathing air, water and the right food have to be provided for.

The European enterprises are also beginning to get good results, often still with the help of NASA. Esro II, renamed Iris, was launched on 5-17-1968 from California with a Scout rocket from NASA.

The eventual meeting with reasonable beings in Outer Space may prove most interesting. The landing on another star requires the special permission of its inhabitants whether beings of minor intelligence, animals, or even plants.

* * * * *

Very important was the "Round Table Discussion" on the determination of scientific factors for defining outer space and its boundaries. The introduction was given by Professor Edmund A. Brun, Paris, and the contributions by Paul A. Campbell (USA), Professor Aldo A. Cocca (Argentina), Dr. Ernst Fasan (Austria), Dr. Valdimir Kopal (CSSR), Professor Alex Meyer (GFR), Walter O. Roberts (USA), Dr. Sanz Aránguez (Espania), F. Zwicky (Vice-President IAA).

Remarkable is the contribution given by Zwicky, who precisely detailed suggestions on the definition of outer space boundaries for incorporation into the Treaty on Outer Space. He said that the main concepts, which must be clearly analyzed and strictly formulated, are the following:

1. What activities, on ground or in space, of the various nations are possible or actually contemplated, and
2. Up to what intensity will other nations tolerate the consequences of such activities.

The last two points of his conclusions were the prerequisites for an acceptable formulation of the various imaginable boundaries of outer space, and "Some of the boundaries of outer space as depending on the activity contemplated." See the following original portion of Zwicky's paper.

...

D. Prerequisites for an acceptable formulation of the various imaginable boundaries of
outer space.

From what was said in the preceding, it becomes obvious that the various detailed specifications of the treaty of outer space can be formulated reasonably if the following directives are being observed.

1. The circumstances and the known facts with which the treaty is concerned must be
sufficiently well established, understood and made available to all of the signatories.

2. Beyond the known facts the scientists with the greatest knowledge and imagination
must review all of the scientific and technical possibilities which may be expected to be
realized during say the next decade for instance. More about this will be said below.

3. All terms must be clearly understood and defined.

4. The terms agreed upon must not involve any impossibilities of observance or execution, both either physically or mentally.

5. Good faith of all of the signatories is indispensable.

The sum total of all of these requirements confronts us with one of those typical large
scale problems which can be satisfactoriy and speedily solved only through the application
of the morphological approach. For this reason the then legal council of the IAA, Mr. A.G.
Haley, asked me to speak to the 1961 Congress in Washington D.C. on the "Morphology of Justice in the Space Age."

This inaugural address was published by the Sandoz Company of Basle, Switzerland in
their Journal KONTAKT, no. 17 (Jan. 1963) in English, German, French and Spanish. It also
appeared in the "Proceedings of the Fourth Colloquium on the Law of Outer Space," University of Oklahoma Research Institute 1963, pages 1-4. Some of the ideas expressed there will
be reproduced in an extended article to appear in one of the next issues of the Astronautica
Acta. In the following we only occupy ourselves with some isolated but characteristic conclusions of the morphological analysis of the legal problems on outer space.

E. Some of the boundaries of outer space as depending on the activity contemplated.

1. Nuclear fusion experiments.

It probably will not be long now before we master the nuclear fusion of the light elements in ordinary rocks for instance, and their transformation into the nuclei of the greatest packing fractions, such as iron for instance. Once we achieve such fusion ignition,
several exceeding dangerous possibilities must be envisaged. For instance, it is conceivable that a whole body of water, such as a river, lake or the whole ocean could be ignited
and its protons and oxygen nuclei fused into heavier elements. If the citizens of a certain nation should engage upon such activities they could not hope for any tolerance from
the neighbors at all.

Or suppose that one could fuse the nuclei of oxygen, nitrogen and argon in the air at
one given point and produce a continued precipitation of solid iron in that limited spot,
the whole of the earth's atmosphere would be sucked in and dropped as a heap of iron or
neighboring chemical element. For the activities just mentioned the tolerance boundary of
outer space granted any nation would be at some very great height above the ground, inasmuch as no nation would be allowed to conduct such experiments anywhere within the atmos-

phere or at best only very far out, if tests are conducted in moderate measure, such as imploding meteors in interplanetary space, or small asteroids like Icarus. But nuclear implosions of entire bigger bodies, like our Moon or the planets, would not be allowed, and outer space, by agreement, would start somewhere beyond Pluto.

2. Where outer space starts for the free use of planes, rockets and so on has actually not yet been agreed upon. A most important decision will, however, soon have to be reached, especially if more and more devices will be launched to populate the outer reaches of the atmosphere.

3. Likewise some boundaries will have to be established for high altitude balloons, depending on their number, the instruments they carry and the activities they engage in. For instance, it would be exceedingly useful for the spotting of jet streams and other atmospheric phenomena to shoot luminous artificial meteors from shaped charges carried aloft by balloons, a technique which we have actually carried out and proved effective (see F. Zwicky, Morphology of Propulsive Power, Monograph no. 1 of the Society for Morphological Research, Pasadena 1962). This kind of testing, however, if done on a large scale and with the traffic increasing at high altitudes will successively be tolerable only at ever greater heights, or again only at very low heights where the direction and range of the artificial meteors can be strictly controlled.

4. The testing of atom bombs and other radioactivity producing devices in the atmosphere and in outer space has already been essentially "outlawed" by agreement, such that the boundary of outer space is somewhere very far out, somewhere perhaps beyond Pluto, nobody has stated exactly where.

5. Next comes the question of the use of bright laser beams, or even the possibility of exciting the whole upper atmosphere to fluorescence, so the night would become day. This obviously would not please the astronomers and would be objected to by many who cannot fall asleep anyway. So, for optical experiments and devices, even search lights, as they become more powerful, some spaces will have to be defined within which these experiments can be conducted freely by this or that nation.

F. Suggestions for preparatory work on the definition of the various boundaries of outer space.

We repeat, there is not just one boundary of outer space but there are many because the depend

a) on the activities envisaged and undertaken by the various nations (and possibly individuals),

b) on the range of the phenomena resulting from these activites,

c) on the tolerance limits accepted by all of the peoples on earth.

The problems related to a) and b) are of the type briefly sketched in section E.

I suggest that a group of competent and imaginative scientists of the IAA be asked to prepare a list of the items involved for presentation at the yearly meeting of the IAA in September 1969.

TWELFTH COLLOQUIUM ON THE LAW OF OUTER SPACE

MAR DEL PLATA, 1969

I. Texts Reproduced

ANNUAL REPORT OF THE PRESIDENT

OF THE INTERNATIONAL INSTITUTE OF SPACE LAW

The extraordinary scientific and technical achievements in the conquest of the Moon had beneficial consequences for developing, among the lawyers and the public in general, a new interest for the legal problems of Space. Lawyers specializing in Space Law were invited to explain to the public, either in conferences, or through radio or television, the legal significance of the first steps of Man on the Moon. Many members of the Institute so contributed to the diffusion of our branch of Law.

1. Membership. The total membership of the Institute, which was 314 members from 50 countries a year ago, has reached 345 on October 1, 1969, from 50 countries (24 European, 12 Latin-American, 8 Asian, 2 North American, 2 African, 2 Australian).

2. Activities of the Institute.

a. Colloquia of Space Law - The XIth Colloquium, held in New York in October 1968, under the chairmanship of Dr. Paul Dembling, General Counsel of NASA, was attended by a large number of lawyers; and it was a great pleasure to see there, with their professor, a complete class of a near-by college where Space Law is taught. The Proceedings of the Colloquium are already printed and distributed.

The XIIth Colloquium is already under way under the chairmanship of Dr. Aldo Armando Cocca.

b. Participation of IISL Members in International Meetings - Several members are representing their governments in the Legal Sub-Committee of the Committee on Peaceful Uses of Space of United Nations.

3. Publications.

a. Bibliography of Space Law - The 1968 issue was printed in July and distributed to the subscribers. We do hope that an increasing number of IISL will buy that scientific publication of the Institute.

b. Survey of Space Law Teaching - The enquiry conducted for the past three years on the teaching of Space Law in the world ended this year, and the results have been published as a Report of the Institute and circulated to all members of the Institute, as well as to a number of law teachers and international organizations interested therein.

c. Legal terms on astronautics - The list of these terms is to be issued before the end of the year; it is a very important work, made under the supervision of Dr. Kopal. The list will be an instrument of the unification of legal terminology in astronautics.

4. Financial situation. During the year the Institute did not receive any grant from private donors, but the von Karman Memorial Fund continued to contribute to the expenses of the Institute. Nevertheless, it was possible for the budget to assume cost of the publication of the 1968 Bibliography and of the Survey of Space Law Teaching.

5. Andrew Haley Gold Medal Award. The 1968 Gold Medal has been attributed to Dr. Gennady Petrovitch Zhukov, Secretary of the Commission on Legal Problems of Outer Space of the USSR Academy of Sciences and also professor of Space Law at the Lumumba University in Moscow.

6. Secrétariat. Finally we should mention the great assistance received from Miss Helene van Gelder and her efficient staff.

The President of the Institute

E. Pépin

*   *   *   *   *

EXTRACT FROM THE INTRODUCTORY REPORT OF PART II (LEGAL PROBLEMS OF TELECOMMUNICATIONS, INCLUDING DIRECT BROADCASTING FROM OUTER SPACE).

by

The Special Working Group with Professor Aldo A. Cocca as Chairman and Rapporteur, Dr. V.S. Vereshchetin and Dr. Pompeo Magno.

... Likewise, it must be remarked that the General Assembly of the International Astronautical Federation adopted in New York, 17 October, 1968, a statement concerning the use of communications satellites, according to the following text:

> The International Astronautical Federation believes that the forthcoming years will see continued and expanded uses of space vehicles for both the exploration of space and its exploitation for practical purposes for mankind.

> The International Astronautical Federation is further of the opinion that maximum practicable use of radio communication techniques is vital to this continued growth and expansion, and that this should be reflected in the regulations, allocations and standards governing use of the radio spectrum.

> The International Astronautical Federation encourages further expansion of the use of communication satellites, and in particular, use of such service in areas of the world not now served or poorly served by terrestrial communication systems.

> The International Astronautical Federation believes that

satellites have manifold uses for domestic and regional services,
as distinct from international services, and urges clarification
of terminology and regulation relating to such systems.

...

III. Direct Broadcast from Satellites

30. In this matter as well, the IISL has offered some concepts. Apart from the
reference made in the reports, in its session of October 1968, in New York, the Rev. Dr. J.
McLoughlin referred to the certainly formidable opposition in the United States to direct
boradcasting from satellites, remarking that when some other countries come forward with a
direct broadcasting system, the economic and educational advantages in such system may
persuade a large block of countries to quit INTELSAT and joint the new body. Professer
Mankiewicz upheld that when direct reception of satellite telecommunication will be a reality, steps must be taken to exercise a certain degree of control over the content of
messages so transmitted. Such control must be an objective, impartial and uninterested one.
Only by a truly international organization - concluded - can it exercise it in that fashion.

31. In the meeting held in May 1969 by a French working group of CNRS, it was upheld
that the principle of freedom of outer space proclaimed in the Treaty of January 27, 1967,
was not absolute, because said Treaty imposes a limitation in paragraph 1 of article I.
By application of the general principles of international law, pursuant to art. III, it is
forbidden for all State authorities to intervene in the internal matters of other States,
ensuring, at the same time, due respect to foreign States. On the other hand, the non-
appropriation rule implies a limitation to the full liberty of States in outer space. Such
is the case concerning the use of geostationary satellites, which imply the appropriation
of a privileged fraction of outer space: the equatorial orbit. Whoever carries out a de
facto occupation must submit, as a counterparty, to precise rules of law. And said working
group concludes by expressing, in view of the fact that direct broadcast from satellites
shall be admitted by the international community, that freedom of space, as well as freedom
of information, are principles to be applied taking into consideration an appropriate international regulation.

34. We may add, as it has suitably been said, that if communication satellites are
meant to bring closer the links of the human family, they cannot do so by themselves alone.
No mean of communication has an intrinsic value when it has nothing to communicate, and
even when man selects something to make known, he does not necessarily favor an approach.
However, if we do not take advantage of the occasion for achieving a better knowledge of
one another offered to us by space communications, ignorance will continue to foster terror,
suspicion and misunderstanding.

35. To this end, it is advisable to take into account that it is not only a reproduc-
tive investment, but a highly human task, conferred upon satellites of communication. That
is why, all effort of the jurist must bear in mind the high destiny of man in his relations
with fellowmen of all the planet, when giving the rules to govern the use of telecommunication satellites.

36. In view of what has been expressed, we believe the following questions may be
stated:

(1) Is it possible to achieve a harmonic action on the part of many

specialized agencies of the UN, in the present and future activities regarding space telecommunications, or is it more adequate to create a new organization involving all activities carried out in outer space and celestial bodies?

(2) Is the INTELSAT action to be restricted to the objectives foreseen in the 1964 Agreements, or extend it to all possibilities and derivations of space communications?

(3) In the case of offering INTELSAT political, social and cultural responsibilities besides the commercial ones held at present, could it act independently or should it form part of a larger international organization, in the capacity of telecommunication organ?

(4) Among the opinions expressed at the Plenipotentiary Conference of March 1969, which are the most advisable for an institutional, financial and operational regime of INTELSAT?

(5) With reference to direct broadcast satellites:

(a) Which should be the legal principle or rule to be established in order that fundamental rights of States and men are respected and that all countries should benefit with the establishment of direct broadcast satellites?

(b) What fundamental norms must a Treaty regulating conduct in direct broadcast contain?

(c) What protection is to be offered from an economical point of view in face of direct broadcast?

(d) Must countermeasures or sanctions be foreseen in the code to be prepared?

(e) Which could be the control organs for the international organization to be created, as well as its constitution and powers?

* * * * *

EXTRACTS FROM "THE RULES GOVERNING THE DIRECT BROADCASTING BY
SATELLITES AT THE UNO"
by
Pompeo Magno

In his introduction Pompeo Magno mentioned that by Resolution No. 2453 B, Par.5, of December 20, 1968, the UN General Assembly authorized at its 23rd session the "Ad Hoc Committee on Peaceful Uses of Outer Space" to set up a Working group for studying the problems and reporting on the technical feasibility of a possible communication by direct broadcasting from or via satellites.

Then literal:

The "ad hoc" Committee, entrusted by the General Assembly with the task of tackling this problem, called the first session of the Working Group, in New York, on February 1969. This session, chiefly dealing with technical matters, was to provide an answer to the questions appearing in the mentioned Resolution No. 2453 B. This first session (Report of February, 1969) came to the following conclusions:

(a) While it is considered that satellite technology has reached the stage at which it is possible to contemplate the future development of satellites capable of direct broadcasting to the public at large, direct broadcasting television signals into existing, unaugmented home receivers on an operational basis is not foreseen for the period 1970-1985. This reflects the lack of technological means to transmit signals of sufficient strength from satellites.

(b) Direct broadcast of television into augmented home receivers could become feasible technologically as soon as 1975. However, the cost factors for both the earth and space segments of such a system are inhibiting factors. For example, the cost to the homeowner/consumer who wishes to augment his home receiver (and antenna) while not precisely measurable at this time, appears to be at least $40 (not including cost of installation) and may be considerably more expensive depending in part, for example, on the frequency employed. Many other factors enter into the cost equation, and in countries lacking large numbers of existing conventional television receivers completely different cost figures apply. As to the space segment, the development and launching of the powerful - therefore heavy - transmitters, which are not yet within the state-of-the-art, involve considerable expenses, which cannot be estimated at this time; the development costs might run as high as $100 million. Therefore, it is most unlikely that this type of system will be ready for deployment on an operational basis until many years after the projected date of feasibility.

(c) Direct broadcast into community receivers could be close at hand. Technology currently under development might allow this in the mid-1970s. Such a system is considered to be less expensive to launch than one intended for reception directly in people's homes. It will also be easier to establish and less expensive for locations where the radio noise level is low.

* * * * *

Having thus disposed of all the prejudicial questions, the Working Group dealt, in its second session, with the subjects under discussion in order to single out the specific problems connected with the projected regulation; a regulation that is all the more urgent because the experts in this field are waiting for it, as they consider it the first step and the guiding line in their work aimed at drafting the new system.

These specific problems, as emerged from the discussions and from the constructive contribution made by all delegations, chiefly refer to the following subjects.

(a) Allocation of frequencies that must be strictly regulated. In this connection, the International Telecommunication Union (I.T.U.), has convened, as early as May 23, 1969, a World Administrative Conference on Space Telecommunications, to be held in Geneva on June 7, 1971, with a view to ensuring, among other things, a national utilization of the spectrum; revising and completing the allocation of the frequency bands appearing in the Regulation of the radio communications;

examining the technical criteria and procedures to be adopted in the parcelling
out of frequencies between space and terrestrial services in order to fix the
criteria and procedures for the allocation to the various space system; studying the feasibility of a coordinated planning of frequencies for radio communication satellites, including those launched into geostationary orbits. A precondi-
tion to this allocation is the right of all nations to use the direct telecasting
satellites; a right that cannot be seriously questioned.

(b) The use of the geostationary orbit where a scarcity of parking space is becoming
manifest. Space is infinite, but begins to be too small for these particular needs.
In fact, since the geostationary orbit is one and is located 36.000 km above the
earth and since the direct broadcasting satellites must be so spaced as to be at
a minimum distance (fixed by the experts) of two degrees from one another, the
number of the available parking places is reduced to 180 (360:2), as against the
ever growing demand on the part of all countries. And even though we have passed
from the 240 circuits of Early Bird to the 1200 circuits of INTELSAT III and to
6000 circuits, on the average, of INTELSAT IV (not to mention the laser, a likely source
of further wonders) international cooperation, in this regard as well as in regard to the limited
geostationary parking place, appears to be of determining importance for the creation of a global network of direct telecasting satellites. It is in this perspective that we must consider the legal problem of the lawfulness of space occupation
by means of satellites--in clear conflict with the principle, as laid down in Art.
2 of the Space Treaty of January 27, 1967, whereby no one is allowed to take possession of space and celestial bodies-- with the so-called "droits de route" for
the physical paths and parking of satellites in outer space and to the utilization
of the frequency spectrum.

(c) The contents of the programs and their level of international acceptability in order
to avoid the possibility that the new system, instead of providing a means for improving
other people's culture and education, may turn into a dispenser of third-rate
broadcasts. While not a basic problem, the choice of the various types of broad-
casts--news bulletins, educational programs, cultural exchanges, entertainment,
etc.--will be made the object of special operational agreements.

(d) Copyrights and similar rights that must be protected, but that presently lack
uniformity in the light of the international conventions in force, in fact of modes
of protection; hence the necessity of entering into generally accepted agreements.

(e) The commercial aspects, a problem that is especially felt by the USA and by all
those other countries where, as everyone knows, television stations earn their
living by selling time to advertisers. An adequate regulation seems advisable to
prevent easy elusions. Also the fiscal angle of the problem - in order to protect
government rights and to avoid double or multiple taxations - may fall
within this subject.

(f) Freedom of information was the focal point of a most spirited debate that
started from the very definition of this principle. In point of fact, freedom
of information, when construed as the right of freely spreading and receiving information, is a concept that can be only found in the Constitution of the most en-

lightened States. At the international level, such a concept is recognized by
Art. 19 of the Universal Declaration of Human Rights, by Art. 19 of the International Pact of the Civil and Political Rights of Man, and by a number of Recommendations issued by the U.N. General Assembly, contained in Resolutions No. 2448
(XXIII), No. 756 (IX), etc., all instruments, however, not yet approved or ratified.

The Soviet Union and other East European countries have repeatedly stressed
the serious consequences of a political, economic and cultural nature that the
projected system might cause as a result of its interference on national sovereignties. In the absence of an effective international regulation preventing
this fact from occurring, the States - it has been said - are left no other choice
for protecting themselves against undesirable broadcasts than that of resorting
to such radical measures as the jamming of same or even the destruction of the
satellite itself.

It has been acknowledged that the best thing to do would be to find a
negotiated solution prohibiting any interferences on the international affairs
of each country, any acts of war propaganda, any infringements of the fundamental
human rights and freedoms, and, possibly, subliminal techniques (being the new
technique in which messages are flashed so fast on a television screen that the
viewer does not see them consciously but absorbs them through the subconscious
mind). It was also recognized that some States object to programs that, in
their opinion, might prove prejudicial to the preservation of peace or to the
status quo, either internal or international and that are deemed to be of such
a nature as to cause social commotions.

Obviously, those other individual rights should be included in this context
which have already been affirmed and sanctioned in the Universal Declaration of
Human Rights: the personality and dignity of Man, his private property and private
life, his own financial means. All need to benefit from a suitable legal protection that must be go beyond the mere defense against defamation, as advocated
by many.

The opportunity was suggested for providing an ethical code or a set of planning rules in the framework of the international cooperation. One thing is certain.
The problem of limiting the freedom of information is one of the most difficult to solve, and in spite of the willingness shown by all countries to find a
solution, which makes us feel optimistic, the work of jurists and political men
will be required for the drawing-up of the relative rules.

As far as we are concerned, we should like to re-affirm the principle, set
forth above, that any limitations of freedom of space and of freedom of information may be justified, provided they are not based on the principle of prej-
udicing other people's interests.

(g) The necessity of preventing any abuses, from the extreme instances of pirate
broadcasting stations to the insidious propaganda broadcasts, has been recognized
by everyone; so the formulation of an appropriate set of rules does not seem at
all difficult.

(h) <u>The method for controlling the enforcement of the agreed regulation</u>, in view of the decisions to be adopted at the international level through suitable future Conventions, represents another major issue. It is too early now to establish what type of control could be launched. A preventive control, besides being in contrast with the rapidity inherent to the system and to the contents of broadcasts, would assume the aspect of a form of censorship. For the same reasons, the opinion ought to be rejected that no telecast by satellite should be made without the consent of all the States in whose territory these telecasts are receivable.

All forms of control must necessarily be carried out jointly and at the international level; and the solution of the problem will depend, in our opinion, on the wise choice of the controlling bodies, the prudent and unbiased attitude and impartiality shown in entrusting the right implementation of the control and repression of all abuses. The sanction against the transgressor, i.e., the exclusion of it, made possible by a global system of direct telecasting, will prevent abuses and the non-observance of the rules laid down in the appropriate Conventions.

* * * * *

Extract from the
DISCUSSION OF THE POSITIONS TAKEN BY THE UNITED STATES IN THE
NEGOTIATIONS OF DEFINITIVE ARRANGEMENTS FOR INTELSAT
by
T. E. Donahue, J.

In general the United States draft agreements proposed that:

1. INTELSAT should remain an unincorporated international commercial joint venture with partners owning undivided shares in proportion to their use of the Organization's facilities.

2. Although established primarily to provide its members and others with satellites to meet their international public telecommunications requirements, INTELSAT should also be authorized to provide INTELSAT financed facilities for international or domestic specialized telecommunications requirements, as well as for domestic public telecommunications requirements. INTELSAT should also be authorized to establish facilities to meet all domestic requirements and international specialized telecommunications requirements at the expense of members requesting such facilities. INTELSAT members would, of course, have certain obligations designed to protect the global system from any adverse effects which might result from the use or establishment of separate facilities by INTELSAT members. The United States proposed, in fact, that the Board of Governors be given the authority to determine whether any proposed separate system would contravene membership obligations and that such decisions be binding on members.

3. INTELSAT would have three organs: an Assembly composed of Signatories to the Operating Agreement (the investors in the system); a Board of Governors, which would have the re-

sponsibility for the design, development, construction, establishment and operation of the satellite system; and a Manager who would implement the Board's decisions.

Annexes A and B to Donahue's "Discussion," concern the functions of the Secretary of INTELSAT headed by a Secretary General, who has the "...legal representation of INTELSAT and is responsible to the Board of Governors for the execution of all of its decisions other than those the execution of which has been entrusted to third parties under contract."

ANNEX A

1. Maintain the INTELSAT traffic data base; convene periodic regional meetings for the purpose of estimating traffic demands.
2. Approve applications for access by standard earth stations; report to the Board of Governors on applications for access by non-standard earth stations; maintain records on new earth station availability dates.
3. Maintain records based on reports submitted by the Signatories, earth station owners, and the contractor performing management services, on the technical and operational capabilities and limitations of all current and proposed earth stations.
4. Maintain an office of record for the assignment of frequencies to users; arrange for the filing of frequencies with the ITU.
5. Based on planning assumptions approved by the Board of Governors, prepare capital and operating budgets and estimates of revenue requirements.
6. Recommend space segment utilization charges to the Board of Governors.
7. Recommend accounting policies to the Board of Governors.
8. Maintain books of account and make them available for audit as required by the Board of Governors; prepare monthly and annual financial statements.
9. Calculate the investment shares of Signatories; bill Signatories for capital contributions; bill allottees for use of the space segment; receive cash payments on behalf of INTELSAT; make revenue distributions and other cash disbursements to Signatories on behalf of INTELSAT.
10. Advise the Board of Governors of Signatories in default of capital contributions, and of allottees in default of payments for utilization of the space segment.
11. Approve and pay invoices submitted to INTELSAT with respect to authorized purchases and contracts made by the Secretariat; reimburse the contractor performing management services for expenditures incurred in connection with purchases and contracts made on behalf of INTELSAT and authorized by the Board of Governors.
12. Administer INTELSAT employee benefit programs and pay salaries and authorized expenses of INTELSAT employees.
13. Invest or deposit funds on hand, and draw upon such investments or deposits as necessary to meet INTELSAT obligations.
14. Maintain INTELSAT property and depreciation records; arrange with the contractor performing management services and the appropriate Signatories for the necessary inventories

of INTELSAT property.

15. Recommend terms and conditions of allotment agreements for utilization of satellite services.

16. Recommend insurance programs for protection of INTELSAT assets, and as authorized by the Board of Governors, arrange for necessary coverage.

17. Analyze and report to the Board of Governors on the economic effects to INTELSAT of any proposed independent satellite system.

18. Prepare the tentative agendas for meetings of the Board of Governors, Assembly, and any advisory committees; prepare the provisional summary records of such meetings; assist the Chairman of advisory committees in preparation of their agendas, records and reports to the Board of Governors and Assembly.

19. Arrange for interpretation and for the translation, reproduction, and distribution of documents.

20. Provide the history of the decisions taken by the Board of Governors and Assembly; prepare reports and correspondence for the Board of Governors and its Chairman, and the Assembly regarding decisions taken during meetings.

21. Arrange for the preparation of verbatim records of meetings, as necessary.

22. Assist in the interpretation of the rules of procedure of the Board of Governors and Assembly, and the terms of reference for any advisory committees.

23. Make arrangements for any meetings of the Board of Governors, the Assembly and advisory committees which may be held away from the INTELSAT headquarters.

24. Recommend procedures and regulations for contracts and purchases made on behalf of IN-TELSAT.

25. Keep the Board of Governors informed on the performance of contractors' obligations, including the obligations of the contractor under Article XI (h).

26. Compile and maintain a world-wide bidders list for all INTELSAT procurements.

27. Negotiate, place and administer contracts necessary to enable the Secretariat to perform its assigned functions, including contracts for assistance from other entities to perform such assigned functions.

28. Provide or arrange for the provision of legal advice to INTELSAT as required in connection with the Secretariat's functions.

29. Provide appropriate public information services.

ANNEX B

1. Recommend research and development programs to the Board of Governors.
2. As authorized by the Board of Governors:
   a) Conduct studies, research, and development, directly or under contract with other entities or persons.
   b) Conduct system studies in the fields of engineering, economics, and cost effective-ness.
   c) Perform system simulation tests and evaluations.
   d) Study and forecast potential demands for new communications satellite services.

3. Advise the Board of Governors on the need to procure space segment facilities.

4. As authorized by the Board of Governors, prepare and distribute requests for proposals, including specifications, for procurement of space segment facilities.

5. Evaluate all bids and proposals submitted in response to requests for proposals and make recommendations to the Board of Governors on such bids and proposals.

6. Pursuant to procurement regulations and in accordance with decisions of the Board of Governors:

   a) Negotiate, place, amend, and administer all contracts on behalf of INTELSAT for satellite system, sub-systems, components, and related terrestrial facilities.

   b) Make arrangements for launch services and necessary supporting activities, and participate in launches.

   c) Arrange insurance coverage to protect INTELSAT spacecraft and associated equipment designated for launch or launch services.

   d) Provide or arrange for the provision of services for tracking, telemetry, and control of the spacecraft, including coordination of the efforts of Signatories and earth station owners participating in the provision of these services, to perform satellite positioning, maneuvers, and tests.

   e) Provide or arrange for the provision of services for monitoring satellite performance characteristics, outages, and effectiveness, and the satellite power and frequencies used by the earth stations, including coordination of the efforts of Signatories and earth station owners participating in the provision of these services.

7. Recommend frequencies for use by INTELSAT satellites and satellite location plans to the Board of Governors.

8. Operate the INTELSAT Operations Center and the Spacecraft Technical Control Center.

9. Recommend standard earth station performance characteristics, both mandatory and non-mandatory, to the Board of Governors.

10. Evaluate applications for access by non-standard earth stations.

11. Allot units of satellite capacity as prescribed by the Board of Governors.

12. Prepare and coordinate system operations plans (including network configuration studies and contingency plans), procedures, guides, practices and standards, for adoption by the Board of Governors.

13. Prepare, coordinate and disseminate frequency plans for assignments to earth stations having access to the system.

14. Prepare and distribute the System Status Report, including actual and projected system utilization.

15. Distribute information to Signatories and system participants on new telecommunications services and methods, e.g., demand assignment.

16. For consideration by the Board of Governors and upon its request, evaluate the technical and operational impact, including frequency and location plans, of any proposed independent satellites upon INTELSAT's space segment.

17. Provide the Secretary-General with the information necessary for the performance of his responsibility to the Board of Governors under par. 25 of Annex A.

18. Recommend policies relating to the acquisition, disclosure, distribution and protection

o   of rights and inventions, and data.

19. Arrange, pursuant to the policies and decisions adopted by the Board of Governors, for licensing of INTELSAT inventions and data to others and enter into licensing agreements on behalf of INTELSAT.

20. Take all operational, technical, financial, procurement, administrative and supporting actions necessary to fulfill the above listed responsibilities.

21. Provide appropriate public information services.

* * * * *

Conclusions of

RIESGOS Y CONTROLES FRENTE A LOS SISTEMAS DE
TELECOMUNICACIONES VIA SATELITE

by

Ricardo Maqueda

TEMA 1. "Problemática legal de las telecomunicaciones por satélite, incluso la trasmisión ultra celeste".

TITULO. "Riesgos y controles frente a los sistemas de telecomunicaciones viá Satélite".

CONCLUSIONES

1. El Derecho Espacial tiene a la Humanidad como sujeto de sus derechos y obligaciones. Hasta tanto la Humanidad esté debidamente representada en un gobierno universal, se hace imprescindible la creación inmediata de una organización internacional para regular las actividades espaciales.

2. Siendo el hombre destinatario final de los beneficios de la actividad espacial, es necesario establecer una regulación internacional, que asegure a los Sectores de Humanidad, nucleados en todos los Estados, la defensa de sus derechos.

3. Cualquiera sea el sistema que se escoja, debe establecerse, con urgencia, una regulación específica y minuciosa de las telecomunicaciones por satélite.

4. Debe fundarse un régimen de estricta igualdad entre todos los Estados. Teniendo particular trascendencia la idéntica posibilidad de acceso al o a los sistemas; equivalentes titularidad dominal del o de los sistemas e igual capacidad de decisión.

5. Incidencia de las telecomunicaciones en el mundo actual exige prever un eficiente sistema de controles. La autorización de emisiones; su contenido; los medios lícitos al alcance de los Estados para autoprotegerse (tanto de las emisiones ilegales, como de las que cuenten con su oposición - pues aquí la mayoría no dá derechos-), el consiguiente sistema de sanciones y la respectiva autoridad de aplicación; son sus principales items.

6. El Derecho debe evitar se repitan lamentables experiencias del pasado. Si al colonialismo y a la guerra convencional secedió la ingerencia económica y la lucha de intereses; compete al Derecho evitar se produzca ahora la más insidiosa y posible de las ingerencias: las comunicaciones.

* * * * *

216

During Part II-A the members occupied themselves with the "Liability for Damages Caused by Space Objects Including Weather Control from Outer Space," and Dr. Jerzy Rajki, Professor of International Public Law at the Varsonia University (Poland) came in his introductory report to the following conclusion:

It should be pointed out in the conclusion to the remarks concerning the subject that unlike many other branches of international law, the international rule of liability for damages in connection with space activities are being formulated with the cooperation of the whole international community of nations. This fact takes on greater significance since, in practice, outer space is being explored and utilized by only a very small number of States. It is to be hoped that this cooperation will continue and that the resulting law on liability for "space damages," recognizing the risks inherent in activities connected with the exploration and use of outer space, will protect the victims of any damges that might be caused, taking account of the common interest of mankind.

Comments on the Rajski Report were given by Michel G. Bourély, who wished to state that the observations given by him represent his own personal view and in no way engage the responsibility of the ELDO, by which he was employed at that time. In the first part of his comments he occupied himself with the current status of negotiations concerning the draft convention on liability and mentioned the international organizations, the damage and losses of nuclear origin, the applicable law in the event of litigation, the limitation of the amount of liability, and the settlement of claims. The second part of his comments he devoted to "Liability Arising out of Weather Control from Outer Space" with the cardinal points: definition of "weather control," principles, and particular problems raised by weather control. The result: hence, the question of compensation for damage and loss in respect of "weather control" deserves more detailed study. With the remark that it applies in more or less similar terms to all applications satellites, Bourély proposes that it be taken up again on the occasion of a later Colloquium of the IISL.

* * * * *

PART II-A LIABILITY FOR DAMAGES CAUSED BY SPACE OBJECTS,
INCLUDING WEATHER CONTROL FROM OUTER SPACE

SUMMARY OF DISCUSSIONS

As the Reporter of this item, Dr. Rajski (Poland), was unable to attend the Colloquium, Professor Cocca was kind enough to take charge of the discussion.

The Reporter, as it was explained by Dr. Cocca, sustained that, in order to establish an appropriate system of legal rules, it would be necessary to deviate from the traditional concepts, because we should make a just and equitable balance between the interests of all the members of the international community. With respect to the subjects of liability mentioned by the Reporter, States and international organizations, Dr. Cocca observed that, in the future, space activities would be exceptionally exercised by States, and therefore it would be of a great importance to settle the problem of liability of international organizations.

The Reporter considered that the elements of liability should be studies with respect to the damages and to the legal causation; he analyzed also the objective or absolute liability and the liability based on fault; he also studied the compensation of damages according to the applicable law and the question of limited or unlimited compensation. He considered it necessary to supplement the application of generally recognized principles of international law by reference to other law, either to the law agreed to between the parties, or to principles "ex aequo et bono." With respect to limited or unlimited compensation, he preferred the principle of unlimited compensation; but, in order to obtain a general consensus, it seemed to him that a ceiling as high as possible (not to be less than $500 millions) might be adopted. As regards the procedure for presentation of claims, he mentioned the three possible claimants already agreed, and suggested the establishment of an arbitration commission, composed of a group of persons elected by the General Assembly of the United Nations.

Dr. Bourély (France) explained his comments on the Report and wished to make special reference to the "Weather Control from Space." On that point, he discussed the definition of "Weather Control" and sustained that the question was dealt with in Article IX of the 1967 Treaty; therefore, if a State or an international organization did not respect that article, it would be guilty of an infraction and the provisions of Articles VI and VII would be applicable. He also considered the case of the bare observation of the weather in order to obtain meteorological forecasts and in relation to the effects, required or not, of space activities on the weather; and he concluded that the compensation for damages in relation to the control of the weather would deserve a more complete study.

Dr. Maldonado (Argentina) concentrated his resumé on the liability resulting from a disaster. He considered that, in the last instance, Mankind was liable for damages so caused, as Mankind is the beneficiary of the exploration and exploitation of the outer space.

Dr. Kaltenecker (German Federal Republic) analyzed the difficult position of the international organizations owing to the divergent opinions concerning their legal nature. He also questioned whether the international organizations might be parties to an international convention. He said that, in spite of the legal difficulties and the opinions, not always concurrent, of the lawyers, the international organizations were existing and working with an entire liability.

Professor Basualdo Moine (Argentina) qualified the problem of liability as the neural point of all the legal branches. With respect to the responsible subjects, he was uncertain whether it would be only the States or only mankind and concurred with those who have the same doubt. He also mentioned that, in the atomic field, the liability was objective and limited, where the project concerning outer space is unlimited and objective. He recalled the action of Dr. Cocca at the discussions in the United Nations on atomic liability in space, and expressed his anxiety that if, in sidereal exploration, an energy more powerful than atomic would appear, what would happen?

Dra. Williams (Argentina) observed that the legal treatment of the space liability appeared more severe than air liability; in the last case the limitation is quasi unanimously admitted, where such limitation is not admissible in space, because its purpose is the integral reparation of the damages. She indicated that the inclusion of the atomic damages in the draft convention should not be postponed.

Professor Sampaio de Lacerda (Brazil) sustained that, as the damages and prejudices suffered by third parties on the surface were regulated by objective liability in aeronautical law, nothing prevents the application of the same criterion to the space liability. But, if in aeronautical law, the objective liability is counterbalanced by the limitation of the indemnity, in space law, the amount should not be limited in any manner.

Dr. Claisse (Argentina) sustained that the liability in space matter should be objective and unlimited, adding that it seemed useless to insist on the point, because a few days ago the Legal Committee of ICAO, when discussing the problem in the aeronautical field, was in favor of a so high a limitation that it was practically admitting an unlimitness. Therefore, the argument was disappearing, sometimes the only argument, frequently produced by those who were in favor of a limitation.

$$* \quad * \quad * \quad * \quad *$$

PART II-B LEGAL STATUS OF EARTH-ORBITING STATIONS
(The Introductory Report was given by Smirnoff)

SUMMARY OF DISCUSSIONS

The Reporter, Dr. Smirnoff (Yugoslavia) presented a synthesis of his Report concerning: the general problem of the legal status of space vehicles, the problem of the legal status of stations on celestial bodies and in orbit in their correlation, and the problem of the legal status of earth-orbiting stations. Therefore, he was submitting to the Colloquium the following questions: a) Is it necessary to differentiate between the legal status of manned or unmanned earth-orbiting stations? b) Is the size of earth-orbiting stations relevant to their legal status? c) Is it necessary to establish a strict definition of earth-orbiting stations? d) Could it be made clear that some categories of vehicles which are orbiting around the Earth (telecommunications satellites) represent a specific kind of orbiting vehicle for which a special legal regime could be established?

Dr. Acuna (Argentina), referring to the difficulty mentioned by the Reporter of finding a definition of an orbital vehicle, said that we must understand by that expression an "ensemble" of movable objects assembled together in order to constitute a homogeneity.

Prof. Ferrer (Argentina) said that, in his opinion, the regime of a cosmic vehicle and the regime of an earth-orbiting station should be the same. He understood that there is no possibility of making a difference between manned and unmanned orbital stations, nor on account of their dimensions. He recalled that the regime of a vehicle and an orbital station should be the same, although a cosmic vehicle would have a right to a trajectory. In the case of an orbital station, it would have a right of maintaining itself at the place assigned to it. Finally, in answer to the fourth question of the Reporter, it seemed to him that there was no reason, in the present stage of the technology, for establishing special regimes for certain vehicles, although in the future other problems should be considered, e.g., the right of privacy.

Dra. Williams (Argentina) said that legal status shouldn't depend either on the dimensions of a station, nor the fact that the station is manned or unmanned. Lawyers should try to establish a definition of a space vehicle, and she preferred the definition submitted to the United Nations (COPUOS) by Argentina because of its contents and its approval by a Colloquium of technicians and lawyers.

Dr. Claisse (Argentina) agreed that there was no reason to establish a difference between manned and unmanned stations. Dimensions and technical methods should not serve to differentiate stations. An exact definition of an orbital station was necessary. It is impossible to compare an orbital station with a station established on a celestial body, because the immovability of the latter constitutes the essence of the problem.

Dr. Kaltenecker (German Federal Republic) understood that the problem might be simplified according to the preceding speakers, but there was still a need for the elaboration of norms, especially for every category of space vehicle.

Dr. Cocca (Argentina) said that he shared the position of simplification of the problem. In fact, it should be taken into account that there was a unique legal status for outer space and for celestial bodies; consequently, as regards the medium in which either a celestial vehicle or station, or an earth-orbiting station is in operation, there would be a legal unity. Arriving on the earth is very different, because a vehicle in operation on the surface is submitted to various regimes: sovereignty of "res nullius" on the surface, in air space and in territorial waters; less strict regimes in waters under jurisdiction and in defense zones; "res communis omnium" on the high seas and in airspace above the high seas. Ultraterrestrial space and the celestial bodies constitute a "res communis Humanitatis." Such advantage should be taken into account. On the other side, we should not believe that the elaboration of norms has been neglected. In fact, the Radiocommunications Conference of Geneva in 1963 has adopted Resolution 2 A, which states that the provisions concerning the cases of assistance and of critical situations--up to the revision of the "reglement" on telecommunications--will be applicable to the cosmonauts and to space vehicles.

* * * * *

Professor Ferrer (Argentina) said that, in his opinion, the regime of a cosmic vehicle and the regime of an earth-orbiting station should be the same. He believes there is no possibility of making a difference between orbital stations because of their dimensions or the fact that they are manned and unmanned. He stated that the regime of a vehicle and an orbital station should be the same, although a cosmic vehicle would have a right to a trajectory. In the case of an orbital station, it would have a right of maintaining itself at the place assigned to it. Finally, in answer to the fourth question of the Reporter, it seemed to him that there there was no reason, in the present stage of the technics, for establishing special regimes for certain vehicles, although in the future other problems should be considered, e.g., the right of privacy.

Dra. Williams (Argentina) understood that no difference of legal status would depend either from the dimensions of a station, nor from the fact that the station is manned or un-manned. She understood that the lawyers should try to establish a definition of a space vehicle, and she recalled the definitions submitted to the United Nations, marking her prefer-ence, on account of its contents and its approval by a Colloquium of technicians and lawyers, for the definition presented by Argentina to the COPUOS in 1967.

Dr. Claisse (Argentina) understood that there was no reason to establish a difference between manned and unmanned stations. The dimensions and the technical methods should not serve to differentiate stations. An exact definition of an orbital station was necessary. It is impossible to compare an orbital station with a station established on a celestial body, because the immovableness of the last one constitutes the essence of the problem.

Dr. Kaltenecker (German Federal Republic) understood that the problem might be simpli-fied according to the preceeding speakers, but there was still a need for the elaboration of norms, especially for every category of space vehicle.

Dr. Cocca (Argentina) said that he was sharing the position toward simplification of the problem. In fact, it should be taken into account that there was a unique legal status for outer space and for celestial bodies; consequently, as regards the medium in which either a celestial vehicle or station, or an earth-orbiting station is in operation, there would be a legal unity. Against, what was arriving on the earth is very different, because a vehicle in operation on the surface is submitted to various regimes: sovereignty of "res nullius" on the surface, in air space and in territorial waters, less strict regimes in waters under jurisdiction and in defense zones, "res communis omnium" on the high seas and in airspace above the high seas, when the ultraterrestrial space and the celestial bodies are consti-tuting a "res communis Humanitatis". Such advantage should be taken into account. On the other side, we should not believe that the elaboration of norms has been neglected. In fact, the Radiocommunications Conference of Geneva in 1963 has adopted the Resolution 2 A, which disposed that, up to the revision of the "Reglement" on telecommunications, the provisions concerning the cases of assistance and of critical situation would be applicable to the cos-monauts and to space vehicles.

* * * * *

SUMMARY OF DISCUSSIONS

Register of Space Vehicles

The Reporter, <u>Dr. da Cunha Machado (Brazil)</u>, said that the space vehicles should be classified in three categories: those which did not remain permanently in space, such as rockets; those used for circulating, such as satellites, vehicles, and platforms; and those which remain on the surface of the Earth, such as launching pads. In his opinion, all these objects should be registered. With respect to the place where these objects should be registered, he conlcuded that it would be necessary to draw up a new legal concept of outer space, and also that the United Nations themselves, or through a specialized organ, should coordinate and control space activities; such control would require a register of matriculation of space vehicles, a register of launchings, already in existence, and a register of platforms, with the understanding that space vehicles may only be registered by the United Nations.

<u>Dr. Maldonado (Argentina)</u> proposed that two registers should exist, one national and one international. The national register should be kept in the State concerned, which should have the obligation to proceed with international registration before the Secretary General of the United Nations.

<u>Prof. Sampaio de Lacerda (Brazil)</u> considered that it would be necessary to give a definition of a space activity. As regards the register, in his opinion, any launching should be registered in writing and no later than the moment when the vehicle is placed into orbit. In addition to the obligation of registration and announcement, the purpose of the launching should be communicated. With respect to the space objects, the State, the launching place, the marks and other particulars should be mentioned.

<u>Prof. Ferrer (Argentina)</u> said that two registers should exist, one national and another international; only one international registration is not possible.

<u>Prof. Monnerat (Brazil)</u> stated that the primordial purpose of registration is to facilitate the identification and the individualization of the space objects. He would not oppose the existence of a national register, but he felt that the international register offers great advantages.

<u>Prof. Ortiz de Guinea (Argentina)</u>, referring to the necessity of defining the space vehicle - as mentioned by the Reporter - said that such objects could be considered as movable things susceptible to registry and that a classification could be formulated referring to things susceptible, or not and thus be individualized. He requested a legal ruling on the subject.

<u>Dr. Kopal (Czechoslovakia)</u> thought that it is necessary to have an authentically international vision in the space field without superceding the national tasks; thinking in this new dimension of the human affairs is critical.

<u>Dra. Williams (Argentina)</u> understood that a national register is indispensable, but it would be ideal if the United Nations, or one of its international agencies, might have the

real function of registration beyond the simple function of public information, which they have at this moment.

Dr. Kaltenecker (German Federal Republic) considered as really complex the registration work to be done by the international organizations, and added that if it is difficult to arrive at an agreement between a few participants, it would be more difficult to find agreement between many.

Prof. Basualdo Moine (Argentina) said that, as regards the registers, the fundamental problem is the publicity. He believes that it is not possible to replace the national register. Therefore, the national register would exist for internal publicity, and the international register for international publicity.

Dr. Claisse (Argentina) mentioned that the problem of the legal regulation of the space vehicles could not be separated from their national registration; it is not possible to abandon the national register.

Dr. Vereshchetin (USSR) introduced a study of Prof. Zhukov, who was of the opinion that registration involved the internal competency of the States, but that fact should not deter the possibility of an international register. He felt that space objects should be identified. The national register of space vehicles is different from the present register of information of the Secretary General of the United Nations. The national registration has certain consequences of a legal character, whereas the U.N. register, as it is presently, does not have any legal consequence.

Prof. Cocca (Argentina) stated that it is not possible to abandon the national register, because this register assigns jurisdiction, which, for the moment, might only be attributed by States. In his opinion, it is absolutely compatible with the existence of an international register, which would complete the system of registration. He recalled that the obligation placed by the General Assembly of the United Nations on the Secretary General was only for information, and he mentioned the paper read at the Eighth Session of the Legal Subcommittee of COPUOS (Geneva, June 1969) on the form of the U.N. Register.

Prof. Fernandez Brital (Argentina) wondered if it would be convenient to have special registers for civil and manned space vehicles. We may entrust the United Nations with the keeping of an international register, but it would be more convenient to entrust an independent organ in order to overcome the difficulties which may occur in relations with non-member States.

*   *   *   *   *

PART IV   ACTIVITIES ON CELESTIAL BODIES INCLUDING THE EXPLOITATION OF NATURAL RESOURCES

Summary of Discussions

The Reporter, Dr. Ferrer (Argentina), said that the time has come to develop in a Treaty the principles included in the 1967 Treaty and concerning the exploitation of the natural resources of the celestial bodies. He believed that it would be convenient to create

223

an administrative body in charge of all space activities under the sponsorship of the United Nations. He divided the resources of the celestial bodies into consumable (minerals) and non-consumable (heat, solar energy); it seems inadequate to use such terminology of civil law when we have in mind exhaustible and non-exhaustible natural resources. He wondered whether a "res communis" on the Earth was of the same nature as in the outer space or in a celestial body. For him, they are of the same nature. But it is impossible to say the same with respect to the appropriation of things taken from one celestial body to another one. With such a transfer we are breaking the equilibrium established in the Cosmos. According to the Law of Lavoisier, in the Earth there exists an equilibrium which would not be maintained if we transported natural resources from one celestial body to another; or at least it is possible that the equilibrium would not be maintained. He added that if the States have renounced their sovereign rights in the new worlds open to human activities, it does not seem difficult to imagine that they might renounce conventions to regulate the exploitation of the natural resources in such places where they have renounced their sovereignty. Such regulation should be established for everyone, for the 1967 Treaty signified the renunciation of such right in favor of all Mankind. As a conclusion to his arguments, Dr. Ferrer said that it would be a magnificent contribution to the problem if the Institute would prepare a draft of an international agreement concerning the exploitation of the natural resources of the Moon and other celestial bodies.

The Reporter also mentioned the papers received on this item, especially from the authors unable to attend the meeting.

Professor Tapia Salinas (Spain) referred to "res communis humanitatis," analyzing each of the three words, and concluded that it is useless to sum up the value of these words because it is a legal expression with a legal range. Analyzing Article II of the 1967 Treaty, he saw a correlation between the appropriation of materials as property of a State, and a claim of sovereignty by the nation which made such appropriation. In his opinion, such materials should be classified according to their utilization: 1) material used "in situ," those necessary for human existence or for the sustainance of establishments settled on the celestial bodies; their utilization should be unlimited, licit and free; 2) other transportable material. These should be further categorized: (a) material of exclusively scientific value—the true "res communis humanitatis," objects of study by the State having priority, but with the obligation to distribute the results to all Mankind; (b) material of exclusively economic value whose nature requires transport for utilization; (c) material of warlike value which could not be utilized according to the 1967 Treaty.

Dra. Williams (Argentina) believed that the utilization, as well as any other form of appropriation, of materials coming from celestial bodies should be coordinated by an international organ. She proposed the inclusion, in the Treaty to be prepared, of meteorites, which up to now have not been submitted to any international regulation. She agreed with division into exhaustible and non-exhaustible materials with only the latter category being open to appropriation without limit.

Dra. Picarel (Argentina) was in favor of regulating the acquisition and utilization of the resources of celestial bodies, the commission of which should be entrusted to an international organization.

Prof. Fernandez Brital (Argentina) said that an international agreement should be prepared on the exploitation of the natural resources of celestial bodies; he was in favor of the creation of an international organ for such purpose and of the idea that the Institute might contribute to the elaboration of a draft agreement.

Dra. Rusconi (Argentina) was also of the opinion that this activity should be internationally regulated with the creation of an international organ for such purpose. The exploitation of a celestial body should not be possible without previous permission of the international community.

Dra. Avila (Argentina) felt that the statutes to be created for the exploration and appropriation of materials of celestial bodies should also resolve the question of the register. Otherwise, such activity might be exercised clandestinely against any regulation which may be enacted.

* * * * *

In PART V (Various) the most impressive explanations were given in

DIE FORSTSETZUNG DES WELTRAUMRECHTS SEIT
DER MONDLANDUNG AM 21. JULI 1969
by
Fr. W. von Rauchhaupt

(Extracts)

II. Das Weltraumrecht.

Das Weltraumrecht, soweit bisher entstanden, soll sich vorzüglich auf eine weiter glückhafte Zukunft der Weltraumtechnik einstellen. Das heisst, dass das bereits entstandene und gegebene Weltraumrech in Geltung bleiben kann. Daraufhin ist es jedoch nachhaltig zu überprüfen; nachhaltiger als es bei der bereits für die nächste Zukunft gleichartig gerüstete Weltraumtechnik nötig erscheint.

1) Die das Weltraumrech schaffenden Kräfte.

Zuerst sind die das Weltraumrech schaffenden und bildenden Kräfte aufzuzeigen. Vielleicht können die bisher entwickelten Blockbildungen beibehalten werden und die Forderungen der Zukunft sind erst in zweiter Linie zu bedenken.

a) An politischen Blockbildungen werden bisher vornehmlich die rivalisierenden Kräfteballungen der USA and Russlands sichtbar, doch sind allmählich in den verschiedenen Teilen der Erde auch zusätzliche oder ausgleichende Unternehmungen erkennbar geworden.

Für den Westen stützt sich die Vormach der USA mit ihren Anhängern in ihrem Inneren auf die NASA nebst den ihr helfenden grossen Firmen der USA, aber auch des Auslandes. Ferner sammelt Europa seine Kräfte in der ESRO und ELDO. In Gross-Amerika tut ein gleiches die Panamerikanische Union, deren Pläne jedoch durch den Geldmangel und die kommunistische Störpolitik leiden.

Für den Osten bindet die slawisch-kommunistische Gruppe um Gross-Russland seine Nachbarstaaten and sich, neuestens auch die arabischen Staaten, doch halten sich Indien und besonders Festland-China fern.

Schliesslich wird die Gesamtheit aller selbständigen Staaten vereinigt in den UN, der nur Festland-China fern bleibt, während Bundesdeutschland zumindest in allen Hauptorganisationen der UN aktiv mitarbeitet. Diese UN haven sich bisher auch bereit gefunden, die Aufgaben der Weltraumerschliessung, vorzüglich die allmähliche Ausgestaltung des Weltraumrechts zu über nehmen. Fachkommissionen und Komitees sind dafür bestellt, die die Anträge für die Vorschläge und Beschlüsse der Generalversammlung vorbereiten.

Nahe liegt dabei ein Vergleich mit der Entdeckung und Erschliessung Amerikas seit 1492, die Jahrhunderte beanspruchte. Erheblich schnellere Entschlüsse und Resultate sind jedoch in der Gegenwart und für den Weltraum möglich geworden durch die erstaunlichen Geschwindigkeiten der Nachrichten- und Bildübertragungen vermittels Satelliten in verschiedenen Höhen; ausserdem auch durch die überaus schnell rechnenden Computer. Für Amerika wurden bisher im wesentlichen nur drei Sprachen benötigt: im Süden Spanisch und Portugiesisch, im Norden Englisch. Ähnlich haben die UN für die Zwecke der Vereinfachung und des Zusammenschlusses die Zahl der offiziellen Hauptsprachen auf fünf zusammengelegt, nämlich Englisch, Spanisch und Französisch fur die westlichen Machte, Russisch und Chinesisch für die übrige Welt. Für die arabischen Völker und die vielen farbigen Völker in Afrika und in anderen Kontinenten gelten zugleich die bereits genannten Sprachen der ehemaligen Kolonialherren dieser vielen Völker. Deutsch besitzt bisher nur inoffiziellen Rang.

2) Der Einfluss des göttlichen Rechts.

Ein neuer Faktor wird indes herangetragen durch die Wieder-Erkenntnis des göttlichen Rechts im Weltraumrecht. Das trat erst neuestens in Erscheinung und zwar fast unmittelbar vor der Astronauten-Landung auf dem Mond am 21. Juli 1969.

Die menschliche Einstellung zum göttlichen Recht.

So bleibt die abschliessende Frage, welches der für das Weltraumrecht wichtige und massgebliche Inhalt des göttlichen Rechtes sei und welcher Platz ihm gebühre.

1) Der Inhalt des göttlichen Rechts.

Der Inhalt des göttlichen Rechts dürfte sich schwerlich gewandelt haben wohl aber die Wirkung auf die Menschheit und deren Einstellung zum göttlichen Recht.

2) Sein Vorrang im Recht.

Wir leben in einer Zeit der menschlichen oder anthropologischen Selbsterkenntnis und müssen deshalb erforschen, welchen gegenwärtigen Inhalt das göttlich Recht insgesamt besitzt und ob es widerum einen Abstieg erdulden und der Vergessenheit anheim fallen soll, oder voll anerkannt, in unsere gegenwärtige Wirklichkeit und Zukunft übertragen und mit in sie hineingenommen werden soll. Das Wesentliche bleibt die Erkenntnis Gottes in seiner Allmacht; wir müssen bemüht sein, seinen Willen nicht nur zu erkennen, sondern auch zu befolgen. Dabei hat unsere menschliche Haltung, wie gesehen, grundlegende Wandlungen erfahren.

Aber Gottes Wille an sich ist vom menschlichen Standpunkt her unveränderlich. Das bedeutet, dass wenn das als göttliches Recht bezeichnete Recht sich ändert oder ändern lässt, es schwerlich göttliches Recht ist, sondern menschliches oder auch Naturrecht, das von den

Menschen abgeändert werden kann, z.B. die Änderung in unserem Leben durch die neuen Verkehrs-
mittel einschliesslich der Astronautik und durch die Erfindung und Verwendung von Kunststof-
en, etc. Es ergibt sich daraus, dass es nebem dem göttlichen Recht, das der menschlichen
Mach entzogen ist, auch rationelles menschliches Recht gibt, das der Mensch neu schaffen
oder abändern kann; aber es darf nicht gegen das göttliche Recht verstossen und das göttliche Recht ist stets das primäre Recht, das den ersten Rang einnimmt und stets zu suchen
und zu befolgen ist.

Das göttliche Recht berührt uns also in verschiedener Art: von Gott her ist est unwan-
delbar, vom Menschen her ist es abhängig von unserem jeweiligen Verständnis und guten oder
bösen Willen. Insofern es als göttliches Recht, das über dem menschlichen Recht steht, er-
kannt ist, gebührt ihm der Vorrang auch gegenüber dem von Gott geduldeten und sogar geseg-
neten menschlichen rationalen Recht.

- - - - -

THIRTEENTH COLLOQUIUM ON THE LAW OF OUTER SPACE
CONSTANCE, 1970

I. Texts Reproduced

ESTABLISHING LIABILITY FOR OUTER SPACE ACTIVITIES
by
Paul G. Dembling

Introduction

The world has had just over 12 years of experience in space exploration with orbiting vehicles launched from earth. How the nations of the world and international institutions have faced their responsibilities in this new environment indicates the shape of the future -- both in outer space and on our planet. It also indicates the directions which should be favored if rational development of the affairs of man are to be promoted and emphasized.

Much progress has been made in the law of outer space activities. The entry into force of the Outer Space Treaty of 1967 and the Treaty on Rescue and Return of Astronauts and Space Objects climaxed almost a decade of efforts to secure widespread international agreement in these areas. The provisions of the Treaties had been advanced previously in the form of General Assembly resolutions, analogous international agreements, domestic legislation, statements by government officials, articles by scholars in the field, and other expressions of views.

Although the Outer Space Treaty contains a provision making any state party to the Treaty internationally liable for damage to another state as a result of its outer space activities, it was generally recognized by the 28 member nations of the Legal Subcommittee of the United Nations Committee on the Peaceful Uses of Outer Space and by the General Assembly that it was necessary to fashion a separate convention on liability. Therefore, the next step in the legal regime for outer space activities is a liability convention.

Throughout the development of the law applicable to activities in outer space, no one has seriously challenged the need to establish criteria for determining liability and procedures for assuring compensation in the event of damage caused by the launching of a space object. Through their systems of domestic law, individual nations are able to establish appropriate rules for compensating their own nationals who are affected by space accidents. However, the movement of objects in outer space is not constrained by national boundaries, and their return to a designated location cannot always be assured. The international consequences of outer space activity are readily apparent. In view of the possibility that residents of any state might suffer personal injury or property damage caused by the space activities of another state, the development of a broad multi-national consensus on criteria and procedures governing international liability is thus required.

Even before the launching of the first Soviet Sputnik in 1957, serious consideration had been given to the appropriate basis for assessing liability in the event of damage caused by a space object. The perceptive European scholar, Vladimir Mandl, proposed in 1932 that owners and operators of space vehicles should be subject to liability without limitation with respect to all personal injury and property damage. Upon the launching of Sputnik I, it became obvious that heavier pieces of space vehicles or spacecraft launched into outer space would not be entirely consumed in the earth's atmosphere upon return. With the likelihood of damage occurring on the surface of the earth having become apparent, the subject of liability for damages caused by space accidents began to receive extensive consideration by scholars and diplomats.

By Resolution 1348 (XIII) dated December 13, 1958, the United Nations General Assembly established an Ad Hoc Committee on the Peaceful Uses of Outer Space consisting of representatives of eighteen nations. The Ad Hoc Committee established a Legal Subcommittee which considered liability for injury or damage caused by space vehicles to be the topic accorded priority treatment. In its report, the Ad Hoc Committee raised several questions, which have been considered up to the present:

First – What are the kinds of injuries for which recovery may be had?

Second – Should liability be based on fault, or without regard to fault
   for some or all activities?

Third – Should different principles govern, depending on whether the
   place of injury is on the surface of the earth, in the air space,
   or in outer space?

Fourth – Should liability of the launching state be unlimited in amount?

Fifth – Where more than one state participates in a particular activity,
   is the liability joint and several?

Sixth – What procedures should be utilized for determining liability
   and ensuring the payment of compensation?

Theories of Liability

Much attention was devoted early in this decade to the question of whether international liability for damages caused by the return to earth of a space object should depend upon a showing of fault on the part of the launching state or states. Essentially three theoretical bases for liability were advanced.

One possibility is that the claimant state would be required to prove at least that the launching state was guilty of negligence, in other words, a failure to exercise the degree of prudence considered reasonable under the circumstances. This is the traditional theory for assessing liability on the basis of fault. The main drawback, however, is that the claimant would have great difficulties in determining the precise malfunction which gave rise to the accident, and in proving that the malfunction was due to the negligence of the launching state or that of an instrumentality under its control. The number, complexity, and interrelationships of components inside a spacecraft would impose, in many instances, prohibitive technical obstacles to determining the exact cause of the accident even if the claimant were able to obtain all of the necessary data, of which some may not be subject to disclosure under domestic law.

In order to alleviate the burden of proof imposed on the claimant, it was suggested that the doctrine known in Anglo-American law as res ipsa loquitur should be employed.

The applicability of this doctrine would create rebuttable presumption of negligence on the part of the launching state, similar to the presumption created in connection with claims for damages under the Warsaw Convention relating to aircraft accidents. Even with the assistance of such a rebuttable presumption, the claimant must persuade the appropriate court, claims commission, or adjudicating entity that the acts or omissions of the launching state were unreasonable under all of the circumstances. In determining what is reasonable, however, it is necessary to consider the technical state-of-the-art generally and the peculiarities of each space vehicle and components therein. In areas of the law where the criterion of reasonableness is relied upon as the basis for decision, prior experience in the relevant activity is relied upon quite heavily. In view of the relative lack of duplicative experience, the rapid advance of space technology, and the peculiar characteristics of each space mission, the validity of applying a reasonableness test as the basis for assessing liability was considered open to doubt.

This brings us to the theory of liability which has grown to be accepted as the appropriate basis for determining whether a launching state should be required to pay damages to a foreign state on whose territory a space object has caused injury or damage -- this is, liability without fault, or, as it is known in Anglo-American law, strict or absolute liability. In order to receive compensation for injury or damage, the claimant need only prove that the damage was caused by the space object or any component or substance therein. The claimant is not required to prove that the launching state was guilty of negligent or willful misconduct.

Assessment of liability on this basis in appropriate circumstances has long been accepted in Anglo-American law and to a lesser extent in Napoleonic Code and other legal systems. Its appropriateness, in situations involving damage caused by space objects, rests on two propositions. First, the claimant is relieved of the prohibitive burden of proof imposed by the traditional negligence test, and there is no need for the claims tribunal to determine whether the conduct of the launching state was reasonable within criteria drawn from the limited relevant experience. Second, and more fundamental, the launching of objects into outer space has been considered to be an extrahazardous area of human endeavor. While no nation doubts the overall social and economic value of space activity, it has been generally accepted that the risk of injury or damage should not be passed from the creator of that risk to the public at large. Except in certain limited exculpatory circumstances, the rationale for imposing liability of the launching state without fault is to require the launching state, which reaps the principal benefits of space activity, to assume the risks imposed on all mankind.

In support of adopting internationally the principle of liability without fault as appropriate in situations involving damages on the surface of the earth caused by space objects, a variety of existing treaties are viewed as possible precedents. A classic statement of liability without fault is provided in Article 1 of the Convention on Damage Caused by Foreign Aircraft to Third Parties on the Surface, concluded in 1952 in Rome. Under that article,

> Any person who suffers damage on the surface shall, upon proof only
> that the damage was caused by an aircraft in flight or by an aircraft
> in flight or by any person or thing falling therefrom, be entitled
> to compensation.

The cause of the particular malfunction giving rise to the accident is irrelevant to recovery under the Treaty.

Since the risks associated with the launching of objects into outer space are often analogized to those incurred in peaceful uses of atomic energy, the treaties dealing with liability to third parties in the field of nuclear energy are also viewed as precedents. The first of several multilateral agreements in this area is the Convention on Third Party Liability in the Field of Nuclear Energy, signed in Paris in 1960. Under this Convention, the "operator" of the nuclear installation is liable, irrespective of fault, for damage or loss caused by nuclear incident involving a nuclear installation. In the 1962 Brussels Convention on the Liability of Operators of Nuclear Ships, a similar basis for assessment of liability is set forth. Article II provides that:

> The operator of a nuclear ship shall be absolutely liable for any nuclear
> damage upon proof that such damage has been caused by a nuclear incident
> involving the nuclear fuel of, or radioactive products or waste produced
> in, such ship.

Liability without proof of fault is also imposed on parties to the International Convention on Civil Liability for Nuclear Damage, signed in Vienna in May 1963, and the Supplementary Convention to the Paris Convention signed in Brussels in 1963. In connection with the approval of all of these treaties, it was believed that the exposed public must receive adequate protection against unknown dangers and that the operators of nuclear facilities should assume all risks of damage up to stated monetary limitations, subject to certain exculpatory circumstances.

The principal effort to develop criteria and procedures for the assessment of liability for damages caused by the launching of space objects has taken place in the Legal Subcommittee of the United Nations Committee on the Peaceful Uses of Outer Space. Throughout the deliberations in the Subcommittee on the matter of liability, beginning in 1962, the principle of liability without proof of fault on the part of the launching state has been accepted as appropriate for application to claims arising out of space vehicle accidents on the surface of the earth. This principle was impliedly adopted in Paragraph 7 of the 1963 Declaration of Legal Principles Governing the Activities of States in the Exploration and Use of Outer Space. While Article VII of the Outer Space Treaty provides only that international liability in connection with launchings is a general legal duty incurred by parties to the Treaty, it is generally recognized that fault need not be proved by the claimant state in order to recover damages against another party.

Notwithstanding the establishment of liability as a general obligation incurred by parties to the Outer Space Treaty, a variety of subsidiary issues, frought with complexities, requires further consideration. While it is comparatively easy to derive the general theory on which liability for damages caused by space objects should be based, difficulties arise when attempting to apply the theory to various categories of possible factual situations. As stated above, the launching state may not be subject to liability under certain exculpatory circumstances. For example, under the Rome Convention, the operator of an aircraft is not subject to liability where acts of persons on the ground cause or contribute to the cause of a crash. In connection with damage caused by space objects, it has been argued that the launching state should not be obligated to compensate the claimant state where the launching state can prove that the damage was caused by the willful misconduct of a resident of the claimant state, or by some event completely outside the control of the launching state, such as a meteor striking the spacecraft while in orbit.

Considerable attention has been devoted to determining the kinds of objects that may be considered space objects for the purposes of assessing liability. Even in the present state of technology, it is no longer a simple matter to make a clear distinction between all spacecraft and all aircraft, particularly if a distinction is sought to be made on the basis of whether the object can be sustained in flight by aerodynamic lift. Eventually, it would appear that some definitional criteria are necessary in order to determine the applicable treaty to determine liability -- the Warsaw or Rome Conventions on the one hand, or the Outer Space Treaty on the other.

Liability of Cooperative Ventures

Where two or more states participate in a single launching, agreement has been reached that the liability of those states should be joint and several. In other words, the claimant state would be entitled to recover full compensation from any one of the participants in the launching. The launching states may provide for indemnification between themselves, either on a pro rata basis or in accordance with some other agreed upon formula. As a modification to joint and several liability, it has been suggested that if the joint launching parties reduce the terms of their cooperation in writing with the Secretary-General of the United Nations, claimant states would be on notice of the proportionate financial responsibilities of each of the launching states and recovery from each launching state would be limited accordingly. However, to the extent that one or more of the joint launching parties fails to make timely payment, the principle of joint and several liability should become applicable.

While the basis for assessing liability against joint launching parties seems fairly clear, there may be instances in which the connection of a particular state with a launching is so attenuated that it should not be considered a participant in the launching and therefore not liable for damage. Questions that might be raised in this connection are whether a state whose only connection with the launch is a minor experiment aboard the spacecraft should be held fully liable for any damage caused by the spacecraft, or whether a state which supplied only a small component in the spacecraft or booster should be liable, or whether a state which had sent a technical observer should bear equal liability. Too broad a definition of joint ventures might affect international cooperation in space. The meaning of substantial participation should be defined, and the questions raised above should all be answered in the negative by the definition. Although some criteria may be provided in treaties, such as in Article VII of the Outer Space Treaty, these kinds of questions are not readily susceptible to precise solutions except in the context of individual factual situations presented to claims tribunals.

Several compromise texts proposed by France, India, Italy are being considered at present to cover the problems just cited.

Collisions of Spacecraft

Most of the issues which have been raised in connection with liability for damage caused by space objects have concerned possible damage caused by impact of such objects on the surface of the earth. A difficult question to decide is whether the principle of liability without fault should also be applied to collisions between spacecraft in outer space, or between a spacecraft and an aircraft within air space. Application of absolute or strict liability to such collision situations would produce an anomalous result. Assuming that the damage to each vehicle is total, the owner of the more valuable vehicle would receive greater compensation solely because its vehicle is more valuable. Where the collision is between spacecraft, the recovery by one state would amount to a windfall since, under the rationale for assessing liability without proof of fault, each of the launching states is considered to have assumed approximately the same risks. To avoid this result, different rules have been suggested.

A useful precedent is afforded by the Brussels Convention of 1910 regarding collisions between ships at sea. Article 2 provides that "if the collision is accidental, if it is caused by force majeure, or if the cause of the collision is left in doubt, the damages are borne by those who have suffered them." Article 3 of the Convention provides that "if the collision is caused by the fault of one of the vessels, liability to make good the damages attaches to the one which has committed the fault." In the case of collisions between aircraft in flight, no similar rule is presently in force. However, a draft convention was prepared by the International Civil Aviation Organization (ICAO) in 1961 which would provide for liability by the aircraft operator on the basis of fault where fault can be ascertained. Both the Brussels Convention and the draft ICAO convention provide for apportionment of the liability in accordance with the relative degrees of fault of each operator and, if it is impossible to determine degrees of fault, the liability would be apportioned equally between them. These precedents lend support to the agreement which has been tentatively reached that liability for damage arising out of a collision between spacecraft in flight, or between a spacecraft and an aircraft, should be assessed on the basis of fault as between the owners or operators of the spacecraft or aircraft. If fault cannot be proved, neither of the damaged parties would have recourse against the other. Of course, even where such a collision has occurred, liability for damage on the surface of the earth through the impact of the spacecraft, or a component thereof, would be assessed irrespective of fault.

Types and Measure of Damage

Once it is determined that the respondent's space activity has caused the damage for which he is liable, it is necessary to determine the elements of damage covered and the amount of compensation due. Ideally a claimant should be restored to his existent condition prior to the damage or injury, and for practical reasons monetary compensation is invariably used.

While it is quite clear that compensation should be provided for death of, or physical injury to, a human being, or physical damage to property, it is not clear that compensation should be afforded for every type of damage that might be perceived. Moreover, defining the measure of damages depends on the particular body of law relied upon to prescribe the kinds of injuries for which recovery may be had, and to measure the amount of the allowable recovery. For example, to what extent should loss of use of property be compensable, as distinguished from damage to the property itself? Should psychic injury to human beings be compensable? How does one measure the damage caused by pollution of the atmosphere by toxic fuels, or radiation? Should some form of what has been called "moral" damages be assessed? An issue of this nature frequently discussed is whether electronic interference with communications caused by a satellite should be compensable, and if so, how does one measure the extent of such interference in monetary terms?

Since none of these questions is answered by Article VII of the Outer Space Treaty, it appears appropriate that the text of a well-drafted treaty on liability should provide, to the extent possible, the types of damages for which compensation will be paid, the methods of evaluating losses suffered, and the limitations, if any, on the amount of recovery. Defining the precise measure of damages in particular factual situations requires recourse to an appropriate body of law. Wide differences of opinion have been expressed on whether a court, claims commission, or other tribunal should look to a particular local law, such as the law of the state of the injured party, or to develop appropriate rules through reliance upon general principles of international law. It has been argued that certainty in defining the measure of damages requires recourse to local law. Where the applicable local law is that of the state of the injured party, a difficulty is created in that two or more persons suffering identical damages in different states might recover considerably different amounts, depending upon the kinds of injuries deemed compensable in each respective state. However, if the claimant is to be restored to his condition that existed prior to the damage or injury sustained by him, as well as monetary compensation is able to do so, it would appear that the law governing his environment should be applicable; therefore, the law of the claimant should be applied. If the law of the launching state is applied, there does not appear to be a relationship between the claimant and his environment. His desire is to be made "whole" within his own frame of reference. The law of the launching state may bear little relationship to his conditions of life. Furthermore, launching states might readily enact domestic laws imposing limits on compensable injuries or amounts recoverable by individual claimants. Moreover, certainty would not be achieved where two or more states are responsible for a particular launching. While reliance upon general principles of international law may, in the abstract, seem to impose a greater degree of uncertainty, decisions of the International Court of Justice and claims commissions in analogous cases may afford some guidance. To the extent that damages caused by space objects might inject novel factors into the substance of decisions, a greater degree of flexibility in the decision-making process would seem desirable.

Claimant States and Injuried Parties

It is well settled in international law that only the state of which the injured party is a national may advance a claim on his behalf.

In determining the international obligation of a launching state to provide compensation for damages, it has been agreed that no duty is owed to nationals of the launching state. Moreover, aliens in the immediate vicinity of the launch or planned recovery area may be considered to have assumed certain of the risks, and also would not recover except perhaps on the basis of proof of fault. However, it is open to question whether alien residents of the launching state should be entitled to press a claim internationally. It would seem fair to provide an international remedy to aliens merely visiting the launching state, or traveling through it at the time of the accident causing damage.

When several states participate in a space activity which has resulted in damage, the parties to the joint launching could agree among themselves as to the treatment to be accorded to their respective nationals.

A nation might represent its "permanent" residents, but not the nationals of the state causing the damage or injury.

Liability arising from space activities is not so unique as to require a legal regime which differs substantially from that applicable to international claims generally. Authorizing states in whose territory damage was sustained to present claims for residents could result in presenting claims for nationals of states not parties to the treaty. This might tend to reduce the incentive for states to become parties to the convention.

Where dual nationality exists, the difficulty could be eliminated by adopting the present procedure of priorities which could be waived in favor of another state or by permitting that only one state represent all of the injured parties.

Since tradition and international politics demand that the state of nationality retain the primary right to present claims for its nationals, it is suggested that this procedure be followed with the right waived by such states to the state of residence or the state where the damage or injury occurred whenever deemed efficacious.

Limitation of Liability

Even though it has been generally agreed that space activity creates extraordinary risks which should not be imposed on the public at large, it has been contended that the further encouragement of the exploration and use of outer space requires the establishment by multilateral convention of an overall monetary limitation, or scale of limitations, on the extent of liability incurred by a launching state for damage caused by a single launch. It is difficult to determine with precision the amount of damages that might conceivably be caused by the return of a space object. One might invoke theories of probability to ascertain the approximate amounts of damages depending on variations in circumstances. Much depends on the size of the space object, and the nature of the components or substances therein. Much also depends on the location of impact. Urban areas with dense population and concentrations of valuable property would suffer far greater damage than elsewhere.

Where a conceivable radiation hazard is imposed by the use of nuclear rocket engines or nuclear power sources in spacecraft, estimates of possible damage caused by impact alone are no longer applicable. Indeed, the strength of arguments in favor of an overall monetary limitation or liability would be lessened were it not for speculations over the possibility of liability in the hundreds of millions of dollars in the event of a nuclear incident. Experience may prove those speculations to be unfounded. Nevertheless, much of the discussion on limitation of liability has been in the context of possible nuclear damage. As precedents for international agreement on an appropriate monetary limitation, one can point to the Brussels Convention on the Liability of Operators of Nuclear Ships, in which the overall limitation is 100 million dollars, and the 1963 Supplement to the 1960 Paris Convention, in which the overall limitation is 120 million dollars. The United States has also entered into bilateral agreements with several states providing for a maximum limitation of 500 million dollars on liability arising out of a nuclear incident involving the nuclear ship Savannah. Even these precedents may be only partially in point, in view of the vast differences between use of nuclear energy in space vehicles, and its use in reactors on land and in ships. If an overall limitation is established, how should account be taken of claims which exceed the limitation? Should all claims be reduced pro rata? Should claims for death and personal injury be satisfied in their entirety before claims for property damage are satisfied? These and similar questions would have to be resolved, probably not in any convention but rather by the state presenting the claims.

However, these questions argue for unlimited liability but some states are of the opinion that without some limit, agreement on a liability convention is not possible.

International Organizations

Although traditionally only states may be parties to actions before international tribunals, this concept has been modified and some treaties give status to nongovernmental entities before such tribunals. In space activities, the question is whether international organizations may be accorded status before international tribunals. Generally the answer is found in international agreements establishing the organization and the tribunal in question.

Article VI of the Outer Space Treaty dealt with this problem by holding State Parties to the Treaty internationally responsible for space activities whether "carried on by governmental agencies or by nongovernmental entities." When nongovernmental entities perform outer space activities, the State Party to the Treaty shall authorize and supervise such activities. Responsibility for such activities, "shall be borne both by the international organization and by the States Parties to the Treaty participating in such organization."

The "Agreement on the Rescue of Astronauts, the Return of Astronauts, and the Return of Objects Launched in Outer Space" also recognizes an international organization whenever such an organization assumes the rights and obligations of the Treaty and a majority of the State Members of the organization are Parties to the Treaty.

With such precedents, agreement has been reached that international intergovernmental organizations should be liable as entities under the convention although differences still exist as to what the relationship should be between such organizations and state parties to the convention.

Procedural Issues

As if the substantive issues regarding liability for damages were not sufficiently complex, several procedural issues have been raised in connection with prosecuting possible claims for damage. On an international level, claims are prosecuted by states or international organizations against other states or international organizations. Should claimants be required to rely on diplomacy, or should a claims commission or other tribunal be established? A combination of both of these procedures appears to be acceptable to many states which have expressed their views on this matter. Claimants would be required to utilize diplomatic channels initially in presenting their claims. However, if satisfaction has not been obtained within a reasonable time, the claimant should have recourse to a claims commission.

Another question concerns the period during which a claimant may present its claim following damage caused by a space object. While a period of one year has been suggested, there may be an interval of many years before the full extent of damage is realized, particularly where injuries are caused by nuclear contamination. Thus it would only be fair to begin the applicable period for presentation of claims only after the facts giving rise to the claim have been identified.

Under international law, claimants are often required to exhaust remedies available under the domestic law of the state that caused the damage before resorting to diplomacy or other international procedures. In order to afford claimants with an expeditious and effective remedy, however, the presentation of a claim diplomatically should not require the prior exhaustion of local remedies. However, a claimant should not be permitted to prosecute its claim concurrently in a domestic forum and before an international tribunal.

Conclusion

It was hoped that a liability convention would have been presented to the General Assembly of the United Nations just concluded. However, while many issues have been decided, there remain several which prevent complete agreement. My own assessment from participating in the Legal Subcommittee sessions since 1964 is that once agreement is reached on the issue of settlement of claims disputes, all the other topics will be readily resolved.

It is obvious that the subject is extremely complex. Yet it is one of practical importance in connection with activity in outer space being carried on at the present time. A large measure of international agreement has been achieved on solutions to many of the issues that have been raised. This agreement has been achieved despite the lack of the extensive experience that ordinarily precedes the establishment of rules governing most areas of human affairs. Thus far, actual experience in outer space activities has been very encouraging. No deaths, injuries, or appreciable property damage cognizable under international law have been caused by space activities, and no international claims have been presented. The establishment of criteria and procedures governing liability for damages affords protection to mankind from the hazards created by the exploration and use of outer space. This protection is essential if people of all nations are to regard space exploration as in the interest of all mankind. Progress in outer space depends upon the lawyers and the policymakers no less than upon the scientists and engineers.

In resolving the issues related to liability, the next major step will have been taken to assure that such progress is attained and the developing legal regime for outer space activities is continuing.

$$* \quad * \quad * \quad * \quad *$$

THE USE OF SPACE COMMUNICATION FOR INFORMATION, EDUCATION AND CULTURAL EXCHANGE

Report by the

United Nations Education, Scientific and Cultural Organization Secretariat

Introduction

1. By extending enormously the range and scope of the mass media, space communication is providing a dramatic opportunity for the transmission of ideas in word and picture to every corner of the globe. The implications of direct broadcasts via satellite into community or home receivers are profound and call for a high degree of cooperation between nations as well as of responsibility on the part of broadcasters.

2. The building of international understanding and cooperation is U.N.E.S.C.O.'s overriding aim and its special interest in space communication stems from its constitutional obligation to promote the free flow of information, the spread of education and greater cultural exchange.

3. In this paper, we provide an outline of U.N.E.S.C.O.'s program in the space communication field. It is recalled that at an earlier Symposium of the International Astro-

nautical Federation - in September 1963 - U.N.E.S.C.O. presented a paper on the Use of Communication Satellites for Information and Education. At that time, we looked forward to the growing use of the new techniques by the mass media, foresaw their early application to provide worldwide live television coverage of "great human events," and expressed our confidence that they would stimulate the use of the media for education. The educational application of space communication is still a matter for the future - hopefully the near future - but there is ample evidence that the early prospect of extensive broadcasting by satellite has had a galvanizing effect on the whole approach to educational reform and the adoption of new techniques to accelerate and improve the educational process.

Types of Satellite Systems

4. Before examining the problems of international regulation and application of space communication in U.N.E.S.C.O.'s fields, it is important to note the difference between the systems by which television transmitters will be linked with receivers through the use of a satellite.

5. In point-to-point communication that signal (consisting of a broadcast or broadcast material) is transmitted via a satellite of relatively low power between powerful and sensitive ground stations. These ground stations which are used for both sending and receiving signals are connected to the terrestrial telecommunication networks through which a television signal is relayed to television broadcast transmitters for distribution to individual receivers just like any other television broadcast.

6. When more powerful satellites become available it will be possible to broadcast programs directly to individual home or community receivers. The Working Group on Direct Broadcast Satellites of the United Nations Committee on the Peaceful Uses of Outer Space in February 1969 reached the conclusion that direct satellite broadcasts into cummunity receivers would be feasible in the mid-1970's. While it was considered possible to envisage the future development of satellites capable of broadcasting to the public at large, direct broadcasting of television signals from satellites into existing home receivers on an operational basis was not foreseen for the period 1970-1985. However, direct television broadcasts into specially equipped home receivers could become feasible technologically as soon as 1975. The use of such systems would be dependent on the costs for both the earth and space segments.

7. Direct satellite broadcasts will introduce a fundamental new element in present broadcasting practices. Broadcasting is now carried out as a national activity with the exception of shortwave broadcasts which, however, have limited audiences. National, public or private bodies are in charge of what is seen or heard within a country. This remains true in the case of point-to-point satellite systems. Technically, a signal originating outside a country is received not by the public at large, but by national bodies which decide what is broadcast to the public. With the advent of direct broadcasting from satellites, however, a situation may arise where the public could receive broadcasts from other countries without the intermediary of a national body. Control of broadcasts might thus shift from within a country to the originating body, i.e., to an extra-national source.

The Need for International Cooperation

8. By adding a new dimension to the mass media, space communication is giving further impetus to the long standing concern about the role of media in society. It has given new

urgency to such continuing issues as program content, the extension of codes of conduct for the profession and, in general, the responsibility of the mass media in serving the public interest.

9. There is general agreement on the objective that space communication should be used conscientiously and effectively for the promotion of international understanding through greater mutual knowledge of each country's culture and achievements. The achievement of this objective will become more and more difficult when it is possible for direct television broadcasts via satellite to be received directly in the homes of peoples all over the world. Sound and visual programs containing opinion as well as news would have enormous possibilities to influence public attitudes on political, religious, educational and cultural matters. Under these circumstances, national legal provisions and existing international arrangements whether in the form of laws, regulations, legal precedents or agreements, will soon prove inadequate to prevent abuses or protect rights. The iminence of these high-powered communication satellites makes international cooperation imperative in the dissemination of programs via space communication.

10. As Professor Terrou, Director of the Institute of the Press of the University of Paris, has affirmed in a Report for U.N.E.S.C.O., direct broadcasting poses a problem that can be solved by only two methods - coercion or international cooperation. Coercion might mean arbitrary jamming, possibly the destruction of instruments for the dissemination of information or even a ban on the manufacture, importation or possession of receiving sets. Cooperation means legal solutions - international agreements and regulations whereby the various States and the bodies responsible for the production and dissemination of information via satellite would accept the discipline and responsibility needed to prevent abuses.

11. The whole problem of content is ultimately linked with that of access to this new telecommunication technique. States have agreed to the principle that space communication should be made available to all nations on a non-discriminatory basis. Space communication agencies are, in effect, "common carriers" and hence subject to the obligations imposed by the international public law to make their service available on an equitable basis. But the machinery and procedures are needed whereby the principle of equal treatment for the mass media may be progressively applied as space communication expands.

12. From the outset U.N.E.S.C.O. recognized the potentialities of space communication to further the organization's aims, and the need to promote international cooperation for its effective use in the interests of all peoples. A series of expert meetings was held, commencing in 1965, which culminated in December 1969 in a Meeting of Governmental Experts on International Arrangements in the Space Communication Field, which was attended by experts from sixty-one States and by observers from a number of international organizations. They examined the problems involved in space broadcasting to promote the free flow of information, the rapid spread of education and greater cultural exchange and steps which might be taken to ensure its orderly use. In the following pages we describe briefly the application of space communication for these purposes, and incorporate some of the recommendations of the governmental experts.

Applications of Space Communication in U.N.E.S.C.O.'s Fields.

    (a) Collection and Dissemination of News

13. In this context, the expression "news" includes not only radio and visual news

items with or without sound, correspondent reports, etc., but also live or taped coverage of major events of the current affairs type, including sports. The relevant activities concern both the collection and dissemination of news and are carried out by broadcasting organizations and by a few news agencies providing coverage for use on television or radio.

14. A comparison between the news coverage in radio and in television demonstrates the importance of satellite communication for the flow of visual news throughout the world. Even if there are still economic, technical or other obstacles to be overcome for radio news coverage, a conventional communications network could allow sound reporting from and to most parts of the world. Television news is much more dependent on satellites.

15. Space communication offers the possibility of world-wide television reporting that can increase and equalize the flow of information and, in conjunction with new video recording techniques, profoundly change present viewing patterns and habits. In the long-term future, the use of space communication, combined with existing electronic techniques, could make possible world-wide electronic distribution of news, newspapers and any other printed and visual information material.

16. Collection and dissemination of international visual news was limited, at the beginning of television, to shipping films by plane. With the development of coaxial cables and microwave networks nationally and regionally, it became possible to transmit visual news within more reasonable delays. However, until the arrival of satellite communication, intercontinental visual news reporting was still largely dependent on aircraft. It is significant that satellite broadcasts have, from the beginning, been primarily used for the transmission of news. The result has been a concurrent increase in the flow of news between the areas that are connected by satellite, principally between North America and Europe. The reverse has been true for continents not connected by satellite. They have experienced a decrease in news coverage because of the difficulties and delays in providing visual information. This imbalance in technical facilities, affecting particularly the capacity for same-day coverage, has had inevitable consequences in patterns of television news reporting.

17. Regions linked by satellite have been able to follow directly the Olympic Games at Tokyo and Mexico, astronauts in space and other events of world interest. Such transmissions have also to be arranged with a view to such factors as the difference of time zones. There is, moreover, the problem of language since commentaries in the language of the receiving countries must be provided either at the point of origin or at the point of reception.

18. A great deal of attention has been devoted to these questions by the professional organizations concerned. There is a consensus that the objectives for the future development of communication satellite systems for international news broadcasts might include:

- making the flow of visual news in the world more balanced, particularly
  with regard to providing news coverage to and from, as well as between
  developing areas;
- ensuring that satellite communication is made available to all countries,
  with special regard to smaller and developing countries;
- providing broadcasters all over the world with the opportunities and
  conditions enabling them to use communication satellite systems for
  the coverage, collection, transmission and dissemination of news;

- providing conditions enabling mass media institutions all over the
  world to cooperate for the exchange of news and coverage of current
  events.

19. It was emphasized, at the U.N.E.S.C.O. Meeting of Governmental Experts, that as
well as subscribing to these principles, the practical problems of implementation must also
be studies, including political, legal and other problems and the attention of governments
and international and regional organizations should be drawn to this need. As long as the
provision of satellite facilities depended on commercial considerations only, this situation
would continue, and it was suggested that development aid be provided to make satellite communication available in regions where commercial traffic did not warrant the service.

20. The Meeting noted that, in the use of satellites for the collection and dissemination of news, all the news media had common interest. A statement from the observer from
the International Press Telecommunication Committee drew attention to the importance of
satellites for the transmission of the printed word and the published photograph as well as
of radio and television. Press agencies used world-wide communications full time and not
spasmodically and were very interested in the opportunity to use satellites for news transmission in place of shortwave radio, especially to increase the flow of news to and from
the developing countires.

(b) Educational Broadcasting

21. No use of modern communication has so interested the planners in developing countries, as well as other individuals and groups concerned with economic and social development, as the possibility of using space communication in support of education by expanded
application of television. In areas where the shortage of teachers and school facilities
is so enormous, only some nationwide instructional communications system seems likely to
make even a start in eradicating illiteracy and training a sufficient number of teachers to
have any significant impact. Where schools are short of teaching aids, a new opportunity
is presented to distribute audio-visual materials and demonstrations from a central studio;
where special courses or special kinds of instruction are required, the chance exists for
production in one place and distribution to all corners of the country.

22. The term "educational broadcasting" lends itself to a multiplicity of interpretations. Here, it is taken to comprise two basic elements:

(i)   instructional or school broadcasting, which involves the trans-
      mission of programs to formal educational establishments, includ-
      ing primary and secondary schools, universities, teacher-train-
      ing institutes, vocational and professional training centers, etc.

(ii) general broadcasting of an educational nature, also called "Public"
      broadcasting. This includes out-of-school education, such as
      agricultural programs, community development, health and family
      planning.

23. The developing countries are placing great hope in the use of satellites for broadcasting because this would enable them to distribute educational television programs to
remote areas not otherwise served. A number of expert missions sent by U.N.E.S.C.O. to
developing countries at their request, to advise governments on the potentialities of a
satellite broadcasting system, concluded that space communication could help provide a

solution to some of the massive problems of national development.

24. A U.N.E.S.C.O. expert mission which visited India at the request of the government at the end of 1967, concluded that a multipurpose satellite system could make a significant contribution to the achievement of national goals. India has since concluded an agreement with the United States for the experimental use of a NASA satellite ATF(F) for one year commencing during 1974. The educational television programs to be used in the experiment will be prepared by India itself and will be broadcast via satellite to 5,000 community sets in selected villages. Two thousand of the villages will receive the programs direct from the satellite, this being the first use of the direct broadcasting techniques.

25. Subsequent to the U.N.E.S.C.O. mission to India to study the possibilities of a satellite system and as part of India's general development plan for educational television, a further preparatory mission on television development and training visited India in 1969, and on the basis of their report, a project has been approved for the establishment of an educational television training and production center by the Government of India, with the assistance of the Special Fund of the United Nations Development Programme and U.N.E.S.C.O.

26. Other U.N.E.S.C.O. missions to assess the potentialities of space communication for education and national development have visited Brazil, Pakistan and a group of countries in Latin America.

27. Following the mission to Latin America a Conference of Ministers of Education of Andean countries held at Bogota January 27-30, 1970, resolved that a request be submitted to UNDP, to have U.N.E.S.C.O., in consultation with ITU and other interested international and regional organizations, carry out a detailed feasibility study for a regional satellite system for educational, cultural and development purposes for the countries of South America. A request has been prepared and submitted to the UNDP Special Fund seeking finance for the study.

28. Immense possibilities are apparent for regional broadcasting via satellite. This will obviously require prior agreement among interested countries on co-production of broadcasts, translation and adaptation, recording and re-use of programs, and, even more essential, on the coordination of educational programs and practices. This is a striking example of the kind of international agreement that might be required for the application of space communication for educational purposes.

29. The U.N.E.S.C.O. meeting of experts in 1969, placed the highest importance on the contribution which the new space technology could make to education, both in-school and out-of-school and in both quantitative and qualitative aspects. Educational planners in developing countries particularly, saw in satellite broadcasting a possibility of overcoming shortages of highly trained teachers and of using the latest teaching aids and audio-visual materials. Thus satellite communication could help make it possible for education to win the race with time and provide high quality instruction to even the most remote areas.

30. While costs now appeared high, tele-education through satellites was considered by the experts to be feasible and economic. They believed that the large numbers of students who could be reached through satellite-based broadcasts could, in due course, reduce the unit cost and promote the use of satellite communication as an effective and economic means for instruction and education generally. Moreover, satellite communication offered new possibilities for the pooling of educational resources through broadcasts to serve regional

needs. An important role for U.N.E.S.C.O. was seen in the need to train a new breed of educator-communicator who could combine the best features of the educator and the mass media professional. Along with those tele-educators, it would be necessary to provide the trained manpower required for the production and broadcasting of educational programs and to develop a new television-oriented pedagogy.

(c) Cultural and Scientific Uses

31. It is difficult to draw a sharp distinction between educational broadcasting, on the one hand, and cultural programs, on the other. Cultural programs, such as opera, ballet and drama, all serve an educational purpose. For the immediate future, the international exchange via satellite of cultural programs is likely in any event to be somewhat limited. Such programs are often relatively timeless, and thus can be transported at lower cost by conventional means. The real impact of cultural television programs by space communication, however, will come in the future, when direct broadcasting satellites are operative.

32. It is clear, that the world can hardly enter into a stage of full cultural exchange, particularly by direct broadcast satellites, until the institutions and patterns of cooperation have been carefully prepared. Some of these patterns already exist in the experience, for example, of the regional broadcasting unions. They have been undertaking for some time program exchanges and transmissions on a continental level. Through the use of satellite systems, and in accordance with the same basic principles adopted by the members of the European Broadcasting Union for Eurovision and by the members of the International Radio and Television Organization for Intervision, these exchanges have been widened to become international in scope. It would seem possible to widen these arrangements for exchange and cooperation to a considerable extent.

33. Anything that can be done to strengthen the programming capabilities of new television systems, or to encourage regional exchanges, will ultimately contribute to world-wide exchange. Such program exchange should, however, take fully into account the need to preserve the distinctive character of each culture.

34. Another possibility for international exchange via satellite is the sharing of scientific information. The opportunity now exists through satellite transmission to share data over long distance as never before in the history of mankind. This occurs at a time of an "information explosion" and attendant requirements for data by scientists and policy-makers. There has been a concurrent advance in the capacity of computers to store this information and retrieve it efficiently.

35. The use of satellites for the transmission of scientific data was believed by many experts at the U.N.E.S.C.O. intergovernmental meeting to be one of the most fruitful areas for satellite communication. Combined with advances in data storage and retrieval and the use of computers, space communication offers the opportunity to bring the major centers of information within reach of laboratories, or institutions of learning in all parts of the world. However, satellite facilities will be needed to accommodate scientific data exchanges, and international cooperation and arrangements will be necessary to realize their full potential.

Problems of Copyright and Protection of the Broadcast Signal

36. U.N.E.S.C.O., in conjunction with the United International Bureau for the Protection of Intellectual Property is studying two aspects of the copyright problems: (1) prob-

243

lems arising from broadcasting by satellites in the fields of copyright and neighboring rights; (ii) the question of the legal protection of satellite transmissions against unauthorized use.

37. The latter problem was examined in considerable detail by the U.N.E.S.C.O. Meeting of Governmental Experts. It was felt that there was an urgent need for international arrangements to protect broadcasting signals transmitted by satellite against uses not authorized by the originating body. It was also emphasized that such protection, to be effective, should be universally applicable.

38. Three possible solutions were discussed: a) providing protection under the International Convention for the Protection of Performers, Producers of Phonogrammes and Broadcasters, ("The Rome Convention"); b) revision to the ITU Convention and Radio Regulations or the addition of a protocol to the Regulations; c) the adoption of a new Convention.

39. It emerged from discussions at the Meeting of Experts that the Rome Convention did not seem to be an appropriate way of solving the problem, but it was agreed that the choice between a separate agreement or revision of the ITU Convention should be the subject of further study.

40. Subsequent to the December Meeting, the second session of the Intergovernmental Committee of the Rome Convention met at U.N.E.S.C.O. Headquarters from December 10-12, 1969, and examined "the protection of performers, producers of phonogrammes and broadcasting organizations in connection with radio and television broadcasts via communication satellites." There was general agreement on the necessity of protection, but participants were divided regarding the way in which this could be provided.

41. The subject was further examined by the Intergovernmental Copyright Committee sitting with the Permanent Committee of the Berne Union in December 1969. The meeting adopted a resolution which declared that "it is not yet possible at present to adopt a definitive position with regard to the steps which should be taken to provide legal protection against uses not authorized by the originating organizations." In accordance with a recommendation of the meeting, it is foreseen that a Committee of Experts will be convened by U.N.E.S.C.O. and BIRPI to examine these problems, and if the elaboration of a new instrument appeared necessary a Diplomatic Conference will be called.

The Promotion of International Agreements

42. The first article of U.N.E.S.C.O.'s Constitution pledges the Organization to work "through all the means of mass communication" and to "recommend such international agreements as may be necessary to promote the free flow of ideas by word and image." Although written well before the space age, this mandate corresponds to U.N.E.S.C.O.'s concern with communication satellites.

43. International agreements designed to promote the free flow of information were in fact among the earliest to be sponsored by the Organization. The Agreement for Facilitating the International Circulation of Visual and Auditory Materials of Educational, Scientific and Cultural Character was adopted by the General Conference in 1948 at Beirut. Two years later, at Florence, the General Conference adopted an Agreement on the Importation of Educational, Scientific and Cultural Materials.

44. Certain of the principles embodied in the Beirut Agreement might be considered to have a bearing on the free flow of information through space communication. Materials cover-

ed by the Agreement must fulfill three conditions to enjoy the benefits provided: their main purpose must be to instruct or inform or to promote the spread of knowledge and international understanding; they must be representative, authentic and accurate; their technical quality must be adequate for use.

45. It will be evident, however, that international agreements in space communication involve broader concepts. At its fifteenth session, the General Conference considered a report which set forth the general objectives of international agreements in space communication as follows:

    (i)   to ensure the use of satellite communication in the public interest for peaceful purposes and for better understanding between nations;

    (ii)   to ensure the availability of satellite communication to all States, irrespective of the stage of their social, economic and technical development, on a global and nondiscriminatory basis;

    (iii)   to promote organizational and administrative forms providing equitable access to communication satellite systems, with special regard to smaller countries and developing areas;

    (iv)   to provide proper access to global and regional communication satellite systems by the United Nations and the Specialized Agencies;

    (v)   to ensure equitable use of the radio frequency spectrum;

    (vi)   to promote harmonious integration of satellite communication facilities into present and planned telecommunication networks used for mass media purposes;

    (vii)   to promote favorable conditions for professional agreements enabling the mass media to increase the exchange of news, programs and program materials;

    (viii)   to encourage the use of satellite communication by different users, with special regard to the development of broadcasting and the flow of educational, scientific, cultural and information materials;

    (ix)   to promote the use of satellite communication for educational and economic development purposes on a national and regional level;

    (x)   to share experience and skills gained by the use of satellite communication.

46. It is evident that many of these objectives go beyond U.N.E.S.C.O.'s own mandate. The report to the General Conference noted, for example, that political and legal aspects of freedom of information in satellite communication are the primary concern of the United Nations and that the regulatory and technical aspects regarding the use of radio frequencies and other technical standards fall within the purview of the International Telecommunication Union.

47. The General Conference of U.N.E.S.C.O. had foreseen that, on the basis of the findings of the meeting of governmental experts, a Draft Declaration might be prepared embodying principles for the use of space communication for the free flow of information, the spread of education and greater cultural exchanges.

48. In the course of discussion during the meeting, experts had been aware that many of the issues under consideration could be dealt with in a draft declaration on guiding

principles, and a number of delegations made suggestions about its contents. The 1970 General Conference of U.N.E.S.C.O. will consider a proposal that such a Declaration should be formulated during the 1971-1972 program period.

* * * * *

II. Other contributions and comments

The thirteenth Colloquium had as its theme "The United Nations Organization and the Legal Problems of Outer Space" in honor of the 25th anniversary of the UN. It goes without saying, therefore, that of the close to 50 papers submitted, those dealing with aspects falling under the said theme hold an important place. And, in fact, practically all subjects dealt with could be put under this subject heading, as the UN through its Secretariat (Outer Space Affairs Division), and in particular through the Outer Space Committee and its Legal Subcommittee, has a big and strong finger in the space law pie. The following, a brief description of the views expressed at the Colloquium, may help the reader to ascertain this unique position of the UN, although, of course, it can never replace the reading of the papers in toto.

In his preface to the proceedings, M. Constantine Stavropoulos, Undersecretary General and Legal Counsel of the UN, pointed to three legal instruments worked out by UN and already endorsed by the international community of states:

> A declaration of legal principles governing the activities of states in the exploration and use of Outer Space, which was adopted by the General Assembly of the United Nations in 1963;
>
> A treaty of the principles governing the activities of states in the exploration and use of Outer Space including the moon and other celestial bodies, which entered into force in 1967; and
>
> An agreement on the rescue of astronauts, the return of astronauts, and the return of objects launched into Outer Space which came into force in 1968.

The president of the International Institute of Space Law, M. Pépin, reported on IISL activities: the preparation of the 12th Colloquium (at Mar del Plata, Argentina, October, 1969), and the First Symposium on the Teaching of Space Law held immediately thereafter. The publications of IISL - Proceedings of Colloquium and Symposium, Worldwide Bibliography on Space Law, Newsletter - include a highly needed Astronautical Multilingual Dictionary containing a list of legal terms.

In his opening address, Dr. Bodenschatz, president of the sessions, pointed to predictions made by Pan American Airlines that between 1985 and 2000, space transportation will be performed by a commercial carrier with a shuttle service between earth and a space station as well as a considerable reduction of cost in the preparation and launching of a space shuttle.

Professor Christol's General Report is the first contribution on the subject, "The United Nations Organization and the Legal Problems of Outer Space." He comments on: the establishment of the Outer Space Committee; the impact of the General Assembly resolutions on space; its close contact with and encouragement to other international organizations and states leading to various space projects; and the impact of concepts and principles developed for outer space on other areas of concern to the UN, such as the sea-bed and ocean-floor. These are, inter alia, the aspects of the UN's role which the author ably describes. Christol (USA) deals with "the social complex theory of international affairs": that is, the (1) social complex forces which work in modern society (scientific and technological revolution - population explosion - growth of international institutions); (2) the functions of international institutions; and (3) the impact of values on the legal and political decision-making process. Historically, UN has been called upon to interest itself in space matters even prior to the successful launch of Sputnik I (1957). The statement of Henry Cabot Lodge Jr., the permanent representative of the United States to the UN, that his government had supported as an objective "the use of space exclusively ... [for] peaceful and scientific purposes" influenced the General Assembly to adopt Resolution 1148 (Nov. 14, 1957), which urged that states engage in a joint study of an "inspection system designed to ensure that the sending of objects through Outer Space shall be exclusively for peaceful and scientific purposes."

The UN-created Committee on the Peaceful Uses of Outer Space, through its Legal and Technical Sub-committee, is responsible for a series of significant unanimous resolutions of the General Assembly, and the drafting of Agreements and Treaties. There is, at the present time, a substantial record of launches (including nature, conduct, locations and result of space activities) in the possession of the Secretary-General. These data - supplied by Australia, France, Italy, the USA and the USSR - are communicated by the UN to the entire world.

UN involvement in space environment prescriptions has also necessitated a cooperative relationship with specialized agencies as well as such bodies as International Astronautical Federation (IAF), International Atomic Energy Agency (IAEA), and the Committee on Space Research (COSPAR). The network of external relationship extends to - among others - the European Space Vehicle Launcher Development Organ (ELDO) and the European Space Research Organization (ESRO).

Under UN sponsorship, the government of India has installed at Thumba, and operates there, an Equatorial Rocket Launching Station (TERLS), maintaining a sounding rocket range, organizing space flight programs and receiving technicians from many states for professional training. At least in part because of UN interest, the World Meteorological Organ (WMO) officially adopted a plan for the World Weather Watch.

The UN, in achieving a system of law and a scheme of public order for the space environment, have contributed to procedural advances in other areas, such as:

   a) Arms control and disarmament;

   b) Peaceful uses of the sea-bed and the ocean-floor beyond the limits of national jurisdiction, i.e., "in the interests of mankind as a whole";

   c) Forum for the exploitation of space capabilities;

   d) Analysis of space environment situations: the importance of this field has produced an academic legal speciality.

As an influential international forum, the UN sees to it that the contributions of all members of the different countries are essential to the emergence of space law. For example, the practice of electing the Chairman, the Vice-Chairman, the Rapporteur of the Committee on the Peaceful Uses of Outer Space, the Chairmen of the two Sub-Committees, and the Chairman of the Working Group on Navigational Satellites and of the Working Group on Direct Broadcast Satellites, from states other than the two resource states - USA and USSR - measurably enlarges the contributions of the non-resource states. Thus the end product has been to ensure that the legal regime for the space environment is a truly international one based on the community of interests of all the participating states.

G. P. Zhukov (USSR) regards the UN as the "center of international cooperation in the elaboration of space law norms." He discusses the machinery by which space law norms are brought about and gives a description of the UN organs - Committee on the Peaceful Uses of Outer Space, the Legal Sub-Committees and the General Assembly. Professor Zhukov speaks about the setting up of a special group in the general legal division of the UN Secretariat's Legal Department "with the purpose of assisting the Legal Sub-Committee on the Peaceful Uses of Outer Space. He continues:

> It should be noted that the Outer Space Affairs Division was set up in the Department of Political and Security Council Affairs of the UN Secretariat; that department services the Committee on the Peaceful Use of Outer Space, its Scientific and Technical Subcommittees and working Groups on Direct Broadcast Satellites and Navigation Satellites, and it is provided that this division should deal with problems of a scientific and technical nature. However ... legal problems of Outer Space were discussed in the Committee on the Peaceful Uses of Outer Space, in the Working Group on Direct Broadcast Satellites, at the UN Conference in Vienna (Exploration and Peaceful Uses of Outer Space, Vienna, 1968): all related to the Outer Space Division of the Department of Political and Security Council Affairs of the UN Secretariat. Therefore important legal problems were withdrawn from the competence of the Legal Department of the UN Secretariat.

Professor Zhukov raised the question "to what extent the distribution of the scientific, technical, and legal problems related to space among divisions of different departments of the UN Secretariat is justified at all?"

In addition, future areas of concern (direct broadcasting, cooperation between Intelsat and Intersputnik, earth resources satellites and the legal status of the moon) are examined. He concludes that though the UN must play an important role in the development of space law norms, much depends on the general political situation in the world and on the readiness of some states to expand international cooperation. However, pointing to the "special role of the leading space powers — the USSR and the United States — in the elaboration of space law norms," he claims that the major international agreements on Outer Space "would hardly have been signed if not for the initiative and tremendous efforts on the part of the Soviet Union."

Particularly qualified to discuss the UN institutions concerned with space activities is the Chief of the UN Outer Space Affairs Division, Abdel-Ghani. In a special report he outlines the structure and organization of these bodies (Outer Space Committee, UN Secretariat, including his own division, in which he is an expert on the application of space technology) and gives some information about the cooperation between the various specialized agencies. In the second part of his report Abdel-Ghani outlines the salient features of the work carried out by these bodies. Specific features are dealt with, such as establishment of a legal regime for Outer Space (liability for damage, use of satellites for transmitting radio and television programs, registration of objects launched into Outer Space, establishment of a scientific and technical program). The UN has taken steps promoting the practical applications of space technology, including the opportunity for developing countries to prepare their own specialists who could participate in the earth resources satellites program.

One of the recurring themes in the IISL discussions is that of the desirability and feasibility of an international space agency to supervise and control all space activities. Tamm explores two approaches to the problem: a first possibility lies within the UN structure, e.g., by expanding the responsibilities of the Outer Space Affairs Division; a second is the creation in the near future of a space agency, the responsibilities of which the author outlines.

One of the main reasons for UN's success in formulating space treaties is, according to Galloway, that the objectives to be attained in developing the new space age were identified shortly after the first satellites were launched into orbit. One of the fundamental objectives was to prevent outer space from becoming an area of hostilities and warfare. Another factor contributing to this success was the fact that the space powers did not adopt a policy of monopoly over outer space and the realization of many other countries that they could — albeit on a small scale — participate in space research. The author concludes her enthusiastic report with appendices in which the status of the Space Treaty and the Rescue Agreement as of September 1, 1970, are given.

Two papers by <u>Gorove</u> follow. The first one concerns the requirement, laid down in the Space Treaty, that the exploration and use of outer space shall be carried out for the benefit and in the interest of all countries. This is perhaps the most important limitation on the principle of freedom of exploration and use of the Treaty. Gorove argues that the phrase "for the benefit" is less restrictive than the negative phrase "not for the detriment" of other peoples: the phrase must be constructively beneficial, in the form of material, political, and other benefits. Must all the results of exploration also be "shared" in order to constitute a benefit to all countires? This and similar questions (the meaning of "all" countries) are discussed by the author in a clear, but - necessarily - not exhaustive, manner. In his short contribution on Art. IV of the Space Treaty, Gorove makes the valuable suggestion to abandon the artificial distinction between "peaceful" and "military" purposes or "peaceful" and "aggressive" purposes and to focus on the prohibition or permission of the particular activity instead; aerial photography is given as an example.

Several articles are devoted to an important problem of the future, namely the rights and obligations of states with respect to the <u>natural resources</u> of celestial bodies, or, as <u>Markoff</u> calls them, space resources. According to this author an agreement in addition to the Space Treaty should be concluded banning all kind of appropriation not only of areas of celestial bodies (Art. II), but also of non-renewable natural resources in space. <u>Williams</u> fully endorses this opinion, and she quotes the example given by Cocca that the sharing of samples of the moon brought to earth by the US astronauts was the performance of an obligation clearly emerging from the Space Treaty and by no means an act of grace. There is however ample evidence that the USA does not share this view, and that is probably one of the reasons why Argentina submitted to the Legal Subcommittee of UNCOPUOS a draft agreement concerning natural resources which establishes that the natural resources of celestial bodies shall be the common heritage of all mankind, and which provides for the distribution of benefits. Dr. Williams, quoting such authors as Professors Goedhuis, Marcoff, Mankiewicz, Cocca, Ferrer, and Wilfred Jenks arrives at the following conclusion: "... [I]n the face of the Outer Space Treaty and rules of positive law contained therein, appropriation of space resources is fully banned ... [and] the liberty of appropriation of non-exhaustible space resources should be unrestricted." Dr. Williams recommends, with reference to space resources, an agreement based on the principles of the Outer Space Treaty and Argentina's draft agreement (presented before UNCOPUOS), as well as the establishment of an international organization for space activities and administration of space resources.

Professor Cocca in "Legal Status of the Natural Resources of the Moon and Other Celestial Bodies" analyses two Argentine proposals presented to the UN Legal Subcommittee of COPUOS. He states that, "... a natural resource, even though it may come from the Moon and other celestial bodies, ... shall always be a natural resource for Earth ... [and] shall be the common heritage of all mankind." Cocca supports the view that exploitation of celestial bodies will produce the same problems as those of the ocean floor and sea bed; these two questions should be merged, therefore, and placed in the hands of the same international agency.

Professor Julio Barboza maintains that the activity of satellites operated by remote control should be of primary international interest because of the illicit information about land, climate, and natural resources they provide about States not involved in such launchings. He concludes that the information obtained of natural resources, without the consent of the interested state, constitutes a violation of the sovereignty of said state, and as a consequence, the international community has to intervene in order to regulate that activity.

Dr. Maria Teresa Curia adheres to the principle that materials brought to earth from outer space are res communis humanitatis, and their use is legitimate only when benefiting all mankind. She appears to agree with her compatriots from Argentina and also advocates the establishment of a special agency on space resources.

Three papers in this volume are devoted to the question of liability for space activities, not much, in view of its importance for particularly the non-space powers, the potential victims of space related accidents. The quality of the contribution submitted by Dembling makes up for the small quantity; his able analysis of the problems involved has been reproduced in full.

Dr. Herczeg (Hungary) discusses reasons behind difficulties in establishing a convention on liability for damages. The 12 article draft convention by the Committee on Peaceful Uses of Outer Space is included in the annex.

Dr. Niciu (Rumania) expresses his personal opinion on some controversial points about liability in space law. Of Niciu's views should be mentioned his insistence on not prescribing the arbitral procedures to be followed in case of conflict, but to leave this to the states concerned; it represents the traditional socialist view on the settlement of disputes between states.

Interesting problems will arise with the putting into orbit of international laboratories launched by international organizations on the basis of an interstate agreement. Such problems are elucidated by Vereshchetin of the USSR Academy of Sciences. He discusses the absence of international registration requirements, right of ownership, liability, and jurisdiction and control over the object and its personnel. The legal regime of an international orbiting laboratory has something in common with all space objects. It has, however, specific characteristics because of its international character, its being placed in orbit around the earth, its mission and the presence of a crew.

A more detailed contribution to the same theme is offered by Professor Magno (Italy). After a concise definition of space objects as well as space stations and space transport, Professor Magno refers to the juridical problems of national and multinational orbital laboratories (e.g., utilization of a space zone and its occupation, pretending sovereignty), and proposes a solution: the defense of occupation should be interpreted as "defense of abuse," to the advantage and interest of all mankind.

Two members on the staff of the Library of Congress, Washington, Dr. C. S. Sheldon II and Mrs. B. M. DeVoe, prepared information about the UN Registry of Space Vehicles. Resolution 1472 (XIV) called for the creation of a Permanent Committee on Peaceful Uses of Outer Space consisting of 24 members: Albania, Argentina, Australia, Austra, Belgium, Brazil, Bulgaria, Canada, Czechoslovakia, France, Hungary, India, Iran, Italy, Japan, Lebanon, Mexico, Poland, Rumania, Sweden, United Arab Republic, UK of Great Britain and North Ireland, USSR and USA. (The Soviet Union had insisted the membership of the Committee be patterned to give equal numbers of members to states associated with the views of the two operational space powers, USA and USSR.) The Committee's purpose was to promote international cooperation for space development and to consider legal problems associated with use of space. On December 20, 1961, Resolution 1721 (which added four members to the committee – Chad, Mongolia, Morocco and Sierra Leone - and sought a compromise in the matter of voting) was adopted by the General Assembly; the Secretary General was requested "to maintain a public registry of the information furnished." Reasons for this registry of space vehicles are, according to Sheldon and DeVoe, to minimize the chance of collision of space objects, to prevent confusion of defense radars, and to identify space objects that cause damage. The authors review the practice of the USA, USSR and other countries in this respect, and, as the Resolution does not say what flights are to be registered and which details are to be given, it is understandable that many differences in reporting are found. Registration practice differs not only in USA and USSR, but also in the smaller countries. Unlike the USA, the Soviet Union does not report the decay of objects or its launch failures. In view of the above reasons it would seem that particularly the practice of reporting a launching after it has taken place makes the existing system highly unsatisfactory. If it is to be used for operational purposes, reports to the register should, according to the authors, icnlude additionally: alerts that launches were about to take place, with intended orbits, and information on radio frequencies employed by the objects. In conclusion, if the nations of the world want an ultimate international space traffic control system, they have to open wider the door of the present register.

Another report on UN registration of space craft by Dr. Isabel H. Ph. Diederiks-Verschoor (Netherlands) points to the establishment of World Data Centers for the IGY program and recommends the suggestions given by Professor da Cunha Machado and Professor R. Menkiewicz of the International Law Association.

An application in space technology of particular importance is the survey from space of earth resources. Smirnoff, Barboza and Brital give their views on this subject. It is interesting to note that Barboza concludes that "la información obtenida por tales medios (by means of satellite) de los resursos naturales, sin consentimento del Estado interesado

252

constituye una violación de la soberanía de dicho Estado sobre tales recursos." Dr.
Fernandez Brital (Argentina) arrives at the conclusion - which seems to be more correct -
that the terms of the Space Treaty do not prohibit the survey from space of natural resources, although these activities must be in conformity with the provisions of that Treaty
(Art. I) and of the Resolution of the General Assembly regarding the sovereignty over natural
resources. Brital investigates the survey of earth resources from space giving an outline
of the various phases preceding the Outer Space Treaty and proposing an adequate legal regime,
either on a regional or an international basis, to govern these activities. The Yugoslav,
Dr. Smirnoff, stresses the importance of the Vienna Conference of 1968, where practical benefits derived from space exploration by ERTS (Earth Resources Survey Satellites) were
assessed. He lists six NASA objectives in its program of earth resources survey. He
states that "the legal regulation of the problem of Earth Resources Survey from Outer Space"
should be the "most urgent task of lawyers."

The protection of satellites and their "right of way," as well as special problems
which might emerge, are investigated by Dr. M.A. Ferrer (Argentina). If a satellite is in
orbit and both the launching and the future orbit have been announced in advance, the
launching state is entitled to keep the satellite in that orbit; that is more or less what
Ferrer calls "el derecho a la trayectoria," based mainly on Art. I(2) of the Space Treaty.

Professor Mango and Dr. Scifoni (Italy) present objective and exact definitions of
space, space objects, and outer space terminology, as well as differing viewpoints of
researchers about this topic; the work performed by UN committees; criteria on division of
space and outer space; navigability in space; and effects of terrestrial gravity. They
also argue the case for investment and individual return on capital outlay.

Pollution of space environment and contaminating agents of the atmosphere, including
radioactive substances as well as noise, are treated by Dr. Estradé (Spain). He pleads
for the extension to Outer Space of already existing norms which protect the earth atmosphere.
SATEMA (Satellites for Technological-Meteorological-Anticontamination Purposes) could be
used also to distribute data on the purity of the air. Dr. Estradé suggests the design of
cosmic programs which would include the use of SATEMA for a more efficient international
meteorological service and the installation of space stations capable of changing the
climate and water conditions of poor earth zones.

After mentioning international law, the UN Charter, the Outer Space Treaty and other
pertinent regulations, Dr. C.E.S. Horsford (UK) summarized "suggested rules of conduct on
celestial bodies" as follows:
   1) all states and their nationals shall be guided in their activities by existing
principles of international law, including the UN Charter and the Outer Space Treaty of
1967;

2) principles of mutual assistance and cooperation ... shall apply equally to activities on celestial bodies as they do to the exploration of outer space;

3) all matters affecting personnel or property of a state which establishes a base on a celestial body may be decided according to the municipal law of that state, but only in so far as it does not conflict with international law or the interests of other states;

4) until the appropriate international machinery is established, all states shall use their good offices and mediation in the settlement of disputes, and shall refrain from belligerent action on celestial bodies or in outer space;

5) a high duty of care is to be implied in the exploration and settlement of celestial bodies, particularly in the field of dangerous experiments and the conservation of natural resources;

6) it shall be the duty of all states which explore or settle on celestial bodies to conserve and have regard to all life forms thereon, at whatever level they may be found, in the interest of those species so long as they are not harmful to the exploring state personnel;

7) no military installations or fortifications shall be erected on a celestial body, and no military operations shall be aimed at or conducted against the property of other states thereon.

In conclusion, he points to two main questions: To what extent, if at all, should there be active UN supervision of planetary and lunar bases? What system of law should apply in a multinational base or settlement, and what powers of legal enforcement should the base commander have, for example, in the trial and punishment of offenders of various nationalities?

Humanity, or Mankind, is a new subject of law, recognized as such by the UN in numerous declarations, resolutions and international instruments on space law; that is the interesting thesis developed by Cocca. In his report "Mankind as a New Legal Subject," after dealing with the historical terminology of Roman law and the creation of a modern legal terminology embracing entirely new situations, Professor Cocca ascertains that the expression "common heritage of all mankind" and similar terms possess "the greatest juridical sense and mean a deep evolution in the field of law." This has been accomplished by the innovative work performed by the UN.

This concept is further discussed by Dr. Maqueda. In "Humanity as Subject of Law" he points out that the UN proclamation is "the cornerstone of space law." There is need of outlining the fundamental bases on which such juridical concept lies: philosophical, religious, and political. Humanity, according to Maqueda, is as capable juridically as a minor that exercises his rights and fulfills his obligations by means of his representatives; the states - and on their behalf the astronauts, it could be added - are in this view the representatives of Humanity. The concept is certainly worth some further thought.

In part IV of this volume a whole series of papers deal with the role and activities of specialized agencies with respect to outer space. Not surprisingly the bulk of these contributions touch in some way or another upon communications by satellites; various aspects of this beneficial space activity fall within the competence of the UN itself, the ITU and UNESCO. A report of the ITU Secretariat, for example, shows that from 1959 on, this organization has been active in this field, particularly concerning itself with the allocation of frequencies to the various space related services. Special Administrative Conferences were organized for that purpose and technical studies of space communications were undertaken.

In the secretarial report of the International Union of Telecommunications (IUT), reference is made to its convention held at Lake Success in 1947, where IUT was recognized by the UN as "the specialized institution to take all the necessary measures ... in order to obtain the aims which it proposes . . . ." There follows an account of the objectives, activities and structure of the IUT. In 1959 an Administrative Conference was held in Geneva to revise radio-communication rules and allot frequency bands for space research. In addition, conditions for the use of these bands were set down. Following this, the Plenipotentiary Committee met, whose purpose it was to inform the UN of IUT's progress, the status of technical studies, and announce the decisions of the Administrative Conference of 1959. In 1963 an Administrative Conference was again held, and at this meeting, for the first time, frequency bands were allotted to satellites. The Worldwide Administrative Conference on Space Telecommunications met in 1971. This conference considered the rapidly changing factors in the realm of outer space and the coordination of existing world systems with regional and national systems. Attention was given to data transmission from great distances, control of space circulation, and assembling of hydrological, meteorological, and oceanographic data, and new prospectives emerging from direct radiodiffusion by satellites. Furthermore, regulations concerning the tasks of the various IUT organs were formulated: the essential tasks of the International Frequency Registration Board (IFRB) are the methodical registration of the frequency assignments delivered from different countries, advice to the members on the utilization of a large number of radioelectric channels in regions with abnormal conditions, assignment and utilization of frequencies prescribed by a conference of the Union (or by the Administrative Board with the consent of the majority of members); tasks of the International Radiodiffusion Consultative Committee (IRCC) and the International Telegraph and Telephone Consultative Committee (IRRCC) are studies of radio-electric space systems and its economics (tariff planning and comparison between cost and value of earth stations).

The IUT provides for technical cooperation in space activities taking advantage of facilities existing in the UN Development Program (UNDP). Technical experts in organization, exploitation, maintenance, and planning are sent to developing countries, and fellowships are given to students and specialists. Furthermore, study groups and seminars are organized. With the help of IUT and UNDP, an experimental terrestrial station for telecommunications by satellite was created in Ahmedabad (India). Two other cooperative missions (UNESCO/IUT) are working in South America and Pakistan.

255

UNESCO, on the other hand, has been - and is - extremely active on the program side of telecommunications, or, in other words, information, education and cultural exchange by satellite. If one talks about communications by satellites, obviously the organization which at present operates these satellites, Intelsat, should be discussed, a task of which one of its officials, Richard R. Colino (USA), acquits himself ably. He gives an extensive report on "The United Nations, Its Specialized Agencies and Communications Satellites," summarizing UN activity in three major fields:

1) establishment of general principles respecting the use of Outer Space;
2) encouragement of the development of space technology;
3) technical assistance to developing nations so that they might benefit from space technology.

These activites are carried out by the UN General Assembly, the Assembly's Committee on the Peaceful Uses of Outer Space, the UN Secretariat, and the UN Development Program.

A Conference of Ministers of Education of Argentina, Chile, Columbia, Ecuador, Peru, Uruguay and Venezuela (1970) requested approval of a study of a Latin-American Communications Satellite System.

ITU, which traces its history back to the establishment of the International Telegraph Union in 1865, is composed of a Plenipotentiary Conference, Administrative Conferences, an Administrative Council and four permanent organs: the General Secretariat, the International Frequency Registration Board (IFRB), the International Radio Consultative Committee (IRCC), and the International Telegraph and Telephone Consultative Committee (ITTCC).

The World Plan Committee and Regional Plan Committees have taken the development of the communications satellite into account in their planning of the international network. The rapidly developing INTELSAT (International Telecommunication Satellite Consortium) satellite system was recognized by the Regional Committees in Rome, Paris, and Mexico City. The World Plan Committee took existing and projected INTELSAT satellites into full and equal consideration with other traditional facilities in developing the general plan for the inter-regional telecommunication network (1967).

UNESCO has undertaken several survey missions to determine the potentialities of satellite communications for educational television. Missions have been sent to India (1967-1969), Brazil (1968), Pakistan and South America (1969).

The International Bank for Reconstruction and Development (World Bank) has given financial assistance to developing countries. The Bank is also a member of the Special Autonomous Group No. 5 of the ITCC which deals with the economic analysis of telecommunication projects. Included within its financial assistance have been loans for the construction of satellite earth stations to increase the INTELSAT satellite system.

The ICAO (International Civil Aviation Organization), a UN specialized agency concerned with the safety of air navigation, has a deep interest in the use of the communication satellite. In 1969, a delegation from INTELSAT met with officials of ICAO to discuss possible aeronautical satellite services.

A future competitor, Intersputnik, is represented by Vereshchetin, particularly, the membership requirement of the ITU and the weighted voting in the governing body of Intelsat is criticized.

The article of Dr. V.S. Vereshchetin (USSR) on "International Space Communications Systems" affirms the advantages of setting up a worldwide space communication system by means of earth artificial satellites. He quotes UN General Assembly resolutions: "Communication by means of satellites should be available to the nations of the world as soon as practicable on a global and non-discriminatory basis. . . ." However, he believes that the principles formulated in Interim Agreements regulating the activities of the International Telecommunications Satellite System (INTELSAT) and the principles laid down in the Draft Agreement on the establishment of an International Communications System using Earth Artificial Satellites by Socialist States differ from each other to a great extent. He states that at the conference on the revision of arrangements for INTELSAT, many of the principles imbued in INTERSPUTNIK found an active support among INTELSAT members, "but forceful resistance to the adoption of those principles on the part of the United States whose voice plays the decisive role in INTELSAT, resulted in their rejection."

Dr. Vereshchetin criticizes the INTELSAT system which admits to its membership only members of ITU - a discriminatory measure "clearly aimed against a certain group of states." On the other hand, "The planned system of INTERSPUTNIK is open for all countries of the world without any discriminatory restrictions whatsoever." In the organization of INTERSPUTNIK, the leading body is the Council. All member states of the organization are represented on it with each of them having one vote. Decisions of the Council are made by at least a two-third majority. Dr. Vereshchetin maintains that at present INTELSAT does not have a body on which all member states of this communications system would be represented; the highest governing body is the Interim Committee; representation and voting therein depends on capital investment on the basis of so-called "weighted voting." Under this "voting of capital" system, one country - the USA - has 53% of the votes.

Furthermore, the draft agreement of INTERSPUTNIK does not preclude the right of states to take part in several communications systems, and it reflects readiness to coordinate the activities of INTERSPUTNIK. On the contrary, Article VIII of the American draft definitive arrangements of INTELSAT suggests that INTELSAT members should be denied the participation in the creation of use of other international systems of space communications.

Dr. Vereshchatin concludes: "For the solution of the set of questions which will arise in the process of interaction and coordination of different space communications systems, both bilateral contacts and arrangements, and existing international organizations whose scope covers the problems of space communications, should be used."

In his "Reply to Mr. Vereshchetin," Richard R. Colino strives to correct and elucidate two aspects of INTELSAT. As to the membership requirement of the ITU, "An examination of the pertinent UN General Assembly resolutions, including No. 1721, fails to disclose any recommendation as to membership in organizations conducting activities in Outer Space. These resolutions, however, do recommend the principle that all nations have non-discriminatory access to communication satellite systems. This principle has been incorporated in the INTELSAT interim arrangements.... It is clear that this principle will also be incorporated into the INTELSAT definitive arrangements."

The requirement that a state be a member of the ITU in order to have membership in INTELSAT means that 137 states (present ITU membership) are eligible to join INTELSAT: INTELSAT's present membership of 77 represents more than half the ITU membership. These

77 states account for more than 95% of the world's international telecommunications traffic. In view of ITU's large membership, the requirement that all members of INTELSAT be members of the ITU and bound by ITU radio regulations is "logical, reasonable, objective and proper." The fact that a few countries are not members of the ITU is a political question for ITU, not INTELSAT, to resolve.

With respect to the use of "weighted voting" in INTELSAT's Interim Communications Satellite Committee (ICSC) and the asserted "violation of sovereign equality": the so-called principle of sovereign equality does not require that all states have an equal voice in international forums. The Charter of UN establishes a Security Council in which the votes of each of the five permanent members have greater weight than others. INTELSAT is an organization operating communications facilities on a commercial basis. The Interim Agreement provisions (adhered to by 77 states) respecting membership and voting on the ICSC are related to a member's investment quota in INTELSAT which is based upon estimates made in 1964 of long-distance telephone traffic, considered suitable for carriage via satellite in the year 1968. The initial investment quotas have been reduced pro rata to accommodate the investment quotas of new members. The principle that a member's investment should be related to its use of the system is probably the most objective criterion in an organization such as INTELSAT; it will also be incorporated into the INTELSAT definitive arrangements.

In another report on direct radio diffusion by satellite, Professor Magno states that great progress has been made by installation of individual as well as community receiving apparatus of mass communication. International Organizations such as the International Union of Telecommunications (IUT), UNESCO, and BIRPI (Bureaux Internationaux Réunis pour la protection de la Propriété Intellectuelle) collaborate closely.

Professor Magno refers to two proposals for regulation presented by France and the Soviet Union. The French suggestion stresses the right of the individual to be informed and to inform others about events of public life in different states, a right which should not be neglected. However, the sovereignty of states which do not want their territory covered by direct radio emissions should be respected.

The Soviet Union's proposal considers "illegal" all radio and television emissions by satellite which contain propaganda in favor of war, militarism, Nazism, national and racial hatred, hostility among nations, immoral emissions and any which interfere with the state's interior affairs. The state's government has the right to adopt all the measures at its disposal to oppose emissions not consented to. The opinion of Canadian and Swedish experts is that an efficient and objective control system would be the best solution to the necessary regulation of direct radio diffusion.

Both WMO and ICAO are interested in the use of satellites. The former organization can utilize them for the purpose of installing meteorological observing equipment to collect data from stations on the earth, and as a telecommunications device for a day-to-day exchange of meteorological data. Airspace is being used both by aircraft and space craft, and that in itself is a reason for ICAO to watch space activities with particular interest: the safety of civil aviation may be at stake. The World Meteorological Organization (WMO)

Secretariat reports on "Developments in Satellite Meteorology." There are three ways in which satellites may be used: a) as platforms on which meteorological observing equipment may be installed as may telemetering equipment for relaying the data back to earth; b) as a means of collecting data from automatic observing stations on the earth's surface or floating in the atmosphere, and as a means of relaying data back to a collecting center on the earth's surface; c) as a telecommunication device for assisting in the worldwide exchange of meteorological data on a day-to-day basis, an essential element in the World Weather Watch.

The TIROS Operational Satellite (TOS) System provides detection of all major storms, information on snow cover, movement of ice packs and ice-locked waterways, all of these being an important aid for navigation and agriculture. For the nighttime cloud data, IR (Infrared) sensors are used which also help to collect solar radiation data. The Satellite Infra-Red Spectrometer (SIRS) provides vertical temperature which can be used for weather prediction. Initially, meteorological satellites were launched in orbits around the equator. The new geostationary satellites now pass over the north and south polar regions.

The USSR plans during 1972-75 to include the direct broadcast of cloud images in the visible and infrared from their METEOR satellites. The USA plans to have a similar direct readout of IR data on the operational ITOS system. A geostationary Operational Environmental Satellite (GOES) is scheduled to be launched with a day and night imager. The World Weather Watch (WWW) plans a global observing system (GOS) by 3 to 4 earth-oriented satellites in quasi polar orbit and 4 geostationary satellites. A global Atmospheric Research Program (GARP) experiment is under way.

Professor Busak (Czechoslovakia), speaking about the juridical aspect of the problem of radioelectric frequencies in space services, gives a detailed picture of the developments in progress, mentioning the experiences of the systems INTELSAT and MOLYNIA. He points to the question of "irate stations," i.e., radiodiffusion stations on board of satellites, operating, despite international regulation, and using frequencies which disturb the authorized services.

The UN Educational, Scientific, and Cultural Organization (UNESCO) Secretariat reported on "The Use of Space Communication for Information, Education, and Cultural Exchange," stating that the implications of direct broadcasts via satellite into community or home receivers calls for a high degree of cooperation between nations as well as of responsibility on the part of broadcasters.

States have agreed to the principle that space communication should be made available to all nations on a non-discriminatory basis. International cooperation means legal solutions: international agreements and regulations whereby the various states and the bodies responsible for the production and dissemination of information via satellite would accept the discipline and responsibility needed to prevent abuses. Space communication agencies are "common carriers" and subject to the obligations imposed by international public law to make their service available on an equitable basis.

The interest of UNESCO in promoting the free flow of information and greater cultural exchange is shown by their activities: collection and dissemination of news; educational broadcasting; cultural and scientific programs (in accordance with principles adopted by Eurovision, the European Broadcasting Union, and Intervision, the International Radio and Television Organization); protection of copyright and broadcast signal; promotion of international agreements.

Julian Verplaetse (Belgium), in his paper on the subject, pays also some attention to the ICAO Panel on Application of Space Techniques relating to Aviation (ASTRA), which concentrated on the feasibility of an aeronautical satellite system. The International Civil Aviation Organization (ICAO), set up by the Chicago Convention of 1944, is developing an interest in Outer Space. In Resolution A 16-11, adopted by the General Assembly at its 16th session in Buenos Aires (1968), it is stated: a) the exploration and use of Outer Space are of great interest to ICAO since many of these activities affect matters falling within the Organization's competence under the terms of the Chicago Convention; b) the space used by or usable for international civil aviation is also used by space vehicles and this necessarily requires adequate coordination to achieve the normal and efficient functioning of both these fields; c) ICAO's participation in space activities directly affecting civil aviation is of growing scope and importance. A Panel on Application of Space Techniques Relating to Aviation (ASTRA), established by the Air Navigation Commission, held meetings in Montreal (1968, 1969) and Paris (1970). It reached the general conclusion that it was necessary to organize a practical aeronautical satellite system. The US Navy had explored the use of a NAVSAT (navigation satellite) in order to pinpoint the location of the fleet's ballistic missiles (FBM) submarines. On the basis of this military experience, civil agencies are working towards the achievement of a combined navigation/traffic control system.

It would seem, however, that particularly important is whether the UN and ICAO - with scientific progress bringing aviation and space activities within the scope of each other's regulatory competence - will start working closely together to deal with questions of common concern. These and other problems (registration, definition of outer space, moon resources) will have to be solved by the organizations concerned, assisted, if possible, by such entities as the IISL, ILA, etc., according to Dr. Kopal (Czechoslovakia). His General Report summarizes, once more, future activities of the various international organizations in the field of space law. He considers in particular the UN agencies, the General Assembly, the role of UNESCO, ITU, IISL, and BIRPI. Projects such as Lunar and Orbital Laboratories, developed by special committees of the International Academy of Astronautics, deserve careful consideration by both space and non-space powers.

The legal counsels of ESRO and ELDO discuss the results of the fourth European Space Conference. Resolutions on future programs and on the establishment of a "European NASA," comprising ESRO, ELDO and CETS, are thus reviewed in some detail. On the topic of "Regional Intergovernmental Organizations," Dr. Bourély (of European Launch Development Organization

- ELDO) reports that the major European countries are united, since 1966, in the European Space Conference attempting the coordination of their efforts and entrusting the practical execution to three bodies: CERS/ESRO is charged with the construction of scientific satellites, CECLES/ELDO is occupied with a European launcher, and CETS/ECTS (European Conference of Telecommunication Satellites) is probing a general position in the field of Telecommunication satellites.

There are two main problems: 1) Should Europe have the capacity of launching a satellite of her own? Unanimity has not been reached so far, in part because of the considerable cost; 2) Should the USA offer to participate in some sector of the post-Apollo program be accepted?

At the 4th session of the European Space Conference (Brussels, 1970) four resolutions were adopted. Since not all member states could make their decisions known, the first resolution referring to the program has interim character. The essential point of the joint program deals with telecommunication satellites in a European operational program which should be working about 1978/1980 and responds to the needs expressed by the European Conference of Post and Telecommunication, as well as the European Union of Radiodiffusion. The Conference established the financing of a general program of research and the costs of its execution by all the participants.

The second resolution regards the institutions. A new European space organization will replace the three existent bodies and the European Space Conference. The third resolution is related to the European participation in the post-Apollo program. The fourth and last resolution reaffirms the interest in the coordination of the European countries' position on the establishment of the definitive INTELSAT regime.

Following Dr. Bourély's report, Dr. Kaltenecker of the European Space Research Organization (ESRO) points to the future of the European Space Organization. The new organization, which is to replace the existing ESC/CES (European Space Conference), CERS/ECSR (European Convention of Space Research), CECLES/ELDO and CETS/ECTS (European Conference on Telecommunication Satellites) will be an intergovernmental organization with a juridical status similar to ECSR and ELDO. Its purpose could be described as follows: elaboration of European spacial politics and harmonization of politics adopted by other bodies, national and international; creation of the necessary facilities to make the European industry competitive, not only in the European but on the world market; execution of programs in the fields of scientific research, practical use of satellites and technological research. All the states which are members of the CSE/ESC will become members of the new organization on the date when the new convention will be open to signatures.

The transportation of passengers and freight in the future may very well take place by means of outer space vehicles, according to Professor Magno (Italy). In his article "Transportation by Space" he points out that space travel does not require motive power. Furthermore, since the additional cost of the rocket launcher is presently due to its consumption and loss in one single trip, new recoverable launchers have been designed to be reused in subsequent trips. Thus the problem of the economic inconvenience of space transport is now likely to be solved. The adventure of Apollo XIII was instrumental in testing the validity of the 1968 agreement bearing on "the rescue of astronauts, the return of astronauts, and return of objects launched into outer space." Many countries who signed that agreement, including Italy, have offered their help according to their means and possibilities. Magno foresees no special difficulties with respect to the legal regulations of outer space travel since the Space Treaty covers most aspects of this earth-outer space-earth traffic. Insofar as the question of liability is concerned, however, we believe that this opinion of optimism is not fully warranted in view of the uncertainty as to the legal regime that should be applied in such cases (dependent on whether the instrument should be considered as an aircraft or spacecraft).

Elio Monnerat Solon de Pontes (Brazil) expresses some thoughts on specific problems in the space law field. The use of armaments in space must be prohibited unless their use is for the defense of future space establishments. The space conquests, largo sensu, must be considered "conquests of humanity." Space activities are overall human activities, but primarily, a national effort. As a matter of international solidarity, all nations and all governments must protect - if necessary - the space instruments used by every other nation in space activities. He believes the UNO is the most representative instrument to consider the present problem.

Professor von Rauchhaupt (Germany) discusses "The Divine Law in the Totality of Outer Space Law." The comparison of the Divine Law with modern human Outer Space Law reveals an irony. There is the fact of the primrodial creation billions of years ago, with its billions of stars and celestial bodies which are now explored by astronauts and scientists. The omnipotence of God the creator is contrasted with the weakness of mankind. Man is still vulnerable and mortal, notwithstanding his progress.

A reliable system of Outer Space Law is still lacking. Many important questions are still unanswered, among them the fundamental understanding of the laws of creation, the Divine Law. The comparison above is analogous to our exploration in Outer Space and our striving to establish an Outer Space Law. In 1958, the Outer Space situation was compared to the discovery of the American hemisphere in 1492. The indigenous population was introduced to Christianity and to European civilization and its law.

The roots of modern Space Law were transplanted from the earth to the Outer Space, and the remainder was created directly for Outer Space by the late A.G. Haley and others. Its purpose is to safeguard living beings or similar intelligences in Outer Space against intruders. The three powers, legislation, jurisdiction, administration, of Divine Law are integrated into modern Outer Space Law. Legislation in Divine Law originates in the Ten Commandments of the Old Testament and their equivalents in other religions. Jurisdiction in Divine Law and in modern Space Law aspire to peace. Administration is embodied in the UN, which admits to the voluntary jurisdiction of the International Court of Justice at The Hague. The many representative states admitted to the UN, therefore, are under the aegis of Divine Law. Modern Space Law would do well to use Divine Law as its foundation.

Of the 5 papers that conclude this volume, one should be singled out, namely the paper of <u>Brooks</u>, which contributes much to our knowledge of the practical possibilities and legal aspects of earth resources satellites. In "New Developments of Earth Satellite Law," Eugene Brooks (USA) states, "Injured in the swamps of Vietnam, the United States space program may, one hopes, ultimately recover its vigor. Non-military space expenditures fell from $5.9 billion in 1966 to $3.3 billion in 1970, while employment by NASA and its contractors dropped from 420,000 to 140,000. Of the ten originally scheduled lunar landings, two have been accomplished, one aborted and three abandoned. If the four remaining moon landings take place, the final American tally will still be 60% of the manned moon journeys originally intended."

Essential to successful space station operation is the space shuttle, a reusable vehicle placed in orbit by a wholly or partly recoverable booster. Carrying up to twelve passengers, the shuttle would reduce the cost of space operations ten-fold, from $1,000 per pound to $100 per pound or less.

The "Grand Tour" on unmanned space craft flight past Jupiter, Saturn, Uranus, Neptune, and Pluto will span the years 1977 to 1985. This "tour" is made possible by the alignment of the planets in space at that time, permitting the gravity of each of the planets to propel the passing capsule on its way with accelerated speed.

Communications, navigation, and meteorological satellites have matured with space flight itself and may soon be joined by air traffic control satellites. The operation of earth resources satellites is based on the electromagnetic manifestations of matter. Various remote sensing systems are listed: panchromatic photography, multispectral photography, infrared photography (used to distinguish water from land), infrared radiometry (measures change in land and water temperatures, used to detect mineral deposits), microwave imagery (assists oceanic and snow mapping).

This new technology is applied to: agriculture and forestry resources to increase crop yeild and help reduce losses due to pests and disease; geology and mineral resources for detecting geological changes, minerals, and erosion on land; geography and cartography of unsurveyed land and for exploration of the Arctic and Antarctic; hydrology and water resources to detect surface and ground water and to analyze temperature, pollution, snow and ice fields; oceanography for detection of fish areas, ocean waves and currents, and oil deposits.

The developing nations feel that a centralized effort is indeed necessary to undertake dissemination of information. Argentina proposed the establishment of a data bank to which all states have access.

Though both the USA and USSR, and perhaps other nations, have used remote sensing devices to detect military installations, there has been no agreement as to whether these actions are consonant with international law. The author gives well documented and detailed information about registration of space vehicles, military surveillance, earth resource uses, and use by states of resource data collected by them.

Important are his conclusions affirming the permissibility of this space activity, debating that it is the duty of states to disclose resource data, and suggesting how to regulate this activity and prevent the misuse of space data. He favors the establishment of a UN Resources Center which would assume the tasks of data reception, reduction, processing and analysis and suggests further the compulsory reporting of all resource data by states which have their own system. An Annex lists the substantive provisions of Argentina's proposal in Legal Sub-Committee.

Summaries of the discussions held during the Colloquium and a few addenda finally conclude this volume and add to its usefulness.

*   *   *   *   *

FOURTEENTH COLLOQUIUM ON THE LAW OF OUTER SPACE

BRUSSELS, 1971

I. Texts Reproduced

CONTAMINATION AND THE OUTER SPACE TREATY

by

Stephen Gorove

The now well-known Outer Space Treaty of 1967 created, for the first time, certain specific international obligations pertaining to the prevention of contamination of outer space from Earth and avoidance of adverse changes in the environment of the Earth resulting from the introduction of extraterrestrial matter.

The relevant provisions have been incorporated in Article IX of the Outer Space Treaty. This article was actually developed from an earlier United Nations' resolution (Res. 1962), which was unanimously passed in December 1963. The article, in a sense, was an attempt to resolve the problem of reconciling the freedom of exploration and use of outer space with the need to ensure that no adverse effects will take place as a result of such exploration, and there will not be any harmful interference with activities in space.

The article contains four sentences and, strictly speaking, only the second sentence seems to deal with contamination problems. However, because of their interrelated nature, it appears essential to give an account of all four sentences.

The first sentence deals with cooperation and mutual assistance and due regard for corresponding interests of all parties. The second sentence deals with pursuance of studies and avoidance of harmful contamination of outer space and adverse changes in the environment of the earth, and the third and fourth sentences deal with what could be regarded as prevention of nuisance, that is, potentially harmful interference with activities in outer space and stipulate international consultation.

As a preliminary remark I would like to observe that Article IX, despite the great importance of the subject matter, is unfortunately limited to the parties to the treaty and nowhere in the article do we find a declaration of some general purpose or intent of a broader scope which we find in some other provisions of the Outer Space Treaty.

Turning specifically to the first sentence, it is stated that in the exploration and use of outer space, including the moon and other celestial bodies, the parties shall be guided by the principle of cooperation and mutual assistance and shall conduct all their activities with due regard to the corresponding interests of all parties.

Of course, just what does a state have to do to live up to this obligation is not specified. Furthermore, what kind of cooperation, what type of assistance, and in what manner, are we talking about? Whether this refers possibly to matters involving pollution or other matters is not stated. Whether the word "guided" means that the state must follow these principles or whether it may consider them is not entirely clear.

What is meant by "due regard," and who determines it? Most likely, it will be determined and left up to each individual state. What is the meaning of "corresponding interests." Does this involve the state's own interest? "Corresponding" usually means something alike or similar in purpose or function, so in that sense it may involve the state's own interest.

The reference to "all parties," of course, raises the question of those who are not parties to the treaty. Do their interests not have to be taken into account?

The second sentence is not derived from the earlier mentioned United Nations resolution. This is a new addition to the Outer Space Treaty which came about as a compromise between Soviet and United States proposals. Perhaps this is the reason for the lack of clarity in this sentence.

The sentence states that the parties to the treaty shall pursue studies of outer space including the moon and celestial bodies and conduct exploration of them so as to avoid their harmful contamination and adverse changes in the environment of the earth resulting from the introduction of extraterrestrial matter and, where necessary, shall adopt appropriate measures for this purpose.

It is interesting to note that this requirement that they shall "pursue studies," is irrespective of whether they engage in any activities in outer space, so apparently all parties must pursue studies.

Presumably, these studies will be pursued by the parties proportionate to their ability, to the costs, values and risks involved, and perhaps the studies will be conducted with the idea to avoid duplication. Just what kind of studies will the parties have to pursue is also not clear. Possibly, the studies could be required to relate to contamination since the rest of the sentence deals with contamination but this is left unclear.

It is interesting to note also that the reference to the word "them" leaves the reader uncertain whether it refers to both outer space as well as celestial bodies. This is something that could have been made clearer.

Furthermore, it should be pointed out that the only obligation is to avoid "harmful" contamination. Therefore other contamination which is not harmful is apparently permissible. Also, there is nothing said about harmful contamination of the earth. The reference is only to harmful contamination of outer space and possibly of celestial bodies.

Also, it is not clear to whom the contamination must be harmful. In a sense, almost anything may be harmful to some people and beneficial to others. People have different value schemes.

What is the meaning of contamination? Does this mean pollution really, or are we dealing here with the spread of impurity as well as infection, in other words, biological types of contamination? It seems unclear.

The parties are not only required to avoid harmful contamination, but also to avoid "adverse changes in the environment of the earth resulting from the introduction of extraterrestrial matter." To whom do the changes have to be adverse? All changes benefit some. Does the sentence refer to climatic changes or all the other types of changes? Furthermore, the reference is to the environment of the earth, but apparently the creation of adverse changes in the environment of celestial bodies is permissible unless the changes would also amount to harmful contamination. Also, it is not quite clear whether or not the "introduction of extraterrestrial matter" has to be intentional.

What about the example of the space mirror? Does this include introduction of extraterrestrial matter? The moon rocket is apparently all right so long as there are no adverse changes in the environment of the earth.

To fullfill their obligation with respect to the avoidance of harmful contamination and adverse changes, the parties are required, "where necessary" to "adopt appropriate measures." But who determines what is "necessary" or "appropriate" and by what standard? How many and what kind of measures are we talking about? Should international consultation be used here? The sentence does not state it, even though the next sentence deals with problems of international consultation. The third sentence states, in fact, that if the party "has reason to believe" that an activity or experiment planned by it or its nationals would cause "potentially harmful interference" with activities of other parties in the peaceful exploration and use of outer space, it shall undertake appropriate international consultations before proceeding with such activity or experiment.

Here again, I believe, the stipulation provides a relatively easy way to get around it for anyone. The phrase "reason to believe" seems to give an opportunity for any party to be lax in censuring itself. What is "potentially harmful interference"" Does this refer to pollution? Perhaps it could include pollution. It may have a much wider scope, and activities similar to the West Ford project could fall under it, perhaps not.

Reference to other "parties" in the third sentence seems to indicate that if only one party is affected no international consultations are required because the word is used in the plural. Actually, instead of international consultations, Japan proposed consultations with the Secretary General of the United Nations. This, however, was not adopted. The reference to "international consultations" does not indicate with whom you have to consult. You may consult with your friends or your enemies. Perhaps COSPAR could have been included as a possible forum of consultation.

Also, there is no indication of how many states a party has to consult. There is no procedure outlined and no authority set up to determine the procedure. There is no provision in case the consultations end in a deadlock. There is no indication anywhere that a party must follow another party's recommendation. So as long as there is consultation, the requirement is satisfied.

The next and last sentence deals with the party which has reason to believe that an activity or experiment planned by another party in outer space would cause potentially harmful interference with activities in the exploration and use of outer space. Such a party may request consultation concerning the activity or experiment.

Again this is a somewhat vague provision, just like the previous one. It does not indicate to whom the party has to turn for consultation. The party may consult with anyone although it would seem very likely that the consultation would include the party whose experiment is interfering with some other experiments or activities in space.

The fourth sentence incorporates a more general provision than the previous one because interference with the activities of any state, not just the activities of a state party to

267

the treaty would be included.

Unfortunately, nothing is said as to what happens if after the request of consultation, the request is turned down. There is no definite obligation involved. One party may request consultation and the other party may turn it down. This also makes it apparent that the other party does not have to follow any recommendation.

The foregoing provisions of the Outer Space Treaty constitute an important initial step toward preventing adverse changes in the environment of the earth from outer space as well as in reducing the chances of harmful contamination of outer space, including celestial bodies. At the same time, our brief scrutiny seems to indicate that further steps will have to be taken by the international community as man's exploration of outer space assumes more significant proportions.

I believe that the formulation of an international code of conduct regarding pollution and contamination from outer space is essential. Also, there seems to be a vital need for the establishment of an international environmental control authority regarding space, to determine and verify and possibly to have powers to adjudicate and halt undesirable interference with the environment.

NOTES

This paper is an elaboration of the author's remarks presented on December 28, 1971, in a panel discussion on "Pollution and Outer Space" before the annual meeting of the Association of American Law Schools in Chicago, Illinois.

Article IX reads as follows:

In the exploration and use of outer space, including the moon and other celestial bodies, States Parties to the Treaty shall be guided by the principle of co-operation and mutual assistance and shall conduct all their activities in outer space, including the moon and other celestial bodies, with due regard to the corresponding interests of all other States Parties to the Treaty. States Parties to the Treaty shall pursue studies of outer space, including the moon and other celestial bodies, and conduct exploration of them so as to avoid their harmful contamination and also adverse changes in the environment of the earth resulting from the introduction of extraterrestrial matter and, where necessary, shall adopt appropriate measures for this purpose. If a State Party to the Treaty has reason to believe that an activity or experiment planned by it or its nationals in outer space, including the moon and other celestial bodies, would cause potentially harmful interference with activities of other States Parties in the peaceful exploration and use of outer space, including the moon and other celestial bodies, it shall undertake appropriate international consultations before proceeding with any such activity or experiment. A State Party to the Treaty which has reason to believe that an activity or experiment planned by another State Party in outer space, including the moon and other celestial bodies, would cause potentially harmful interference with activities in the peaceful exploration and use of outer space, including the moon and other celestial bodies, may request consultation concerning the activity or experiment.

* * * * *

SPACE PROGRAMS AND INTERNATIONAL ENVIRONMENT PROTECTION

by

Peter H. Sand

1 INTRODUCTION

The "human environment" has become fashionable with lawyers, at a price: chances are that the volume of legal theory surrounding and obscuring the topic will soon outscore the comparable record achievements of Space Law. Before joining in the endeavour, it may be useful to define the subject of this paper by way of progressive elimination.

1.1 First, a distinction needs to be drawn between the cosmic environment at large and our terrestrial environment stricto sensu. With due respect to the scientific merits of a "clean universe," and without attempting to draw another magic line, we may conveniently exclude from our present discussion the legal problems pertaining to what Jenks describes as the "cluttering and contamination" of outer space and celestial bodies, and concentrate instead on matters directly relevant to the quality of life on Earth.

1.2 The second distinction concerns the information impact and the action impact of space technology. Space Science has begun to make important contributions to Earth Science: besides a certain amount of technological spin-off, the data obtained by application satellites for meteorology, earth resources and pollution monitoring are becoming a vital basis for environmental decision-making, possibly including "anthropogeneous modification of the environment." Yet the legal consequences of this new "information impact" are not essentially an environmental problem, but rather part of a more general problem of international law and politics: vis., the sharing of knowledge which directly equates power (Wissen ist Macht, from some horses's mouth). We may disregard them here, in view of the fact that they are to be discussed at a subsequent session of this Colloquium.

1.3 Having thus narrowed down the subject, we can now focus our attention on a different, but equally important environmental dimension of current space programs. Beyond the neutral tasks of scientific observation and data-gathering, space technology is gradually advancing towards a position from where it can actively interfere with the natural condition of our biosphere -- for better or worse. Experimentally, accidentally, and for the most part inadvertently, certain space activities have already begun to affect the terrestrial environment; and ultimately, outer space may indeed become another medium for planned "ecomanagement." This change of roles, from exploration to interference, from reflection to action, is the real innovation.

1.4 The environmental impact of space programs may be incidental (i.e. unintended), or deliberate; it may be caused by terrestrial sources utilised in the course of space activities, or by extraterrestrial sources introduced into the biosphere as a result of such activities. Rather than summarily ranking these types of impact on a blacklist of "global threats to the environment," each should be viewed as part of a continuum, within which its environmental significance may vary from zero to kogai (the now proverbial Japanese term for environmental disruption).

1.5 What aggravates the potential risk from individual types of impact is their co-existence with each other and with an infinite variety of unrelated other types of environmental impact (human and natural), all of which may have cumulative and possibly synergetic

269

effects on the biosphere. Perhaps the most urgent problem, therefore, is <u>monitoring</u> of all conceivable types of impact, quite regardless of their individual significance.

2 INCIDENTAL INTERFERENCE WITH THE EARTH'S ENVIRONMENT

In this first category we shall include those interfering (polluting) side-effects of space programs which are not part of the intended objectives of such programs. The term "incidental" interference seems more appropriate than the frequently-used term "inadvertent," for in most cases the interfering party is quite aware of the interference he causes, although he may not consider it as significant from his viewpoint and consequently will treat it as a calculated (sometimes unavoidable) risk of his space programs.

2.1 Pollution from terrestrial sources

2.1.1 <u>Hardware</u>. With the increasing number of space launchings, returning space instrumentalities, boosters and debris have become a problem in the Earth's airspace and on the surface. The current procedure of U.N. registration of launchings, in spite of several shortcomings, at least helps to keep an <u>ex post facto</u> record of how much hardware is going up, and the new "U.N. Convention on International Liability for Damage Caused by Space Objects" will take care of legal responsibility for surface and collision damage, including explosion of unexpended fuel.

2.1.2 <u>Rocket exhausts</u>. Neither the U.N. registration system nor any other international data exchange system includes information on the nature and amounts of pollutants introduced into the atmosphere by space instrumentalities. Pursuant to the U.S. National Environmental Policy Act of 1969, and the Executive Order on "Protection and Enhancement of Environmental Quality" of 1970, NASA is now under an obligation to submit to the Council on Environmental Quality "environmental impact statements" for any major project significantly affecting the quality of the human environment. NASA has issued policy guidelines for the preparation of these statements, and has already submitted in draft form statements for 21 projects, including on-going programs for rocket engine testing and altitude exhaust system testing. Although some of the statements are extremely general and were actually returned to NASA by the C.E.Q. for more detailed redrafting, they provide useful illustrative data. E.g., the Draft Environmental Impact Statement for the Apollo Program (submitted in February 1971), lists the amounts of pollutants released in the course of a normal Saturn V launch as follows:

Product	0-20 KM 0-10.8 NM	20-67 KM 10.8-36.2 NM	Above 67 KM Above 36.2 NM
Carbon Dioxide	623,720	316,860	890
Carbon Monoxide	1,398,840	699,420	400
Water	734,420	367,210	643,560
Hydrogen (H_2)	36,200	18,100	37,800
Hydrogen (H)	4,000	2,000	–
Oxygen (O_2)	19,440	9,720	–
Oxygen (O)	9,200	4,600	–
Hydroxyle Radical (OH)	68,660	34,330	–
Carbonaceous Products	133,000	67,000	–
Carbonyl Sulfide	–	–	14
Hydrogen Sulfide	–	–	112
Nitrogen	–	–	427
Sulfur Dioxide	–	–	42
Sulfur (S_2)	–	–	85
Hydrogen Chloride	–	–	1,029
Aluminum Oxide	–	–	107
Metal Oxides	–	–	175

1 KM = 0.53961 NM

The statement adds that material released above the stratosphere (60 km) "will effec-tively never reach sea level," because its residence time at this altitude is in excess of ten years.

Normally, an additional amount of residual kerosene (RP-1 fuel) "not exceeding 5,000 gallons" is dispersed at the time of first stage separation, and ends up as a thin film on the ocean surface covering approximately one square mile. In the case of an aborted flight, however, a maximum of 230,000 gallons of RP-1 could reach the ocean. In addition, approxi-mately 170 pounds of toxic propellant are combusted or evaporated at the time of re-entry of the Apollo command module, starting at an altitude of about 10,000 feet.

Based on these and other data, NASA concluded that the quantities released "are two or more orders of magnitude below the recognized levels for concern" and that the Apollo Program "does not have any significant detrimental impact on the human environment."

On the whole, this conclusion (repeated in virtually all NASA statements) would seem to confirm the earlier general conclusions of the COSPAR "Consultative Group on Potentially Harmful Effects of Space Experiments," which in 1964 has examined reports on rocket pol-lution of the upper atmosphere and reported to the U.N. Committee on the Peaceful Uses of Outer Space that "harmful contamination of the upper atmosphere on a long-term global basis is unlikely on present and expected scale of firings of super rockets and the release of experimental seeding."

However, the COSPAR group had made it clear then that its study did not include three possibly significant contingencies: (a) the use of nuclear-powered rockets and nuclear reactors in satellites; (b) the extensive use of high-flying supersonic transport aircraft; (c) the extensive use of completely disintegrating meteorological rockets. It also recom-mended continued studies of the following matters: (a) evaluation of exchange times between the various regions of the upper atmosphere, especially between 60 and 100 km; (b) short

271

and long term local and zonal effects of rocket contamination in the upper atmosphere; (c) the possibility of any catalytic effects which might trigger chemical and photochemical processes in the upper atmosphere; and (d) radiation balance in the upper atmosphere and its dependence on changes in composition there.

Although this report was endorsed by the U.N. Committee on the Peaceful Uses of Outer Space, it does not seem to have generated any international follow-up action since 1964. The fact that pollution by rocket exhausts should continue to be a matter of concern (particularly with the prospect of rocket "shuttles" multiplying the present volume of space traffic through the atmosphere) was underscored in 1966 by a report from the U.S. National Academy of Sciences on "Weather and Climate Modification: Problems and Prospects." While tentatively discarding the likelihood of appreciable disturbance by supersonic transport aircraft (a conclusion which may have to be qualified in the light of more pessimistic recent evaluations), the report continues:

> Rocket-exhaust contamination of the higher atmosphere is, however, a much more complex problem, primarily because the chemistry of the mesophere and thermosphere (including the radiational roles played by the minor constituents), and the processes in those regions that disperse or remove impurities are so little understood. Since rocket activity will increase, and since we are already capable of doubling, in a single year, the quantity of some exotic constituents (e.g., atomic sodium), vigorous investigation of aeromomy and high-atmosphere dynamics is a clear prerequisite to settling the issue of rocket-caused contamination.

2.1.3 <u>Radiation</u>. Nuclear radiation is the least publicized among the environmental hazards of space programs. The small radioisotope thermoelectric generators (RTG) which provide electrical power for Apollo lunar experiments use a fuel capsule containing 8 pounds of 238 Plutonium Dioxide Microspheres, which involves exposure to neutron emission and gamma rays during normal operations. The added risk of accidental burning (short of nuclear explosions, which would require about four times that amount of fuel) was illustrated when 2 pounds of 238 Plutonium aboard a satellite vaporized upon re-entry in April 1964, distributing the material in the atmosphere for an estimated residence time of two years. Far more serious operational safety problems will arise with the advent of nuclear propulsion systems for rockets (and particularly with nuclear explosion propulsion), the development of which currently accounts only for some cryptic references in the environmental impact statements filed by NASA research centers. According to von Braun, "the problems of man-made radiation connected with these space ships will prove far more challenging in the long run than those of the natural radiation in space."

2.2 <u>Pollution from extra-terrestrial sources</u>

2.2.1 <u>Back contamination</u>. Both the U.S.S.R. and the U.S. until recently conducted intricate quarantine and decontamination measures to safeguard returning space instrumentalities against the risk of contaminating the biosphere by extre-terrestrial micro-organisms. Article IX of the "Treaty on Principles Governing the activities and Use of Outer Space Including the Moon and Other Celestial Bodies" provides that all States Parties to the Treaty shall conduct exploration of outer space and celestial bodies, and shall make use of those resources, in such a manner "as to avoid their harmful contamination and also adverse changes in the environment of the Earth resulting from the introduction of extra-terrestrial matter and, where necessary, shall adopt appropriate measures for this purpose." It has been pointed out, however, that the Treaty's subsequent provisions for consultation only relate to "interference...in the peaceful exploration and use of outer space," but do not technically apply to potential contamination of the Earth from extra-terrestrial matter. In the United States, an Interagency Committee on Back Contamination (ICBC) was established in August 1967, "in order to protect the public's health, agriculture, and other living resources against the possibility of contamination resulting from returning lunar astronauts or lunar explosed material." NASA's environmental impact statement for the Apollo Program in February 1961 concluded that there had been "no evidence of any possible contaminants" and noted that deletion of the quarantine procedure was already under consideration; quarantine and decontamination for lunar missions was actually discontinued after Apollo 14, and beginning with the return of Apollo 15 in August 1971. This decision was taken unilaterally and without international consultations.

      2.2.2 _Radiation_. Contrary to the more optimistic conclusions of the U.S. National Academy of Sciences in 1966, the Williamstown "Study of Critical Environmental Problems" (SCEP) in July 1970 found that the combusion products (particularly water vapor) or supersonic air transport in the stratosphere could produce significant environmental disturbance, including increases in stratospheric cloudiness, alterations of the stratospheric heat balance ("greenhouse" effect) and depletion of the ozone cover which shields the earth from harmful ultraviolet radiations. The Stockholm "Study of Man's Impact on Climate" (SMIC) in July 1971 endorsed these conclusions, with additional emphasis on the need for further research on the problem of ozone depletion and its potential health consequences. If the _a fortiori_ reasoning of the U.S. National Academy of Sciences regarding rocket exhausts is correct, these recommendations are equally applicable to space programs; i.e., "answers to these questions should be produced before large-scale aircraft operation [or space shuttle operation] in the stratosphere becomes commonplace."

3 DELIBERATE INTERFERENCE WITH THE EARTH'S ENVIRONMENT

      In this category we shall include those space programs which are intended to create certain environmental effects, for experimental or operational purposes. "Deliberate interference" thus refers to all man-made alterations of the ecological balance, whether their objective is perceived as beneficial or detrimental. (The typical source of legal problems will be, in fact, deliverate interference perceived as beneficial by some and as detrimental by others.)

      3.1 _Interference by terrestrial means_

      3.1.1 _Hardware_. A notorious example of man-made space objects deliberately "dumped" in orbit was Project West Ford, the ill-fated attempt to place a band of copper needles (dipoles) around the Earth for communication purposes. The project was severely criticized because of its potential interference with radio astronomy, the radiospectrum being viewed as a protected environmental "resource."

      3.1.2 _Chemicals_. While cloud-seeding by chemicals has become a widespread method of experimental and operational weather modification in the lower atmosphere, no attempts appear to have been made to use space technology for articial weather or climate modification

as envisaged in theory. However, several of NASA'S sounding rockets are being used to release chemicals at various altitudes for the purpose of determining the composition and
dynamic behaviour of the atmosphere and the characteristics of the Earth's magnetic field.
The chemicals used are sodium, lithium, cesium, barium, nitric oxide and tri-methyl aluminum.
E.g., the joint U.S.-German Barium Ion Cloud Project (BIC) launched from Virginia in Sept.
1971 released 36 pounds of barium-copper oxide mixture at an altitude of 20,000 miles over
Central America (a previous release in March 1969 involved 6 pounds of barium at 46,000
miles). The barium project was reviewed and cleared by a committee report on potential contamination and interference from space experiments by the U.S. National Academy of Sciences
in July 1967, and NASA claims in its draft environmental impact statements that all these
chemical releases are negligible in comparison with the overall amounts of chemicals released by meteorite burning and other natural sources, and in any event are rapidly dispersed
and removed by oxidation and precipitation. The least that can be said about this claim is
that the natural occurrence of these exotic constituents is very low at the specific altitudes given (which is the very reason why an artificial release is readily observable) and
that there are major uncertainties about their residence times, mixing and removal processes. The disquieting aspect of these chemical releases, again, is not their individual environmental significance but the fact that in spite of their unquestionably "global" effects
and mounting frequency (NASA alone launches approximately 80 sounding rockets annually from
bases in the U.S., Canada, Sweden, Brazil and India), they do not appear to be subject to
any standard procedure of international consultation _ex ante_, nor even to the U.N. system
of registration _ex post_ (which only records the hardware launched).

    3.1.3 _Radiation_. The high-altitude nuclear explosions carried out by the major
space powers prior to 1963 and since continued by France and the People's Republic of China
were at least partly designed as unilateral "environmental experiments" in the global dis-
persion of radioactive matter. Against this deliberate interference, the 1963 Nuclear Test
Ban Treaty strongly emphasized what has since become known as the "ecological" viewpoint.
In spite of its incomplete political success, the Test Ban Treaty may thus in many respects
be considered as the first powerful manifestation of contemporary international concern
with the human environment.

    3.2 _Interference by extra-terrestrial means_.

    According to the classification suggested by von Ciriacy-Wantrup and adopted by
McDougal and others, the resources of extra-terrestrial space which are potentially amenda-
ble to human use may be divided into two major categories: stock resources (i.e. non-
renewable resources such as solid minerals) and flow resources (i.e. renewable resources
such as cosmic radiation). The plain physical categories are matter and energy.

    3.2.1 _Matter_. In view of present technological limitations, the risk of upset-
ting the Earth's ecological balance by the introduction and commercial exploitation of extra-
terrestrial stock resources is as remote as the prospects of lunar mining. There is, however, the related contingency that even minor quantities of such matter may have physical/
chemical characteristics so "beneficial" for specific purposes on earth (on a somewhat less
innocuous scale than the unusual fertilizing qualities reportedly found in lunar dust) that
they can indeed be utilized with significant environmental effectiveness. At that point, a
case may have to be made for international ecological controls on utilization.

3.2.2 <u>Energy</u>. Our major and vital extra-terrestrial flow resource is, of course, solar radiation. Proposals to utilize space technology for "beneficial" interference with this resource have seriously envisaged orbiting reflecting satellites ("space mirrors") to illuminate the dark areas of the world at night, to melt the polar ice caps, or literally to burn an enemy country on Earth. While the latter folly at least seems to be ruled out by the 1967 Space Treaty, other methods of tapping solar and non-solar radiation in space for energy production and utilization in the biosphere may indeed become available in the more distant future, which could potentially affect the energy balance of the Earth.

4 CONCLUSIONS

Space activities occupy a peculiar position in the international environmental context. On the one hand, the potential active "polluters" represent a very small and very powerful group of states (vis., the space powers and their associates), whose willingness to accept ecological responsibility varies greatly, depending at least in part on national economic capabilities (as the test ban precedent indicates, the marginal space powers may in fact turn out to be more reluctant than the super-powers to submit to global environmental controls). On the other hand, the wide and seemingly powerless group of states who are potential passive "victims" cuts across all political boundaries, alliances and cliches, including the alleged East-West and North-South polarizations.

4.1 <u>Available sources of law</u>

The basis of positive international law to protect the terrestrial environment against incidental or deliberate interference by space programs is narrow indeed. The only outright prohibitions of environmentally hazardous activities in space are contained in the 1963 Test Ban Treaty (for nuclear explosions) and in the 1967 Space Treaty (for military weapons). The Space Treaty's mild attempt to prevent "adverse changes in the environment of the Earth" limits itself to the problem of back contamination by extra-terrestrial matter. The manner in which lunar quarantine procedures were unilaterally discontinued by the United States indicates the ineffectiveness of the Treaty's consultation provisions for this purpose, and the absence of any foreign protest against this way of proceeding would seem to indicate a total lack of international concern, too. The only international body appointed for the purpose of considering potentially harmful effects of space experiments, the COSPAR group, has been virtually inactive with regard to Earth protection since its 1964 report. The three U.N. agencies (WHO, WMO, IAEA), who according to legal commentators would be expected to bear responsibility for studying "measures for preventing adverse effects of space experiments upon terrestrial environment" have not shown any greater interest in the matter.

Regarding state responsibility, the new UN Liability Convention on Space Objects may be interpreted as establishing the "launching state's" absolute liability for all damage, including environmental damage, caused to other states, persons or organizations, and in this regard would obviate the need to rely on legal precedents and analogies drawn from the law of international aviation, air pollution, water resources, nuclear energy or telecommunications. A similar argument for extensive interpretation of the term "damage" (as including proven environmental damage) can be made for a number of bilateral agreements where the term occurs in connection with space activities. This does not, however, cover potential damage caused by space programs to such common international resources as the ocean environment or

Antarctica, which lie beyond the limits of national sovereignty and therefore are not protected by our traditional "territorial" concepts of international law.

4.2 Recommendations for action

A number of proposals for global environment protection have been put forward, several of which are directly concerned with, or applicable to, interference from space activities. Among the international legal and scientific institutions which have formulated guidelines to this effect ar the Institute of International Law, the David Davies Memorial Institute of International Studies, the World Peace Through Law Conference, and the Study Group for Man's Impact on Climate (SMIC). The recommendations which follow draw on these guidelines with a view to identifying the course of international action required.

4.2.1 Monitoring and data interchange. What seems to be abundantly clear from our foregoing survey is the lack of adequate factual information on the extent of environmental interference caused by current space programs. Neither the U.N. registration of launchings nor the COSPAR reports and pre-launch announcements contain information on the nature and amounts of rocket fuels, rocket exhausts, radioactive payloads, tracers and other chemicals released in the atmosphere during space launchings and re-entries. There is no up-to-date information on the continued effects of these activities and substances on the composition and dynamics of the atmosphere, including its radiation and heat balance. An international body charged with the compilation, processing and dissemination of this information is urgently needed, so that its overall environmental significance and its relation to and interaction with other types of environmental factors can be assessed. A useful national model for the procedures required for this purpose are the "environmental impact statements" currently submitted by NASA under the U.S. Environmental Policy Act.

Conceivably, a system of post-launch environmental monitoring could be extended to voluntary pre-launch notifications similar to the COSPAR "Spacewarn" system for satellite observation, or eventually into a non-mandatory standard procedure of international pre-launch consultations. For certain categories of space programs, such a procedure could actually be attractive from the point of view of launching states, as a device to obtain routine international clearance and thus to rule out subsequent objections by other states.

4.2.2 International controls. It seems unrealistic to suggest a general prohibition of all space programs designed or likely to cause specific changes in the terrestrial environment (including the upper atmosphere), in view of the multitude of current small-scale experiments that would be affected by such a rule. Instead, agreement should be sought to subject this type of space program at least to certain mutually acceptable standard conditions: (a) routinge submission of scientific evidence to the effect that any environmental modifications caused by the program would either be technically reversible/reparable when necessary, or self-corrected/repaired by natural processes within a tolerable time limit; (b) advance international consultations for all large-scale programs designed or likely to have persistent or longterm effects. The current legal situation under the restrictive (loop-hole) interpretation of the 1967 Space Treaty -- according to which consultations are required for the environmental protection of the Moon, yet not required for the environmental protection of the Earth -- certainly is absurd and should be remedied. The institutional reference point could be the same as for monitoring purposes.

4.2.3 <u>International responsibility</u>. Environmental damage should clearly be recognized as coming within the terms of the 1971 U.N. Convention on International Liability for Damage Caused by Space Objects. While this recognition would confirm the principle of absolute liability (for causation regardless of fault), it leaves the important burden of proof for causation on the claimant. <u>De lege ferenda</u>--it would be desirable to extend this liability to certain types of environmental damage which Fawcett describes as a matter of "public international order" rather than a matter between individual states; viz., interference with common resources of mankind, such as ocean resources, Antarctica or global atmospheric resources. This question of principle, however, -- which would also require designation of an international "ombudsman" acting on behalf of mankind in the absence of individual claimants -- hardly seems appropriate for separate codification in the limited context of space activities. It would first have to be clarified as a general proposition, possibly in the framework of the "Universal Declaration on the Human Environment" at the 1972 U.N. Conference in Stockholm.

*   *   *   *   *

II. Other Contributions and Comments

1. <u>Establishment of orbiting laboratories</u>: Although Part II of the Proceedings deals with laboratories on the moon, suggesting that different problems arise, <u>Ferrer</u>, in Part I believes that the same legal regime applies to both kinds of laboratory, namely the rules applicable to space vehicles. Thus, the freedom to place or replace the station wherever it is deemed necessary applies to both situations. Also in both cases the ownership is not affected by the fact that the laboratory is in outer space (Art. VIII, Space Treaty); and, furthermore, the rules of liability as laid down in the Draft Convention (adopted by the Legal Sub-Committee in 1971) are the same for both. The last thesis particularly is debatable, as it presupposes that both laboratories can be considered as space objects.

<u>Iványi</u> sees another similarity: all these stations cannot do without radiocommunications and are in that respect subject to the provisions of the International Telecommunication Convention and to other rules established by the ITU. And, according to the author, this also will apply when communications will be provided by means of laser.

An orbiting laboratory can, and will, be used for the survey of the earth's natural and human resources. This use should be in accordance with the principle of Art. I of the Space Treaty, states <u>Markoff</u>, and he adds that observational activities are surely not acts of war - although military intelligence through these means remains an unlawful activity and contrary to Art. I of the Space Treaty - but they may serve in international relations as expression of mistrust, ill-will and similar cold-war antagonisms if carried out without the consent of a given country.

Short papers by <u>Smirnoff</u> and <u>Von Rauchhaupt</u> on the subject of orbiting laboratories conclude Part I of the Proceedings.

2. Establishment of laboratories on the moon: The Space Treaty will apply to these installations, but special problems may remain, according to Diederiks-Verschoor. She mentions the problem of jurisdiction and ownership in case of laboratories built in cooperation with other states or with an international organization. The position of the state of registry and the launching state in case of damage caused by the laboratory should also be considered in this connection. An international agreement may be required to deal with these and other problems.

Similar considerations are expressed by Niciu, who compares the provisions of the Space Treaty with those of the Soviet draft treaty concerning the moon.

In a detailed and intelligently written article, Robinson illuminates the human problem areas anticipated in prolonged space flights and gives examples of situations in which new legal rules will be necessary. Examples of these problem areas are failure of individuals to adjust to confinement in isolation and unsatisfactory relations between crew members. In this connection the concept of active or passive "survival homicide" in isolated situations of extreme duress is being discussed by the author on the basis of two cases in Anglo-American jurisprudence. Although the subject of this contribution may seem to go beyond the usual space law discussions, it is not science fiction and definitely deserves the attention of space lawyers.

Part II is concluded with a short paper in which Zhukov outlines the provisions of the Soviet draft treaty concerning the moon. One of the novelties of this draft is the article which provides, in case of damage caused to persons or property on the moon, for a rebuttable presumption of fault on the part of the state that caused the damage.

3. Protection of the earth's environment: In a very short time the issue of environmental protection of the earth has become one of major concern for scientists, politicians and lawyers alike. Space technology affects both sides of the problem: it may be the cause of pollution or contamination, but it may also contribute to the prevention or cure of cases of envrionmental damage. Space law can undoubtedly be of some help in regulating both aspects, and the fact particularly that outer space itself may become an environmental victim should be an incentive to work on this problem. The papers on this subject mainly concentrate on the effects of space activities on the earth's environment. A good example is the excellent article by Sand, which contains an analysis of the various types of environmental impact - under the headings of incidental and deliberate interference with the earth's environment- and after a short description of the few existing legal provisions, recommendations for the course of international action to be taken. (This article has been reproduced in this volume.) Hardly any rules exist with respect to this question: some of them are self-imposed (US Environmental Policy act of 1969, the NASA Quarantine Regulations); others, of an international character, are only concerned with one kind of pollution (the 1963 Nuclear Test Ban Treaty) or are extremely vague (Art. IX of the Space Treaty). On the latter provision Gorove gives his comments which have been reproduced in full. Estradé suggests various measures such as selection of clean engines and propellants and atmospheric tests concurrently with launchings; and, to prevent contamination of celestial bodies, sterilization measures are recommended. Fasan argues that even without Art. IX, international law already forbids acts of negligence which endanger life and health and security of mankind (the catchword here is "negligence"; it may be very difficult to prove such behavior). His suggestion

is to forbid all experiments which could endanger the environment as long as there is no international consensus that the particular activity is not dangerous. <u>Poulantzas</u> suggests that the General Assembly asks the International Court of Justice for an advisory opinion with regard to the interpretation of Art. IX, whereas <u>Kraus-Ablass</u> expresses the view, on the basis of the Trail Smelter Arbitration, that the principle of neighbourliness provides that any actions in the terrestrial environment producing harmful effects on the territory of another state must be avoided.

4. <u>Evaluation, conservation and development of earth resources</u>: It is impossible to discuss the above subject without paying attention to the US Skylab and ERTS programs and the NASA policies with respect to participation of other countries in the scientific experiments of these programs; they form the practical elements which have to be taken into account when questions of (space) law arise. This US policy was described as follows by a Department of State official: "We are committed to develop our earth resource surveying program openly, and to make available to other countries the data and experience which it produces." The US puts this policy into practice by concluding bilateral agreements with the states whose proposals are to be incorporated in the ERTS programs. Although this takes care of the position of those states who accept this invitation to cooperate in the survey activities, that activity in general should be regulated, in order that both the surveying state and the overflown states - whether participating in the project or not - have a clear picture of their rights and obligations. In this connection, one of the conclusions arrived at during a meeting on air and space law in 1970 in Argentina should be mentioned: the information on natural resources obtained by means of satellites without the consent of the state concerned is a violation of the sovereignty of such state over its resources. It shows the strong views held on the subject and indicates that internationalization may be needed to prevent serious conflicts between the surveyer and the surveyed. The fact that the surveying state considers its activities as being in conformity with international law and space law is, with respect to this basically more political than legal problem, - although possibly the more correct view - not as relevant as lawyers would wish.

The above formulated thoughts were raised, either directly or indirectly, by <u>Fernandez-Brital</u>, <u>Cocca</u> and <u>Vereshchetin</u> in their papers on the subject.

5. <u>Space telecommunications</u>: Without Intelsat the discussion on this subject would have been highly theoretical and, as such, to some extent sterile. <u>With</u> Intelsat an interaction between theory and practice developed which had a positive effect on both sides. The full and detailed description of the long and winding road which led from the 1964 Interim Agreements and the Intelsat Consortium, via long and difficult negotiations, to the Agreements relating to the International Telecommunications Satellite Organization "Intelsat" of August 20, 1971, is therefore essential material for the students of satellite communications law. The article, written by <u>Doyle</u>, also contains a discussion of the powers and functions of the newly created organization.

The creation of a European satellite system is one of the aims of the European space program. However, for the launching of its satellite, Europe may well have to rely on US launchers, and that country will take into account the European system's technical, and particularly, economic compatibility with the Intelsat system, as seen by the Intelsat Assembly. Art. XIV of the Intelsat Agreement deals with that subject, but can be interpreted in different ways. That, in short, is one of the problems raised by Bourely & Thynne of ELDO. Other questions briefly dealt with concern the various responsibilities of the members of the satellite organization to be established. The European satellite system is also the subject of a short paper by Kaltenecker & Arets of ESRO, in which ESRO's competence in this matter, participation of non-ESRO members, the use of the system by CEPT end EBU, and the manager Eurosat are discussed.

Direct broadcasting by satellite may lead to an infringement of a state's sovereign right to control the kind of information transmitted to its population, according to Dudakov, and should therefore be regulated. The ITU held in June/July 1971 its World Administrative Conference on Space Telecommunications, at which frequency bands were allocated to the various space services of the present and the future, some provisions on notification and registration of frequencies have been modified, and among others, the provision on the cessation of useless emissions has been amended. Busak is the author of a paper on this subject, in which he also involves the relevant provisions of the Space Treaty.

6. Related problems: Part VI of the Proceedings contain papers on a variety of subjects. It commences with another contribution on the problems of European cooperation in space. Bourely outlines the question which, at the 1970 European Space Conference, stood in the way of agreement; the conclusion appears to be that the countries involved cannot make up their minds on the main program. Man's activity on the moon may set the model for ventures farther afield. "In this view," according to Brooks, "the moon is a test case for international action." Hence, the importance of the new regulations supplementing in greater detail the provisions of the Space Treaty. Brooks analyzes two drafts, the Argentinian draft agreement on the natural resources of the moon and other celestial bodies and the Soviet draft treaty concerning the moon, by scrutinizing article by article what innovations both drafts bring. His contribution is followed by a paper entitled "Space Flight and the Problem of Vertical Limit of State Sovereignty," submitted by Emin, in which it is stated that the activities which are carried out by spacecraft are space activities all the way through, regardless of the altitude and location, which leads the author to the interesting conclusion that the fact of the flight of a spacecraft in the superjacent space of a foreign state cannot be qualified as a violation, because the internal regulations which forbid flight in superjacent space are not applicable to space activities which are in accordance with international law.

A long and very interesting paper by Galloway contains a comparison of the provisions of the Space Treaty, the Rescue Agreement, the Draft Convention on Space Liability and the Soviet draft treaty concerning the moon. The latter treaty is also separately analyzed. Among the many questions the author raises at the end of her paper with respect to future space treaties, the first one reflects not only her attitude towards the Soviet proposal, but also toward other new treaties in general: "In view of the fact that many of the provisions proposed for the moon treaty are identical or similar to provisions in the two space treaties already in force, is it necessary to have a new international agreement concerning the moon?"

Herczeg describes some concepts and institutions of international law which have to be reconsidered as a result of space activity and its legal regulation and some new principles which have appeared.

The paper "Outer Space and Outer Space Law - An Intermediate Balance of March 1971" of Von Rauchhaupt contains a survey on the development of space law, followed by some suggestions for the future. Simic writes on the international coordination for the launching of space craft according to international law, touching the important problems of registration, whereas Safavi suggests future work for the IISL. Verdacchi gives interesting thoughts on the use of cosmic space and the natural resources of the moon and other celestial bodies. Williams writes one of the first comments on the convention on space liability.

- - - - -

FIFTEENTH COLLOQUIUM ON THE LAW OF OUTER SPACE

VIENNA,1972

I.   Texts Reproduced

INTRODUCTION

par

C. Verdacchi

Les thèmes à l'ordre du jour des quatre "sessions" du quinzième "Colloquium" de droit spatial, sont:

- Problèmes juridiques de la télédétection par satellites;
- Récentes tendances dans le droit des communications spatiales;
- Problèmes connexes avec l'interprétation et l'application de la Convention sur la responsabilite;
- Nouveaux sujets pour la réglémentation de l'espace extra-atmosphérique.

On peut bien dire qu'il s'agit de thèmes étroitement en ligne avec le thème général du Congres de la I.A.F.: "L'espace extra-atmosphérique pour le développement du monde".

En ecoutant les claires relations, nous nous sommes de plus en plus convaincus que le droit spatial, quoique de nature "composite" comme le dernier des droits, constitue déjà un "corpus juris" qui aura bien d'influence, à sa fois, sur les autres branches du droit. Cette affirmation bien s'harmonise avec le discours d'ouverture de Monsieur le Président de la République Fédéral d'Autrich, selon lequel aucune autre champ a influencé plus à fond la vie humaine, en peu de temps, que ce que derive des technologies et des recherches spatiales.

Le thème a été développé aussi dans le discours prononcé dans la même occasion par M. Jaumotte, Président de l I.A.F., qui a rappelé le "tremendous" développement des sciences spatiales de 1964(année du précédent Congres de la I.A.F., de même à Vienne) a 1972, et a fait mention, en argument, des difficiles problèmes de l"Europe pour ses propres programmes spatiaux et pour ceux envisagés dans le programme Aerosat USA-Europe. L'impact de l'espace sur le développement du monde (titre du travail du Dr. Stever, dont nous parlerons) c'est l'impact de la recherche pure sur la recherche appliquée: de la Terre à l'espace, de l'espace à la Terre.

*   *   *   *   *

LE ROLE DES N.U. EN MATIERE DE SATELLITES POUR LA
TELEDETECTION DES RESSOURCES NATURELLES

par

Eilene Galloway

Le 23 juillet 1972 a été lancé l'"ERTS-A de "Western Test Range", en Californie.

Les buts poursuivis concernent: recherches sur l'agriculture, la géologie, l'idrologie, l'océanographie, la géographie.

Les photos, les "data" et les copies sont considerées de publique domaine, aussi au moyen d'accord bi- et multi-latéraux.

Une résolution (2778) du 29 novembre 1971 de l'Assemblée Générale des N.U. a sanctionné la constitution d'un Groupe de Travail sur la "télédétection" terrestre par satellites, accueillant la relative décision du Sous-Comité scientifique et technique.

Président de ce Group est l'Italien Franco FIORIC.

L'Assemblée Générale, "expérant que le Groupe de Travail entreprendra bientôt ses activités", prie les Etats de fournir au Groupe renseignements en matière; invite le Groupe a "s'enquérir des points de vues des organes appropriés" des N.U. etc.; "prie le Secrétaire Général de présenter au Groupe ses observations" et "le Comité des utilisations pacifiques de l'espace extra-atmosphérique, ainsi que le dit Sous-Comite, de faire en sorte que le Groupe entreprenne bientôt ses activités proprement dites et de tenir l'Assemblée Générale au courant." Cela en particulier pour les Pays en voie de developpement.

Les N.U. ont constitue un certain nombre d'organismes pour l'espace. Rappelons: ledit Comité; le Groupe de Travail pour les satellites des services de Navigation; le Groupe de Travail pour les communications directes par satellites; la Division des affaires de l'espace extra-atmosphérique etc.

Bien d'importance a eu, en matiere, aussi la Conference de Stockholm (5-16 juin 1972) sur le "milieu".

Les N.U. pourraient examiner la possibilite d'élaborer un "schema" de traité sur la télédétection en argument. A ce propos, certains principes du "Traité Spatial" et la Convention sur la responsabilité peuvent être considerés aussi en matière de télédétection.

On a prévu aussi une agencie "ad hoc". A ces propos les points de vue peuvent être "pro" ou "contre".

En analisant la question du "nombre" des traités, on peut considerer quatre types de lois internationales: lois exclusives pour l'espace extra-atmosphérique; lois applicables aussi à la terre et a l'atmosphère; lois applicables à l'espace extra-atmosphérique et occasionellement à l'atmosphère; lois exclusives pour la terre en consequences d'activités spatiales.

* * * * *

L'ETUDE DES RESSOURCES TERRESTRES PAR DES OBJETS SPATIAUX
ET LE DROIT INTERNATIONAL

par

Marco G. Marcoff

Les capacités de détection multidimensionelle par des objets spatiaux ouvrent de larges perspectives à l'étude et à la connaissance non seulement des conditions naturelles de l'environnement terrestre, mais aussi des ressources minérales, biologiques et économiques se trouvant en surface et dans le sous-sol de la terre ferme, ainsi que dans les étendues océaniques.

Malgré travail exploratoire et expérimental dans ce domaine, il n'existe pas encore de règlement international concernant l'utilisation des techniques spatiales aux fins de télédétection scientifique et économique, sauf les normes générales du droit conventionnel de l'espace.

Les possibilités de la télédétection par satellites en matière d'identification des récoltes agricoles (état de la vegetation, espèces cultivées, degré de maturité etc...), des ressources biologiques terrestres et aquatiques et des gisements minéraux ont été démontrées de façon suggestive par l'expérience aérospatiale combinée effectuée en 1969, à l'aide de l'avion "HB-57F" et le vaisseau spatial "Apollo 9".

Afin de créer les conditions juridiques nécessaires a une collaboration dans ce domaine, le Brésil et le Mexique sont entrés en rapport contractuels avec la NASA. Les expériences ont cependant montré que les opérations de télédétection par scanners ultrasensibles ne peuvent pas se cantonner sur le territoire précis de l'Etat qui a donné son consentement, mais qu'elles touchent les intérêts économiques, politiques et stratégiques des Etats voisins. La portée des capteurs déborde les confins de l'Etat visé par l'observation.

L'étude spéciale préparée par le Secrétariat des Nations Unies à cette fin, souligne que c'est surtout l'utilisation simultanée d'aéronefs et d'objets spatiaux, qui permet à présent d'obtenir des résolutions au sol accrues et, partant, des informations utiles.

Le stade dit "expérimental" des opérations actuelles n'empêche pas d'y entrevoir les menaces réelles surgies pour les Etats tiers. De graves problèmes de souveraineté liés à la reconnaissance économique ou stratégique se posent.

Le fait que 32 Pays et 300 savants de nationalité différente prennent part au programme ERTS-A, n'apporte aucune assurance que les intérêts légitimes des autres Etats seront dument sauvegardés. Il y a lieu d'espérer que le Sous-comité juridique des Nations Unies ne tardera plus à s'acquitter de ses devoirs et qu'il ne laissera plus ce soin uniquement au Sous-comité des N.U. scientifique et technique, ou au Conseil économique et social.

* * * * *

ASPECTS JURIDIQUES DE L'ESTIMATION, CONSERVATION ET DEVELOPPEMENT
DES RESSOURCES DE LA TERRE AU MOYEN D'OBJETS SPATIAUX

par

Giovanni Meloni

Malgré l'émotion profonde suscitée dans le monde entier par le drame des astronautes péris le premier juillet 1971 à bord du "Soyuz" envoyé par l'Union Soviétique dans l'espace, et la stupeur et l'enthousiasme qui ont accompagné l'entreprise de Apollo XV, une partie du public commence a regarder d'une facon désenchantée la succession de ces entreprises.

Dès le début, mais surtout pendant les cinq dernières années, la communauté des savants, des juristes et d'hommes d'état s'est engagée a donner aux expériences spatiales un sens plus complet et à rechercher et a découvrir, au dela des motivations théoriques, les raisons pratiques de ces activités.

Dans un sens et dans cette perspective, au delà de toute méfiance a l'égard de l'ordre juridique des Nations Unies, nombreuses propositions officielles et la doctrine la plus autorisée envisagent la gestion et le contrôle des activités spatiales sous les auspices de cette Organisation.

Les dites propositions visent, comme on le verra ensuite, a créer des nouvelles compétences du Secrétariat Général, ou bien a instituer une nouvelle section de l'organisation même.

La voie est à nouveau ouverte a deux possibilités: a celle de la coopération scientifique et à celle de la création d'un instrument de garantie du droit existant.

Comme nous avons déjà eu l'occasion de l'affirmer, un accord entre Etats, qui prévoie un organ pour garantir les droits et les intérêts des Parties signataires des traités du 1967 et du 1968, est essentiel. La Convention du 29 mars 1972, relatif à la responsabilité internationale dans le domaine des activités spatiales, a comblé une lacune sur le plane du droit spatial.

"De jure condendo", l'internationalisation des dits objets spatiaux, sous la forme d'une organisation international spatiale, à côté d'un organ de solution des différends éventuels, avec une juridiction permanente, obligatoire et à compétence générale, serait, sur le plan opératif, le meilleur instrument.

Dans cet ordre d'idées, on trouve les propositions de l'Argentine au mérite d'un projet d'accord international sur la télédétection au moyen d'objets spatiaux.

De ce qui precède, il nous semble de pouvoir affirmer que l'étude de l'emploi des satellites de télérévélation des ressources de la Terre, conduise ou puisse conduire à une phase nouvelle des relations internationales.

* * * * *

L'ESPACE EXTRA-ATMOSPHERIQUE POUR LE DEVELOPPEMENT

par

Carlo Delle Sedie

Le thème de cette année comporte un ultérieur examen de l'exploration de l'espace et de ses applications, objet d'étude de la Conférence de Vienne tenue du 15 au 27 aout 1968, qui avait pour objectif:

- les avantages de la recherche et de l'exploration spatiale et la mesure dans laquelle les Etats "non-spatiaux" et les Pays en voie de développement peuvent en profiter;

- participation des Etats "non-spatiaux" à la coopération international, dans le cadre des N.U.

Dans cette occasion le Prof. MATSCH, déjà Président du Comité des N.U. pour "l'usage" pacifique de l'espace extra-atmosphérique, tint une allocution sur les avantages de cet "usage" et, en parlant des entreprises spatiales, observa que tous les efforts étaient concentrés envers la Lune. Et l'année suivant, Armstrong, Collins et Aldrin posèrent, premiers des hommes, leurs pieds sur notre satellite naturel.

Le Commandant célebra cet évent avec les mots "We come in peace for all mankind".

Le Pape, Paul VI, en recevant les participants a la Conférence Internationale sur l'exploration et utilisation pacifique de l'espace, communiqua son émotion et ajouta que les progrès scientifiques et techniques doivent toujours être suivis par le progrès morale, juridique et de la coopération international. Il loua le Traité Spatial en notant que pour cela aussi le Saint Siège avait contribué.

*   *   *   *   *

AVENT DES "NAVETTES" POUR LA TELEDETECTION DES RESSOURCES NATURELLES

par

John R. Tamm

Avant que la décade en cours soit terminée, comme suite a la mission SKYLAB on prévoit qu'un unique avion, apte pour voler au dedans ou au dehors de l'orbite terrestre pourra effectuer des transports continus d'hommes et de provision dans ladite orbite. (On entend parler d'un moyen semblable à une "navette", pour assimilation au terme "textile" n.d.r.).
De l'emploi de la "navette" peuvent être dérivees certaines questions légales. Par example:

- Si, lorsque la "navette" rentre dans l'atmosphère, elle vient d'assumer la condition d'avion, est elle légale en volant aérodinamiquement?

- Peut-elle être employée pour deplacer, sans consentement, un satellite de télédétection, d'un autre Etat, abandonné, ou pour le dommager?

- Peut l'équipage d'une "navette" inspecter une station "spatiale" avec ou sans équipage, d'un autre Etat, sans permission ou préavis?

- Quelles règles opératives il faut appliquer pour ce moyen qui peut voler également dans et extra-atmosphere?

Certaines des questions indiquées ne peuvent pas être posées selon les règles en vigueur et demandent un "agreement" "ad hoc". Cependant on peut les étudier, pour en trouver une solution légale, à la lueur des traités en principes généraux de droit.

Maintenant nous pouvons observer que l'activité en argument va augmenter et que le but des opérations va changer.

La "navette" donnera une nouvelle dimension a l'occupation par les hommes du proche milieu spatial et permettra une vaste observation des conditions existant sur la Terre, dans l'orbite terrestre et dans le système du soleil.

A ce propos, il faut tenir compte du fait que sans moyens de transport d'équipage, d'équipement et de provisions a coût relativement bas, la permanence des hommes dans l'orbite terrestre sera bien limitée.

* * * * *

PERSPECTIVE DE LA TELEVISON ET DE LA RADIODIFFUSION
DIRECTE PAR SATELLITE
par
Jan Busak

Après avoir rappele les initiatives précédentes l'Auteur parle de la Conférence réunie sous l'égide de l'UIT en 1971.

Les principes qui pourraient servir comme base d'une réglémentation international peuvent être résumés comme suit:

1. Chaque Etat a le droit d'utiliser l'espace extra-atmosphérique pour les émissions de radiodiffusion par satellite sur le pied d'égalite et sans discrimination.

2. Pour les émissions de radiodiffusion par satellite les principes généraux du droit international sont applicables.

3. Les émissions pour les autres Pays ne peuvent être effectuées qu'avec accord formel de ceux-ci.

4. Les émissions de radiodiffusion par satellite doivent servir aux intérêts de la paix et du progrès.

5. Les émissions ne doivent constituer ni incitation à la guerre ni incitation aux actes susceptible d'y conduire, ni nuire a la bonne entente international ou contenir des informations d'immixtion dans les affaires intérieures d'autres Pays ou contraires aux bonnes moeurs ou des idées contraires aux droits fondamentaux de l'homme.

* * * * *

LES NECESSITES POUR SYSTEMES DE SATELLITES DE TELECOMMUNICATION
DE LA COMMUNAUTE INTERNATIONAL
par
Gunter B. Krause-Ablass

La quantité des satellites internationaux de télécommunication est limitée par deux raisons: limitée du nombre des positions avantageuses pour les satellites avec orbite stationnaire; limitée du nombre de fréquences à disposition.

La restriction des positions avantageuses c'est domaine des lois qui concernent l'ordre dans l'espace extra-atmosphérique; la restriction des fréquences concerne les lois internationales des télécommunications.

Par conséquent, les principes juridiques relatifs a la distribution des "chances" concernent deux champs légals, c'est-a-dire: les lois de l'espace extra-atmosphérique et les lois des télécommunications.

Le principe de la liberté et de l'égalité d'usage de l'espace extra-atmosphérique dérive du Traité Spatiale. De ce principe découle une pareille réduction de la souveraineté de chaque Pays.

Toutefois, le même principe comporte aussi le droit, pour l'Etat intéresse, d'exclure d'autres Etats. Cela c'est bien important, compte tenu du fait que le nombre des fréquences est limité et ainsi limitée devient - pour ainsi dire - l'application pratique du principe d'égalité. On dérive que, au present, on ne peut pas établir un complet système de satellites nationaux pour radiocommunications internationales. Donc le droit des Nations d'être directement parties des télécommunications internationales se limite à pouvoir participer (a l'utilisation) d'un système international.

* * * * *

LA CRISE SPATIALE EUROPEENNE
par
M. Bourely

Au cours du "colloquium" tenu l'année dernière, on avait résumé ainsi les facteurs de cette crise:
- En premier lieu, la difficulté de répartir les différentes formes de l'activité spatiale a l'intérieur de l'enveloppe financière, assez restreinte, que l'Europe peut consacrer aux activités spatiales entreprises à titre collectif.
- En second lieu, le problème de la disponibilité des moyens de lancement, c'est-à-dire celui de la fourniture par les Etats-Unis de lanceurs pour satisfaire l'ensemble des besoins de l'Europe.

Nous ajoutons que ce qui importe vraiment est ceci: comme les Américains l'ont dit très clairement, le fait que l'Europe participe ou qu'elle ne participe pas à la réalisation du post-Apollo, n'aura pas d'influence sur les conditions dans lequelles elle pourra utiliser les moyens de lancement des Etats-Unis - qu'il s'agisse des lanceurs conventionnels ou du nouveau système de transport spatial.

Cependant une reunion des ministres de la Conférence Spatiale Européenne s'est tenue à Paris.

Les discussions ont permis de dégager un accord général sur les points suivantes:

1. Les membres de la réunion ont reconnu la nécessité d'un programme spatial européen cohérent et d'une organisation spatiale européenne unique chargée de l'exécuter.

2. Les Etats membres de la C.S.E. qui souhaitent poursuivre, avec le soutien de la C.S.E. la phase de définition du Laboratoire de Sortie, ont la possibilité de la faire dans le cadre de la C.S.E.

3. Les Etats membres de la C.S.E. qui sont actuellement engagés au titre des programmes de lanceurs du CECLES/ELDO soutiendront ces programmes jusqu'à la fin de 1972.

4. La prochaine Conférence Spatiale Européenne se réunira a Bruxelles vers le 15 decembre 1972 pour décider sur la participation d'autres Etats aux études sur les laboratoires et sur la continuation des programmes de lanceurs européennes.

* * * * *

LE PRINCIPE DU "PLEIN DEDOMMAGEMENT" DANS LA CONVENTION
SUR LA RESPONSABILITE POUR LES DOMMAGES CAUSES PAR DES
OBJETS LANCES DANS L'ESPACE EXTRA-ATMOSPHERIQUE
par
Armando Cocca

...

Le principe du "plein dédommagement" est un des mérites plus grands de la Convention sur la responsabilité. Il s'agit non seulement d'un progrès dans les lois internationales mais aussi d'une conferme du droit comme science a l'égard des considérations politiques et d'autres.

L'idée du "plein dedommagement" fut avancé, d'abord, par le Sous-Comité. Initialement elle était étendue, par la Délégation de l'Argentine, aux dommages indirects et retardés, en 1965. Le Japon présenta un document en matière en 1969. Les N.U. ont, depuis, favorisée cette idée.

La responsabilité absolue est établie, à l'art.II, non seulement pour les dommages à la surface de la terre, mais aussi pour les avions en vol.

La réparation, prévue à l'article XII de la Convention, tend a "rétablir la personne, physique ou morale, l'Etat ou l'organisation internationale demandeur dans la situation qui aurait existé si le dommage ne c'était pas produit". (N.d.r.: il s'agit de l'application du principe latin de la "restitutio in integrum).

C'est important de rappeler, à ce propos, une proposition avancée en 1970, par Argentine, Autriche, Belgique, Canada, Italie, Japon, Royaume Uni et Suède: proposition largement semblable mais pas identique.

En considération du fait que la Convention se réfère au dommage causé "par des objets lancés dans l'espace", il était nécessaire de définir ces "objets" causant dommage.

Argentine, France, Italie et Mexico présènterent un document de travail qui comprenait dans cette locution:

- chaque objet spatial;
- chaque personne à bord d'objet spatial;
- chaque part d'objet spatial, part à bord, détachée our tombée d'un objet spatial ou du véhicule de lancement, ou part de ceci.

Cette définition ne fut pas acceptée.

Cependant, la Convention peut être considérée comme document de grande importance.

D'autre part, la clause de revision permettra d'en améliorer le texte, comme, par exemple, pour ce qui concerne le caractère de la décision dont à l'article XIV, que l'Argentine aurait voulu amender au cours de l'élaboration.

* * * * *

LA CONVENTION SUR LA RESPONSABILITE POUR LES DOMMAGES CAUSES PAR LES OBJETS LANCES DANS L'ESPACE EXTRA-ATMOSPHERIQUE
par
I.H.PH. Diederiks-Verschoor

...

Dès 1959 la Commission "ad hoc" des N.U. pour l'usage pacifique de l'espace extra-at-mosphérique avait considéré avec attention l'élaboration d'une convention sur la responsabi-lite pour dommages.

A propos de cette Convention, viennent d'être considérées: les définitions; les fonde-ments de la responsabilité; la responsabilité conjointe; l'exonération de responsabilité; les organisations internationales; le dédommagement, l'exception au principe de total com-pensation; l'exclusion de limites dans le dédommagement; les demandes pour ceux derniers; la loi applicable, la Commission des demandes.

La Convention développe questions du Traité Spatial et de la Convention sur la respon-sabilité pour les dommages causés par les objets lancés dans l'espace summairement consi-dérées dans ces deux documents.

(Nous renvoyons à la relation (n.d.r.)), en concluant que nous pouvons dire que la Con-vention montre quelque lacune et ne résulte pas complètement satisfaisante, toutefois il est souhaitable qu'un grand nombre de Pays la ratifie.

Il faut observer que les Etats non signataires pourraient avoir, tout de même, avantages de la Convention, sans avoir assumé obligations. Cela peut conduire à des faux résultats.

Enfin on voudrais demander s'il ne serait pas désirable de constituer de fonds inter-nationaux pour dédommager les victimes. Resterait à établir comment et en quelle mesure les Etats devraient contribuer.

Il s'agirait d'un procedure simple pour la réparation ainsi prévue dans la Convention en faveur des victimes qui ne seraient pas de plus en plus "victimisées par des compliquées et longues procédures."

Aussi le dédommagement pour les conséquences sur la climatologie et pour d'autres dommages causés par résidus radio-actifs d'objets lancés dans l'espace extra-atmosphérique doit être règle bien soigneusement. A cet égard apparait la nécessité indérogable de prévoir la régistration de ces objets, en défaut de quoi chaque mesure serait inutile.

*　*　*　*　*

INTERPRETATION DE QUELQUE ARTICLE DE LA CONVENTION

SUR LA RESPONSABILITE INTERNATIONALE POUR LES

DOMMAGES CAUSES PAR DES OBJETS SPATIAUX

par

Cristian Patermann

Cette relation entend discuter en detail des articles XII et XXII de la Convention sur la responsabilité, dont le contenu et les locutions, à notre avis, soulèvent un certain nombre de problèmes.

L'article XXII dispose que la Convention, le cas echéant, s'applique aussi aux organisations internationaux.

La responsabilité des Pays membres de ces organisations est secondaire et conditionnée:
- à la demande presentée, premièrement, a l'organisation;
- a l'accomplissement d'un periode de six mois sans que l'organisation ait payé dédommagement fixé.

Nous pensons que, pour la future, on soulèvera bien de problèmes connexes avec la question si la réglémentation relative a la responsabilité des Organisations et des Etats parties, tel qu'est prévue dans la Convention, satisfait ou non les exigences pratiques des activités de ces Organisations internationales dans le domaine de l'espace extra-atmosphérique et dans autres.

A ce propos l'on fait une distinction entre Organisations 1) reconnues, 2) ou moins comme subjets de droit international.

Nous sommes favorables au principe de la responsabilité exclusive plutôt qu'à celui de la responsabilité conjointe.

Pour ce qui concerne les notes sur l'art. XII, nous renvoyons a la relation.

*　*　*　*　*

QUELQUE PROBLEMES DE LA CONVENTION SUR LA RESPONSABILITE
INTERNATIONALE POUR LES DOMMAGES CAUSES PAR DES OBJETS
LANCES DANS L'ESPACE
PAR
Istvan Herczeg

...

A mon avis son importance faisant-epoque entre les lois internationales peut être syn-
thetisée en cinque points, disposés en ordre de priorité:

1. en point de fait la Convention a levé la responsabilité civile au niveau de responsabilité statuelle et ainsi a élargi notablement le champ de cette responsabilité;

2. la Convention a établi la règle de la responsabilité absolue des Etats, auparavant inconnue;

3. la Convention a introduit la règle de la responsabilité solidaire et particulière des
Etats, également inconnue en champ international;

4. la Convention a crée une nouvelle forme d'arbitrat international avec la "Commission de
règlement des demandes";

5. les organismes internationaux peuvent adhérer à la Convention en déclarant d'accepter les
droits et les obligations y prévus.

Puisque la matière est reglée chez certains Etats avec lois intérieures, en beaucoup de
cas bien differéntes, on dérive que ces lois ne sont pas toujours conformes aux règles internationales, particulièrement lorsqu'elles ne résultent pas développées au point d'être
applicables a ce nouveau champ de l'activité humaine.

Dans la Convention manque l'unique rémède possible qu'on pouvait introduire: c'est-à-
dire une regle générale qui établit la lois à appliquer aux cas non prévus dans la réglémentation de ladite Convention.

*   *   *   *   *

ULTERIEURES NOTES SUR LA RESPONSABILITE SPATIALE.
LE PROBLEME DE LA PROTECTION DU MILIEU
par
Silvia Maureen Williams

...

C'est l'opinion presqu'unanime que l'entrée en vigueur de la Convention sur la responsabilité ait été saluée comme "pierre miliaire" dans la codification des lois réglant les
rapports qui dérivent des entreprises spatiales.

A ce propos nous voudrions signaler, toutefoir, deux observations.

La première c'est que plusieurs membres du SousComité juridique auraient préféré que la
Convention établisse le caractère définitif de la décision finale, non conditionnée à l'ac-
ceptation préventive des parties. (En matière rappelons que les représentants de l'Argentine
avaient proposé une solution alternative qui rendait obligatoire la décision, sauf different
accord des parties).

La deuxième concerne la position des organisations internationales et, en particulier, des Etats parties de ces organisations qui ne soient pas parties aussi de la Convention.

On pourra éliminer, nous l'espérons, les deux raisons de critique par la revision prévue a l'article XXVI.

On peut discuter aussi sur les limites des activités spatiales intéressées à la Convention. On peut conclure que la protection de l'humanité, de chaque dangereuse conséquence des dites activités est clairement reconnue avec les mots de la même Convention. Le Prof. Saud considère que cette admission confirme le principe de la "responsabilité absolue", quoiqu'.elle passe sur l'important argument du charge d'épreuve.

* * * * *

NOTES ET OBSERVATIONS A PROPOS DE LA "CONVENTION SUR LA
RESPONSABILITE INTERNATIONALE POUR LES DOMMAGES CAUSES
PAR DES OBJETS SPATIAUX", AVEC REFERENCE: AU TRAITE SPA-
TIAL; A LA CONVENTION SUR LE SECOURS, ETC.; AUX SYSTEMES
JURIDIQUES DE CHAQUE ETAT, DANS LE CADRE DES PRINCIPES
GENERAUX DE DROIT
par
Cesare Verdacchi

L'Assemblée Générale des N.U. a approuvé pendant la vingt-sixième session et adressé aux Gouvernements des Etats pour être signé le projet de convention sur la responsabilité pour les dommages causés par des objets spatiaux.

Il s'agit d'un autre important pas pour la coopération internationale. Nous souhaitons donc, que tous Etats la signent tout de suite, c'est-à-dire, avec la vitesse qui caractérise les objets spatiaux ....

Sur le texte de la convention on peut faire quelque notes, et nous avons fait ainsi avec l'uni texte italien.

Premis cela et en renvoyant aux observations en detail contenues dans la relation, nous soulignons seulement les considérations qui suivent:

- Le réglement des demandes, dont a la convention, implique, aux termes de la loi, une vraie transaction.

Comme on sait, la transaction vaut seulement pour les personnes qui en sont parties.

Cela entraine que l'Etat intéressé devra en voie préliminaire obtenir, le cas échéant, un mandat par la personne, fisique our morale, qui demande la réparation.

- Le délai nécessaire pourrait faire dépasser les termes internes de péremption.

Pour obvier à cette inconvénience il faudra disposer que le terme de péremption ne court pas pendant l'expérimentation du système réglé par la convention.

- Un principe latin dit: "cui sunt commoda ei sint onera".

Ce principe, envisagé dans le cadre des solennelles déclarations sur la destination à l'avantage de tout le monde de l'exploration de l'espace extra-atmosphérique, pourrait paraître contraire a l'esprit de la convention, c'est-à-dire, puisque les avantages sont destinés à "toute l'humanité" aussi les dommages (alias "onera") devraient être à la charge de "toute l'humanité", au moins de celle qui a approuvé le "Traité Spatial".

Donc, l'approbation de cette convention par les Etats protagonistes des entreprises spatiales destinées à "toute l'humanité" fournit une épreuve remarquable de bonne volonté! -"Last but not least"! Chaque Etat devrait traduire, dans sa langue, les mots "objets spatiaux" dont au title, comme s'il y ait écrit "objets lancés dans l'espace extra-atmosphérique". Cela, parce que, par exemple, les météorites ne sont pas objet de la convention, bien qu'ils soient "objets spatiaux".....

* * * * *

LE TRAITE DU 17 JANVIER 1967 ET LES CONVENTIONS QU'EN DERIVENT
par
Pompeo Magno

...

L'actuelle réglémentation se base sur le Traité du 27.1.1967. Principe premier c'est que l'espace et les corps célestes sont "res communis omnium civium", c'est-à-dire, ils appartiennent à toute l'humanité.

Nous avons déjà conclu la Convention sur les astronautes et celle sur la responsabilité pour dommages par activité spatiale. Aujourd'hui, nous preparons deux autres Conventions qui doivent se placer dans le cadre du Traité Spatial: la première sur l'identification et l'immatriculation des objets spatiaux; la seconde sur le règlement juridique particulier de la Lune et, si l'on voudra, des autres corps célestes, ainsi que sur l'exploitation des ressources de ceux-la.

Plus particulièrement, on peut dire que quelque difficulté est née à propos: des moyens d'identification des objets spatiaux a immatriculer, et, sur le plan strictement juridique, de la définition des mêmes objets spatiaux.

Mais cela est la confirmation de l'importance que toutes les délégations attribuent a ces questions. La préoccupation de la délégation de l'Italie a été et est d'inserrer les deux nouvelles Conventions dans le cadre de la "Magna Charta" déjà existante, c'est-à-dire du Traité Spatial, qui a été une grande conquête de l'ONU et de l'humanité.

Autre préoccupation c'est d'éviter toute possibilité de différences d'interprétation et d'application des principes déjà choisis et affirmés.

Le droit spatial a la chance d'être complètement nouveau et original, outre que mondial; et il ne doit pas permettre la prolifération de textes sur le même sujet.

Nous devons conserver, dans la construction des divers protocoles internationaux, cette unité des principes et des méthodes toujours appliquée, et qui a fait du droit spatial, autonome ainsi qu'international, la plus jeune mais aussi la plus claire de toutes les branches du droit et de toutes les disciplines juridiques. On peut atteindre ce but par une formule, à inserrer dans le préambule des Conventions à venir, qui considère le Traité Spatial comme accepté.

NECESSITE D'UN TRAITE SUR L'ETAT (STATUT) JURIDIQUE DE LA LUNE
par
Michel Smirnoff

...

On écouta, avec bien d'intérêt, l'illustration du "schéma" du Traité sur la Lune (elabore par l'URSS), faite par le Prof. Zhukov, au cours du XIVième Colloquium de droit spatial.

Mr. Gromyko, dans sa lettre de transmission du projet du traité, demanda: d'écrire l'argument à l'ordre du jour de la 26e Session de l'Assemblée Générale des N.U. sur le titre: Préparation d'un Traité international concernant la Lune; d'envoyer le "schéma" du Traité au Sous-Comité des N.U. pour l'usage pacifique de l'espace extra-atmosphérique, dont la Session était prévue auparavant de distribuer, à propos du "schéma", un document des N.U.

Certains, pendant la discussion, ont observé qu'il s'agissait d'une pféposition prématurée; d'autres ont donné une différente interprétation au Traité du 1967.

Comme soutien du "schéma" de part soviétique, on a souligné: les entreprises Apolla et Lunakhod; qu'il y avait différence d'interprétation sur des questions très importantes du Traite Spatial, comme à propos des activités militaires, etc...

Dans la lettre de Mr. Gromyko sont indiqués 6 principes du "schéma" de la Lune qu'on peut voir dans le texte complet de cette relation (exploration au bénéfice aussi des futures générations; exclusion des activités dangereuses pour l'humanité; défense de poser sur la Lune des armes nucléaires et d'appropriation de la surface de la même; mesures pour sauvegarder la vie humaine sur la Lune).

Nous soulignons les conclusions suivantes pour démontrer la nécessite du nouveau Traité:
- il faut éclaircir, tout de suite, le sens de certaines règles du Traité;
- le "Traité Spatial" est un document de caractère général, qui consent d'émaner des Conventions et des accords d'exécution;
- l'idée de la "démilitarisation" est bonne, toutefois il faut considérer la nécessité d'établir le sens exact de cette parole;
- quant à l'exportation des ressources lunaires, on doit considerer qu'une éventuelle défence en matière peut conseiller aux Etats intéressés de mettre fin aux explorations ou d'ignorer ces défences.

* * * * *

LE PROGRAMME "INTERCOSMOS" A LA LUMIERE DES
PRINCIPES PLUS IMPORTANTS DU DROIT SPATIAL
par
V.S. Vereschetin

Les neuf Pays socialists pendant cinq années ont réalisé des buts du programme "Intercosmos", qui a entrainé questions légales et organisatives. A ce propos se posent les interrogatifs suivant:

-1'"Intercosmos" est-il une organisation internationale?

- quelle connexion existe, à l'intérieur des structures "Intercosmos", entre l'activité des Etats intéressés?

- 1'"Intercosmos" peut-il agir dans les relations internationales comme "entité" di distinguee?

En renvoyant au texte de la relation, nous pouvons dire que:

1) 1'"Intercosmos" est un programme (élaboré conjointement et en suite approuvé) qui prévoit la collaboration entre neuf Pays socialists pour l'exploration et l'utilisation de l'espace extra-atmosphérique. Existe une organisation apte à réaliser ce programme qui s'exerce par "meetings" annuels des Directeurs des organismes nationaux de coordonnement, sessions annuelles des quatre Groupes de Travail de spécialistes, régulières réunions d'experts;

2) cause le défaut d'un certain nombre d'éléments qui caractérisent les organisations internationales intergouvernementales, 1'"Intercosmos" ne peut pas être classifié entre ces organisations. Toutefois, quant au paragraphe qui précède, les accords entre les Gouvernements et les organisations nationales etc., peuvent faire considérer 1'"Intercosmos" comme organisation international "sui generis" aussi dans les rapports internationaux.

3) les activités de 1'"Intercosmos" rentrent sous la catégorie des activités conjointes dont à l'article XIII du "Traité Spatial" et à l'article X de la Convention sur la responsabilité pour dommages;

4) aussi les principes plus importants du "Traite Spatial" et certaines règles sur le secours des Astronauts et sur la responsabilité peuvent être appliqués à 1'"Intercosmos";

5) au cours de l'exécution du programme "Intercosmos", on peut avoir des relations entre les Etats participants, entre les mêmes et Etats tiers.

* * * * *

PROBLEMES JURIDIQUES DE L'EMPLOI DE VOLS SPATIAUX HUMAINS,
DE STATIONS SPATIALES ET ENTREPRISES HUMAINES AU MOYEN D'INI-
TIATIVES PRIVEES ET DE FINANCEMENTS NON PUBLICS
par
George S. Robinson

(Nous nous limitrons a reproduire l'intuitif "grafic" de la relation de 36 pages, dont a pag. 14, et la part essentielle des conclusions).

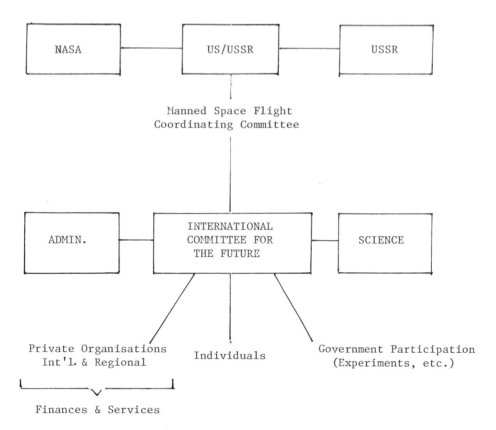

Toutes les observations générales et particulières, affirmations et propositions conduisent
aux conclusions qui suivent:

- on observe que bien des hommes sont concaincus que c'est essentiel un programme rationel
  et positif de recherches;
- un programme d'exploration spatiale doit contenir une précise indication en vue des béné-
  fices scientifiques et aussi des réponses aux interrogatifs philosophiques et théologiques;
- les Organisations ont traité des recherches spatiales comme ressortissant d'un club;
- experts de lois et Organisation pourront aider "grouper embrionaires" de recherche.

* * * * *

DROIT DIVIN ET DROIT NATUREL HUMAINE DANS LE DROIT
DE L'ESPACE EXTRA-ATMOSPHERIQUE
par
W. Von Rauchhaupt

...

Une bombe explosant "par accident" ou bien lancée pour un certain but cause destruc-
tions, grande désordre et, par conséquent, l'urgente exigence de pleine réparation des dommages provoqués. La raison est purement négative; le résultat tout au plus produit une restitution, mais rarement plus que cela.

L'explosion originale de la création, le cas échéant d'une telle hypothèse, produirait la préparation et la formation d'une nouvelle matière primaire et matériel pour construire étoiles avec leur admirable ordre dans leurs orbites circulaires et elliptiques et avancées spirales et aussi rayons de différentes directions qui se mouvent de millions d'années lumière.

Ça suffit cette premisse, pour donner une idée de la différente portée des lois humaines et des lois divines.

Les sources du droit spatial sont principalement tes trois suivantes:

- le droit rationnel étudié et formulé par les Nations Unies à New York et la NASA, à Washington, D.C., d'une part, et par la Russie Soviétique d'autre part;
- le droit acquis par la costume. Ce droit en grande partie industriel, se forme lentement, et n'a pas encore de structure stable et a besoin de l'approbation de la juridiction regulière ou d'un arbitrage spécial;
- le droit devin est la source la plus importante et existe dans une sphère plus élevée. L'homme ne peut l'altérer. Son existence a été reconnue peu à peu et acceptée comme droit de première importance dans l'Espace.

Le droit naturel est donc différent, à l'égard du droit divin, étant toujours formulé par les paroles conventionnelles de l'homme, dont l'importance est nettement moindre que celle de son Créateur et de son droit divin. Le droit divin existe depuis que Dieu créa le monde.

La première excursion de l'homme dans l'Espace ne s'est pas réalisée avant 1958, et la première visite à la Lune se fit en 1969, (année de notre ère... et non de la Création...) Ces excursions seront suivies par d'autres selon les Droits divin et humain, afin, nous l'espérons vivement, d'assurer la paix et de perfectionner le vrai développement du Monde.

*   *   *   *   *

II. Autres Contributions et Commentaires

Nous voulons rappeler aussi, entre autres, les interventions et relations de: C. Terzani (Italie), qui a parlé des conséquences favorables des technologies spatiales pour le développement de l'éducation de la culture, et de l'intérêt de 1/UNESCO pour cette matière; A.Franchina (Italie), qui a établi aussi un rapport entre les problèmes de la télédétection au moyen de satellites et ceux relatifs à la photographie aérienne; H. G. Stever (U.S.A.), qui a illustré une relation bien circonstanciée sur les perspectives spatiales, l'éthique spatiale, les expériences et les "leçons" relatives, etc...; I. Hall (U.S.A.), qui a parlé sur les implications sociales, économiques, etc.., de ladite télédétection et de l'utilisation des données; C. Verdacci (Italie), qui a décrit les traits essentiels du "Programma S. Marco", exemple de collaboration internationale comprenant aussi Pays en voie de développement technique: cela dans l'esprit du "Traité Spatial", art. 4. etc...

Nous rappelons, enfin, les relations des autres très illustres auteurs en regrettant que l'Espace" (non extra-atmosphérique, ... mais de ce volume) ne permet pas de les développer dans le mesure que nous voudrions.

Le volume des "Proceedings" du XVIème Colloquium, auquel nous renvoyons, vaudra pour suppléer a telle manque. Cependant, pour le respect que nous devons à si éminents auteurs, nous traiterons de la matière de leurs relations à titre de synthèse conclusive personelle, en tenant compte des derniers développements connus chez les N.U., et du caractère "architectonique" de nos buts et de ceux de chaque auteur, buts confluent "in unum", c'est-à-dire vers le progrès des sciences spatiales (aussi juridiques) pour le bien de toute l'humanité.

Leonardo da Vinci, dans un de ses Traités, dit que "Aucune chose peut être aimée ni haïe si auparavant l'on n'a pas connaisance d'elle"; enseignement qui, en certaine mesure, correspond au latin "nil volitum quin praecognitum". Et puisqu'aussi la science spatiale, pour être aimée par tous, entraine premièrement un problème de connaissance, nous souhaitons, d'abord,que les questions de la téléradiodiffusion directe par satellites (aussi pour ce qui concerne les informations) puissent être résolues, dans l'esprit du Traité Spatial - compte tenu aussi des projets présentés, en matière - en élaborant un code déontologique. Cela, en superant par des règles appropriées les difficultés connexes avec la souveraineté, la politique, la morale, les droits d'auteur et personnels, la distribution des fréquences, le commerce, le controle, etc. Le Groupe de Travail "ad hoc" (chez le N.U.) a décidé de "adresser principalement son attention aux problèmes juridiques et politiques bien qu'on continue l'examen des développements de la technologie de la télédiffusion directe". Ledit Groupe de Travail se réunira de nouveau avant la 13e Session du Sous-Comité Juridique. Il va sans dire que, à leur fois, les questions de toute nature qu'en dérivent - et spécialement juridiques - auront importance et reflexes différents (dans le cadre du "Traite Spatial", ainsi que des conventions "sur la responsabilité internationale pour les dommages causés par objets lancés dans l'espace extra-atmosphérique" et "sur le secours aux astronautes et la restitution des astronautes et des objets lancés dans l'espace extra-atmosphérique") selon qu'il s'agit de différents types de "moyen spatiaux" et d'entreprises nationales ou internationales; intergouvernementales; réalisées par organisations douées de personalité juridique ou non; d'organisations limitées ou d'une portée bien générale; d'organismes qui disposent, ou non, de moyens financiers, d'assurances, etc.. Ainsi l'ELDO, l'ESRO, l'INTELSAT (dans ses phases expérimentale et commerciale), l'INTERSPUTNIK, se trouvent,à ce regard, en position differente. (P. Magno, O.F. Brital, R.R. Colino, S.E. Doyle, B.C. Dudakov, G.M. Kolosov, G.P. Zhukov, T. Kozlnk, M. Bodenschatz, J. Gal, F.G. Rusconi, D.M. Poulantzas, J. Rajski, H. Kaltenecker).

Problèmes presque mêmes se présentent en matière de télédétection des ressources naturelles, de l'état de l'espace, etc., par satellites. A ce propos il faudra tenir compte aussi (particulièrement pour la diffusion éventuelle des informations par ce moyen obtenues): de l'utilité générale de la télédétection, à l'intérieur et en champs international (pour vérifier l'état des glaciers, la pollution intra- et extra-atmosphérique, les conditions de la mer et de la flore et faune, etc.); de la particulière convenance d'un seul Etat; du caractère publique ou privée, spontane (à l'arbitre de l'Etat lanceur) ou à demande, sur commission, gratis ou à paiement, de l'activité de télédétection; des accords déjà existants, généraux our particuliers; des renseignements que Etats tiers peuvent en obtenir; de la langue usée; de la régistration (qu'on souhaite) des objets lancés; du principe de la liberté de l'espace; des perspectives après 1'an 2000; de la nécessité d'éviter phenomènes criminaux (traditionels our nouveaux); du danger de la prolifération des conventions (une pour la lune,

une pour l'espace, une pour chaque corps céleste...) - nous croyons - à détriment de la poli-validité du "Traité Spatial". (V.G. Emin, S. Beresford, S. Estrade, C. Horsford, G. Jacquemin, P. Magno, M. Marcoff, G.P. Zhukov, B. Sands Corring, S. Gorove, E. Pepin).

Et maintenant, pour conclure, nous revenons a la relation de W. Von Rauchhaupt pour retourner des "Lois divines" à l'espace et aux corps célestes, de ceux à la "mère Terre", de cette a l'humanité, de l'humanité à nous hommes; des hommes au droit human, du droit humain aux nécessités et aux expoirs humains qui visent aux sciences spatiales quasi comme à un "boomerang" bienfaisant. Et cela nous avons senti dans les mots des astronautes et enfin dans la noble allocution finale du Dr. Von Braun - bien justement optimiste - toute vouée à envisager ce que l'homme pourra obtenir en échange de ce qu'il a donné et donne à l'espace.

Conditions déterminantes sont, non seulement que l'homme puisse disposer d'un droit apte à régler cette nouvelle matière (et nous pensons d'en disposer) mais, aussi qu'il l'applique sans reserves....

- - - - -

CONCLUSIONS

TO

THE DEVELOPMENT OF THE

LAW OF OUTER SPACE

The first phase of man's exploration of outer space had a great deal of similarity to man's early conquest of the Antarctic. There was the challenge of the South Pole, a place no human foot had yet trod upon. Brave men were ready to risk their lives to be the first to plant the flag of their respective country on that distant and elusive goal. Scientific objectives of their expeditions clearly had to take a back seat.

Whether we look at it from a technical or a logistic standpoint, cr just from the angle of human endurance, to reach the South Pole and return alive was a most marginal proposition at the turn of the century. Reaching the Antarctic continent by sailing ship was difficult enough and a chapter in itself. But the basic mathematics behind the subsequent dog sled trek from the Antarctic coastline to the South Pole and back was remarkably similar to that of a multistage rocket launching of a small spacecraft into orbit. Just compare the small number of huskies (propulsion) and the weight of the few nearly empty sleds that ultimately returned from the Pole (empty weight of the rocket) with the ten times larger number of huskies pulling the massive caravan that departed many weeks earlier.

During the last decade and a half, the first phase of a multi-national, multi-faceted space program has demonstrated that man can orbit the earth, fly to the moon, do useful work in a space station, soft-land unmanned probes on distant planets, and do all sorts of useful things in outer space for the direct benefit of man on earth. Many people deplore the fact that mankind seems to have become somewhat blasé at all these accomplishments and is getting tired of hearing so much about space. But maybe this is just a sign of a healthy maturing process. For was it really much different with the other great scientific and technological breakthroughs of the 20th Century? Have we not become just as blasé about former miracles such as radio, television, commercial aviation, nuclear power plants or the conquest of epidemics? Particularly for the younger generation, all these things have lost their flair of the miraculous and become a natural part of the new world into which they have been born.

The second phase of man's accomplishments, whether in the Antarctic, in wireless communications, commercial aviation or the control of epidemics, has another feature in common: To enable mankind to fully benefit from these new opportunities, the need invariably arises for a body of International Law describing the ground rules for their use. Just as it was the case with the Treaty on Antarctica, the various international agreements on the use of the electromagnetic radiation spectrum, or on the vaccination requirements for international travel, a body for a Law of Outer Space can come into being only through patient and repeated deliberations between competent representatives from countries all over the world. It is gratifying to learn from the preceding pages that the 1973 Colloquium on the Law of Outer Space in Baku, USSR (the sixteenth yearly meeting of its kind after the stage had been set in 1958 at The Hague), has made another great contribution in this vital field.

International cooperation in outer space has long ceased to be merely a pious hope. The Intelsat consortium for worldwide telephony and television services via satellite now includes 88 nations, and whereas for some highly developed countries those satellites may provide just additional communications channels, many of the emerging new nations have found their Intelsat ground station, which enables them to communicate with the satellites, to be the one and only link to the rest of the world.

The date for a joint rendezvous and docking between a USSR Soyeuz and a USA Apollo spacecraft has now been firmly set and the project is implemented on both sides with great enthusiasm and dispatch.

A sizable number of countries have expressed great interest in establishing a system of domestic direct-broadcast TV satellites for audiovisual school and adult education as well as for domestic communications. More and more countries are subscribing to the imagery mailing service of earth resources satellites, such as ERTS-1, hoping to more accurately assess their crop auspices or their domestic resources in minerals or fossil fuels. Improved global weather monitoring and prediction via satellite have become another space activity of vast international significance.

During its first phase, outer space seemed to many to be just a far-out region of little practical value, accessible only to two competing super powers capable of supporting these costly ventures with massive technological and financial support. In the second phase, which we now have entered, we see a proliferation of countries getting in the act with programs tailored to their particular needs and budgets. It has become very obvious to many countries that outer space is not a playground reserved for the super-rich, but a vantage point which offers the most needy regions on earth to more effectively help themselves.

# # # # #